What could you accomplish during
a semester / year abroad in the

FACULTY OF THEOLOGY AND
RELIGIOUS STUDIES'

undergraduate program?

STUDY THEOLOGY AT
ONE OF EUROPE'S MOST
PRESTIGIOUS INSTITUTIONS

Since 1432, K.U.Leuven (Catholic University of Louvain, Belgium) has been at the center of Christian theology, from Erasmus to Vatican II and beyond. Our world-renowned library and programmes make the Faculty of Theology and Religious Studies a destination for American students. Come see Europe, perform critical research, and tap into a rich history to one of Europe's oldest universities. And with tuition less per semester, it's affordable too!

D1249033

KATHOLIEKE UNIVERSITEIT
LEUVEN

admissions@theo.kuleuven.be
Or visit us on the web at
http://theo.kuleuven.be/en/spring_semester

SERVANT OF THE GOSPEL

Servant of the Gospel

STUDIES IN HONOR OF HIS ALL-HOLINESS ECUMENICAL PATRIARCH BARTHOLOMEW

Contributions by the Faculty of Holy Cross
Greek Orthodox School of Theology

Edited by
Thomas FitzGerald

Foreword by His Eminence Archbishop Demetrios

HOLY CROSS ORTHODOX PRESS
Brookline, Massachusetts

In appreciation: Publication of this book was made possible in part through a generous contribution of an anonymous donor who gave this gift "with deep gratitude for the ministry of His All-Holiness Patriarch Bartholomew and the higher education ministry of Hellenic College and Holy Cross, and with the fervent prayer that their service to God and His Church will continue to bear fruit abundantly."

Published by Holy Cross Orthodox Press
50 Goddard Avenue
Brookline, Massachusetts 02445

ISBN-13 978-1-935317-27-2
ISBN-10 1-935317-27-X

Cover photo by John Mindala.

Library of Congress Cataloging-in-Publication Data
Servant of the Gospel : studies in honor of His All-Holiness Ecumenical Patriarch Bartholomew : contributions / by the faculty of Holy Cross Greek Orthodox School of Theology ; edited by Thomas FitzGerald.
  p. cm.
 ISBN-13: 978-1-935317-27-2
 ISBN-10: 1-935317-27-X
1. Orthodox Eastern Church. I. Bartholomew I, Ecumenical Patriarch of Constantinople, 1940- II. FitzGerald, Thomas E., 1947- III. Holy Cross Greek Orthodox School of Theology.
 BX325.S47 2011
 230'.19--dc23
                                                        2011033747

CONTENTS

Foreword

But I am among you as one who serves.
(Luke 22:27)

When a dispute arose among the disciples during the Last Supper, the Lord made this extremely significant statement: "But I am among you as one who serves" (Luke 22:27). Previously, He had made a similar statement centered on the meaning of *serving* when He declared that "the Son of Man came not to be served but to serve" (Matt 20:28; Mark 10:45).

With these very important statements, our Lord Jesus Christ established the meaning of *serving* as the fundamental and ultimate meaning of His Incarnation and mission on earth, and as the eternal and absolute criterion of defining the genuine and true mission of the servants of the Gospel throughout the ages.

As an individual and as a clergyman, but mostly throughout the twenty years of his glorious ministry, His All-Holiness Ecumenical Patriarch Bartholomew is the *servant patriarch*. He is literally the fine imitator of the *servant* Lord Jesus Christ, *serving among us* day and night.

His All-Holiness is the *servant patriarch* as manifested in his intense, eloquent, and continuous offering of the Gospel of Jesus Christ to every corner of the earth and consequently to every human being.

He is the servant patriarch as he works indefatigably and painfully for unity, cooperation, and common witness of faith amongst the Orthodox Churches worldwide.

He is the *servant patriarch* by his industrious and systematic work for the salvation of the wounded natural environment and for the stoppage and reversal of ecological destruction.

He is the *servant patriarch* by his vigilant and loving pastoral care for his immediate and broader flock, and for both individual people in distress and general groups in need of urgent assistance.

I congratulate the Dean of Holy Cross Greek Orthodox School of Theology and the professors of its faculty for the beautiful initiative of this volume in honor of His All-Holiness Ecumenical Patriarch Bartholomew. The title of the volume, *Servant of the Gospel*, completely describes the wonderful reality of the twenty years of his patriarchal ministry as a true *servant patriarch*. We intensely pray that the years that follow will be years of long and bright continuity of the superb patriarchal *diakonia* of our Ecumenical Patriarch, years of a march "from glory to glory" (2 Cor 3:18) in imitation of the serving God.

+DEMETRIOS
Archbishop of America
October 2011

ΠΡΟΛΟΓΟΣ

Ἐγώ δέ εἰμι ἐν μέσῳ ὑμῶν ὡς ὁ διακονῶν
(Λουκᾶ 22:27)

Κατά τήν διάρκεια τοῦ Μυστικοῦ Δείπνου, ὁ Κύριος ἐξ ἀφορμῆς φιλονικείας μεταξύ τῶν μαθητῶν του, ἔκαμε τήν ἑξῆς βαρυσήμαντη: *Ἐγώ δέ εἰμι ἐν μέσῳ ὑμῶν ὡς ὁ διακονῶν* (Λουκᾶ 22:27). Τήν ἴδια αὐτή δήλωση μέ κέντρο τήν ἔννοια τοῦ διακονεῖν, εἶχε κάμει καί προηγουμένως ὁ Κύριος ὅταν διεκήρυξε ὅτι *ὁ Υἱός τοῦ ἀνθρώπου οὐκ ἦλθε διακονηθῆναι ἀλλά διακονῆσαι* (Ματθαίου 20:28 καί Μάρκου 10:45).

Μέ τίς σπουδαιότατες αὐτές διακηρύξεις Του, ὁ Κύριος Ἰησοῦς Χριστός καθιέρωσε τήν ἔννοια τοῦ διακονεῖν ὡς θεμελιώδη καί κορυφαία ἔννοια τῆς ἐνανθρωπήσεως καί τοῦ ἔργου Του ἐπί τῆς γῆς καί ὡς αἰώνιο καί ἀπόλυτο κριτήριο γνησίας καί ἀληθινῆς ἀποστολῆς τῶν ἀνά τούς αἰῶνας ἐργατῶν τοῦ Εὐαγγελίου.

Ὁ Παναγιώτατος Οἰκουμενικός Πατριάρχης κ.κ. Βαρθολομαῖος εἶναι ὡς ἄνθρωπος καί ὡς κληρικός, ἀλλά κυρίως ὡς Πατριάρχης κατά τήν διάρκεια τῆς εἰκοσαετοῦς λαμπρᾶς προσφορᾶς του, ὁ *διακονῶν Πατριάρχης*. Εἶναι κατά κυριολεξίαν ὁ ἔξοχος μιμητής τοῦ *διακονοῦντος Θεοῦ ἡμῶν Ἰησοῦ Χριστοῦ, διακονῶν ἐν μέσῳ ἡμῶν* ἡμέρας καί νυκτός.

Ὁ Παναγιώτατος Πατριάρχης εἶναι *διακονῶν* μέ τήν ἔντονη, εὔγλωττη καί συνεχή προσφορά τοῦ Εὐαγγελίου Ἰησοῦ Χριστοῦ σέ κάθε σημεῖο τῆς Γῆς, καί, κατ'οὐσίαν, πρός πάντα ἄνθρωπον.

Εἶναι διακονῶν μέ τόν ἀδιάκοπο μόχθο καί πόνο γιά ἐνότητα, συνεργασία καί κοινή μαρτυρία πίστεως μεταξύ τῶν ἀνά τόν κόσμο Ὀρθοδόξων Ἐκκλησιῶν.

Εἶναι διακονῶν μέ τήν ἄκρως ἐπιμελῆ καί συστηματική ἐργασία γιά τήν σωτηρία τοῦ τραυματισμένου φυσικοῦ περιβάλλοντος καί τήν ἀνάσχεση καί ἀντιστροφή τῆς οἰκολογικῆς καταστροφῆς.

Εἶναι διακονῶν μέ τήν ἄγρυπνη καί στοργική ποιμαντική του μέριμνα ὑπέρ τοῦ ἀμέσου καί τοῦ εὐρυτέρου ποιμνίου του, ὑπέρ τῶν ἑκάστοτε συγκεκριμένων ἐμπεριστάτων ἀτόμων ἀλλά καί γενικωτέρων συνόλων τά ὁποῖα χρήζουν ἀμέσου βοηθείας.

Συγχαίρω τόν Κοσμήτορα τῆς Ἱερᾶς Θεολογικῆς Σχολῆς τοῦ Τιμίου Σταυροῦ καί τούς Καθηγητάς της γιά τήν ὡραία πρωτοβουλία ἐκδόσεως τοῦ παρόντος Τόμου πρός τιμήν τοῦ Παναγιωτάτου Οἰκουμενικοῦ μας Πατριάρχου κ.κ. Βαρθολομαίου. Ὁ τίτλος τοῦ Τόμου *Διάκονος τοῦ Εὐαγγελίου*, ἀποδίδει πλήρως τήν ὑπέροχη πραγματικότητα τῆς εἰκοσαετοῦς προσφορᾶς του ὡς τοῦ κατά κυριολεξίαν καί κατ'ἐξοχήν *Διακονοῦντος Πατριάρχου*. Προσευχόμεθα ἐκτενῶς, τά χρόνια πού ἀκολουθοῦν νά εἶναι χρόνια μακρᾶς καί λαμπρᾶς συνεχείας ἀγλαοκάρπου Πατριαρχείας τοῦ διακονοῦντος Οἰκουμενικοῦ μας Πατριάρχου, χρόνια πορείας *ἀπό δόξης εἰς δόξαν* (2 Κορ. 3:18) ἐν μιμήσει τοῦ διακονοῦντος Θεοῦ.

+Ὁ Ἀρχιεπίσκοπος Ἀμερικῆς Δημήτριος
Ὀκτώβριος 2011

Introduction

SERVANT OF THE GOSPEL: ECUMENICAL PATRIARCH BARTHOLOMEW OF CONSTANTINOPLE

Rev. Dr. Thomas FitzGerald
Dean of Holy Cross Greek Orthodox School of Theology and
Professor of Church History and Historical Theology

E cumenical Patriarch Bartholomew is a Servant of the Gospel of Jesus
Christ. As one of the great religious leaders of our day, he is a person
of deep faith who has a global vision and sees beyond boundaries. With
wisdom and humility, he has led the historic Ecumenical Patriarchate
of Constantinople since 1991. As Patriarch, he has represented the Orthodox Church on the world stage. But more than this, his patriarchal
ministry has been one through which he has moved beyond historic limitations with a personal witness that has been healing and reconciling.
His leadership reveals the positive contribution that persons of faith and
good will can make to peace and reconciliation, the healing of divisions,
and the well-being of society.

A Follower of Christ

The Patriarch is first and foremost a faithful Orthodox Christian
whose life and ministry are rooted in the person of Jesus Christ and
guided by His gospel as proclaimed by the Orthodox Church. This
is clearly evident in the pages of his book *Encountering the Mystery:
Understanding Orthodox Christianity Today*.[1] It is also evident in his
Festal Encyclicals and Lenten Addresses. In a recent encyclical, he has
pointed to the centrality of Christ, saying:

> Our Risen Lord Jesus Christ, the new Adam and God, con-
> stitutes the model for the beneficial influence of a saint on

the natural world. For Christ healed physical and spiritual illness, granting comfort and healing to all people, while at the same time bringing calm and peace to stormy seas, multiplying five loaves of bread to feed the five thousand, thereby combining the reconciliation of spiritual and natural harmony. If we want to exert a positive impact on the current negative natural and political conditions of our world, then we have no other alternative than faith in the Risen Christ and fulfillment of his saving commandments.[2]

The rich legacy of Orthodox Christianity is always expressed in the teachings and the ministry of the Patriarch. He praises the Triune God, who is loving and compassionate, the *philanthropos theos*. He honors the human person, created in the divine "image and likeness" (Gen 1:26–27) and blessed with inherent dignity and value. Furthermore, he treasures the creation at the divine gift and the context of salvation. At his Enthronement Address in 1991, the Patriarch said, "Orthodoxy has much, much more to offer the contemporary world. In Orthodoxy one can find not only the correct faith in the true God, but also the correct perception of humankind as the image of God, of the world, of the creation." For two decades, these convictions have been at the heart of the ministry of the Patriarch.

Precisely because of his faith, Patriarch Bartholomew has been able to challenge divisions among Christians and has emphasized the value of dialogue. He has repudiated violence and urged mutual respect for all peoples, religions, and cultures. He has called for an end to the abuse of the environment. Precisely because of his deep faith, Patriarch Bartholomew has been able to engage religious leaders and heads of state, diplomats and journalists.

The First Bishop

Ecumenical Patriarch Bartholomew is the senior bishop of the worldwide Orthodox Church, which has about 300 million members. His holds the historic title "Archbishop of Constantinople-New Rome and Ecumenical Patriarch." All other Orthodox patriarchs, archbishops, and bishops acknowledge the Ecumenical Patriarch of Constantinople (present-day Istanbul, Turkey), as the first bishop of their Church. The title "Ecumenical Patriarch" dates from the sixth century and indicates his distinctive ministry of leadership within the Church. As a faithful shepherd of the Church, he is the 270th successor to St. Andrew the First-Called Apostle.

Ecumenical Patriarch Bartholomew presides at the Holy Synod of the Ecumenical Patriarchate of Constantinople, the ranking Church within the communion of the fourteen Autocephalous Orthodox Churches that presently comprise Orthodox Christianity. Bishops from throughout the world are part of the Holy Synod of the Ecumenical Patriarchate and the wider Synaxis of Hierarchs, which he often convenes.

The Ecumenical Patriarchate includes episcopal jurisdictions—metropolitanates, archdioceses, and dioceses—not only in Turkey and Greece, but also in other regions, including the Americas, Western Europe, Australia/Oceania, and the Far East. The Ecumenical Patriarchate has pastoral responsibility for all Orthodox Christians living in areas beyond the canonical borders of other Autocephalous Orthodox Churches. The vast jurisdiction of the Ecumenical Patriarchate is multiethnic, multicultural, and multilingual.[3]

Patriarch Bartholomew was elected to his office on October 22, 1991. Born on the small island of Imbros, Turkey, on February 29, 1940, he completed his preliminary theological studies at the renowned Patriarchal Theological School on the island of Halki. From there he pursued further studies at the University of Munich, the Bossey Ecumenical Institute in Geneva, and the Institute for Oriental Studies in Rome, where he received his doctoral degree. Ordained a deacon in 1961 and a priest in 1969, he was guided by the late Patriarch Athenagoras (1886–1972). He subsequently served as a close advisor to the late Patriarch Dimitrios (1914–1991). In 1973, he was elected a bishop and served as the Metropolitan of Philadelphia and later of Chalcedon. As Ecumenical Patriarch, he has inherited the rich legacy dating back to the time of the Apostle Andrew the First-Called. As a patriarchal center, the Church of Constantinople dates from the fourth century. His predecessors include such luminaries as St. Gregory the Theologian, St. John Chrysostom, St. Methodios, and St. Photios the Great.

Each day brings its own challenges for the Patriarch. On most weekdays he welcomes to his office a wide variety of persons: pilgrims, heads of state, diplomats, and journalists. On Sunday and holy days, he usually travels to one of the parishes in Istanbul for the Liturgy and to meet with parishioners. Indeed, one of his major concerns has been the return of churches and Church property that were confiscated by the Turkish government in the past. He has urged the government to recognize the legal status of the Patriarchate and to eliminate any restrictions on its activities. Of particular concern is the Patriarch's insistence upon the reopening of the Theological School of Halki, which was closed by the Turkish government in 1971.

Guardian of the Bond of Unity

Ecumenical Patriarch Bartholomew recognizes his unique responsibility for serving the unity of the entire Orthodox Church and for identifying challenges that require attention by the entire Church. He has acted wisely and judiciously to strengthen the bond of unity and to deepen the spirit of conciliarity among the Autocephalous Orthodox Churches. Not intruding upon the rightful responsibilities of other primates or the integrity of the other Autocephalous Churches, he has exercised his own responsibility as the first bishop of the Orthodox Church. While strengthening the bonds of unity and witness, Patriarch Bartholomew has led the entire Orthodox Church in addressing common challenges and in giving a united witness to Christ and His gospel. As he has said, the Ecumenical Patriarchate "bears a primacy of honor and service within Orthodox Christianity throughout the world. Its authority does not lie in administration, but rather in coordination. This is not a sign of weakness, but precisely of conciliarity. For the Church of Constantinople serves as primary focal point of unity, fostering consensus among the various Orthodox Churches."[4]

Since the early years of the twentieth century, the Ecumenical Patriarchate has convened a series of meetings designed to overcome disharmony and to deepen the unity among the Autocephalous Churches. A significant improvement in these relations began to take place under the leadership of the late Ecumenical Patriarch Athenagoras during the 1960s. In 1961, a number of topics were identified for study by Church representatives in anticipation of a "Great and Holy Council." Under the leadership of the late Patriarch Dimitrios, this list eventually was revised in 1976 to include ten major topics for study. Since then, a number pan-Orthodox conferences and meetings addressed most of these themes. The most recent Pre-Conciliar Pan-Orthodox Conference was held in 2009 and dealt with the topic of the so-called Orthodox Diaspora.

Since his election in 1991, Ecumenical Patriarch Bartholomew has committed himself to strengthening pan-Orthodox unity and witness. The cooperation among the Churches had been shaken by internal difficulties in many Orthodox Churches following the fall of communism in Russia and in other Eastern European countries, beginning about 1989.

Despite the recent tensions, Patriarch Bartholomew consistently returned to the critical topics of Orthodox unity and the witness of the Church today in his meetings with the representatives of the other Orthodox Churches. His own personal dialogues with others did much to strengthen the spirit of conciliarity.[5]

The Patriarch was determined not to let these tensions continue to stand in the way of progress in moving towards the Great and Holy Council and in addressing the situation of the so-called Diaspora. This refers to the presence of Orthodox Churches in regions, such as North America, which are beyond the canonical boundaries of the Autocephalous Orthodox Churches. The Ecumenical Patriarchate has the pastoral responsibility for all Orthodox in these regions according to the canonical tradition and historical precedent. At the same time, however, the Ecumenical Patriarchate wisely has recognized that a pan-Orthodox agreement must be found to organize the Church in these regions, so that there is a more united witness to the gospel of Christ.

With the patient leadership of Bartholomew, new opportunities for cooperation were established. He presided at extraordinary synods of patriarchs and archbishops to address difficulties in the Church of Bulgaria (1998), Jerusalem (2005), and Cyprus (2006). The Patriarch also acted to re-establish the Church of Albania in 1991–1992, to regularize the situation in the Church of Estonia in 1996, and to strengthen Orthodox unity in Ukraine in 2008.

Most recently, Ecumenical Patriarch Bartholomew convened a meeting of the fourteen Orthodox primates or their representatives in Constantinople on October 10–12, 2008. This was the fifth time that such a synaxis was held at the initiative of Patriarch Bartholomew. Previous meetings were held in Constantinople in 1990, on Patmos in 1995, and in Jerusalem and Constantinople in 2000. These gatherings of the primates of the Autocephalous Orthodox Churches have been significant events. They have expressed in a very visible manner the unity of the Orthodox Church and the willingness of the Primates to address challenges facing the entire Church today. Speaking of his own role in these meetings, the Ecumenical Patriarch said that he has "regarded it as his sacred duty to strengthen the bonds of love and unity of all those entrusted with the leadership of the local Orthodox Churches."[6]

At this gathering, Patriarch Bartholomew emphasized the need for unity and greater witness of the Orthodox Churches. He also called for the reaffirmation of the process leading toward the Great and Holy Council. Within this context, he urged the primates to act in addressing the topic of the so-called Diaspora. In their own statement, the primates approved the proposals of the Ecumenical Patriarch.

Under the leadership of Ecumenical Patriarch Bartholomew, the hierarchs representing the fourteen Autocephalous Churches at the synaxis affirmed that the *status quo* in the so-called Diaspora was no longer acceptable. This affirmation set in motion the plans to convene the Fourth Pre-Conciliar Pan-Orthodox Conference, which met in 2009. This meeting subsequently sanctioned the establishment of an Assembly of Bishops in specific regions of the so-called Diaspora that are beyond the boundaries of the other Autocephalous Churches. These assemblies will bring great unity to the developing church in each region and will set the stage for a full canonical resolution.

The recommendations of the Fourth Pre-Conciliar Conference also marked a renewal of the process leading the convocation of a Great and Holy Council. Patriarch Bartholomew has emphasized the need of the entire Orthodox Church to complete the Pre-Conciliar discussions so that plans can be formulated soon for the meeting of the Great and Holy Council.

Advocate for Recociliation

The Ecumenical Patriarchate has a special responsibility for guiding and coordinating Orthodox participation in the contemporary ecumenical movement. The Patriarchate has consistently affirmed that the divisions among Christians are a scandal that weakens the witness of Christians in the world. At the same time, the Patriarchate has affirmed that the restoration of unity and full communion among divided Christian Churches and communities can only come about through the clear resolution of doctrinal differences, a resolution nurtured by prayer and expressed in common acts of witness.[7]

Through a series of letters dating back to 1902 and especially in the historic Encyclical of 1920, the Patriarchate has encouraged the participation of the entire Orthodox Church in a renewed dialogue with other Christian Churches and communities. The Patriarchate was one of the founding members of the World Council of Churches in 1948. It has also led Orthodox participation in bilateral theological dialogues between the Orthodox Church and the Oriental Orthodox Churches (1961, 1975), the Church of Rome (1979), the Old Catholic Church (1964), the Anglican Communion (1964), the Lutheran World Federation (1976), and the World Alliance of Reformed Churches (1988).[8]

Speaking of the role of the Ecumenical Patriarchate in the quest for the unity of the Churches, Patriarch Bartholomew has said,

> The Ecumenical Patriarchate has been an ardent proponent of genuine efforts among Christians to overcome animosity and misunderstandings. The Patriarchate has called upon the churches to come out of their isolation, and to enter into dialogue for the sake of reconciliation and the restoration of visible unity. The Ecumenical Patriarchate has reminded the followers of Christ of the prayer of the Lord for their unity. He prayed "that they may be one even as you Father are in me and I in you, may they also be one in us, so that the world may believe that you sent me" (John 17:21). We all need to hear clearly this powerful prayer of our Lord today.[9]

Ecumenical Patriarch Bartholomew has had much firsthand experience of dialogue with other Churches. As a young deacon, he studied in Rome during the time of the Second Vatican Council. He also studied at the Bossey Ecumenical Institute of the World Council of Churches. Some years later, as a metropolitan, he served with distinction as a member of the Council's Faith and Order Commission, and as a member of its Central Committee and Executive Committee. As a key advisor to Patriarch Dimitrios, he took an active role in the establishment of the International Orthodox-Catholic Dialogue in 1979. In these positions, he came to be recognized by Roman Catholic and Protestant theologians as being a thoughtful and articulate spokesman for Orthodoxy.[10]

Ecumenical Patriarch Bartholomew has been especially concerned with the relationship between the Orthodox Church and the Roman Catholic Church, which have been divided formally since 1484. He was elected as Patriarch at a time when this relationship was under severe strain, especially in Eastern Europe. In the wake of massive political changes, there was a resurgence of the Eastern Rite Catholic Churches in many parts of Eastern Europe. Sometimes known as "Uniates," these Churches entered into communion with the Catholic Church at various times, particularly between the sixteenth and nineteenth centuries. These Churches generally follow Eastern liturgical practices but accept the ultimate authority of the pope. In a number of places, there were accusations of proselytism and sharp clashes between Eastern Catholics and Orthodox over the control of church buildings and property rights.

Some Orthodox viewed the revival of the Eastern Catholic Churches as an attempt by Rome to undermine the Orthodox Church in those regions, and this gravely jeopardized the work of reconciliation.[11]

In addition to this, there were tensions among the Autocephalous Orthodox Churches themselves, tensions that also impacted upon pan-Orthodox cooperation and ecumenical dialogue. These tensions reflected internal changes in some Churches as well as the political developments in the Balkans.

Against this difficult background, Ecumenical Patriarch Bartholomew met with Pope John Paul II in Rome in 1995; this was the first papal visit to the Patriarchate since 1979. This visit continued the tradition established by Patriarch Athenagoras and followed by Patriarch Dimitrios. Patriarch Bartholomew found in Pope John Paul II a person who was also committed to the process of reconciliation between Orthodoxy and Catholicism. They subsequently both supported the restoration of the International Theological Dialogue in 2000.[12] They met again at a historic meeting in Assisi, Italy, in 2002, for a "Day of Prayer for Peace in the World." The two issued a historic joint declaration on the protection of the creation simultaneously in Rome and in Venice in 2002. Ecumenical Patriarch Bartholomew again met with Pope John Paul II in Rome on June 29, 2004.

Only a few months later, Pope John Paul II and Ecumenical Patriarch Bartholomew presided over a historic celebration in St. Peter's in Rome on November 27, 2004, marking the return to the Orthodox of the relics of St. Gregory the Theologian and St. John Chrysostom, saints who are honored by both Orthodox and Roman Catholics. The relics solemnly were placed in the patriarchal cathedral on November 30. The return of the relics was a vivid reminder of how much the two Churches share in common, including the veneration of the saints. This event clearly indicated that the relationship between the Churches had improved greatly.

When Pope John Paul II died, Ecumenical Patriarch Bartholomew led the Orthodox delegation at the funeral in Rome on April 8, 2005. It was truly a dramatic gesture of respect for the pope who had served his Church in that office for about twenty-seven years.

Elected on April 19, 2005, Pope Benedict XVI led the delegation of the Catholic Church to meet with Ecumenical Patriarch Bartholomew and to participate in the observance of the feast of St. Andrew on November 30, 2006. The pope was present in the Cathedral of St. George for the festal Liturgy led by Ecumenical Patriarch Bartholomew, who was joined by members of the Holy Synod from throughout the world.

The Patriarch and the pope later proceeded to the balcony near the Patriarch's office, where they jointly blessed those who were gathered in the courtyard below.

At the invitation of the pope, Ecumenical Patriarch Bartholomew was present for the feast day of Sts. Peter and Paul in Rome in 2008. Only a few months later, Ecumenical Patriarch Bartholomew was invited by the pope to address the Catholic Synod of Bishops meeting in Rome in October 2008. This was the first time in history that a patriarch was invited to address a world Synod of Catholic Bishops.

Within the beautiful Sistine Chapel and in the presence of Pope Benedict XVI, Ecumenical Patriarch Bartholomew spoke to over four hundred cardinals, archbishops, and bishops, as well as to monks, nuns, and laypersons from throughout the Catholic Church. During the course of his lecture, the Patriarch said, "It is the first time in history that an Ecumenical Patriarch is offered the opportunity to address a Synod of the Bishops of the Roman Catholic Church, and thus be part of the life of this sister Church at such a high level. We regard this as a manifestation of the work of the Holy Spirit leading our Churches to a closer and deeper relationship with each other, an important step towards the restoration of our full communion."[13]

Messenger of Peace

Ecumenical Patriarch Bartholomew has also affirmed the critical need for mutual respect and understanding among the religions of the world. Deeply sensitive to the many incidents of terrorism and fanaticism, he has spoken out boldly against violence and injustices, especially those carried out in the name of religion. Condemning all aspects of religious fanaticism, he has affirmed the need for mutual respect of races, faiths, and cultures. He has called for all to honor places of prayer, cemeteries, and historic religious buildings of all faiths. He has called upon all religious leaders to support human rights and to oppose all forms of discrimination.

The Ecumenical Patriarchate has sponsored six pan-Orthodox meetings with Jewish leaders since 1977. Likewise, the Patriarchate has sponsored ten pan-Orthodox meetings with representatives of Islam since 1986. These meetings have provided valuable opportunities for the representatives to meet together in an atmosphere of mutual respect to discuss critical issues facing the relationship among the religions. Referring to the unique witness of his Church, Patriarch Bartholomew has said that "even at the cost of defamation for 'betraying' the Gospel, we have never restricted such engagements merely to Christian confessions. Standing as it does on the crossroads of continents, civilizations, and cultures, the Ecumenical Patriarchate has always served as a bridge between Christians, Moslems, and Jews."[14]

During the past two decades of his service, Patriarch Bartholomew has personally participated in many conferences that have gathered religious leaders from a wide variety of traditions. Among the most prominent was the "Conference on Peace and Tolerance" convened by the Patriarch and held in Istanbul on February 9, 1994. It brought together in dialogue prominent Christian, Jewish, and Muslim leaders.

This meeting produced the now historic "Bosphorus Declaration." Signed by Patriarch Bartholomew, the Declaration boldly reaffirmed the conviction that "a crime committed in the name of religion is a crime against religion." The Declaration also said, "We stand firmly against those who violate the sanctity of human life and pursue policies in defiance of moral values. We reject the concept that it is possible to justify one's actions in any armed conflict in the name of God."[15]

Addressing the danger of religious fanaticism, Ecumenical Patriarch Bartholomew has boldly said,

> There has never been a greater need for spiritual leaders to engage in the affairs of the world. We must take a visible place on the stage, especially because too many crimes today are taking place in the name of faith . . . Religious extremists and terrorists may be the most wicked false prophets of all. Not only do they commit horrible crimes against humanity, but they do so in the name of a lie. When they bomb, and shoot, and destroy, they steal more than life itself; they also undermine faith, which is the only way to break the cycle of hatred and retribution. International spiritual leaders must play an active role in discrediting false prophets and in healing the wounds of our people As Rabbi Hillel asked: "If not us, then who? If not now, then when?"[16]

Steward of God's Good Creation

Ecumenical Patriarch Bartholomew has been very active in promoting greater care for the environment, which is God's good creation. Speaking especially to Christians, the Patriarch has reminded the faithful that the creation is gift from God to be treasured, not abused. Our relationship with the Triune God and with one another always takes place within the context of the created reality. Each of us shares in the created reality. While we affirm a distinctive quality and dignity of the human person, therefore, we are never detached from the rest of the created reality. The human person shares in the reality of entire creation with all of God's creatures. Creation is the sacred context in which our growth in holiness takes place, and growth in holiness does not draw us away from the creation; the physical world is not by nature an obstacle to our growth in holiness. Far from rejecting the body and the rest of the material creation, the Orthodox Church especially looks upon the physical as the work of God and the medium through which the divine is manifest.

At the same time, the Patriarch has also addressed all persons of good faith, regardless of their religious convictions. He has pointedly argued that the very future of humanity depends upon the care that we show to the creation today. This care requires that the dangers of consumerism, greed, and selfish individualism be overcome.

Often referred to as the "Green Patriarch" because of his concern for the well-being of the creation, Patriarch Bartholomew has organized a number of conferences that highlight the importance of the environment and the responsibility of men and women to be good stewards of the creation. He has called upon Church leaders, the faithful, and governments to address the degradation of the environment and to support programs that reverse this tragic tendency.

Among the many recent initiatives of the Ecumenical Patriarchate was the formal recognition of September 1 as a day of prayers for the environment. An encyclical from Patriarch Dimitrios in 1979 established this tradition. Patriarch Bartholomew has continued the practice of issuing an encyclical on September 1, the first day of the Orthodox Church year, calling upon the faithful to be especially thoughtful of the need to protect the environment as expression of their Orthodox Christian faith. At the meeting of Orthodox Primates in 1992 under the leadership of Patriarch Bartholomew, they solemnly affirmed Constantinople's initiative.

Patriarch Bartholomew has personally led a number of environment seminars at the Patriarchal Theological School on the island of Halki between 1992 and 1998. These seminars brought together Church leaders, theologians, and environmentalists. "For us Orthodox," Ecumenical Patriarch Bartholomew said in 1992, "every destruction of the natural environment caused by humanity constitutes an offence against the Creator Himself and arouse a deep sense of sorrow. In relation to the degree to which people are responsible for their actions, *metanoia*—a radical change of course—is demanded of us all. For this reason, each human act that contributes to the destruction of the natural environment must be regarded as a very serious sin."[17]

Since 1995, Patriarch Bartholomew has led nine environmental symposia in various parts of the world. Entitled "Religion, Science, and the Environment," these historic gatherings have brought together an international body of theologians, scientists, researchers, governmental leaders, and journalists to examine the tragic consequences of such factors as pollution, climate change, and economic policies, especially on the great bodies of water. The most recent was held on the Mississippi River in 2009.

No long after this symposium, the Patriarch boldly declared,

> Nature is a book, opened wide for all to read and to learn, to savor and celebrate. It tells a unique story; it unfolds a profound mystery; it relates an extraordinary harmony and balance, which are interdependent and complementary. The way we relate to nature as creation directly reflects the way we relate to God as Creator. The sensitivity with which we handle the natural environment clearly mirrors the sacredness that we reserve for the divine. We must treat nature with the same awe and wonder that we reserve for human beings. And we do not need this insight in order to believe in God or to prove His existence. We need it to breathe; we need it for us simply to be.
>
> At stake is not just our ability to live in a sustainable way, but our very survival. Scientists estimate that those most hurt by global warming in years to come will be those who can least afford it. Therefore, the ecological problem of pollution is invariably connected to the social problem of poverty; and so all ecological activity is ultimately measured and properly judged by its impact upon people, and especially its effect upon the poor.[18]

Herald of the Gospel

From the earliest days of Christianity, the witness of the Ecumenical Patriarchate of Constantinople has enriched the entire Church and Western civilization. The Patriarchate has been a center of learning and theological reflection, of dialogue and engagement, of philanthropy and mission, of iconography and architecture. The historic churches, shrines, and monasteries of Constantinople have been a destination for pilgrims from throughout the world. Even in difficult times of oppression and persecution, the Patriarchate has been a faithful witness to the message of the gospel of Christ.

Ecumenical Patriarch Bartholomew is truly a follower of Christ and a servant of the gospel. He is also deeply rooted in the profound witness of the Patriarchate across the centuries.

The path that the Patriarch has followed has certainly not been an easy one. It has required of him both love and forgiveness, both wisdom and patience. Although many honor him because of his courage and determination, others have unjustly criticized him, and even accused him of betraying the gospel. With this in mind, he has said, "There is always much more than meets the eye when we consider human life and the natural environment. We must at all times be prepared to create new openings and to build bridges, ever deepening our relationship with God, with other people and with creation itself. We must never rest complacent in the ivory towers of either our academic or ecclesiastical institutions."[19]

And so he believes that the Church is called to bear witness to Christ and His gospel in the midst of the challenges and opportunities of life today. The "Light of Christ" cannot be hidden. For Patriarch Bartholomew, the follower of Christ is truly meant to be the "salt of the earth" and the "light of the world" (Matt 5:13–14). Such a person is one whose life bears witness to the loving, healing, and reconciling gospel of Christ.

The Patriarch again speaks to each of us when he says,

> The challenge before us is the discernment of God's Word in the face of evil, the transfiguration of every last detail and speck of this world in the light of Resurrection. The victory is already present in the depths of the Church, whenever we experience the grace of reconciliation and communion. As we struggle—in ourselves and in our world—to recognize the power of the Cross, we begin to appreciate how every act of justice, every spark of beauty, every word of truth can gradually wear away the crust of evil. However, beyond our own frail efforts, we have the assurance of the Spirit, who "helps us in our weakness" (Rom 8:26) and stands beside us as advocate and "comforter" (John 14:6), penetrating all

things and "transforming us," as St. Symeon the New Theologian says, "into everything that the Word of God says
about the heavenly kingdom: pearl, grain of mustard seed,
leaven, water, fire, bread, life and mystical wedding cham-
ber." Such is the power and grace of the Holy Spirit.[20]

Notes

1. His All-Holiness Ecumenical Patriarch Bartholomew, *Encountering the Mystery: Understanding Orthodox Christianity Today* (New York:
Doubleday, 2008).

2. Ecumenical Patriarch Bartholomew, "Patriarchal Proclamation
for Pascha 2011."

3. Thomas FitzGerald, "The Orthodox Church Today: An Overview,"
Origins 33, no. 7 (2003): 105–110.

4. Ecumenical Patriarch Bartholomew, "Councils and Conciliarity,"
October 1, 2010, Kadirga Center for Visual Art, Istanbul.

5. Thomas FitzGerald, "Conciliarity, Primacy and the Episcopacy,"
St. Vladimir's Theological Quarterly 38, no. 1 (1994): 17–43.

6. "Address by His All Holiness Ecumenical Bartholomew at the
Synaxis of the Heads of Orthodox Churches," *Greek Orthodox Theological Review* 53, nos. 1–4 (2008): 293.

7. See Thomas FitzGerald, *The Ecumenical Movement: An Introductory History* (Westport, CT: Praeger, 2004).

8. See Thomas FitzGerald, *The Ecumenical Patriarchate and Christian Unity* (Brookline, MA: Holy Cross Orthodox Press, 2009).

9. "Address of Ecumenical Patriarch Bartholomew at the Orientale Lumen Conference," in *The Ecumenical Patriarchate and Christian
Unity*, 93.

10. Thomas FitzGerald, "The New Ecumenical Patriarch and Orthodox Ecumenical Witness," *Ecumenical Trends* 21, no. 1 (1992): 3–6.

11. Thomas FitzGerald, "Orthodoxy Theology and Ecumenical Witness," *St. Vladimir's Theological Quarterly* 42, nos. 3–4 (1998): 339–361.

12. The Orthodox-Catholic Dialogue in North America began in
1965 and was not interrupted until the 1990s.

13. Ecumenical Patriarch Bartholomew, "The Unity of the Church
Is Unbreakably Related with Her Mission," *Greek Orthodox Theological
Review* 53, nos. 1–4 (2008): 313.

14. Ecumenical Patriarch Bartholomew, "The Imperative of Inter-
Religious Dialogue in the Modern World," The John Paul II Catholic
University of Lublin, August 20, 2010.

15. "The Bosphorus Declaration: Joint declaration of the Conference on Peace and Tolerance," in John Chryssavgis, ed., *Cosmic Grace, Humble Prayer: The Ecological Vision of the Green Patriarch Bartholomew I*, revised ed. (Grand Rapids, MI: Eerdmans, 2009), 114.

16. Ecumenical Patriarch Bartholomew, "Fundamentalism and Faith," in *Cosmic Grace, Humble Prayer*, 136.

17. Ecumenical Patriarch Bartholomew, "The Power of Joint Prayer and Action," Halki Symposium, June 1, 1992, in *Cosmic Grace, Humble Prayer*, 84.

18. Ecumenical Patriarch Bartholomew, "Religion and the Environment: The Link Between Survival and Salvation," October 19, 2010.

19. Ecumenical Patriarch Bartholomew, "Theology, Liturgy, and Silence: Fundamental Insights from the Eastern Fathers for the Modern World," *Greek Orthodox Theological Review* 53, nos. 1–4 (2008): 238.

20. Ecumenical Patriarch Bartholomew, "The Unity of the Church is Unbreakably Related with Her Mission," 322–323.

Chapter 1

THE PRESBYTER AND THE ESSENTIAL ACTIVITIES OF THE CHURCH

"AND HE SAID TO THEM, GO INTO ALL THE WORLD AND PREACH THE GOSPEL TO THE WHOLE CREATION."

Rev. Dr. Alkiviadis Calivas
Emeritus Professor of Liturgics

Introduction

I am grateful to the Presbyters Council for giving me the honor to ad-dress you this evening with a reflection on preaching, which is the theme and focus of this year's Clergy Retreat. I was asked to base my remarks on the words of our Lord Jesus Christ recorded in the Gospel of Mark: "Go into all the world and preach the gospel to the whole creation" (Mark 16:15). Because you have already heard a good deal from several distinguished speakers about the art of preaching, allow me to place the topic in a larger context by referring to the four essential activities or ministries of the Church, one of which is preaching the Word of God.

My comments will have little to do with sermon style, structure, and content, and more to do with "God's trumpets" (1 Thess 4:16; Rev 8:2): the bishops, presbyters, and deacons of the Church, the hierarchical priesthood, charged by the Lord Christ to announce the Good News of salvation to a broken, wounded, and disoriented world, heralding the coming judgment and God's Kingdom, made present to us in the Church through the sacraments. My comments will focus on "God's plowmen" (1 Cor 9:10), the leaders of God's people; these leaders are the burden bearers and the feeders of the flock, who plow the hearts and souls of people, sowing the seeds of divine knowledge, holiness, love, peace, joy, and hope as they proclaim God's wonders with zeal, eagerness, and joy, as the Prophet Isaiah did when he heard the voice of the Lord saying, "Whom shall I send, and who will go for us?" Then Isaiah said, *"Here am I! Send me!"* And the Lord said, "Go . . ." (Isa 6:8–9).

The Four Essential Activities of the Church

Of the many activities the Church enacts in the world, four are constitutive of her nature and are therefore indispensable. They are: to gather
humbly and joyfully before God in prayer and solemn feast, or *worship*;
to proclaim the gospel with power and conviction, or to *preach* the word
of God; to do theology or to teach the faith effectively, or *catechesis*;
and to initiate and accomplish works of love, or *philanthropy*. Indeed,
in every generation the very effectiveness of the Church's mission in the
world is (or should be) measured against her ability to perform these
four fundamental activities or ministries with due diligence, competence, vigor, faithfulness, confidence, and boldness. And the responsibility for doing these activities faithfully, effectively, and dynamically
rests chiefly with the clergy, and more specifically with the bishops and
the presbyters, as the rites of ordination testify.

The Unique Relationships Born of Ordination

Through the rite of ordination, the Church sets apart qualified and
tested members of the faith community, assigning them to a particular place that defines their relation to the community of which they
are themselves members.[1] Through the dignity of their office, ordained persons exercise specific leadership roles within the community and execute certain functions and responsibilities for, with, and
on behalf of the people, inasmuch as all ministries in the Church
are relational, linked organically to one another. No ministry in the
Church stands above or outside the community. As Metropolitan
John of Pergamon has shown, "Ministry as a whole is a complexity of
relationships. No ordained person realizes his ordo in himself but in
the community."[2]

    As with every human relationship, the unique relationships born of
ordination must be cultivated and cared for if they are to bear fruit and
fulfill their sacred purpose. Meaningful relationships spring and flow
from persons who love as God loves: freely and unconditionally, even
if imperfectly. Relationships go awry when love falters or is betrayed.
When this happens authority is abused, privileges are misused, responsibilities are abdicated, and duties are neglected. But as the Scriptures
tell us, when one abides in love, one abides in God and God abides in
him (1 John 4:16). Then the light shines, and there is no cause for stum-
bling (1 John 2:10). The priestly ministry is, above all else, an event of

communion, a vocation for edification, a ministry for service, and an instrument of unity.

Of the various relationships born of ordination, one alone is central and unique. Through the action of the Holy Spirit, ordination relates the ordinand directly to the priesthood of Christ, to reflect and project His saving work within a concrete community—within a concrete diocese or parish—and through this community to the life of the whole Church.[3] Indeed, because of this unique relationship with Christ, the true test of a clergyman who desires to fulfill his ministry is the extent to which he manifests Christ in his demeanor and speech (2 Cor 4:1–12).

The Ordination Prayers for the Presbyter and the Church's Constitutive Activities

As with all divine services, and especially the sacramental services, the essential meaning and purpose of each rite is found especially in the prescribed prayers of the rite, through which the action of God and of the Church is made manifest. And so it is with holy orders. The rites of ordination affirm the Church's belief that the priesthood is a calling initiated by God and authenticated and confirmed by the Church, although this does not always happen with absolute accuracy owing to human frailties.

The meaning of ordination, what it accomplishes, and what gifts it bestows upon the recipient are found in summary form in the ordination prayers for each order. For example, the second of the two prayers for the ordination of a presbyter in our Byzantine, or Constantinopolitan, Rite provides us with a concise list of the gifts, functions, and responsibilities that pertain to the office of presbyter. It also underscores the fact that the ministry of the presbyter—and for that matter of every order in the Church—is constituted by the Holy Spirit, "who heals that which is infirm and supplies that which is lacking,"[4] and enables the presbyter to do certain things, all of which are linked to the four essential ministries of the Church. The prayer reads as follows:

> O God, great in power and unsearchable in understanding, wonderful in Your counsels over and beyond the sons of men, You the same Lord, fill this man, whom You have willed to enter into the rank of presbyter, with the gift of Your Holy Spirit so that he may be worthy to stand blamelessly at

> Your altar, to proclaim the gospel of Your Kingdom, to exer-
> cise the sacred ministry of the word of your truth, to offer
> You gifts and spiritual sacrifices, and to renew Your people
> by the washing of regeneration; so that he also being pres-
> ent at the Second Coming of our great God and Savior Jesus
> Christ, Your only-begotten Son, he may receive the reward of
> the good stewardship of his office in the abundance of Your
> goodness. For blessed and glorified is Your most-honored
> and majestic name . . .[5]

The essential responsibilities of the presbyter described in the
prayer coincide with the Church's four constitutive activities. The presbyter, according to the prayer, presides over the priestly people to unite
their priestly prayer at every divine service and to sanctify their lives
through the celebration of the holy sacraments. He preaches the gospel
so that he may enchant people with Christ and set their hearts aflame
with divine passion. He teaches the truths of the faith and guides the
faithful in the Christian life so that they may better discern the teachings of the Church, the ethical dimensions of the life in Christ, and the
purposes God's creation.

Whereas the prayer of ordination makes an explicit reference to
three of the four essential activities of the Church (worship, preaching, and teaching), the fourth, philanthropy or good deeds, is implied
in the phrase "he may receive the reward of the good stewardship of
his office." According to St. Paul, one of the several qualifications for
the priestly office is that the candidate be a "model of good deeds"
(τύπον καλῶν ἔργων; Titus 2:7); as one who teaches by example, who
exhorts the people by deed and word "to apply themselves to good
deeds, so as to help cases of urgent need, and not to be unfruitful"
(Titus 3:14). Patriarch Bartholomew reminds us that we are all "imperfect beings who lead an imperfect life." Only God, he adds, "offers us the possibility of perfect love and brotherhood. And only by
struggling to emulate that perfection ourselves is it possible to lend
dignity to our flawed existence."[6] The presbyter, as a good steward
of the office he holds, struggles to interiorize the life of Christ in
himself and in others, whereby he creates and inspires godly action
among the people, fostering a ministry of good works and generous
service to the world, which, as the prayer of ordination affirms, will
be made evident at the Second Coming of our Great God and Savior
Jesus Christ (Matt 25:31–46).

The Qualities Required of a Priest

Because of the magnitude of the task, St. Paul tells us in his Pastoral Epistles that every candidate for holy orders should be graced with certain virtues and abilities. He states that a candidate should be above reproach and well tested; that he be dignified, sensible, moderate, fervent and sincere in faith, theologically knowledgeable, and pastorally skilled; that he be an apt teacher, a skillful apologist of the faith, and a good steward, who can effectively manage and actively direct the affairs of the faith community entrusted to his care (1 Tim 3:1–13; 4:11–16; 2 Tim 1:13–14; 4:1–5; Titus 1:5–9).

For St. Gregory the Theologian, it is not enough that a priest possess such virtues and talents. The priest, he says, must also be worthy of the grace of priesthood. Such worth arises from hearts that are humble, contrite, loving, and devoted to the rule of God. "A man," he says, "must himself be cleansed before cleansing others; himself become wise, that he may make others wise; become light, before he can give light; draw near to God, before he can bring others near; be hallowed, before he can hallow them; be possessed of hands, before leading others by the hand, and of wisdom, before he can speak wisely."[7]

Perhaps, as Professor John Erickson once noted,[8] nothing summarizes best the criteria and the qualities required of a priest and are more vital to him as the shepherd of the flock than the virtue of solicitude (φροντις), an all-embracing passionate concern and love for the people entrusted to his care by God and the Church. Such passionate love generates in the priest respect for the people and a genuine openness to their needs, reverence for the ministry itself, and a strong desire to perform the responsibilities of the office with sincerity, seriousness of purpose, and competence according to his true ability.

The priesthood requires hard work, patience, determination, and resolve. It is not an office for the timid, the indifferent, the cynical, the acquisitive, or the indolent, but for those who live life humbly, zealously, and fearlessly for God as servants of redemption. The priest is motivated above all else by a deep sense of purpose and by an abiding love for the Lord and Author of life, whose voice he hears in the deepest chambers of his heart: "Do you love Me more than these?" (John 21:15). And "You did not choose Me, but I chose you and appointed you that you should go and bear fruit" (John 15:16). In the depths of his soul, the priest knows that the command to bear fruit is accompanied by a warning and a promise: "He who abides in Me, and I in him, he it is that bears much fruit, for apart from Me you can do nothing" (John 15:5). The Church is God's vineyard. It is He who tends the vine. The clergy are His plowmen.

The Responsibilities of the Priestly Office

Doing and overseeing the four essential activities of the Church is not an option. The clergy do them because they must, because they have been clothed with the grace of priesthood, a priceless gift, entrusted to them by God and the Church "for building up the Body of Christ" (Eph 4:12). The gift of priesthood, which every recipient must honor, cherish, elevate, and protect "as the apple of the eye," carries with it certain non-negotiable responsibilities, which Christ requires of every ordained person, so that the work of salvation may be perpetuated through the Church until the close of the age. "And Jesus came and said to them, All authority in heaven and on earth has been given to Me. Go therefore and make disciples of all nations, baptizing them in the name of the Father and of the Son and of the Holy Spirit, teaching them to observe all that I have commanded you; and lo, I am with you always, to the close of the age" (Matt 28:18–20).

The clergy celebrate the sacred mysteries, preach the gospel, teach the faith, and create works of love because these activities constitute the indispensible responsibilities of the priestly office and are absolutely vital to the life of the Church in her unique mission to the world. Whatever else the clergy may do in the service of God's people, nothing is more crucial than these four activities. Indeed, every other activity worthy of the Church emanates from them and is an extension and an expression of them.

In the Church there is no ministry other than Christ's ministry.[9] Jesus said, "Truly, truly, I say to you, he who believes in me will also do the works that I do" (John 14:12). The Church's indispensable activities are, in fact, related to our Lord's own saving work. The Gospels describe these works succinctly with these words: "And Jesus went about all the cities and villages, teaching in their synagogues and preaching the gospel of the Kingdom, and healing every disease and infirmity." And the Evangelist continues, "When He saw the crowds, He had compassion for them, because they were harassed and helpless, like sheep without a shepherd. Then He said to His disciples, The harvest is plentiful, but the laborers are few; pray therefore the Lord of the harvest to send out laborers into His harvest" (Matt 9:35–38).

In every generation Christ charges every Local Church through powerful prayer to generate worthy pastoral workers to gather His harvest. Every bishop, presbyter, and deacon exercising faithfully his respective role is the laborer sent by the Lord of the harvest into His harvest to reap what He has sown.

The four fundamental activities or ministries—worship, preaching, catechesis, and philanthropy—are interconnected and interdependent. Each serves the same purpose and goal: to place us within the mystery of God's Kingdom by doing the works of Christ. And the Eucharist reveals the Kingdom, which is future to us, in the form of the present.[10]

The Liturgy: The Matrix in which the Essential Activities Are Formed, Taught, and Enacted

Clergy know by experience that worship, itself a constitutive activity of the Church, is the matrix, or the setting, in which the other three activities are formed, informed, taught, and enacted. To be sure, as Fr. Alexander Schmemann was fond of saying, it is faith that gives birth to and shapes liturgy (worship), but it is liturgy that bears testimony to faith and becomes its true and adequate expression and norm. Indeed, as one theologian asserts, "The liturgy is the bodily form of dogma, and dogma is the soul of the liturgy."[11] The Liturgy, as participation in the mystery of communion with God, shapes and informs the other three indispensible activities of the Church.

In an article written several years ago, Bishop Kallistos Ware posed three questions, to which he gave a succinct but powerful answer. "What is the purpose for which the Church exists?" he asked. "What is her unique and characteristic role, which no one else and nothing else can fulfill? What is it that the Church attains that ethnic assemblies, youth clubs, and charitable works cannot? The answer can only be one: The Church exists in order to bring us salvation in Christ Jesus; to bring us salvation not by some abstract or theoretical means—since the Church does not constitute a philosophical system or ideology—but with a concrete and visible form, through the celebration of the Divine Liturgy. Behold the unique and characteristic role of the Church, that which the Church alone can accomplish: to offer the Holy Eucharist . . . [And] the Holy Eucharist, which is the quintessence of the Church, is realized visibly only within the local parish."[12]

Who among us does not recall daily the simple truth we learned in our classes as seminary students, a truth which we have come to affirm personally through experience in the exercise of our pastoral ministry? The truth of which I speak is that the Church is primarily a worshipping community and that Christians are above all liturgical, or worshipping, beings. In the words of Patriarch Bartholomew, "Orthodox spirituality is liturgical, sacramental, and eucharistic . . . Holy men and women are those persons who have discovered the meaning of their life as liturgical beings, as ecclesial persons."[13]

Clergymen have come to know from personal experience that the miracle of the new life in Christ, acquired through Baptism and lived in community, is built on and around the Table of the Lord. The life of the parish community and its members is centered basically on the weekly celebration of the Divine Liturgy, with its two essential foci: the *amvon* and the Table, which is to say, the proclamation of God's word and the Eucharist. Inasmuch as the reading of the Scriptures is a constitutive element of the Divine Liturgy, so is the homily, or sermon.

This fact is underscored by the prayer of the Divine Liturgy before the reading of the Gospel: "Shine within our hearts, loving Master, the pure light of Your divine knowledge that we may comprehend the message of Your Gospel. Instill in us also reverence for Your blessed commandments, so that having conquered all sinful desires, we may pursue a spiritual life, thinking and doing all those things that are pleasing to You. For You, Christ our God, are the light of our souls and bodies . . ."[14] A careful reading of the prayer indicates that the sermon, or homily, is an integral part of the Divine Liturgy because it helps the faithful delve into the mysteries of the faith contained in the Scriptures and tradition.

Whereas the message of the Gospel may be understood directly or immediately—inasmuch as the word of God speaks by and for itself— its deeper meanings are drawn from the explanations provided by the preacher, who is charged to open the Scriptures, to stir the souls of the faithful, and to contribute to their edification in the faith (Luke 24:32). The record of the Scripture and tradition is apprehended and understood correctly only within the context of the living faith of the Church, because the Church alone is "the pillar and bulwark of the truth" (1 Tim 3:15), the sole repository of faith.[15] Or, as Archbishop Demetrios (Trakatelis) puts it, "The complete and the whole content of the divine revelation in Christ [has been] preserved intact in its unsurpassed beauty and integrity for twenty centuries by the Church."[16]

There is more to preaching than retelling the narrative and applying its truths to everyday living. As St. Hilary of Poitiers noted, "Scripture is not in the reading, but in the understanding."[17] Thus, as Gordon Lathrop tells it, the priest's task, as preacher and teacher, "is not so much about things to do as it is [to offer] an utterly new way to understand the world, and so an utterly new way to conceive and thus live our lives."[18] The mere dry recital of facts will not alone create a living and vibrant faith. The "slowness of heart" of people will be transformed into joyful commitment only when Jesus' life is interpreted as the fulfillment of God's promises in all the Scriptures (Luke 24:13–35).[19]

Between the narrative and its application comes the hard work of interpreting and teaching the deeper meanings of God's word, a task and a mission entrusted to the clergy, even as the whole people of God (the λαός) are the guardians of tradition and piety.[20] Precisely because the task of preserving, teaching, and spreading the faith is so vital a task of the bishop and presbyter, a classical and theological education is a desired precondition for ministry. However, whatever intellectual abilities and other competencies and gifts a clergyman may bring to his task, none is more vital than a deep and abiding love for Christ, or as Fr. Georges Florovsky put it, "no one profits from the Gospels unless he be first in love with Christ. For Christ is not a text but a living Person, and He abides in His Body, the Church."[21]

The Divine Liturgy: Encountering Christ, the Word and Son of God

Divine grace flows through the Divine Liturgy to constitute, renew, and sustain the Church in her permanence. The Church finds her fullest expression and realization through the Holy Eucharist, because there the community of believers is continually formed to be the mystical Body of Christ. In every liturgical event, but most especially at the Divine Liturgy, by the grace of the Holy Spirit who constitutes the Church that Christ established, we encounter Christ, who renders present both His past saving acts and their fulfillment. In and through the sacred rites of the Liturgy, God acts to take us to Himself, to enfold us in His self-giving, that we may become partakers of divine nature (2 Pet 1:4), sharers in the divine qualities of incorruptibility and immortality (1 Cor 15:53–55).

At the Divine Liturgy,[22] celebrated in faith every Sunday and feast day, we hear God's word, which calls us to repentance. Made clean by the word (John 15:3), our souls and hearts are cleansed from evil consciousness. At the Divine Liturgy we express our indissoluble unity in love and confess our common faith. We find another life and receive the seeds of holiness to bear fruit commensurate to the gift. We experience the transfiguration of our being by communicating in the Lord and realize ever more fully our ecclesial identity, by which "we subsist in a manner that transcends every exclusiveness of a biological and social kind."[23] In and through the Eucharist, we are fashioned continually into a new creation, whereby the self-giving, unconditional, and sacrificial love of God made manifest in the Christ event becomes the new inner principle, source, and guide of life.

Liturgy Forms Identity and Lives

Although attending divine services is itself good, being energized by liturgy for the good and for increased faith is a greater good. Some people complain that the Liturgy is repetitious. But so are most, if not all, of life's essential activities. For the attentive worshipper, however, the Liturgy is anything but tedious routine. It is an epiphanic, revelatory event, an opportunity for conversion and transcendence. Enacted reverently and joyfully, authentic worship brings us to the ultimate frontier, to the outer limits of our creatureliness, where we meet the loving embrace of the living God and bathe in the glorious light and beauty of His Kingdom. That is why clergy and laity alike must make sure that every liturgical service is liturgy at its best, which is to say an enriching experience aesthetically, intellectually, emotionally, and spiritually, if people are to move beyond the ordinary, beyond the confines of naive religiosity.

Liturgy builds faith and forms personal and communal identity. As Steven Platten observed, "Liturgy at its best forms lives . . . Liturgy helps shape our knowledge of the faith, our confidence in the faith, and our capacity to live the faith."[24] But we must ask ourselves, is the worship practiced in our parishes a liturgy at its best? Does it induce the inner and exterior involvement of the people? Does it stir the soul, enlighten the mind, and strengthen the will for the good and the holy? Or has our worship become opaque, burdened with ritual formalism? Has our liturgy ceased to be dangerous, as someone once asked, leaving us and the world in which we live unaffected and unchanged?[25]

Liturgy at its best issues from strong faith, which in turn is nurtured by effective catechesis. Hence, bishops and presbyters, as guides and shepherds of the people of God, are obliged to offer the faithful sound instruction helping them become, to the degree possible for each, theologically and liturgically literate.

Dignified and inspiring liturgical rituals, elegant and lucid liturgical texts, and stirring and uplifting liturgical music help to make good liturgy. But so do meaningful, challenging, and persuasive liturgical homilies that mine the inexhaustible riches of the Scriptures and the doctrines of the faith. Homilies that are full of meaning—and not platitudes and shallow talk—contribute greatly to the making of good liturgy, to the making of a restorative and transformative environment in which we are given the possibility to experience both the simplicity as well as the radicality of the gospel: that in Christ we have become a new creation, a gift realized ever more fully through the ongoing conversion of the heart.

We must not forget that preaching is an essential component of Orthodox worship and is itself an act of prayer and a transforming event, because it engages the people with the essential truths of the faith. But so do all the constitutive elements of the Liturgy, and most especially the prayers and hymns, which are replete with biblical language and imagery, theological insights, and ethical imperatives. Superbly didactic and inspirational, they constitute a string of tiny sermons that allow the truths of the faith to nestle in the hearts of people, informing their way of thinking, so that sluggish faith may be rekindled and active faith may be strengthened.

Preaching the Word of God Cannot Be Neglected

Preaching the word of God and preserving the unity of the faith must never be neglected or depreciated. From the start, preaching and teaching were of utmost importance to the Church, as the Scriptures (Luke 24:13–35; Acts 2:42, 46; 6:2–4) and the early Church Fathers tell us. And both these ministries together with philanthropy were intimately related to worship. The sermon, as some think, is not incidental to the Divine Liturgy, and I would add to any liturgical service, but an integral part of it, as St. Justin the Martyr, writing in the middle of the second century, affirms:

> On the day named after the sun, all who live in city or countryside assemble. The memoirs of the apostle or the writings of the prophets are read for as long as time allows. When the lector has finished, the president addresses us and ex-

horts us to imitate the splendid things we have heard. Then we all stand and pray. As we said earlier, when we have finished praying, bread, wine, and water are brought up. The president then prays and gives thanks according to his ability, and the people give their assent with an "Amen!" Next, the gifts over which the thanksgiving has been spoken are distributed, and everyone shares in them, while they are also sent via the deacons to the absent brethren. The wealthy who are willing make contributions, each as he pleases, and the collection is deposited with the president, who aids orphans and widows, those who are in want because of sickness or some other reason, those in prison, and visiting strangers— in short he takes care of all in need.[26]

The witness of St. Justin is of special interest on several counts. The community he describes is similar to the community in the book of Acts; both are established on the teaching of the apostles and the "breaking of bread" (Acts 2:42). His description of the liturgical actions contains the essential components that comprise the Divine Liturgy: reading the Word of God, the homily, prayer, and the Eucharist. Finally, his description also links the Church's concern for the needy, her philanthropic work, to the Eucharist.

In an age such as ours[27] when countless voices through a myriad of media seek to lay claim to people's thoughts, hearts, and souls, every bishop and priest must take to heart St. Paul's admonition to his beloved disciple Timothy: "I charge you in the presence of God and of Christ Jesus who is to judge the living and the dead, and by His appearing and His Kingdom: preach the word, be urgent in season and out of season, convince, rebuke, and exhort, be unfailing in patience and in teaching . . . Always be steady, endure suffering, do the work of an evangelist, fulfill your ministry" (2 Tim 4:1–2, 5).

Preaching the word at every Divine Liturgy and sacred service with fervor and joy, reaching out to those of faith, or of little faith, or of no faith, and teaching the truths of "the faith which was once for all delivered to the saints" (Jude 3) is of paramount importance today, as it was in every previous generation. Like St. Peter, we need to be persistent and tireless in our desire to bear testimony to the truth: "I intend always," St. Peter wrote, "to remind you of these things, though you know them and are established in the truth that you have. I think it right, as long as I am in this body, to arouse you by way of reminder" (2 Pet 1:12–13).

St. Paul tells us that "faith comes from what is heard, and what is heard comes by the preaching of Christ" (Rom 10:17). But he says, "How are men to call upon Him [Christ] in whom they have not believed? And how are they to believe in Him of whom they have never heard? And how are they to hear without a preacher? And how can men preach unless they are sent?" (Rom 10:14–15).

Bearing Witness to the Light

Divine revelation is encoded and transmitted through the medium of human language. Words matter in the Church; they carry meaning, convey truths, and foster communion. Hence, we need to use them wisely and correctly. The Lord we worship is the Word and Son of God made flesh, who "dwelt among us full of grace and truth" (John 1:14). The mission He entrusted to us is to preach and teach the word of God. The kerygma of the apostles and the dogmas of the Fathers—which contain the words of life—bring us into contact with ultimate meanings. It is the clergy's task, by vocation, education, and training, to contemplate, absorb, and apply these truths to the real, practical, everyday life of the Church and of the people they serve through sound and effective preaching and teaching.

The role of the preacher and the content of the homily, as Professor Dimitra Koukoura suggests,[28] are defined by St. John the Evangelist and Theologian in his Gospel from beginning to end, and more succinctly in his description of the ministry of John the Baptist: "There was a man sent from God, whose name was John. He came for testimony, to bear witness to the light, that all might believe through him. He was not the light, but came to bear witness to the light" (John 1:6–8). In every liturgical service, whether it is the Divine Liturgy, a sacrament, a funeral, or another prayer service, the priest is sent "to bear witness to the light," to preach and to teach not his ideas and thoughts, but "the words of eternal life" (John 6:68).

At every divine service we meet people who have heard the words of life and have believed, but who have need for further assurances, encouragement, and comfort, or have the need for greater and richer nourishment to satisfy their spiritual longings and hunger. At every divine service we also encounter people who have heard the words of life but have forgotten them, and people who have never heard them but need to hear them. Hence, no opportunity should be lost to tell the story of God's goodness, even briefly, and to recount His manifold blessings and His providential love for the world. Like the psalmist, the heart of every preacher/priest should overflow with a "goodly theme" (λόγον ἀγαθὸν; Ps 44/45:1).

To be effective, the preacher must come to know his people/audience well; he must be aware of the times and of the people's needs, concerns, worries, desires, choices, and aspirations. He must engage their hearts, minds, imaginations, and wills in ways that the Scripture will be fulfilled in their hearing (Luke 4:21). In the inner recesses of their hearts, all people—including the priest/preacher—secretly yearn to hear a truth that is larger than death, a truth that frees them from the profound sense of alienation and failure that lurks in the depths of their being as the result of the ancestral sin. They yearn to hear a truth that transcends their doubts and prejudices and the hidden fears, anxieties, illusions, and lies that burden their souls and bind them to the appearances of life. They yearn to hear a truth that lifts them out of the dark and joyless pits of enmity and thrusts them into the mystery of divine love that opens them to the possibility of becoming the dwelling place of God, so that they may share in the plenitude of divine life.

Preaching Is an Act of Evangelism

The *amvon* in our churches is an ever-present reminder to the clergy and the people of the apostolicity and catholicity of the Church— a reminder that the word of God will not be silenced, and that Jesus' command "Go into all the world and preach the gospel to the whole creation" (Mark 16:15) must be fulfilled. Preaching is not a choice, but an essential act to be performed with dedication, due care, imagination, and a joyous heart.

Now, the preaching ministry of the Church is not confined to the hearing of the people assembled in a given place or service. The *amvon*—like the petitions for the catechumens in the Divine Liturgy— is a reminder to all, clergy and laity alike, of the missionary dimensions of community life. Mission, as Archbishop Anastasios (Yannoulatos) has emphasized, "is a basic expression of our ecclesiastical self-awareness and self-consciousness."[29] The starting point of every missionary activity, as he says, "is the promise and commandment of the risen Lord in its Trinitarian perspective: 'As the Father has sent me, even so I send you . . . Receive the Holy Spirit' (John 20:21–22)."[30] And he adds, "The work of Christ is not simply an announcement[;] it is an event, the event *par excellence* of world history, which opens the way for the ultimate end, for the completion of the upward evolution of the world. It is a matter of the assumption of human nature, for its regeneration within the life of the Holy Trinity. This assuming in love, the continuous transfer of the life of love, the recreation of all things in the light of God's glory, is being continued in space and time through the mission of the Church, the body of Christ."[31]

Preaching the word of God in and out of the Liturgy is an act of evangelism. The Church is always a Church-in-mission,[32] because through her God calls all creation to share in the freedom from bondage to decay and to obtain the glorious liberty of the children of God (Rom 8:21). Everything the Church does is for the life of the world. Thus, as Metropolitan Methodios noted in a message to the clergy of the Metropolis of Boston, "We must open the embrace of every community to welcome the sojourners of life to quench their spiritual thirsts at the well of Orthodoxy . . . Opening our embrace . . . means finding all those not connected with the Church wherever they may be . . ."[33]

In his keynote address at the 39th Biennial Clergy-Laity Congress of the Greek Orthodox Archdiocese of America, Archbishop Demetrios gave special emphasis to the theme of evangelism. "We are no longer a Church community looking for survival," he said. "Such an understanding of ourselves belongs to the past. We cannot be a self-centered, self-enclosed Greek Orthodox ecclesiastical body, limited to itself and directing its energy exclusively within itself. We cannot be a Ghetto Church. God calls us to gather His people. In order to gather God's people we have to go out, to look for them, to search places and find them and lead them to God's home. The theme of the Congress [Gather My People to My Home] calls us in no uncertain terms to reach out, to move out and start gathering the souls who look for a spiritual home, for a living community, and ultimately for a communion with God . . . Let us be the voice of Christ, everywhere, for everyone, at any time, at any place of the wide-world of God."[34]

Indeed, Patriarch Bartholomew, in his address at the Synaxis of the Heads of Orthodox Churches in 2008, emphasized the importance "of the duty of mission." He said, "There are many useful conclusions that we may gain from [the] ecclesiology of St. Paul. We confine ourselves to pointing out, first, the importance—for the life of the Church in general and for the ministry of us all in particular—of the duty of mission. The evangelization of God's people, as well as of those who do not believe in Christ, constitutes the supreme obligation of the Church . . . So we must in every way encourage and support the external mission of the Church wherever it is practiced."[35]

The Realities of Life Should Not Be Ignored

The Church is a living and dynamic organism. Hence, to fulfill their ministry of service—as celebrants, preachers, teachers, and motivators for the good—bishops, priests, and deacons have to be open, engaged, versatile, flexible, and resourceful. Sadly, however, some among us are trapped in some idealized past, satisfied with things as they are either by ideology, fatigue, indolence, or habit. Some others among us, with a "museum view" of ministry and ecclesial life, remain aloof from the demands, the problems, and the challenges of the times. Fearful of change and skeptical of new ideas, they are reluctant to try new ways of thinking, looking, and doing. But when the realities of life are ignored, horizons are limited, capacities are diminished, and ministries are impoverished. We must love, honor, and learn from the past because history is part of revelation, at once a mystery and a tragedy. As Orthodox Christians, however, our sights must be set not on the past, but on the future, on God's Kingdom, from whence we draw our identity. The Kingdom, although not yet perfectly manifest, is the focus and orientation point of the Church's activities, forming the present in the direction of the Kingdom. We must remember that tradition is not only a protective and conserving principle; it is also a principle of regeneration and growth.[36] Hence, creativity is not a departure from tradition, but the very manifestation of it.

The portrait of the priesthood that I have painted may appear to some as too idealistic, as removed from the realities of life, for who among the clergy possesses perfectly every required gift and talent enumerated in the Scriptures and the writings of the Fathers? We are, after all, frail and imperfect human beings. As practitioners of the sacred ministry, we know full well that our priesthood is often inadequately realized due to our limitations. But the power for effective ministry does not rest wholly with us. At the very beginning of the rite of ordination, we each heard from the mouth of the ordaining bishop the wonderful promise of the Lord, expressed succinctly but superbly in the words of the proclamation that the Holy Spirit, "who heals that which is infirm and supplies that which lacking," will be at work in us, so that the purposes of God may be fulfilled through earthen vessels. Anchored in this hope, we can pray fervently at every Divine Liturgy, "I implore You, look upon me, Your sinful and unworthy servant, and cleanse my soul and heart from evil consciousness. Enable me by the power of Your Holy Spirit . . ."[37] Our task is to be worthy of the grace by discharging our responsibilities faithfully, conscientiously, and courageously, mindful of the fact that whatever good and noble things we do, we do them by the inspiration and power of the Holy Spirit.

When strength eludes us and we find ourselves wanting in the exercise of our duties, we need only to turn to the Lord Christ, remembering St. Paul's words, "I can do all things in Him who strengthens me" (Phil 4:13). Christ is merciful and kind. He asks of us only three things: to keep Him, whose priesthood we bear as a gift, always in mind; to remain steadfast and immoveable in our faith; and to ceaselessly cultivate our intellect, our heart, and our will, which we freely dedicated to His service on the day of our ordination. As priests we must never stop praying, loving, hoping, or learning as we seek, by the power of the Holy Spirit, to fulfill our calling to the fullest, and not the least, of our God-given abilities.

Conclusion

Let me complete this reflection with one further note. It is hard to imagine how people can worship in Spirit and in truth, hear the word of God, and live by the truths of the faith when the community's commitment to translate its devotional and instructional acts into works of justice is lukewarm, or worse, lacking. Liturgy at its best does not end with the "Δι' εὐχῶν." Neither does good preaching and good teaching end in the church or the classroom. The truths of the faith, proclaimed by the apostles (the kerygma) and taught by the Fathers (the dogmas), must be lived. Liturgy not only rehearses the fundamental truths of the faith, which the Church has believed, preached, taught, and confessed from the beginning, it also trains people, as Walter Burghardt noted, to recognize justice or injustice when they see it and to stimulate them to live justly.[38]

In other words, having exposed us to the all-embracing love of the Triune God, the ultimate truths of our faith, and the imperatives of the Gospel, true worship, good preaching, and effective teaching, necessitate the performance of "the liturgy after the liturgy," to use the phrase originated by Archbishop Anastasios (Yannoulatos)[39] in 1963 and popularized in subsequent years by the late Romanian theologian Fr. Ion Bria, who repeated it and the ideas behind it in various conferences and publications of the World Council of Churches.[40] Good liturgy, challenging and inspirational preaching, and persuasive teaching call for a mission to the world—for the liturgy after the Liturgy—by a people who, having heard the word of God and having experienced His unconditional love, are eager to go into the world to engage it in all its complex realities and situations, to enter into its achievements as well as its miseries, contradictions, and anomalies; and, as Archbishop Demetrios once noted, "to stand up for suffering humanity and proclaim redemption in uncompromising faithfulness to God . . . expressing [His] immutable, dynamic, and redeeming love."[41]

Celebrating the mysteries faithfully, preaching the word of God with prophetic boldness, teaching the faith of the Church persuasively, and doing good works joyously are the primary activities by which the Church actualizes her sacred mission to the world and transmits the Orthodox faith, ethos, and identity to people from one generation to the next. The intent and aim of all that the Church does is the glorification of God through right worship and through the correct explanation and inspired application of divine revelation to particular life situations and circumstances.

The evangelization of the world begins locally through the life of one person and one community. Therefore, let us not hesitate, let us not fear; but with joy and confidence let us "go into all the world and preach the gospel to the whole creation . . . And they went forth and preached everywhere, while the Lord worked with them and confirmed the message by the signs that attended it" (Mark 16:15, 20).

Notes

It is a distinct honor to contribute an essay to this volume, which commemorates the twentieth anniversary of the elevation of His All-Holiness Patriarch Bartholomew to the Patriarchal Throne of Constantinople. During his tenure as Ecumenical Patriarch, in addition to his pioneering work for the protection of the natural environment and the promotion of world peace, His All-Holiness has been a visionary leader dedicated to the advancement of inter-Christian dialogue, inter-faith understanding, and especially inter-Orthodox collaboration by strengthening the bonds of love and unity among the Local Churches. An eloquent and convincing preacher, Patriarch Bartholomew has touched the hearts of countless people through his spoken and written word, bringing them hope and inspiring them to embrace all of God's creation with care and love, while strengthening their faith and increasing their desire for the good. This essay is based on a presentation I made in 2010 at the Annual Clergy Retreat of the Greek Orthodox Archdiocese of America, the subject of which was "Preaching the Word of God."

1. See John D. Zizioulas, *Being as Communion* (Crestwood, NY, 1985), 214–225.

2. Ibid., 220, 233.

3. See Constantine B. Scouteris, *Ecclesial Being: Contributions to Theological Dialogue*, ed. Christopher Veniamin (South Canaan, PA, 2005), 74–75.

4. From the proclamation, or αναρρησις, with which every ordination to the hierarchical priesthood begins.

5. See Panagiotis Trembelas, *Μικρόν Ευχολόγιον*, vol. 1 (Athens, 1950), 231; Ioannis Fountoulis, *Χειρονονία Πρεσβυτέρου: Κείμενα Λειτουργικής*, vol. 4 (Thessaloniki, 1977), 27; and Paul F. Bradshaw, *Ordination Rites of the Ancient Churches of East and West* (New York, 1990), 135. See also Pierre-Marie Gy, "Ancient Ordination Prayers," in *Ordination Rites: Past and Present*, ed. Wiebe Vos and Geoffrey Wainwright (Rotterdam, 1980), 70–93.

6. Ecumenical Patriarch Bartholomew, *In the World, Yet Not of the World* (New York, 2010), 49.

7. Cited in Robert Payne, *The Holy Fire: The Story of the Fathers of the Eastern Church* (New York, 1957), 179. For more on St. Gregory and the priesthood, see Lewis J. Patsavos, *A Noble Task: Entry into the Clergy in the First Five Centuries*, trans. Norman Russell (Brookline, 2007), 118–128.

8. John Erickson, *The Challenge of Our Past* (Crestwood, NY, 1991), 82–84.

9. See Zizioulas, *Being as Communion*, 210; and C. Scouteris, *Ecclesial Being*, 74.

10. John D. Zizioulas, *Lectures in Christian Dogmatics*, ed. Douglas Knight (London, 2008), 137.

11. Regin Prenter, "Liturgie et dogma," *Revue d'histoire et de philosophie religieuses* 38 (1958): 115–128, in Gordon Lathrop, *Holy Things: A Liturgical Theology* (Minneapolis, MN, 1998), 10.

12. Bishop Kallistos Ware, "Ενορία και Ευχαριστία," in *Ενορία, προς μία νέα Ανακάλυψή της* (Athens, n.d.), 126.

13. Ecumenical Patriarch Bartholomew, *In the World, Yet Not of the World*, 59.

14. Although this beautiful prayer is meant for all the people, it is, I believe, especially applicable to the preacher/priest, who by vocation, education, and training is charged to guide and instruct the people.

15. See, for example, The Confession of Faith, Definition 12, of Patriarch Dositheos of Jerusalem, which was ratified by the Council of Jerusalem in 1672: "We believe the Catholic [Orthodox] Church is taught by the Holy Spirit, for He is the true Paraclete, whom Christ sends from the Father in order to teach the truth and to drive away darkness from

the mind of the faithful . . . Therefore, not only are we persuaded, but do profess as true and undoubtedly certain that it is impossible for the Catholic Church to err, or at all be deceived, or even choose falsehood instead of truth. For the all-holy Spirit operates continually through the holy Fathers and Leaders faithfully ministering, delivers the Church from error of every kind" (in Ioannis Karmiris, Τα Δογματικά και συμβολικά μνημεία της Ορθοδόξου Καθολικής Εκκλησίας, vol. 2 [Athens, 1953], 755). See also Jaroslav Pelikan, *The Christian Tradition: A History of the Development of Doctrine* (Chicago, 1987), 334.

16. Archbishop Demetrios of America, *Ways of the Lord: Perspectives on Sharing the Gospel of Christ* (New York, 2010), 151.

17. Cited by Fr. Georges Florovsky, *Bible, Church, Tradition: An Eastern Orthodox View* (Belmont, MA, 1972), 17.

18. Gordon W. Lathrop, *Holy Things*, 32.

19. Luke 24:13–35 contains the story of Jesus' post-Resurrection appearance to Cleopas and the other disciple on the road to Emmaus. Compare Acts 8:26–40, which contains the story of the conversion of the Ethiopian eunuch. In the first instance, the risen Christ Himself "opens" the Scriptures and reveals the deeper meanings of God's word to the two disciples. In the second instance, Philip the deacon does the same for the Ethiopian eunuch.

20. The power to discern between truth and falsehood is given to the whole people who are engaged actively in the life of the Church. This principle was noted by the Patriarchs of the East in a statement issued in 1848: "Among us, neither Patriarchs nor Synods have ever been able to introduce novelties, because the defender of the religion is the body of the Church, that is to say, the people, which want its religion to remain eternally unchanged and of like form to that of the Fathers" (in Ioannis Karmiris, Τα Δογματικά και συμβολικά μνημεία της Ορθοδόξου Καθολικής Εκκλησίας, 920). The final authority rests upon the conscience of the whole Church guided by the Holy Spirit. This said, it is equally important to make certain distinctions. The laity are neither the arbiters nor the official public teachers of the faith. Their task to receive and acknowledge the truth and safeguard the faith from innovations and distortions. It is the responsibility chiefly of bishops, either singly or corporately, to proclaim and define the truth, which has been present always in the conscience of the Church. See Kallistos Ware, "The Ecumenical Councils and the Conscience of the Church," *Kanon: Jahrbuch der Gesellschaft für das Recht der Ostkirchen* 2 (1974): 228–233; and A. Calivas, "Theology and Theologians: An Orthodox Perspective," in Rodney L. Petersen and Nancy M. Rourke, eds., *Theological Literacy for the Twenty-First Century* (Grand Rapids, MI, 2002), 23–38.

21. Georges Florovsky, *Bible, Church, Tradition*, 14.

22. For more on the Divine Liturgy, see A. Calivas, *Aspects of Orthodox Worship* (Brookline, MA, 2003), 162–192.

23. Zizioulas, *Being as Communion,* 60.

24. Stephen Platten, "The Uses of Liturgy: Worship Nourishing Mission," *Worship* 83, no. 3 (2009): 234.

25. See David B. Baltchelder, "Holy God, Dangerous Liturgy: Preparing the Assembly for Transforming Encounter," *Worship* 79, no. 4 (2005).

26. Justin the Martyr, *Apology* 1.67, in Lucien Deiss, *Springtime of the Liturgy* (Collegeville, MN, 1979), 93–94.

27. For the challenges facing the preacher/priest today see, for example, J. Sergius Halvorsen, "The Context of the Eucharistic Liturgy," in Michael Monshau, ed., *Preaching at the Double Feast: Homiletics for Eucharistic Worship* (Collegeville, MN, 2006), 111–149; and Nikos Kokosalakis, "The Eastern Orthodox Tradition in Non-secular, Secular, and Post-secular context," *International Practical Theology* 9 (2008): 106–109, and the same article in Greek translation, "Θρησκεία και πλουραλιστική κοινωνία," *Συναξη* 110 (April–June 2009): 64–69.

28. Dimitra Koukoura, *Σπουδή και χριστιανική ομιλία,* vol. 1 (Thessaloniki, 2009), 109–110.

29. Archbishop Anastasios, *Mission in Christ's Way* (Brookline, MA; Geneva, 2010), 210.

30. Ibid., 211.

31. Ibid., 211–212.

32. See Emmanuel Clapsis, "The Holy Spirit in Creation: Missionary Implications," in *The Holy Spirit and Mission* (Geneva: WCC, 1990); and A. Calivas, *Challenges and Opportunities: The Church in Her Mission to the World* (Brookline, MA, 2001), 1–5.

33. Metropolitan Methodios, "Thoughts for the New Ecclesiastical Year," August 2009, The Metropolis of Boston.

34. Archbishop Demetrios of America, *Ways of the Lord,* 79–80 and 88. The keynote address was delivered at the 39th Clergy-Laity Congress of the Archdiocese in Washington, DC, on July 14, 2008.

35. "Address of His All Holiness Ecumenical Patriarch Bartholomew at the Synaxis of the Heads of Orthodox Churches: The Ecumenical Patriarchate, October 10, 2008," *Greek Orthodox Theological Review* 53, nos. 1–4 (2008): 299.

36. See A. Calivas, *Theology: The Conscience of the Church* (Brookline, MA, 2002), 23–27. For a more extensive treatment on the meaning of holy tradition in the Orthodox Church, see John McGuckin, "The Orthodox Sense of Tradition," in *The Orthodox Church: An Introduction to Its History, Doctrine, and Spiritual Culture* (London, 2008), 90–119.

37. From the Prayer at the Cherubic Hymn of the Divine Liturgy. See *The Divine Liturgy of Saint John Chrysostom* (Brookline, MA, 1985), 13.

38. Walter J. Burghardt, "Worship and Justice Reunited," in Anne Y. Koester, ed., *Liturgy and Justice: To Worship God in Spirit and Truth* (Collegeville, MN, 2002). The *Shepherd of Hermas* (Eighth Mandate: 8–11), an ancient Christian text, provides us with a succinct description of the good in which we are called to walk. "Sir, make clear to me also the nature of good . . . The deeds of goodness that you are to perform and from which you are not to hold back [are the following]. In the forefront are faith, fear of the Lord, love, concord, upright speech, truthfulness, patience. There is nothing superior to these in the life of human beings . . . Let me enumerate also the consequent good actions: the assistance of widows, visiting orphans and the poor, ransoming God's servants in their difficulties, showing hospitality . . . non-resistance to anyone, being of a quiet disposition, being poorer than all men, honoring the aged, practicing justice, exercising fraternal charity, enduring insult, being long-suffering, abstaining from spite, comforting those who are troubled in spirit, not rejecting those who have stumbled in the faith, but winning them back and encouraging them, calling sinners to order, not oppressing debtors in their needs—all this and more besides . . . Walk in them, then, and do not hold back from them and you will live to God." The text is found in *The Apostolic Fathers* (New York, 1947), 272. As I have noted elsewhere, the intercessions in the Anaphora of the Divine Liturgy of St. Basil also provide us with a succinct but powerful summary of the pastoral ministry and of the works of love that we are called to do.

39. For the origins and meaning of the phrase, see Archbishop Anastasios, *Mission in Christ's Way*, 94–96. The phrase was used to convey the following meanings: "The event (of the Divine Liturgy) must not be lost as an instantaneous emotion, but the Liturgy must be extended into daily life. And all of life must be transfigured into a liturgy . . . The Liturgy has to be continued in the personal, everyday situations . . . Without this continuation the Liturgy remains incomplete. Since in the Eucharistic event we are incorporated in Him who came to serve the world and to be sacrificed for it, we have to express in concrete *diaconia*, in community life, our new being in Christ, the Servant of all. The sacrifice of the Eucharist must be extended in personal sacrifices for the people in need, the brothers for whom Christ died . . ."

40. Ion Bria, ed., *Martyria-Mission: The Witness of the Orthodox Churches Today* (Geneva, 1980); and Ion Bria and Petros Vassiliades, Ορθόδοζη χριστιανική μαρτυρία (Katerini, Greece, 1989).

41. Bishop Demetrios Trakatellis, "Theology in Encounters," *Greek Orthodox Theological Review* 32, no. 1 (1987): 36.

Chapter 2

THE DIGNITY OF THE POOR AND ALMSGIVING IN ST. JOHN CHRYSOSTOM

Rev. Dr. Emmanuel Clapsis
Archbishop Iakovos Professor of Orthodox Theology

General Remarks

Among of the central pastoral concerns that St. John Chrysostom has addressed in his exegetical writings are the impoverished conditions of the poor and the need for all Christians to care for them. In his voluminous writings, he spoke forty times on almsgiving alone, some thirteen times on poverty, more than thirty times on avarice, and about twenty times against wrongly acquired and wrongly used wealth.[1] Of Chrysostom's exegetical homilies, the majority of these on which we will rely in this paper were delivered in Antioch between 386 and 398, while he was still only a presbyter.[2] At that time, Antioch was one of the most important and prosperous cities of the Roman Empire: an occasional imperial residence, a city of merchants, administrators, and scholars. Along with its economic and social prosperity, Antioch had its own social and economic problems, and poverty was one of the most salient.

The content of the sermons discloses the preacher's view of his congregants' needs, what they must know about their faith, and the practical implications of their faith for their lives either in the church or in the world at large. Incidental comments made during the delivery of the exegetical homilies—such as praise or criticism of the audience, responses to commonly asked questions, and references to life outside of church—provide useful information about the composition of the congregation and its reaction to the religious precepts of the sermon. Focusing on the homilies of Chrysostom, the mid-fifth-century

23

historian Sozomen wrote, "John attracted the admiration of the people, while he strenuously expiated against sin, and testified the same indignation against all acts of injustice as if they had been perpetuated against him. This boldness pleased the common people, but grieved the wealthy and the powerful, who were guilty of most of the vices he denounced."[3] His prophetic criticism against the abuses of wealth and his strong advocacy of the needs of the poor lead us to wonder who the audience of Chrysostom was. Did he try to appease the possibly overwhelming presence of the poor in the congregation by denouncing the abuses of wealth? In response to the fact that Chrysostom frequently addressed and discussed the wealthy, Wendy Mayer[4] asks whether these references reflect the social dominance of the wealthy in that community or whether such concentration upon this group means that its members were numerically dominant in the Church. She argues for the former case. Disproportionate attention to socially dominant groups does not prove that other types of people were not present. Mayer's interpretation of Chrysostom's congregation includes upper class women as well as men, their slaves, clergy, and at times ascetics. Artisans and soldiers also listened to the sermons, but not the extremely poor who begged outside of the church and in the market. Chrysostom, through his preaching, assumes the responsibility of making visible the invisible poor, whom the better-off in his congregation had bypassed, either by ignoring their presence or demeaning their dignity as human beings.[5]

Scholars assessing the theological writing of Chrysostom and his pastoral ministry have referred to him as the most significant moralist and ethical preacher of his time.[6] Louis Bouyer states that "Chrysostom betrays a 'distressing poverty' of spiritual depth; that he merely crosses Christian ideals with stoic sobriety, and an indifference to terrestrial fortune; and in favoring the monastic way of life, he proposes a Hellenistic idea of virtue devoid of mystical meaning, and limited to sheer moralism."[7] Such a view reflects the travail of modern theology, which suffers from its disjunction from ethics and its separation from the fullness of ecclesial life. For John Chrysostom and for the Fathers of the early Church, theology and ethics are inseparably united, expressing and communicating as an ecclesial act the totality of the Church's faith.

In this paper I will argue that Chrysostom's views on the dignity of the poor and the importance of almsgiving are grounded on his theological anthropology as it is formed in Baptism and lived in the Church.

Christians by virtue of their Baptism ought to perceive their personal and communal life in the world from the perspective of their participation in God's Kingdom, which they already have began to experience in the Church. In other words, their identity is primarily shaped not by what they were or continue to be in the world, but by what they become through Baptism, by which the enter into a communion with God and become citizens of His Kingdom. This is the basis of Chrysostom's understanding of the dignity of all people and the care that they should have for one another, especially for the poor.

Anthropological and Theological Premises

Baptism, for Chrysostom, inscribes the faithful on the citizen lists of heaven.[8] They become the visible sign of the new creation, as St. Paul states in 2 Corinthians 5:17: "If any man is in Christ, he is a new creature."[9] Chrysostom exhorts those who have been baptized to think and do things that lead them into the heavenly world or indicate that they deserve to be its citizens.[10] They are "alien citizens"[11] as far as their life in the world is concerned. This means that they neither reject the world in its totality, because they continue to be its citizens, nor do they wholeheartedly accept the world even in its best or ideal expression. This critical appreciation and reception of the world is built into the vision of life that they derived from their beliefs about what the world is and will become in the coming reign of God. He attributes this transformation of the baptized faithful to be the primary effect of God's grace:

> Did you see how a new creation has truly taken place? The grace of God has entered these souls and molded them anew, reformed them, and made them different from what they were. It did not change their substance, but made over their will, no longer permitting the tribunal mind's eyes to entertain an erroneous notion, but by dissipating the mist, which was blinding their eyes, God's grace made them to see the ugly deformity of evil and virtue's shining beauty as they truly are.[12]

God's grace, for Chrysostom, plays a primary role in enabling the faithful to establish and to enhance their unity with God without ignoring their human responsibilities toward their brethren.[13]

In the reign of God, every human being is welcome regardless
of his or her social status. Distinctions of power, class, gender, age,
and bodily health are cast aside; they lose their worldly significance in
God's love:

> Come to me . . . His invitation is one of kindness, His good-
> ness is beyond description. Come to me all, not only rulers
> but also their subjects, not only the rich but also the poor, not
> only the free but also the slaves, not only men but women,
> not only young but also the old, not only of those of sound
> body but also the maimed and those with mutilated limbs,
> all of you, He says, come! For such are the Master's gifts; He
> knows no distinction of slave and free, nor of rich and poor,
> but all such inequality is cast aside.[14]

Based on God's acceptance of all human beings in His Kingdom, Chrysostom exhorts those entering the Church to adopt the same kind of
sensibility and attitude toward the others, their brethren. In Christ, he
notes, "every difference of honor is cancelled out; there is one esteem
for all, one gift, one brotherhood binding us together, the same grace."[15]
Chrysostom attributes the overcoming of all differences and distinctions in
the Church to the transformation of the faithful into a new creation as a result of their denunciation of the devil and their entrance into the "world of
the Spirit":

> It is certainly marvelous and contrary to expectation, but this
> rite [exorcism] does away with all differences and distinction
> of rank. Even if a man happens to enjoy worldly honor, if he
> happens to glitter wealth, if he boasts of high lineage or the
> glory which is his in this world, he stands side by side with
> the beggar and with him who is clothed in rags, and many at
> time with the blind and the lame. Nor is he disgusted by this,
> because he knows that all these differences find no place in
> the world of the spirit, where one looks only for the soul that
> is well disposed.[16]

The new outlook of life that people derive from grounding their
lives in the coming reign of God transforms them into "guardians of
the poor." Chrysostom believes that persons who have transposed
themselves into the future life are well disposed and prepared to be
guardians of the destitute:

> For he who can philosophize about the resurrection, and can remove himself entirely to the future life, will account the present circumstances as nothing: neither wealth, nor plenty, nor gold, nor silver, nor the covering cloths, nor luxuriousness, nor expensive tables, nor any other such thing. And he who accounts these as nothing will more readily abound in the guardianship of the poor.[17]

His claims about the equal status of all human beings in the Church because of their Baptism and their current participation in the future reign of God cannot be empirically observed in the life of the Church. The desired goal of Chrysostom is to transform the life of the Church and of the faithful to reflect the new creation that they have become in their unity with God. Yet, this vision is not a utopia. Chrysostom believes that the monastic life he had experienced manifests the egalitarian spirit of the Christian faith. A visit to a monastery, he suggests, could teach humility to the powerful people and reassure the poor of their dignity: "A farm laborer and one who has no experience with worldly affairs sit near the commander of troops, who thinks much of his authority, all sitting on a pallet of straw."[18] In his commentary on Matthew 23:11–12, which defines the Christian understanding of humility, Chrysostom asserts that humility as it is described by Jesus is lived in the "the city of virtue,"[19] by which he means the monastery. Thus he says, those listening to his homily will find the illustrious and rich having laid aside all worldly rank, serving "those that come there." No one asks whether a person is slave or free. "No man there is great or mean." There is one table for all. "There is no wealth and poverty there, no honor and dishonor." Because of this "there is great equality amongst them, wherefore also there is much facility for virtue." Several scholars argue that Chrysostom's own experience of the monastic life makes him take on a more progressive position about the poor and the rich.[20]

The intention of Chrysostom was not to abolish hierarchical social structures, but to instill in the people a sense of human solidarity grounded on their "heavenly citizenship," their participation in God's Kingdom.[21] The equality and the dignity of all people is, for Chrysostom, a gift of God that entails an active concern and care for the welfare of all human beings, but especially for the most vulnerable, the poor.[22] Being compassionate and caring for the poor and the needy is a sign that discloses the conscious participation of its practioners in the reality of the new creation that God has granted to the world. Thus, for Chrysostom the ethic of compassion and active care for the poor expressed in almsgiving is theologically grounded upon the eschato-logical vision of the coming reign of God.

The fact that the faithful do not reflect in their lives the heavenly citizenship that they have acquired through Baptism motivates Chryso-stom to address issues of wealth and poverty. Worldly citizenship, with all that it entails, has overshadowed their eschatological ethos. He ad-dresses this matter by reminding his congregants of their heavenly citizenship. In this response, we can grasp Chrysostom's response to people's questions concerning whether the possession or lack of wealth reflected God's judgment.[23] People were debating whether the existence of wealth and poverty actually reflected God's judgment, in the context of the belief that life's events were not random. Chrysostom begins his pastoral response on this matter by affirming initially that wealth is a gift of God. The reality of life with all its injustices led Chrysostom to ques-tion whether all wealth could be understood this way. He tried to resolve the dilemma by defining the nature of wealth as either a gift from God or simply something permitted by him.[24] Chrysostom draws this distinc-tion between the wealth acquired as God's gift and that acquired with God's permission in order to explain the improper use of possessions by the rich.[25] Russell Edward Willoughby argues that Chrysostom draws this distinction possibly to refrain from attributing the evils that accom-pany misused wealth to the work of God.[26] Concerning wealth, the ma-jor argument of Chrysostom is that wealth itself is neutral; whether or not it is good depends on how one uses it:

> Wealth will be good for its possessor if he does not spend it
> only on luxury, or on strong drink and harmful pleasures; if
> he enjoys luxury in moderation and distributes the rest to the
> stomachs of the poor, then wealth is a good thing.[27]

Consequently, Chrysostom distinguishes the wealthy that use their riches rightly from the covetous.

> I do fasten upon the rich: or rather not the rich, but those
> who make a bad use of their riches. For I am continually say-
> ing that I do not attack the character of the rich man, but
> of the rapacious. A rich man is one thing, a rapacious man
> is another: an affluent man is one thing, a covetous man is
> another. Make clear distinctions, and do not confuse things
> which are diverse. Art thou a rich man? I forbid thee not. Art
> thou a rapacious man? I denounce thee.[28]

Frequently, Chrysostom shows that the possession of great wealth can be a great misfortune. Riches are dangerous because they often undermine the virtue of compassion.[29] He argues that one who enjoys such luxury and neglects others who are in need due to hunger lives in wickedness and inhumanity. Chrysostom depicts the rich who do not practice almsgiving as crueler than wild beasts. He describes this cruelty as the worst kind of wickedness; it is an inhumanity without rival.[30]

To transform the attitudes of the wealthy toward the destitute and to encourage them to share their wealth, he reminds all that God will judge the people based on their beneficence and their practice of almsgiving. The prospect of judgment and retribution is of central importance in Chrysostom's understanding of Christian moral life; if goodness is not rewarded and evil punished after this life—particularly because the good so often suffer, and the wicked prosper, in the present world—then our most basic sense of justice will be rendered absurd, and our faith in God's provident care of the world contradicted.[31]

The Suffering of the Poor

Chrysostom is determined to help his congregants to become cognizant of the suffering of the poor. His admirable endeavors on this matter reflect not only his theology and his uncompromising commitment to the gospel, but also his personal experience of the suffering of the poor to whom he had while distributed alms as a deacon in Antioch (381 AD).[32] Frederick Farrar observes, "From his work as a deacon, Chrysostom derived an ever-deepening impression of the misery of the world."[33] His personal contact with the poor as a deacon distributing the aid of the Church to them had an immense impact upon his preaching on wealth and poverty.[34]

Chrysostom describes the economic conditions. He states that in Antioch about a tenth of the population was abjectly poor. The very rich also represented about a tenth of the population. The Church in Antioch had an income not exceeding that of "one of the lowest among the wealthy"—and it had to maintain more than three thousand widows and virgins, not including the prisoners, the sick, and the poor.[35] Chrysostom comes to the conclusion that if ten wealthy people were willing to distribute their money, "there would be no poor."[36]

> Let us distribute then amongst the poor the whole multitude of the city, and ye will see the disgrace how great it is. For the very rich indeed are but few, but those that come next to them are but few. But those that come next to them are many; again, the poor are much fewer than these. Nevertheless, although there are so many that are able to feed the hungry, many go to sleep in their hunger, not because those that have are not able with ease to succor them, but because of their great barbarity and inhumanity. For if both the wealthy, and those next to them, were to distribute amongst themselves those who are in need of bread and raiment, scarcely would one poor person fall to the share of fifty men or even a hundred.[37]

Chrysostom takes the initiative to be an advocate of the extremely poor, who most probably were either outside of the gates of the church waiting for alms or seeking alms in the agora. He is concerned for the beggars that wander uncared for in the market place in harsh winter. He brings to the church, through his homilies, their suffering with the intention to motivate his audience to recognize their responsibility to provide to the poor at least the minimal necessities for survival.

> Today, I stand before you to make a just, useful, and suitable intercession. I come from no one else; only the beggars who live in our city elected me for this purpose, not with words, votes, and the resolve of a common council, but rather with their pitiful and most bitter spectacles. In other words, just as I was passing through the marketplace and the narrow lanes, hastening to your assembly, I saw in the middle of the streets many outcasts, some with severed hands, others with gouged-out eyes, others filled with festering ulcers and incurable wounds, especially exposing those body parts that, because of their stored-up rottenness, they should be concealing. I thought it the worst inhumanity not to appeal to your love on their behalf.[38]

He describes the dehumanizing means to which beggars resort to when seeking alms from the better off, while at the same time he denounces the attitudes of those who amuse themselves with the suffering and the indignities of the desperate poor:

> There are other poor people . . . who, when their begging
> yields them nothing, start to do tricks, some eating the
> leather from worn out shoes, others driving sharp nails into
> their heads; still others plunging their naked bodies in wa-
> ter frozen by the cold—or doing other even more senseless
> things in order to present a wretched spectacle. But while
> these things are going on, you stand there laughing and mar-
> veling—being entertained by the miseries of others . . . And
> in order that he may perform his tricks better, you give him
> money more liberally.[39]

The better-off, however, are not readily ashamed. The spectacle of
the poor and the indignities that they are undergoing is for them an
amusement, an entertainment, and this generates anger in Chrysostom.
At the same time, he repudiates their inhumanity and cruelty, elevating
the status of the poor by identifying them with Christ. He encourages all
to be charitable and compassionate to the poor, because through them
they communicate directly with Christ.

Chrysostom defends the poor against the charges of the rich that
their impoverished life is the result of their idleness. He argues that
God continually gives the sun, moon, fountains, rain, and His other
gifts to all, including the idle. The rich are rebuked for their idleness
and for giving money to vain entertainers and jugglers.[40] When he
hears from the rich that the poor engage in many lies and inventions,
he replies that this only means that the poor must be pitied because
it is their poverty that has forced these things upon them.[41] However, even though Chrysostom is protecting the poor from attack
by the rich, he is not advocating a life of idleness for the poor. He
clearly describes his attitude as one "very earnestly wishing all to be
employed; for sloth is the teacher of all wickedness."[42] What Chrysostom opposes is humankind's inhumanity: "But I beseech you not to
be unmerciful, nor cruel."[43] Chrysostom shows that the wealthy are
likewise hardened:

> But we [the rich], so far from pitying, add even those cruel
> words, "Hast thou not received once and again?" so we talk.
> What then? Because he was once fed, hath he no need to be
> fed again? Why dost thou not make these laws for thine own
> belly also, and say to it likewise, Thou wert filled yesterday,
> and the day before, seek it not now?[44]

This raises the question of whether charitable giving should be discriminate or indiscriminate. Certainly, Chrysostom seems to be in favor of indiscriminate giving. Alms given to the undeserving poor at least have the chance of changing their hearts and making them deserving.

The Value of the Poor

Chrysostom portrays the poor, who are recognized as having nothing material to contribute, as being necessary for the spiritual well being of the rich. Referring to the rich, he advises them, "For if there were no poor, the greater part of your sins would not be removed. They are the healers of your wounds; their hands are medicinal to you . . . You give money, and with it your sins pass away."[45]

In an effort to be better seen and to be fed, many of the poor would congregate outside of the churches on the days of worship. Chrysostom, afraid that the better-off would still ignore them and anxious to enhance even further their visibility, reminds his audience of the importance of the poor for the being of the Church.[46] Elaborating on Paul's metaphor of the ecclesiastical body, he states,

> And in fact, in the body even the small members seem to contribute no small service; when they are removed, they often harm even the great ones. What, for example, is more insignificant in the body than the hair? Nonetheless, if you remove these insignificancies from the eyebrows and eyelids, you spoil the entire grace of the countenance, and the eye will no longer appear as beautiful as it did. Despite the trifling nature of the loss, all the comeliness is destroyed— and not only the comeliness, but much of the use of the eyes . . . And in fact, in the church as well there are many different members: some are more valued; some less . . . What, for example, is more insignificant than the beggars? Nonetheless, even these perform a great service in the church, fastened to the doors of the sanctuary and providing a great adornment. Without these, the fullness of the church would not be completed.[47]

As eyelashes beautify the eye and optimize its function, so the desperately poor adorn and perfect the Church. The eye whose eyelashes have been physically plucked loses some sight of the world below; the Church whose impoverished have been conceptually deleted loses some sight of the world above. Opening one's eyes to the broken bodies of the poor that cluster outside of the doors, Chrysostom insists, brings into the people the riches of God. He believes that the Church is incomplete without the presence and participation of the poor in its life.

Chrysostom, commenting on the presence of the destitute at the entrances of the churches, reminds his audience of the lessons that their presence conveys:

> Anyone sober and willing to pay attention learns no small lesson even from the houses of prayer. Indeed, the poor sit before the entrances of the churches and shrines of the martyrs so that we may derive great benefit from their spectacle. Reflect that, when we enter earthly palaces, it's impossible to see anything like this: noble, famous, wealthy, intelligent men are rushing about everywhere. Into the true palaces, however—I mean the church and the oratories of the martyrs—go the possessed, the maimed, the poor, the old, the blind, and the crippled. And why is this? So that you may learn from the spectacle of these people. If you've come dragging along any arrogance from outside, after you've looked at these people, you should learn to cast aside your pride and humble your heart as you enter so that you may hear what's said. (Someone that prays with arrogance cannot be heard.) When you see an old man here, you should learn not to consider your youth a great thing, since these old men too were once young. When you boast a good deal about your military command or your imperial power, you should consider that from these people spring those that have become illustrious at the emperor's court. When you're confident about your body's health, an encounter with these people should teach you to repress your confidence: the healthy man that continually comes in here will not become overconfident about his body's health; the sick man will receive no trifling consolation.[48]

The spectacle of the indigent at the gates of the churches provides opportunities for the faithful to remember the contingency of life and be humble. By eradicating earthbound pride, they efficaciously prepare the observant churchgoer to hear God's word within.

Chrysostom continues to expound on the didactic importance of the poor who cluster at the entrances of the churches:

> But they sit here not for this reason alone. They are also sitting here to make you compassionate and move you to pity. They sit here to make you marvel at God's benevolence: If God is not ashamed of them but has set them at his entryways, much less should you be ashamed of them. They sit here too so you don't exult in earthly palaces. Do not be ashamed at a poor person's call. And if he approaches, if he grasps your knees, don't shake him off—these are the extraordinary dogs of the royal courts. I have called them dogs not to dishonor them—far be it—but to praise them magnificently. They guard the king's court. Feed them. The honor rises to the king. There is pride—in earthly palaces, that—here all is humility. Especially from the very entryways, you learn that human affairs are nothing. From the very persons that sit before them, you are taught that God takes no pleasure in wealth. Their seated assembly is essentially an admonition, sending out a clear voice about the nature of all human beings, saying that human affairs are nothing, no more than a shadow and smoke.[49]

Chrysostom suggests that the righteous poor sit at the church doors not because God (or the Church), frowning on their straitened circumstances, contemptuously refuses to allow them inside, but because they have little need to hear God's word proclaimed and explained. Long ago heedful of that word, they now live it. Voluntarily they cede the church interior to the morally suspect wealthy—hard-of-hearing, slow-learning folk. By remaining outside, the destitute dangerously afford the affluent a better opportunity to listen, understand, and reform. Whatever their spatial or economic location, however, Chrysostom emphasizes that all people are invited to share the Eucharistic meal:

> Yet the crippled, the maimed, and the old man with a runny nose that's clothed in rags and filth all come to share the table with the young, the beautiful, and even the man that's wearing a purple robe and a diadem. All are thought worthy of the spiritual feast. Both sorts of people enjoy the same benefits; there is no difference. If then Christ does not disdain to call the poor to the table along with the emperor—for both

are called—do you perhaps disdain even to be seen giving to them, even to be seen talking with them? Enough of your madness and pride![50]

Does John Chrysostom encourage passivity by stressing that out of adversity come good things?[51] The answer is unequivocally no. Chrysostom stresses the benefit of adversity because difficulties in life are simply unavoidable.[52] Because the poor suffer superlatively, the mere sight of them reveals the miseries of all other human beings, whether physical, emotional, or financial, as petty. The intensity of their pain trivializes, and therefore soothes, less intense pains. Yet, however didactic this may be, it pales beside the instruction they offer to those who train their ears as well as their eyes upon them. With their voices, the poor teach the better-off equanimity, even gratitude, in the face of adversity. They also teach how to pray. From God they ask nothing more than He wishes that they have; from the passerby they ask only for the barest minimum that they need to live. Although the hardhearted refuse to listen, they neither cease entreating nor begin cursing them. These better-off, however, demand of God not what He deems fit, but everything that they themselves desire; then they indict Him for cruel dereliction when He does not immediately endow them. In particular Chrysostom exhorts his audience:

> When you are encumbered with poverty or sickness, if from nowhere else, at least from those that beg and wander the alleyways, learn to give thanks to the Lord. Though they spent their entire life begging, they do not blaspheme, they do not get angry, and they do not register annoyance. Instead, they devote the whole narrative of their mendicancy to thanksgiving, calling God great and merciful. While someone wasting with hunger calls God merciful, you, living with abundance, call him cruel if you cannot seize the possessions of all. How much better is the poor man! How will he someday condemn us! God sent the poor throughout the world as common teachers and consolers in our misfortunes. Have you suffered anything you wish you had not? Nevertheless, it is nothing like what the poor man suffers. Have you lost an eye? The poor man has lost both. Have you had a long-lasting illness? That poor man has one that is incurable. Have you lost your children? That poor man has lost even the health of his own body. Have you suffered a great financial loss? Nonetheless,

you have not yet reached the point begging from others. So give thanks to God. You see them in the furnace of poverty, begging from all but receiving from few. When you get tired of praying because you do not receive what you ask for, consider how often you've heard a poor man calling to you and you haven't listened; consider how he hasn't gotten angry at you or insulted you. And you don't listen out of cruelty whereas God doesn't listen out of mercy.[53]

Beyond the educational value of the extremely poor who cluster outside the churches and beg in the marketplace for alms, what elevates their dignity and gives them a pre-eminent position and importance in the Church and in the world is their identification with Christ. This identification, in Chrysostom, is ontological, iconic, and sacramental in nature, and demands the better-off to respect their dignity and acknowledge in them the active presence of Christ. This does not allow anyone to be indifferent to their suffering and obliges those who want to be with Christ to actively care for them. For the early Fathers, the identification of Christ with the poor does not only refer to the spiritual excellence of poverty, but also it strongly exhorts and encourages the rich to give alms. Chrysostom makes both of these points. He points out: "And if you give to the poor, do not dislike yourself for giving, for it is not to the poor that you give, but to Christ; and who is so wretched, as to disdain to stretch out his own hand to Christ?"[54] The identification of Christ with the poor is a direct critique to those rich people who by refusing to share their material resources with the poor make Christ hungry, because He lives in the poor:

> You eat in excess; Christ eats not even what he needs. You eat a variety of cakes; he eats not even a piece of dried bread. You drink fine Thracian wine; but on him you have not bestowed so much as a cup of cold water. You lie on a soft and embroidered bed; but he is perishing in the cold . . . You live in luxury on things that properly belong to him . . . At the moment, you have taken possessions of the resources that belong to Christ and you consume them aimlessly. Don't you realize that you are going to be held accountable?[55]

It is obvious that for Chrysostom, the poor are the icon of Christ in a way that the rich are not. He asks the faithful to recognize the presence of Christ in the poor and care for them as an act of faith and love for Him.

He asks them to give priority in recognizing and serving God by feeding the poor moreso than by the practice of expressing their faith and dedication to God by decorating His Church with gold and silk ornaments.

> Do you really wish to pay homage to Christ's body? Then do not neglect him when he is naked. At the same time that you honor him here [in Church] with hangings made of silk, do not ignore him outside when he perishes from cold and nakedness. For the One who said "This is my body". . . also said "When I was hungry you gave me nothing to eat". . . For is there any point in his table being laden with golden cups while he himself is perishing from hunger? First fill him when he is hungry and then set his table with lavish ornaments. Are you making a golden cup for him at the very moment when you refuse to give him a cup of cold water? Do you decorate his table with cloths flecked with gold, while at the same time you neglect to give him what is necessary for him to cover himself? . . . I'm saying all this not to forbid your gifts of munificence, but to admonish you to perform those other duties at the same time, or rather before, you do these. No one was ever condemned for neglecting to be munificent: for the neglect of others hell itself is threatened, as well as unquenchable fire . . . The conclusion is: Don't neglect your brother in his distress while you decorate His house. Your brother is more truly his temple than any Church building.[56]

For Chrysostom, to gaze upon the bodies of the poor is to gaze directly upon Christ's body. The bodies of the poor belong to God, through whom He becomes present and discloses Himself to the world. They make Christ more immediately apprehensible. He catechizes,

> Do you wish to see his altar (θυσιαστηριον) too? . . . This altar is composed of the very members of Christ, and the body of the Lord becomes an altar . . . venerable because it is itself Christ's body . . . This altar you can see lying everywhere, in the alleys and in the agoras and you can sacrifice upon it anytime . . . invoke the Spirit, not with words but with deeds. Nothing kindles and sustains the fire of the Spirit as effectively as this oil poured out with liberality.[57]

So convinced is St. John of Christ's identity with the poor that he does not hesitate to put words in the mouth of Christ:

> It is such a slight thing I beg . . . nothing very expensive . . .
> bread, a roof, words of comfort. [If the rewards I promised
> hold no appeal for you] then show at least a natural compas-
> sion when you see me naked, and remember the nakedness
> I endured for you on the cross . . . I fasted for you then, and I
> suffer hunger for you now; I was thirsty when I hung on the
> cross, and I thirst still in the poor, in both ways to draw you
> to myself and to make you humane for your own salvation.[58]

The identification of the poor with Christ acknowledges their dignity
as icons of Christ and encourages wealthy Christians to actively care for
them. Chrysostom advises his audience: "When you see an impoverished
Christian believe that you see an altar. When you see a beggar, far from
abusing him, reverence him (Ὅταν οὖν ἴδῃς πένητα πιστόν, θυσιατήριον
ὁρᾶν νόμιζε· ὅταν ἴδῃς πτωχόν τοιοῦτον, μή μόνον μή ὑβρίσῃς, ἀλλά καὶ
αἰδέσθητι)."[59]

Even though it appears that Chrysostom loves the poor, so much
so that he is called the defender and the lover of the poor, he believes
that the poor are not righteous simply because they are poor. Chrysostom understands Paul's teaching as an exhortation to marvel at the
poor when they are pious and to call the poor saints when they are
reasonable and moderate.[60] Poverty does not necessarily produce
these virtues, and instead is more likely to cause discouragement and
complaint. In his work *The Rich Man and Lazarus*, Chrysostom points
out that Lazarus was rewarded by God not because he was poor, but
because of his patient endurance of poverty.[61] Thus, while Christ is actively present in the suffering poor, the poor do not always in their attitudes reflect the presence of Christ in them. This, however, does not
mean that the better-off Christians have the liberty to be indifferent to
their situation and to not recognize the dignity of the poor as bearers
of Christ.

Almsgiving

Chrysostom refers to almsgiving as an "excellent counselor, the queen of
the virtues, who quickly raises human beings to the heavenly vaults."[62]
Almsgiving is for him an art and especially the best art among the arts:

> Let us show how almsgiving is an art, and better than all arts.
> For if the peculiarity of art is to issue in something useful,
> and nothing is more useful than almsgiving, very evidently

this is both an art, and better than all arts. For it makes for us not shoes, nor doth it weave garments, nor build houses that are of clay; but it procures life everlasting, and snatches us from the hands of death, and in either life shows us glorious, and builds the mansions that are in Heaven, and those eternal tabernacles.[63]

He also refers to almsgiving as the "the best of all virtues," because it is the strongest and most powerful means for the remission of sins. He makes the observation that ascetic practices such as virginity, fasting, and sleeping on the ground are more difficult than giving alms. But these practices are not required of all, whereas almsgiving is a duty for all Christians. In fact, nothing is more characteristic of a Christian life than almsgiving. It is "the mother of love, of that love, which is the characteristic of Christianity, which is greater than all miracles, by which the disciples of Christ are manifested."[64] It makes those who practice it to be like God. It is an indispensable aspect of an authentic human life. "A human being is great; and it is honorable for a man to be merciful. But if he does not practice almsgiving he loses his humanity."[65] He asserts that "nothing is so strong and powerful to extinguish the fire of our sins as almsgiving."[66] It has the power to ascend unto the heavens and seek from God on behalf of its practitioners forgiveness of their sins.

> Almsgiving's wings are great. She cleaves the air, surpasses the moon, and goes beyond the sun's rays . . . She surmounts heaven and overtakes the multitudes of angels, and the choirs of archangels, and all the higher powers, and she stands next to the royal throne. And you shall be taught from this very Scripture that says, "Cornelius, your prayers and your alms have ascended before God" [Acts 10:4]. "Before God" means that even if you have many sins, you should not be afraid if you possess almsgiving as your advocate. For no higher power opposes it. She pays the debt demanded by sin . . . For it is the Lord's own voice that says, "As you did it to one of the least of these, you did it to me." Therefore, regardless of how many other sins you have, your almsgiving counterbalances all of them.[67]

Chrysostom compares almsgiving with Baptism and expresses the belief that it has the same efficacy as Baptism in cleansing people's sins: "Almsgiving has the efficacy of Holy Baptism. As the holy bath cleanses the people's sins, in the same manner almsgiving cleanses the sins of those people who give alms."[68]

Chrysostom, commenting on his favorite story of the Last Judgment (Matt 25:32–37) points out to his audience the pre-eminence that beneficence has over all other godly virtues and the fact that the Judge considers inhumanity and unmercifulness as the most evil acts. Questioning why the Lord gives such exclusive emphasis to the virtue of beneficence for those who are entering into God's Kingdom and to inhumanity and unmercifulness for those who are sent into hell, Chrysostom puts in the mouth of the Lord the following response:

> "I do not judge the sin," He says, "the inhumanity. I do not judge the ones who have sinned, but the ones who did not repent. I judge you severely for your inhumanity, because you disregarded such beneficence, although you had almsgiving as a great medicine of salvation, by which all sins are blotted out. I reproach, therefore inhumanity as the root of wickedness and of every piety. I praise love toward mankind as the root of all goods, and I threaten the inhumane with the eternal fire; to the beneficent I promise the Kingdom of the Heavens."[69]

He insists that unless people are led to Christ's special representatives, the poor, on earth, they will find themselves possessing nothing, stripped of everything valuable in the afterlife. "After we depart this life, we shall be able to appear rich in the next life if we don't leave our money here but transport it to secure treasuries through the hands of the poor; if, that is, we lend to Christ."[70] Chrysostom presents the destitute as bankers that deserve to be trusted,[71] and he admonishes his audience,

> Don't transact any business yourself, since you don't know how to make a profit. Instead, lend to someone that offers interest greater than the principal. Lend where there is no envy, no accusation, no plotting, and no fear. Lend to someone that needs nothing yet for your sake exhibits need. Lend to someone that feeds everyone yet is hungry so that you don't go hungry. Lend to someone that is poor so that you may become rich. Lend where it's possible to reap a profit of life rather than death. While this kind of usury procures the kingdom, worldly usury procures hell. This usury springs from wisdom; the other from avarice. This usury springs

from charity; the other from cruelty . . . I really do, however, want you to have a reward—and not a cheap or small one, but one far greater. Instead of gold, I want you to receive heaven as your interest. So why confine yourself to poverty, crawling around the earth and demanding small change rather than great profit? This is the mark of someone that doesn't know how to become rich.[72]

For the unheeding scrooges in his congregation at Antioch, John Chrysostom paints an uncomfortably grim picture of what awaits them before God's tribunal.

Keep in mind that day when we shall stand before the tribunal of Christ begging for mercy. Then Christ will bring the poor forward and say to us: "For a single loaf of bread or a single obol you raised an immense disturbance in these souls." What will we say? What defense will we offer? Listen to what he says, proving that he is going to bring them into our midst (Mt. 25.45): "To the extent that you didn't do it to one of these, you didn't do to me." They will no longer say anything to us, but God will accost us on their behalf. After all, the rich man saw Lazarus as well as Abraham, but while Lazarus said nothing to him, Abraham spoke to him. So it shall be in the case of the poor that we now despise. We shall not see them pitifully stretching out their hands, but at rest. We instead shall assume their former state—and would that it were only that state rather than a state far worse—as our punishment.[73]

Although the destitute do not speak in this world, they nevertheless cut off an uncharitable person's defense. The Judge himself takes their cause. Without uttering a word, the poor silence every defendant that has failed to feed them. On the other hand, the poor freely and readily volunteer their aid to those that have cared well for them. Interchangeably representing almsgiving and the destitute as defenders of the charitable, Chrysostom himself urges,

Give bread, and receive paradise. Give a pittance, and receive a jackpot. Give what perishes, and receive what does not die. Give what decays, and receive what cannot be destroyed . . . Give to the poor so that, even if you are silent, countless mouths may rush to your defense—as almsgiving

> stands in the way of your condemnation and acts as your
> advocate. Almsgiving ransoms the soul.[74]

Chrysostom here accents the disparity of the gifts exchanged. Though
earthly donors may think of themselves as generous patrons of the
poor, he forcefully reminds them that they are no more than proleptic
clients are, tendering trifles to genuine patrons they can never hope to
repay. He unequivocally states, "It is impossible, utterly impossible—
even if we perform innumerable other good deeds—to pass through
the doors of the kingdom without almsgiving."[75] Yet, giving alms does
not mean to distribute to the poor what it has been unjustly grabbed
from the poor: "Turning to the pride that money generates: First let us
keep hands off from greediness and then do almsgiving. Let us not simply confuse everything, the same hands that grabbed to pretend giving
alms, practicing here one virtue and there another. This is shameful
and foolish."[76]

The importance of almsgiving for someone's entry into God's Kingdom is illustrated by Chrysostom in his commentary on the Gospel story
of the ten virgins (Matt 25:1–12). He states that the five foolish virgins
who lack oil for the lamps were actually lacking almsgiving. The foolish
virgins, despite the fact that "they had achieved so many virtues, trained
in virginity, elevated their bodies to heaven, and competed for superior-
ity over the heavenly powers," did not have the "light" to welcome the
bridegroom because they lacked almsgiving: "Virginity is extinguished
when it lacks almsgiving."[77] Chrysostom informs his audience that the
oil that is needed for participation in the heavenly banquet is offered by
the poor who sit "in front of the Church in order to ask for alms," and
its price is affordable. "I do not put a price on it so that you can afford.
Buy as much as you can."[78] One gets the impression that for Chrysostom
almsgiving is a virtue that only the rich can adopt and practice because
of their wealth, and this impression may be justified, because Chrysostom intends through his homilies to motivate the rich to become charitable and caring towards the poor. This, however, is not accurate, because almsgiving is grounded upon his eschatological vision of the unity
of humankind in God's love that the aspiring citizens of heaven must
live and communicate in the world in the same way that God expresses
His love, compassion, and care for His people. Thus, the "art of arts," the
"chief virtue," must be practice by all Christians regardless of their possessions and social status. For this reason, the notion of almsgiving is
not limited only to the distribution of material wealth:

> Give as much bread as you can. You do not have bread? Give
> one obol. You do not have an obol? Give one glass of refresh-
> ing water. You do not have even this? Grieve with the afflicted
> and you have a reward to collect. For the reward is not pro-
> portionate to your necessity, but to your free will.[79]

Should Christians practice almsgiving indiscriminately, extending it
to all people in need regardless of their race, nationality, or religion?
Chrysostom exhorts the faithful to give alms to the destitute without
investigating whether it is just or worthy to do so in some instances.
He fears that this may lead some people to refuse inadvertently alms to
people in real need, in whom Christ is actively present. Faithful to this
understanding, he advises the people to enhance this practice and offer
alms generously not only to monastics and anchorites, but to all people
in need, regardless of their affiliation with the Church, their nationality,
race, or religion.[80]

For Chrysostom, virtues that edify particular persons alone have a
secondary importance compared to those virtues and practices that sustain life for others. "And as men could not sail on the sea, if harbors and
roadsteads were blocked up; so neither could this life hold together, if
you take away mercy and compassion, and love to man."[81] He considers
almsgiving as chief among these because it contributes to a great degree
to the well-being and sustenance of the neighbors in need.

> Let us see amongst good works, which are confined to our-
> selves, and which pass over from us to others. Fasting then,
> and lying on the bare ground, and keeping virginity, and a
> self-denying life, these things bring their advantage to the
> persons themselves who do them; but those that pass from
> us to our neighbors are almsgiving, teaching, charity.[82]

It is the vocation of Christians to live according to the principles
and values of God's Kingdom, to "mind the things of above." This entails
first prayer[83] and then almsgiving.[84] He believes that "prayer together
with almsgiving can furnish us with countless good things from above;
they can quench the fire of sin in our souls and can give us great freedom."[85] He regards almsgiving as the completion of prayer. The prayer
does profit the neighbor, but by almsgiving, it is made efficacious and
furnished with wings, because the alms ascend for a memorial before
God. All virtues such as fasting, virginity, and practicing self-denial are
meaningless if they are not accompanied by almsgiving:

> Though you practice self-denial, though you practice virgin-
> ity, you are set without the bridal chamber, if you do not have
> almsgiving. Yet what is equal to virginity, which not even in
> the new dispensation hath come under the compulsion of
> law, because of its high excellence? But it is cast out, when it
> has not almsgiving.[86]

The preaching of Chrysostom on almsgiving was not always welcome by his audience. In fact, there was opposition and disagreement
with his persistent speaking about almsgiving and with his criticism
of the wealthy for their avarice, covetousness, and reluctance to care
for the poor. Chrysostom is aware of this criticism, and occasionally he
will directly respond and explain his motives and what he really expects
from the wealthy people of his audience.

> Perhaps one of the senseless, accustomed to scoff, will criti-
> cize what I've said and altogether ridicule me, saying, "How
> long will you continue introducing the poor and destitute
> in your speeches, prophesying misfortunes to us, predicting
> poverty, and trying to make us destitute as well?" I am not
> trying to make you destitute when I say these things, but try-
> ing to open to you the riches of heaven.[87]

He asserts that, in reality, he would prefer not to speak often of
almsgiving. That is, if the people willingly concerned themselves with
giving alms, he would not need to address this advice to them. "What
do you say? Am I forever speaking of almsgiving? I would wish myself
that there were not great need for me to address this advice to you . . .
but when ye are not yet sound how anyone can arm you for the fight?"[88]
He recognizes that his preaching on almsgiving has a minimal effect
upon his audience, but he is determined to keep preaching:

> I am now ashamed of speaking of almsgiving, because that
> having often spoken on this subject, I have affected noth-
> ing worthy of exhortation. For there has been some increase,
> but not so much as I wished. For I see you sowing, but not
> with a liberal hand, and I fear that you will also "reap spar-
> ingly" (2 Cor 9:6).[89]

The goal of his preaching is to establish among the faithful habits of virtues, "to let the deed become a law and immovable custom: For discourse
and advice do not have the power to achieve these things as much as the

habit that is established firmly with time."[90] Thus, he is determined to continue to preach on almsgiving as long as it is necessary. It seems that he embraces the thesis that repetition is the mother of all learning.

> But perhaps some one will say, "You are every day discours-
> ing to us of almsgiving and humanity." Neither will I cease to
> speak of this. For if you had attained to it, in the first place,
> not even so ought I to desist, for fear of making you the more
> remiss; yet had you attained it, I might have relaxed a little;
> but if you have not arrived, even at half; say not these things
> to me, but to yourselves. For indeed you do the same in blam-
> ing me, as if a little child, hearing often of the letter alpha,
> and learning it, were to blame its teacher, because he is con-
> tinually and for ever reminding him about it.[91]

Notes

1. Chysostomus Baur, *John Chrysostom and His Time*, vol. 1, trans. Sr. M. Conzaga (Westminster, MD: Newman Press, 1959–60), 217; B. Leyerle, "John Chrysostom on Almsgiving and the Use of Money," *Harvard Theological Review* 87 (1997): 29–47; idem, "John Chrysostom: Sermons on City Life," in R. Valantasis, ed., *Religions of Late Antiquity in Practice* (Princeton, NJ: Princeton University Press, 2000), 247–260; O. Andren, "On Works of Charity in the Homilies of St. John Chrysostom," in G. Swensson, ed., *Kyrkona och diakonien. Nagra Ekumenica och Internationelle Perspektiv. Festskrift till diakonissan Ingra Bengtzon* (Uppsalla: Pro Veritate, 1985), 39–52; T. Barrosse, "The Unity of the Two Charities in Greek Patristic Exegesis," *Theological Studies* 15 (1954): 355–388; G. Bebis, "Saint John Chrysostom: On Materialism and Virtue," *Greek Orthodox Theological Review* 32 (1987): 227–237; M. J. De Vinne, "The Advocacy of the Empty Bellies: Episcopal Representation of the Poor in the Late Roman Empire," Ph.D. diss., Stanford, 1995; R. Finn, *Almsgiving in the Later Roman Empire* (Oxford: Oxford University Press, 2006); Methodius Fouyas, "The Social message of those homilies of St. John Chrysostom which were delivered in Constantinople from A.D. 398 to A.D. 404," diss., Manchester, 1962; idem, *The Social Message of St. John Chrysostom* (Athens, 1968); R. S. M. Greeley, "St. John Chrysostom, Prophet of Social Justice," *Studia Patristica* 17, no. 3 (1982): 1163–1168; A. D. Karayiannis, "The Eastern Christian Fathers (AD 350–400) on the redistribution of wealth," *History of Political Economy* 26 (1994): 39–67; D. S. B. Krstitch, "St. John Chrysostom as the Theologian of Divine Philanthropy," Th.D. diss.,

Faculty of Divinity, Harvard University, 1968; D. Kyrtatas, "Prophets and priests in early Christianity: Production and transmission of religious knowledge from Jesus to John Chrysostom," *International Sociology* 3 (1988): 365–383; Wendy Mayer, "Poverty and Society in the World of John Chrysostom," in L. Lavan, W. Bowden, A. Gutteridge, and C. Machado, eds., *Social and Political Archaeology in Late Antiquity*, Late Antiquity Archaelogy 3 (Brill, 2006), 465–484.

2. See Soc. 6.3 (PG 67:668A–669A); L. Maxwell, Christianization and Communication in Late Antiquity: John Chrysostom and His Congregation in Antioch (Cambridge: Cambridge University Press, 2006); Wendy Mayer, "Who came to hear John Chrysostom preach? Recovering a late fourth-century preacher's audience," *Epherides Theologicae Lovanienses* 76 (2000): 73–87. On the difficulties in dating the sermons, see Wendy Mayer, "The Provenance of the Homilies of St. John Chrysostom: Towards a New Assessment of Where He Preached What," Ph.D. thesis, University of Queensland, 1996; idem, "John Chrysostom and His Audience: Distinguishing Different Congregations at Antioch and Constantinople," *Studia Patristica* 31 (1995): 70–75.

3. Sozomen, *HE* 8.5.

4. Wendy Mayer, "Who Came to Hear?"

5. De Vinne, "The Advocacy of the Empty Bellies."

6. Ibid.

7. Louis Bouyer, *The Spirituality of the New Testament and the Fathers* (New York: Desclee, 1963), 440–449.

8. John Chrysostom, *Baptismal Instructions*, trans. Paul W. Harkins (Westminster, MD: Newman Press, 1963), 68. Rodgerson Phyllis Pleasants, "Making Christian the Christians: The Baptismal Instructions of St. John Chrysostom," *Greek Orthodox Theological Review* 34 (1989): 379–392; Raymond F. G. Burnish, "Baptismal Preparation Under the Ministry of St. John Chrysostom in Fourth-Century Antioch," in *Baptism, the New Testament and the Church: Historical and Contemporary Studies in Honour of R. E. O. White*, ed. Stanley E. Porter and Antony R. Cross (Sheffield Academic Press, 1999), 379–401.

9. Chrysostom, *Baptismal Instructions* 4.12, p. 71.

10. Ibid., 2.27, p. 53.

11. For example, John 17:11–19; Rom 13:1–8; 1 Cor 5:9–13; Gal 4:26; Phil 3:20; Heb 12:22–24; 1 Pet 2:11–17.

12. Chrysostom, *Baptismal Instructions* 4.12, p. 71.

13. Σ. Ι. Γκόσεβιτς, "Η Περί Θείας Χάριτος διδασκαλία Ἰωάννου τοῦ Χρυσοστόμου," *Θεολογία* 27 (1956): 206–239, 367–389.

14. Chrysostom, *Baptismal Instructions* 1.27, p. 33.

15. Ibid., 11.21, p. 167.

16. Ibid., 2.13, p. 48.

17. John Chrysostom, *John Chrysostom on Repentance and Almsgiving*, trans. Gus George Christo, *The Fathers of the Church*, vol. 96 (Washington, DC: Catholic University of America Press, 1998), 133.

18. Chrysostom, *In Mattheum hom.* 69.54 (PG 57:635–637).

19. Ibid., *Homily* 72 (PG 58:671); English translation in *Homilies on the Gospel of Saint Matthew*, vol. 10 of Nicene and Post-Nicene Fathers, First Series, ed. Philip Schaff (repr., Peabody, Massachusetts: Hendrickson Publishers, 1994), 438.

20. F. X. Murphy, "The Moral Doctrine of St. John Chrysostom," *Studia Patristica* 11 (1972): 52–57; Joseph F. Kelley, *The World of the Early Christians* (Collegeville, MN: Liturgical Press, 1977); Frances Young, *From Nicaea to Chalcedon: A Guide to the Literature and Its Development* (London: SCM, 1983); Rebecca H. Weaver, "Wealth and Poverty in the Early Church," *Interpretation* 41 (1987): 368–381.

21. Rowan A. Greer, *Broken Lights and Mended Lives: Theology and Common Life in the Early Church* (University Park: Pennsylvania State University Press, 1986), 155.

22. Ibid.

23. Peter Robert Lamont Brown, *Power and Persuasion: Towards a Christian Empire* (Madison: University of Wisconsin Press, 1992), 71–117.

24. Chrysostom, *Homilies on the Gospel of Saint Matthew* (NPNF[1] 10:454).

25. Ibid.

26. Russell Edward Willoughby, "The Use and Misuse of Wealth in Selected Homilies of John Chrysostom," *Church Divinity* (1987): 4.

27. John Chrysostom, *On Wealth and Poverty* (Crestwood, NY: St. Vladimir's Seminary Press, 1984), 137.

28. Chrysostom, *Homilies on Eutropius*, 254.

29. John Chrysostom, *On Wealth and Poverty*, 21.

30. Ibid., 21–22.

31. Chrysostom, *In Matt. hom.* 13.5; Brian E. Daley, *The Hope of the Early Church: A Handbook of Patristic Eschatology* (Cambridge: Cambridge University Press, 1991), 106; C. A. Hall, "John Chrysostom's *On Providence*: A Translation and Theological Interpretation," diss., Drew University, Madison, N.J., 1991.

32. Baur, *John Chrysostom and His Time*, 155–156.

33. Frederic W. Farrar, *Lives of the Fathers: Sketches of Church History in Biography*, vol. 2 (London: Adam and Charles Black), 638.

34. Willoughby, "The Use and Misuse of Wealth, 2.

35. Chrysostom, *Homilies on the Gospel of Saint Matthew* 66.3 (NPNF[1] 10:407).

36. Ibid.

37. Ibid.

38. John Chrysostom, "A Sermon on Almsgiving," 1.1, in *John Chrysostom on Repentance and Almsgiving*, 131. In a homily on the Gospel of Matthew (*Hom.* 61.3, PG 58:591), Chrysostom focuses the eyes of his audience upon the impoverished agricultural workers hat suffer the landlord's abuse: "How then are these people? They are the ones that own fields, the ones that pluck the wealth that springs from the earth. And what could be more unjust than these? If anyone should examine how they treat their wretched, hard-suffering tenant farmers, he will see that they are more cruel than barbarians. On those wasting away with hunger and toiling throughout their entire lives, they levy continuous, intolerable payments and impose oppressive burdens. Like asses or mules—or rather like stones—they use their bodies, not even allowing them to catch their breath: both when the earth bears its fruit and it does not, they alike wear them out; they grant them no respite. What could be more pitiable than this? When they have labored the whole winter, their strength utterly spent in frost, rains, and night watches, they go away with empty hands—and still owing money. Yet more than this hunger and shipwreck they fear and dread the torments, seizures, demands, arrests, and inescapable tasks to which the overseers subject them."

39. John Chrysostom, *Homilies on the Epistles of Paul to the Corinthians* 63 (NPNF[1] 12:124).

40. Chrysostom, *Homilies on the Gospel of Saint Matthew* (NPNF[1] 10:235): "But if there come to thee a poor man wanting bread, there is no end of reviling, and reproaches, and charges of idleness, and upbraidings, and insults, and jeers; and thou considerest not with thyself, that thou too art doing somewhat . . . But if thou tellest one of money-getting, and of traffic, and of the care and increase of thy goods, I also would say unto thee, Not these, but alms, and prayers, and the protection of the injured, and all such things, are truly works, with respect to which we live in through idleness. Yet God never told us, 'Because thou art idle, I light not up the sun for thee; because thou doest nothing of real consequence, I quench the moon, I paralyze the womb of the earth, I restrain the lakes, the fountains, the rivers, I blot out the atmosphere, I withhold the annual rains' . . . When therefore thou seest a poor man, and sayest, 'It stops my breath that this fellow, young as he is and healthy, having nothing, would fain be fed in idleness; he is surely some slave and runaway, and hath deserted his proper master:' I bid thee speak these same words to thyself; or rather, permit him freely to speak them unto thee, and he will say with more justice, 'It stops my breath that thou, being healthy, art idle, and practisest none of the

things which God hath commanded, but having run away from the commandments of thy Lord, goest about dwelling in wickedness, as in a strange land, in drunkenness, in surfeiting, in theft, in extortion, in subverting other men's house.' And thou indeed imputest idleness, but I evil works; in thy plotting, in thy swearing, in thy lying, in thy spoiling, in thy doing innumerable such things."

41. Ibid., 234.

42. Ibid., 232.

43. Ibid., 235.

44. Ibid.

45. Chrysostom, *Homilies on Timothy* (NPNF[1] 12:455).

46. For a mere glimpse at this broad concern of his, see Chrysostom, *Hom. 45.4 in Act. Apost.* (PG 60:319–320); *Hom. 15.6 in Ep. ad Rom.* (PG 60:547–548); *Hom. 18.7 in Ep. ad Rom.* (PG 60:582–583); *Hom. 1.3 in Ep. ad Coloss.* (PG 62:303–304); and *Hom. 14.2–3 in Ep. 1 ad Tim.* (PG 62:573–574). Scholars have concluded that most of Chrysostom's exegetical homilies were delivered at Antioch between 386 and 398, while he was still only a presbyter. See Soc. 6.3 (PG 67:668A–669A); Wilken, 9–10; and Quasten, 433.

47. Chrysostom, *Hom. 30.3–4 in Ep. 1 ad Cor.* (PG 61:253–254).

48. Chrysostom, *Hom. 11.4 in Ep. 1 ad Thess.* (PG 62:466).

49. Ibid.

50. Ibid., 11.4–5, cols. 466–467.

51. J. Brian Benestad, "Chrysostom on Wealth and Poverty," *Diakonia* 24, no. 3 (1991): 204.

52. Ibid.

53. Chrysostom, *Hom. 11.3 in Ep. 1 ad Thess.* (PG 62:465–466).

54. Chrysostom, *Homilies on Timothy* (NPNF[1] 12:455).

55. Chrysostom, *Homilies on the Gospel of Saint Matthew* (NPNF[1] 10:301).

56. Ibid., 313.

57. Chrysostom, *Hom. 20.3 in Ep. 2 ad Cor.* (PG 61:540).

58. Quoted by W. J. Burghardt, "The Body of Christ: Patristic Insights," in R. S. Pelton, ed., *The Church as the Body of Christ* (South Bend, IN, 1963), 97.

59. Chrysostom, *Hom. 20.3 in Ep. 2 ad Cor.* (PG 61:540).

60. Chrysostom, *On Repentance and Almsgiving*, 133.

61. Chrysostom, *On Wealth and Poverty*, 23.

62. Chrysostom, *On Repentance and Almsgiving*, 30.

63. Chrysostom, *Homilies on the Gospel of Saint Matthew* (NPNF[1] 10:324).

64. Chrysostom, *Homilies on Titus* (NPNF[1] 12:541).

65. Chrysostom, *In Mattaeum* (PG 58:524).

66. Chrysostom, *Homilies on Titus* (NPNF[1] 12:542).
67. Chrysostom, *On Repentance and Almsgiving*, 31.
68. Chrysostom, *De Eleemosyna* (PG 60:750).
69. Chrysostom, *On Repentance and Almsgiving*, 109.
70. Chrysostom, *Hom. 25.3 in Johan.* (PG 59:152).
71. Roman bankers not only accepted money on deposit, but also occasionally paid interest on an account. More commonly, though, they did no more than keep cash that had been deposited with them sealed in bags or chests; for this security they charged a nominal fee. Bankers also made payments on behalf of their depositors in accord with written instructions and transfer funds (sometimes over greater distances) between their own customers or between a customer and a non-customer known to them. Their principal gain was derived from lending money at interest.
72. Chrysostom, *Hom. 55 in Matt.* (PG 57:61–62).
73. Chrysostom, *Hom. 77. 4 in Johan.* (PG 59:419). A similar story can be found in *Hom. 40.4 in Johan.* (PG 59:234).
74. Chrysostom, *Eleem. et decem virg.* 2 (PG 49:294).
75. Chrysostom, *Hom. 23.3 in Johan.* (PG 59:144).
76. Chrysostom, *In Epistulam ad Hebraeos* (PG 63:172.13).
77. Chrysostom, *On Repentance and Almsgiving*, 32.
78. Ibid.
79. Ibid.
80. Chrysostom, *De Eleemosyna et Hospitalitate, Hom.* 23 (PG 63:728): "Μή τοίνυν μηδέ συ πολυπραγμόνει· διά γάρ τόν Χριστόν δέχῃ· ἄν γάρ ἀεί περιεργάζεσθαι μέλλῃς, πολλάκις καὶ δόκιμον ἄνδρα παραδραμῇ, καὶ τόν ἐκ τούτου μισθόν ἀπολεῖς. Μηδέ τῶν οἰκείων μόνων τῆς πίστεως φροντίζωμε, τῶν δέ ἄλλων ἀμελῶμεν, ἀλλ᾽ ἐάν τινα ἴδωμε πάσχοντα κακῶς, μηδέ ἕτερον περιεργαζώμεθα· ἔχει γάρ τὸ δικαίωμα τῆς βοηθείας τὸ κακῶς πάσχειν αὐτόν. Ἀλλ᾽ οὐκ οἶδα πόθεν αὕτη κεκράτηκεν ἡ συνήθεια· κἄν μέν κοσμικόν ἴδωμεν ἐν περιστάσει, οὐκ ὀρέγομεν χεῖρα· πρός δε τοὺς ἐν ὄρεσι μόνον καθημένους ἐσμέν σπουδαῖοι. Κἄν Ἕλληνα, κἄν Ἰουδαῖον, κἄν ἕτερον τινα ἴδῃς ἐν περιστάσει, εὖ ποιεῖν δεῖ. Καί γάρ τούς μονάζοντας μόνους ἐπιζητῶν, κἀκείνους μόνους εὖποιεῖν ἐθέλων, κἀκείνους δέ πάλιν περιεργαζόμενους, ἐάν μή ᾖ ἄξιος, ἐάν μή ᾖ δίκαιος, ἐάν μή ᾖ σημεῖα ποιῶν, καὶ οὐκ ὀρέγων χεῖρα, τὸ πλέον τῆς ἐλεημοσύνης ἐξεῖλες· καὶ τοῦτο σὲ αὐτό τῷ χρόνῳ τῆς ἐλεημοσύνης ἐξεῖλες."
81. Ibid., 325.
82. Chrysostom, *Homilies on the Gospel of Matthew* (NPNF[1] 10:468).
83. Ibid., *Hom. 7.25, p. 115.
84. Ibid.
85. Ibid.
86. Ibid., 468–469.

87. Chrysostom, *Hom. 30.5 in Ep. 1 ad Cor.* (PG 61:255–256).

88. Chrysostom, *Homilies on the Gospel of Matthew* (NPNF[1] 10:523).

89. Ibid., 407.

90. Chrysostom, *On Repentance and Almsgiving*, 39.

91. Chrysostom, *In Mattheum hom.* 87 (PG 58:779.41).

Chapter 3

THE IMAGERY OF PATRIARCH IGNATIOS' LEAD SEALS AND THE *ROTA FORTUNAE* OF NINTH-CENTURY BYZANTINE ECCLESIO-POLITICAL POLICIES

V. Rev. Archimandrite Dr. Joachim (John) Cotsonis
Director of the Archbishop Iakovos Library

Εἰς πολλὰ ἔτη, Δέσποτα!

I t is a great honor to contribute to this celebratory volume marking the twentieth anniversary of the election and enthronement of His All-Holiness Bartholomew, Archbishop of Constantinople-New Rome and Ecumenical Patriarch. Anyone who is even slightly aware of His All-Holiness' writings, homilies, addresses, liturgical celebrations, conferences, visitations, and archpastoral ministry during these years has quickly discerned the Patriarch's great interest in and love for the rich Byzantine Christian heritage to which he and his See belong, and his heroic endeavors in preserving this unbroken tradition. Among his many undertakings, His All-Holiness has expressed interest in the revival of a traditional Byzantine-inspired patriarchal seal, and, in keeping with his sigillographic appreciation, this article focuses on the imagery and inscriptions of the official lead seals of one of Patriarch Bartholomew's sainted predecessors, those of Patriarch Ignatios (847–858 and 867–877) (figs. 1, 2, and 3),[1] as they reflect the ecclesio-political policies of mid-ninth-century Byzantium.

A few introductory remarks about Byzantine seals would be appropriate at this point.[2] In the Byzantine Empire, seals were made either of gold, silver, lead, or wax.[3] Examples of gold and silver are rare—gold seals were issued solely by the emperor and were intended only for certain documents (*chrysobulls*) and for specific recipients, and silver seals were issued for only a limited time by the Greek despots of Epiros and the Peloponnesos—while only few specimens of wax seals survive due to the fragility of the medium. It is the lead seal that survives in the greatest number, literally into the thousands.[4] Lead seals served a variety of purposes in Byzantium: to guarantee the privacy of correspondence, to validate official documents, to function as the counter-signature of a superior official by conveying authority on the issuance of his or her subordinates, in securing goods for commerce, and to be used as tokens that were distributed to the needy in exchange for food and services at charitable foundations.[5]

The largest number of surviving lead seals bear inscriptions on both their obverse and reverse, often beginning with an invocation, such as "Lord, help" or "Theotokos, help," and include the name of the owner and frequently the owner's office or title. There are a good number of surviving seals that bear an image of the cross on their obverse,[6] some examples exhibit animal figures,[7] a few specimens display classical personifications,[8] and only rarely does a secular portrait of the owner of the seal appear.[9] Often the owner of a seal chose for its obverse a religious figural image, either that of Christ, the Virgin, or a saint, while the reverse bore an invocative inscription frequently accompanied by the owner's office or title.[10] Thousands of such examples survive, and my database includes 9,200 specimens drawn from the major published collections.

Within this last category belong the lead seals of Patriarch Ignatios (figs. 1–3). The seal in figure 1 measures 35 mm in diameter. The obverse bears an image of Christ standing on a dais with His right hand before His chest in a blessing gesture, while He holds a Gospel book with His left. Flanking the image of Christ is the vertical inscription Ο ΘΕΟC - ΗΓΟV, while on the reverse appears the continuation of the invocation in five lines: +ΙΓΝΑΤΙΟV – ΑΡΧΙΕΠΙCΚΟΠ - ΚWΝCΤΑΝΤΙΝΟV – ΠΟΛΕWCΝΕΑC - ΡWΜΗC+. Transcribed, the full inscription reads: ὁ Θεὸς ἡγοῦ Ἰγνατίου ἀρχιεπισκόπου Κωνσταντινουπόλεως Νέας Ῥώμης ("God, lead Ignatios, Archbishop of Constantinople-New Rome").

For the example in figure 2, measuring 34 mm in diameter, the obverse bears a bust image of Christ, who blesses with His right hand and holds a Gospel book in His left. Flanking the image of Christ is the vertical inscription ΙV|ΧΕ| ΚΕ – [Η]|Γ|Ο|V, while on the reverse appears the continuation of the invocation in five lines: ΙΓΝΑΤΙ – [Ο]V[Α] ΡΧΙΕΠΙCΚ, - [Κ]WΝCΤΑΝΤΙΝΟV – [Π]ΟΛΕWCΝΕΑC - ΡWΜΗC+. This inscription reads: Ἰ[ησο]ῦ Χ[ριστ]ὲ Κ[ύρι]ε ἡγοῦ Ἰγνατί[ο]υ [ἀ]ρχιεπισκ[όπου] [Κ] ωνσταντινου[π]όλεως Νέας Ῥώμης ("Jesus Christ Lord, lead Ignatios, Archbishop of Constantinople-New Rome").

Fig. 1.
Christ standing, lead seal of Ignatios, Archbishop of Constantinople-New Rome, M-11915, Hermitage, St. Petersburg (photo: Hermitage)

Fig. 2.
Christ bust, lead seal of Ignatios, Archbishop of Constantinople-New Rome, Fogg 862, Arthur M. Sackler Museum, Harvard University Art Museums, Cambridge, MA (photo: Dumbarton Oaks)

The third specimen (fig. 3), with a 37 mm diameter, bears a similar bust image of Christ blessing and holding a Gospel book and flanked by the identical vertical inscription: IV|XE| KE – H|Γ|O|V; the reverse has the same five-line inscription as the other two examples: IΓNA[T] I – OVAPXIEΠ[ICK], - KWNCTANTINOV – ΠΟΛΕWCNEAC - PWMHC+. This inscription also reads: Ἰ[ησο]ῦ Χ[ριστ]ὲ Κ[ύρι]ε ἡγοῦ Ἰγνα[τ]ίου ἀρχιεπ[ισκόπου] Κωνσταντινουπόλεως Νέας Ῥώμης (Jesus Christ Lord, lead Ignatios, Archbishop of Constantinople-New Rome). It has been

6c

Fig. 3.
Christ bust, lead seal of Ignatios, Archbishop of Constantinople-New
Rome, Zacos Collection (photo: G. Zacos, *Byzantine Lead Seals*, vol. 2
[Bern, 1984], no. 6c)

noted that these seals issued by Ignatios are the first among the patriarchal seals to bear the title ἀρχιεπισκόπου Κωνσταντινουπόλεως Νέας
Ῥώμης, that is, *Arch*bishop of Constantinople-New Rome, whereas his
predecessors employed the title "bishop of Constantinople" or "bishop
of Constantinople-New Rome" for their seals.[11] In addition, editors of
these seals have observed that it is impossible to determine to which of
Ignatios' two patriarchates they should be assigned, either 847–858 or
867–877.[12] It is also possible that they were issued contemporaneously.

At the time of publishing our seal figure 2 in 1946, Thomas Whittemore noted that the combination of the invocation Ἰησοῦ Χριστὲ Κύριε
("Jesus Christ Lord")—instead of either Ἰησοῦ Χριστὲ ("Jesus Christ") or
Ἰησοῦ Κύριε ("Jesus Lord"), found on the obverse—is unknown among
published sigillographic specimens, and that most likely the source for
such an invocation is liturgical in origin.[13] In the sixty-five years since
his article appeared, thousands more seals have been published. Among
the published specimens bearing religious figural iconography, only
one other seal bears a closely similar invocation: the eleventh-century
seal issued by Leo, Metropolitan of Chalcedon, where the incipit of the
invocation reads Κύριε Ἰησοῦ Χριστὲ Ὑιὲ Θεοῦ.[14] Thus the invocation on
two of Ignatios' seals is rare indeed. Whittemore also observed that the
imperative form "ἡγοῦ" of the verb "ἡγοῦμαι" likewise is not found on
seals, and this proves to remain valid at the present time.[15] When the
imperative "ἡγοῦ" ("lead") is encountered in texts, it is most frequently
employed in the context of spiritual authority, and often employed for
leading a monastic community.[16] As the leading churchman of the Byzantine Empire, it was appropriate for Ignatios to invoke the Lord to lead

him for inspiration, strength, and guidance as he in turn as patriarch led all the faithful under his spiritual care. As will be discussed below, the monastic connotation of the imperative form "ἡγοῦ" will also prove to be significant for Ignatios.

These seals, bearing the patriarch's name and office, when attached to any of his documents or letters not only served to secure the privacy of the texts, but also validated their authenticity and endowed their contents with his authority. By placing an image of Christ with its accompanying invocative inscription on his seals, the patriarch gives visual expression to his personal devotion to the Lord and his faith in His guiding powers. But Patriarch Ignatios was not only a personal believer within the framework of Byzantine culture. He was a public official, indeed the highest-ranking ecclesiastical figure of the Byzantine Empire. His official seals, therefore, represented his office, and their imagery and inscriptions were weighted with meaning and significance. In this regard it is instructive to observe what his predecessors and successors chose for their official seals. Also critical to this discussion is the fact that Ignatios was only the second Iconophile patriarch following the final liquidation of Iconoclasm in 843 because Methodios, his predecessor, was patriarch for only three years until his death in 847.[17] When a search is made for examples of patriarchal seals from the pre-Iconoclastic period that bear religious figural imagery, only one example comes to light: the seal issued by Eutychios (552–565 and 577–582), with its worn depiction of an unidentified bearded saint.[18] For the Iconoclastic period, when religious figural images were officially banned, seals belonging to three Iconoclastic patriarchs are known: Theodotos (815–821), Anthony I (821–837), and John VII (837–843).[19] No image appears on these pieces: the obverses display cruciform invocative monograms, and five-line inscriptions occupy the reverses. The invocative monograms begin with the prayer Κύριε βοήθει ("Lord, help"). With the final Iconophile victory in 843, beginning with Methodios I and followed by all of his successors—even those after the fall of the empire, except for Ignatios—all the patriarchs placed an image of the Theotokos on their seals.[20]

The choice of the image of Christ for Ignatios' seals is, therefore, unusual. He was the only post-Iconoclastic Constantinopolitan patriarch to select such an image. It was, however, the custom of emperors after Iconoclasm to place the Lord's image on their seals. This began with specimens of Michael III after the end of his minority (856–867) and was followed by all of his successors until the end of the empire in 1453.[21] In the pre-Iconoclastic period, emperors did not employ the image of Christ on their seals. From the reigns of Justin II (565–578), if not that of Justinian I (527–565), through that of the early years of Leo III's (717–720), before his ban against holy images, emperors placed some type of image of the Virgin on their seals.[22] Her image on imperial seals replaced the older classical figure of *Nike*, or Victory.[23] During the Iconoclastic period (720–843), emperors replaced the image of the Mother of God on their seals with that of the cross and a prayer to the Trinity.[24] During the Iconophile interlude (787–815), three emperors—Nikephoros I (802–815), Michael I Rangabe (811–813), and Leo V (813–815) until his renewal of the ban on images in 815—again took up the image of the Theotokos for their seals, but now she is flanked by the cruciform invocative monograms, Θεοτόκε Βοήθει, and the reverse of these seals bear the sign of the cross.[25] Thus from the middle of the sixth century through the early ninth century, excluding the Iconoclastic period, emperors employed some form of Marian imagery for their official seals, whereas after Iconoclasm imperial seals bore an image of Christ.

Michael III and his mother, the regent Theodora, also restored the image of Christ on coins after the end of Iconoclasm,[26] reviving the short-lived innovation of the emperor Justinian II (685–695 and 705–711).[27] Justinian II's immediate successors did not employ this numismatic practice. It appears to have been of little interest,[28] and the evidence of the seals tends to corroborate this view. Not only do pre-Iconoclastic emperors not employ Christ's image on their seals (nor did Justinian II himself); the image of Christ likewise does not appear on seals in general at this time. No parallel chronological sigillographic interest or imitation is observed. Only five seals from my database bearing the image of Christ belong to the seventh and early eighth centuries. The figure of Christ on seals is a small percentage of the *total* number of religious figural seals: 666 out of 9,200, or 7.2%. During the pre-Iconoclastic period, no emperor chose this image for his seals. But after the Triumph of Orthodoxy, the majority of sphragistic images of Christ belong to emperors: 494 of 642, or 76.9%. Thus the image of Christ had little sphragistic appeal in Byzantine society, being closely associated with the person of the emperor after Iconoclasm. This connection is reinforced by the fact that post-Iconoclastic emperors placed His image on coins as well.[29]

Elsewhere I have attempted to explain why emperors first selected an image of the Virgin for their seals only to change to that of the image of Christ after Iconoclasm, whereas post-Iconoclastic patriarchs then took up the image of the Virgin for their seals.[30] There has been much

scholarly literature demonstrating that by the middle of the sixth century, the cult of the Theotokos had been grafted onto that of the imperial
and civic cults: she became identified as the patron of Constantinople,
protector of the empire, and most sure guarantor of imperial victory.[31]
The imperial identity was closely associated with the person of the Theotokos, and this development is clearly reflected in the seals.

In addition to the close imperial connection with the cult of the
Theotokos in the pre-Iconoclastic centuries, it must be remembered
that during the period of Iconoclasm (ca. 730–787 and 815–843), con-
siderable debate centered on the intercessory powers of the Virgin in
addition to the legitimacy of her image.[32] According to Alexander Kazhdan, the most likely cause of the clash between the Iconoclast emperor
Leo III and the Iconophile patriarch Germanos in 730 was the nature of
the veneration of the Mother of God and the role that she played in the
life of the empire.[33] The Iconophiles, on the other hand, were quick to
defend both the Virgin's intercessory role and her images.[34] They rea-
soned that the Theotokos must be revered, because it was from her that
Christ assumed flesh, and thus His body was circumscribable and could
be depicted. For the Iconophile, any hostility toward the venerable icons
was therefore an attack against the Theotokos: she became identified
with the legitimacy of image veneration. Unsurprisingly, the majority of
seals assigned by George Zacos and Alexander Veglery in their catalogue
to the years of the Iconophile interlude of 787–815 (34 out of 39 seals, or
87.2%) bear an image of the Virgin and Child.[35] After the final victory
of the Iconophiles in 843, Patriarch Methodios placed the image of the
Theotokos on his seal, as noted above, and his successors would do so
as well. The representation of the Theotokos, not the image of Christ,
became the Iconophile emblem *par excellence*.[36]

After the final Iconophile victory in 843, a new pattern of imperial and patriarchal sphragistic iconography appears. The emperor now
places an image of Christ on his seals, not that of the Virgin as before.
This begins with specimens of Michael III after the end of his minority
(856–867) and continues with all of his successors until the end of the
empire in 1453. Meanwhile, after Iconoclasm, beginning with Methodios
I and followed by all of his successors, even after the fall of the empire,
the patriarchs placed an image of the Theotokos on their seals. Only
Ignatios I (847–858 and 867–877), immediately following Methodios
on the patriarchal throne, was the exception: he preferred the image of
Christ for his seals. His successor, Photios, returned to the example of
Methodios and selected an image of the Mother of God for his seals, as

did all subsequent patriarchs of Constantinople. It appears that a period of transition occurred before the stabilization of the respective imperial and patriarchal sigillographic iconographic choices. Yet, as made by the two highest individuals in the Byzantine politico-ecclesial hierarchy, the choice of images for imperial and patriarchal seals reflects official and far-reaching ideology.

On one level, it is in the spirit of the Iconophile victory discussed above that Methodios placed an image of the Virgin on his seals, because the representation of the Virgin was the Iconophile emblem *par excellence*. This can be clearly seen in the *Canon of Orthodoxy*, composed by Methodios himself to commemorate the Triumph of Orthodoxy, in which the Marian references succinctly reiterate the Iconophile position regarding the Theotokos: she is the source of Christ's flesh, the image of which can be venerated, in addition to her own, and that she is the universal intercessor.[37]

As outlined above, however, by the middle of the sixth century the Theotokos was also clearly understood as the heavenly patron and defender of the empire's capital city. Her cult was closely tied to that of the emperor and the fortunes of the city. Devotion to the Virgin had been built up, layer by layer, taking on all the attributes and honors of the imperial cult as the object of public veneration in Constantinople.[38] As Kate Cooper has suggested, already in the debates concerning the title "Theotokos" in the fifth century between the imperial family and Nestorios, the conflict reflected the struggle over who would actually mediate the power of Christ: the imperial family or the Church.[39] Recently, Liz James has discussed how beginning with Leo I (457–474), emperors, and not empresses, actually displayed a greater activity in enhancing the cult of the Virgin; as the Theotokos developed a greater and more powerful significance in the civic life of the capital, the great mediating power of Christ that the Theotokos has as intercessor would be controlled by the emperor.[40] Thus both the Virgin and the emperor were seen to have access, as intercessors, to the mediating power of Christ. According to Nike Koutrakou, during the debates between the Iconoclasts and Iconophiles, the arguments over the intercessory powers of the Virgin reflected a response to a fundamental contemporary understanding of imperio-ecclesial polity, that of the intercessory role of emperors.[41] Leo III is described by the Iconophiles as claiming himself to be both "emperor and priest" (ὅτι βασιλεὺς καὶ ἱερεύς εἰμι).[42] In the *Ecloga*, the law code issued by Leo III and his son Constantine V, the role of the emperor is described as one commissioned by God to be "the shepherd to the most faithful

flock" (ποιμαίνειν ἡμᾶς κελεύσας τὸ πιστότατον ποίμνιον).[43] Later, Leo V
(813–820), who initiated the second phase of Iconoclasm, was credited
with the phrase, "I am a child of the Church and as intercessor I shall
hear" (τέκνον εἰμὶ τῆς Ἐκκλησίας καὶ ὡς μεσίτης ἐπακροάσομαι).[44] Thus
pre-Iconoclastic emperors placed the image of the Virgin on their seals
to identify with her role as protector and intercessor for the empire. The
seals are one of the strongest pieces of evidence for the grafting of the
cult of the Theotokos onto that of the emperor during this period and
for indicating the extent to which these cults overlapped. Although the
emperor may have ruled his earthly realm as Christ's representative,[45] in
the pre-Iconoclastic period the role of the emperor was likened to that
of the Virgin: as mediator between the divine and human worlds.[46] In
his discussion of the biased trials against Pope Martin and Maximos the
Confessor in the 650s, John Haldon noted the significance of the false
accusations brought against these opponents of the imperial Monothe-
lite position: treason and slandering both the emperor and the Virgin.[47]
In the symbolic universe of the mid-seventh century, the imperial values were closely linked to that of the Theotokos, and to undermine one
of these authorities would be understood as an attack on both. It was
the Iconoclast emperors who claimed the sole authority of mediation.
It is also noteworthy that during Iconoclasm the Iconoclastic patriarchs,
as previously observed, employed the use of the cruciform invocative
monograms, Κύριε βοήθει ("Lord, help"), also rejecting the intercessory
powers of the Mother of God.[48]

    With the end of Iconoclasm and the Triumph of Orthodoxy, the
seals indicate a new pattern. Beginning with Emperor Michael III, emperors now place the image of Christ on their seals, whereas the patriarchs, beginning with Methodios I, place an image of the Virgin on
their seals (except for Ignatios I, as noted above). Michael III and his
mother, the regent Theodora, also restored the image of Christ on coins

    It appears, therefore, that after the liquidation of Iconoclasm, there
was a new sphragistic iconographic repertoire established for the emperor and the patriarch. The consistent separate choice of images reflects the roles of these two highest and most powerful officials in the
Byzantine Empire. This sigillographic development parallels the same
thought-world in which Patriarch Photios composed, sometime between 879 and 886, the *Eisagoge/Epanagoge*, a legal manual that for the
first time clearly defined the separate roles and spheres of the *imperium*
and *sacerdotium* that departed radically from previous law codes, now
redefining their activities in favor of the patriarch.[49] The emperor is now

defined as a "legitimate authority" (ἔννομος ἐπιστασία),[50] subject not only to the teachings of the Gospels, Ecumenical Synods, and canons, but also to the juridical tradition (because Christ is seen as the lawgiver), whereas at the same time he is regarded as chosen by God to participate in a special way in this divine truth.[51] As various scholars have noted, in the years following the liquidation of Iconoclasm, the emperor's status has changed: on the one hand he is promoted to a quasi-divinized status as an initiate and participator in the truths of God's divine law, but at the same time he has lost his legislative independence and serves to execute Christ's legislation.[52] Nowhere in the text is the emperor's role characterized as that of an intercessor, as in the pre-Iconoclastic and Iconoclastic periods. In this light it is understandable that after Iconoclasm the emperor's image is associated with that of Christ on coins and seals. Although the emperor's divine status has been enhanced and he enjoys a proximity to Christ, simultaneously he has been relieved of certain powers and functions as an agent of His will and thus is found on the reverse, or secondary, position on the coins and seals; Christ, as the source of the law, enjoys the privileged field of the obverse.[53] At the same time, the patriarch is now described as a "living and animate image of Christ" (εἰκὼν ζῶσα Χριστοῦ καὶ ἔμψυχος);[54] he must preserve those that he has received from God (. . . οὓς ἐκ Θεοῦ παρέλαβεν εὐσεβείᾳ καὶ σεμνότητι βίου διαφυλάξαι),[55] he is the salvation of those souls that have been entrusted to him (τέλος τῷ πατριάρχῃ ἡ τῶν καταπεπιστευμένων αὐτῷ ψυχῶν σωτηρία),[56] the care of all spiritual matters depends on him (τῶν ψυχικῶν ἁπάντων ἡ πρόνοια τῷ πατριάρχῃ ἀνάκειται),[57] and he alone acts as the arbitrator and judge concerning matters of repentance and the return of sinners and heretics (ὡσαύτως δὲ καὶ μετανοίας καὶ ἐπιστροφῆς ἀπό τε ἁμαρτημάτων καὶ αἱρέσεων αὐτὸς καὶ μόνος καθίσταται διαιτητής τε καὶ γνώμων).[58] From these descriptions, the patriarch now takes on the characteristics of the powerful intercessor. As Marie-France Auzépy[59] and Gilbert Dagron observe, all that the patriarch has gained with the Triumph of Orthodoxy is at the expense of the emperor.[60] Immediately after Iconoclasm, the prestige of the patriarch was privileged over that of the emperor.[61] Although the text of the *Eisagoge* characterizes the patriarch as the "living and animate image of Christ," his role is clearly defined as that of the universal intercessor. It is fitting, therefore, that his seals now bear an image of the Theotokos, the intercessor *par excellence*.[62]

Marie-Theres Fögen and Dagron have also noted that the context of the *Eisagoge/Epanagoge*, with its newly articulated emphasis on the separate spheres of the *imperium* and *sacerdotium* that privilege the patriarch, is actually a concept introduced from contemporary papal Rome.[63] In addition, Dmitry Afinogenov observed that Methodios, in his second letter addressed to the Stoudites, was the first patriarch of Constantinople to stress apostolic succession, an ideology that the hierarch came to know during his earlier years in Rome (815–821): "up to the Apostles, and their successors, that is the patriarchs, are also Apostles" and "for a bishop is a common name and thing, whereas that of the Apostles and their successors is rare and very infrequent, masterful and sovereign."[64] This ecclesio-political setting may help to explain another aspect of the inscription found on Methodios' seal that was presented at the outset of this article: δούλῳ τῶν δούλων τοῦ Θεοῦ ("servant of the servants of God"). This phrase was an innovation for patriarchal seals, and Methodios actually appropriates a title that was employed by the popes of Rome beginning with Gregory I (590–604): *Servus servorum Dei*.[65] Here a further observation may also prove insightful. As discussed above, the choice of an image of the Theotokos on Methodios' seal reflects Iconophile teachings with regard to the Virgin's depiction as well as the patriarchal appropriation of the role of intercessor previously belonging to the emperor. Yet, like the ideology of two powers, *imperium* and *sacerdotium*, and the title "servant of the servants of God," the use of an image of the Virgin for the patriarch's seal likewise could reflect papal practices. Various scholars have demonstrated that a particular type of Marian iconography, the *Maria Regina*, dressed in imperial garments, was cultivated by popes of the eighth century as a means of expressing the emerging claim of their political independence from the imperial control of Constantinople.[66] Although not an example of the *Maria Regina* iconography, the image of the Theotokos found on Methodios' seal echoes similar statements of the first post-Iconoclastic patriarch's enhanced position over imperial authority.[67]

The practice of placing an image of the Theotokos on the seals of patriarchs, and their identification with her role as intercessor beginning after the liquidation of Iconoclasm, chronologically parallels another significant development: the greater emphasis on images of the Mother of God in the mosaic decoration of the cathedral of Hagia Sophia, the Church of Holy Wisdom.[68] Even the various Marian iconographic types found on patriarchal seals over time have been employed to study the history of the sanctuary's imagery.[69] Hagia Sophia is clearly seen as a, indeed, *the* patriarchal church, and the sphragistic material supports the work of Nicholas Oikonomides[70] and Dagron,[71] who see the cathedral's mosaic program as messages reflecting patriarchal policies, rather than the work of Robin Cormack,[72] Andreas Schminck,[73] and Alexei Lidov,[74] who preferred to interpret the mosaics as imperial statements. Dagron rightfully emphasizes the fact that in the late ninth- and early tenth-century mosaic of the southwest vestibule, the figures of Constantine I and Justinian I offer their models of the city and church, respectively, to the Theotokos, the "supreme intercessor," and not to Christ alone.[75] Although Hagia Sophia was originally dedicated to Christ as Holy Wisdom, the Logos of God,[76] as noted above, after Iconoclasm the presence of the Virgin in the figural decoration of the cathedral took on greater prominence. The Virgin as the vehicle of the Incarnation has long been understood as the temple or house of Christ, the Wisdom of God, especially in light of the biblical text Proverbs 9:1: "Wisdom has built a house for herself and set up seven pillars."[77] At least as early as the ninth century, this chapter of Proverbs was incorporated into the vesperal readings for feasts of the Theotokos.[78] It is not surprising, then, that the Virgin as the personification of the temple of Wisdom became associated with the cathedral church of Hagia Sophia, Holy Wisdom, as its secondary legitimate patron.[79] Because the Hagia Sophia was the church of the patriarch, this would be another reason for Methodios I and his successors to claim the Virgin's image for their official seals. Other ecclesiastical officials linked to the cathedral likewise selected images of the Mother of God for their seals.[80] Of 76 seals (excluding the patriarchal seals) belonging to individuals linked to Hagia Sophia from my database, 59, or 77.6%, depict an image of the Theotokos.[81]

Why then did Ignatios not follow the practice of Methodios, who placed an image of the Virgin on his seals, and why then did Photios, his successor, return to this practice? One suggestion is that because Methodios was the first post-Iconoclastic patriarch, and he served as patriarch for only three years, that no official practice had yet been established concerning the design of patriarchal seals. Such a view would explain Ignatios' choice as freely based on the preference of his personal devotions. Yet this could not be a complete explanation for producing the official seals of the highest-ranking churchman of the empire, on which image and text would be loaded with meaning. One must recall, however, that Methodios and Ignatios represented two different factions within the Iconophile party after 843, and this difference is not due just to the dichotomy of their characters, as moderate scholar and monastic and rigorous monastic, respectively. Methodios was selected to be patriarch by the empress Theodora and her close associates with a local ecclesiastical assembly that met in the private residence of Theoktistos, Theodora's chief counselor.[82] Methodios was a member of this inner circle. Despite the fact that he suffered persecution and exile during the reign of the Iconoclast emperor Michael II (820–829), he was later pardoned by the succeeding Iconoclast emperor Theophilos (829–842), the husband of Theodora, and brought to live in the palace on account of his extensive learning.[83] Although earlier scholarship viewed Methodios as a moderate who was chosen to oversee a smooth reconciliation between Iconoclast clergy and those who remained firm Iconophiles during the period of banned images,[84] more recent studies have revealed the patriarch to be a staunch Iconophile who did not compromise with the lapsed bishops and priests and who took the rigorist position of permanently excluding them from the ranks of the clergy after the victory over Iconoclasm in 843.[85]

Yet Methodios had also come into conflict with the Stoudite monks who had not forgotten that he lived in the palace under the Iconoclast Theophilos. Methodios was elected patriarch as the candidate preferred by Theodora, but the Stoudite monastery had hoped to have one of their own placed on the patriarchal throne, most notably John Katasambas/ Kakosambas, and when this did not occur, they threatened schism.[86] This was a repeat of recent history: in 806 Nikephoros had been elected patriarch over the Stoudite candidate, most likely Theodore himself, and the Stoudites strongly protested.[87] They had already been in disagreement with Nikephoros' predecessor, Patriarch Tarasios (784–806), concerning his leniency in dealing with the repentant Iconoclast hierarchs from the first phase of Iconoclasm, and now the Stoudites turned against Nikephoros, too, because he, like Tarasios, was a layman raised to the patriarchal throne and not one of their own.[88] The tension was exacerbated with the "Moechian" schism that pitted Theodore and the Stoudites against the patriarchs Tarasios and Nikephoros over the uncanonical second marriage of the emperor Constantine VI; this schism continued for sixteen years as a divisive political, religious, and legal dispute (795–811).[89] Thus there was a pre-existing conflict below the surface of the recent alignment for the Triumph of Orthodoxy in 843, and this division preoccupied Methodios throughout his short, four-year reign as patriarch. With Methodios, the Stoudites, deprived once again of their candidate for the patriarchal throne, questioned the canonical standing of Methodios' election as well as his ordination of many replacements of deposed Iconoclast hierarchs, who were perceived as unworthy, while simultaneously not appointing any Stoudite candidates.[90]

Methodios, who employed the image of the Virgin and Child for his seals, died in 847 and was succeeded by Ignatios, who took up the image of Christ for his seals. This rejection of the iconography of the official patriarchal seals of Methodios parallels the rejection of his ecclesiastical policies and those of his supporters who brought him to the throne, and represents the other camp within the Iconophile victors, the Stoudites. It must first be remembered that Ignatios was the son of the emperor Michael I Rangabe (811–813) and the grandson of the emperor Nikephoros I (802–811).[91] Both of these emperors ruled during the Iconophile interlude of 787–815, and as Iconophiles they employed the image of the Virgin and Child for their seals.[92] Because Ignatios was of imperial descent from both sides of his family, he may well have desired to proclaim visually his prestigious royal lineage. His choice of the image of Christ for his seals reflects contemporary post-Iconoclastic *imperial* practice, unlike that of the image of the Virgin and Child on his grandfather's and father's imperial seals from at least nearly forty years before.[93] It is known that Ignatios was particularly valued for his Iconophile imperial dynastic credentials, especially at a time when the young emperor Michael III was under the regency of his mother Theodora, because the sons of the previous Iconoclastic emperor, Leo V (813–820), were passed over as candidates for the patriarchal office.[94] Later in his career, when Ignatios was recalled from exile by the emperor Basil I to begin his second term as patriarch in 867, he was installed for a two-month waiting period in the imperial Mangana palace, which had originally been his patrimonial home, created by his father Michael I.[95] Thus, even though Michael I abdicated in 813 and entered the monastic life—as did his son Ignatios, born Niketas, who was forcibly castrated in order to prevent him, as a eunuch, from subsequently claiming the throne[96]—his strong imperial links and aura were never diminished or forgotten. Decades later, when selecting the image of Christ for his patriarchal seals, as current emperors now did, Ignatios adopted this official and public means of recalling and claiming his imperial ties.

In addition to his rigorous monastic career, which aligned Ignatios with the Stoudites, it was being Michael I's son that also strongly forged the patriarch's support of Theodore's followers. Michael I himself was greatly influenced by Theodore the Stoudite, even turning to him on matters of political importance.[97] Most significantly, it was Michael I who had ended the "Moechian" schism, in 811, shortly after ascending the throne, recalling Theodore and the Stoudites who had been exiled since 809 by the emperor Nikephoros I. Recording this event in the *Life* of Theodore the Stoudite, composed by Michael the monk, Michael I is described as a "Christomimetic" intercessor on behalf of those monks who had been previously separated.[98] Therefore, in the recent memory of Stoudite history, this emperor was portrayed as a Christ-like figure defending Theodore and his supporters, and this Christomimetic portrayal of his father would have been another factor predisposing Ignatios to employ an image of Christ for his seals.

Although from an Iconophile imperial family, Ignatios was not actively involved in the struggle against Iconoclasm, having been during those years following a strict ascetic regimen in his monastery, a monastery that had been in communion with the Iconoclasts, while his spiritual father had been the community's leader. Eventually Ignatios became its abbot.[99] As discussed earlier in this paper, the presence of the imperative form of the verb "ἡγοῦ" ("lead") in the invocation found on Ignatios' seals is unique, but within Byzantine texts it is usually employed to refer to leading with spiritual authority, especially in a monastic context. Theodore the Stoudite himself used this imperative in his letters when instructing other monastic leaders and his spiritual children.[100] As an abbot, too, and as an ardent defender of the Stoudite legacy, Ignatios could easily have appropriated the imperative for his seals as a means of invoking the Lord's guidance as he undertook his patriarchal duties and as a linguistic allusion to his monastic and Stoudite sympathies.

Given Ignatios' ambiguous religio-political pedigree from a monastic house that had been in communion with Iconoclasts, the empress Theodora, who had appointed Ignatios, hoped that he would reconcile the former Iconoclast clergy, because Methodios' policy of permanently excommunicating them was considered too rigid and untenable.[101] From the day of Ignatios' patriarchal consecration, the new ecclesiastical and imperial climate was manifested: Ignatios expelled from among those metropolitans gathered for the ceremony Gregory Asbestos, Archbishop of Syracuse, who may have been a schismatic, but who had been a strong supporter of Methodios. Subsequently Ignatios was accused of maligning the memory of Methodios; his actions were labeled those of a "parricide," because he supported the Stoudites and called into judgment those clergy that Methodios had spared.[102] In addition, recently it has been convincingly argued that the patriarchal archive built up by the Iconophile patriarchs Tarasios, Nikephoros, and Methodios had been transferred to the Stoudios monastery by Ignatios upon his ascension to the throne in 847. This archive contained polemical works by Methodios and others, works written during the Stoudite schism that

Ignatios preferred to keep safely hidden away out of the hands of his own detractors and in order to safeguard the memory of his friends of the Stoudite community.[103] Thus, Ignatios' family connections, election, and Stoudite-favoring policies clearly represent a rejection of Methodios' spiritual heritage. In this light, one can understand his decision to change the imagery of his official seals from that of his predecessor.

As mentioned above, it is uncertain to which of Ignatios' two patriarchates his surviving seals belong or if the two types of seals, that with the figure of the standing Christ and that with the bust of Christ, were simultaneously issued. But it is known that during the time of his second patriarchate, Ignatios was especially interested in the image of Christ of the Chalke gate. In 867 Ignatios was restored to the patriarchal throne. In 869 he commissioned the writing of the *Passion of the Martyrs of Chalke* in response to finding the martyrs' relics after receiving instructions in a dream as to their whereabouts. The text reflects the ninth-century belief in an earlier icon of Christ at the Chalke gate before the empress Irene's installation of an icon of Christ ca. 800.[104] According to the *Passion*, in his dream Ignatios is visited by a female figure who reveals that she and her friends are the martyrs killed by the soldiers of the emperor Leo III in 730 when the soldiers attempted to prevent them from removing the icon of Christ from the Chalke gate of the imperial palace. She tells Ignatios that they have been buried in the now-ruined church of Saint Demetrios attached to the monastery of Saint Aninas, which is in the western part of the city, near the Stoudios monastery.[105] The patriarch and his entourage proceed to the site and, after an earthquake opens the ground for them, they discover the bodies, which exude a wonderful fragrance. The text magnifies the role of the earlier Germanos, the patriarch at the time Leo III initiated Iconoclasm, whose memory by now was greatly celebrated as the last Orthodox patriarch before the onset of Iconoclasm. Germanos, like Ignatios, was a monk and eunuch, and the latter benefitted from this prestigious association, because Germanos' immediate followers, Tarasios and Nikephoros, were laymen who became patriarchs, as was Photios, the nemesis of Ignatios.[106] Although Methodios was also a monastic, as noted above, Ignatios was not of the same mindset and pursued different policies, and therefore did not attempt to associate himself with his memory. Now two years into his second patriarchate, the earthquake and the discovery of the relics of the martyrs for the icon of Christ *Chalkites* are used by Ignatios at a politically astute moment to enhance his restored position.

The Christ *Chalkites* icon was of particular interest to both Theodore the Stoudite and Methodios. When the icon of Christ *Chalkites* was first placed on the Chalke gate by the empress Irene, ca. 800, to replace the image of the cross and epigrams erected by the Iconoclasts,[107] Theodore composed epigrams to accompany this image.[108] Although Theodore's poems reinforce the reality of Christ's human nature as the means by which His image is made possible, Theodore makes no *specific* mention of the Virgin as the vehicle of Christ's Incarnation that justified the production of his image.[109] When the image of Christ was removed by Leo V just before Christmas of 814[110] and replaced by the sign of the cross and a set of Iconoclast epigrams, Theodore also composed another set of five epigrams as a critical response to the five Iconoclastic ones, as well as a longer refutation of the Iconoclastic epigrams (ca. 815).[111] Only in these texts, after the removal of the Christ *Chalkites* icon, do references to the Virgin appear more directly in the texts, though not frequently, and not by name or a title such as "Virgin," "Mother of God," or "Theotokos"; two of the epigrams refer to her role in the Incarnation, one of which forms an acrostic "Theotokos," while in the text of the refutation she is referred to twice, briefly, and toward the end of the text she is again invoked when Theodore elaborates upon the article of the Creed "incarnated by the Holy Spirit and the Virgin Mary."[112] It is important to recall, too, that Theodore's second refutational epigrams were not publicly visible like his first set, which appeared on the Chalke gate along with Irene's icon of Christ. When the image was restored after 843 by the empress Theodora,[113] Methodios, for his part, also composed a long epigram that was placed adjacent to the image on the Chalke gate.[114] In this public poem celebrating the icon, the divine and human natures of Christ are acknowledged, but here Methodios directly includes the role of the Virgin in giving Christ his depictable flesh: ἐκ μητρὸς ὤφθης ἐν χρόνῳ βροτὸς φύσει ("but because of your mother, you are seen in time and mortal by nature").[115] As noted above, he likewise emphasized in his canon to the Theotokos the role of the Mother of God as the source of Christ's flesh that could be represented and, as previously discussed, Methodios placed her image on his seals. Ignatios, although interested in the history of the Christ *Chalkites* icon, nevertheless appears to follow the Stoudite focus of interest on Christ Himself; he preferred the image of Christ for his seals without employing the image of the Virgin as had his immediate patriarchal predecessor, whose policies he rejected.

Another example of Ignatios' interest in images of Christ is the use of *enkolpia*—pendants, often cross-shaped, that usually contained a relic of the True Cross and frequently had sacred images on their exterior—which had begun to be employed as Iconophile reactions to the Iconoclasts.[116] The term *enkolpion* is rare in the ninth century, where five references are known, all found in texts written by sympathizers of Ignatios.[117] *Enkolpia* were usually historiated with an image of Christ's Crucifixion, although other images of the Virgin and or saints could be present or included.[118] In one of the texts, that of the *Vita Theodorae*, the account of the Iconoclast emperor Theophilos' repentance and death-bed scene is narrated, in which Theophilos kisses the *enkolpion* worn by the chief minister Theoktistos, and this *enkolpion* is described as bearing an image of Christ.[119] From one of the other sources, it is known that Ignatios himself was given an *enkolpion* by the emperor Michael III.[120] In 861, a time when Ignatios had been deposed and was in hiding due to a death sentence issued against him by the emperor, there was a great earthquake that lasted forty days, and the authorities then took it as a sign to end the mistreatment of Ignatios. As an emblem of surety, Bardas, the uncle of the emperor, sent Ignatios the emperor's *enkolpion*, which Ignatios then wore around his neck. When he came out of hiding and Bardas enquired why the patriarch wandered about like a fugitive, Ignatios paraphrased a Gospel text: "Christ, our Lord and Savior, commanded us, saying, 'If they persecute you in the city, flee to another' " (Matt 10:23). Although the text does not describe this *enkolpion*, it most likely bore an image of Christ, if not other holy figures, and it is noteworthy that the patriarch invokes Christ's own words when he appears before his former persecutor wearing the *enkolpion*.[121] Ignatios' use of and familiarity with *enkolpia*, with their Iconophile Christocentric images, accords well with his sphragistic images of Christ.

Ignatios' first term as patriarch was from 847 to 858. He was appointed by Theodora without being elected by a synod.[122] He was sympathetic to the Stoudites, thus creating opposition from the moderates, especially Gregory Asbestos, as noted above. In 856 Michael III came of age and aligned himself with his uncle, Bardas, the brother of Theodora. Michael III and Bardas supported the moderate position against Theodora and Theoktistos, who backed the monastic rigorists and Ignatios. Bardas, with the complicity of Michael, assassinated Theoktistos and forced Theodora into monastic orders. When Ignatios refused to bless her taking of the veil, the patriarch was then regarded as an enemy of the new political regime. Subsequently he was accused of treason and banished to the island of Terebinthos, and eventually he was forced to resign from the patriarchal throne and was replaced by Photios.[123] In 867 Basil I became sole emperor, after assassinating Michael III, and sought the support of Ignatios' followers and the papacy who had previously stood by Ignatios. Thus he removed and exiled Photios and restored Ignatios to the patriarchal throne in the same year. When Ignatios died in 877, Photios once more succeeded him on the patriarchal throne, until he was exiled again in 886 by the new emperor Leo VI. Leo reversed his religio-political policies to favor again the extremist followers of Ignatios, who had not accepted Photios' return to the throne. Photios died in exile in 891.[124]

For his patriarchal seals, Photios employed images of the Virgin and Child, returning to the practice established by Methodios and expressing the new ecclesio-political thought-world of imperial and patriarchal post-Iconoclastic Byzantium as outlined above. All succeeding patriarchs would place an image of the Virgin and Child on their seals down to the end of the empire and even beyond, as already observed. Photios chose two different iconographic types of the Virgin and Child for his seals: on the obverse of one, a standing image of the Virgin and Child, as the Hodegetria type, accompanied by the circular inscription [+Υ]ΠΕ[ΡΑ] ΓΙΑΘΕ ΟΤΟΚΕΒΟΗΘΕΙ; and on the reverse the inscription in six lines is: +ΦWΤΙ-WΑΡΧΙΕΠΙС-ΚΟΠWΚWΝС-ΤΑΝΤΙΝΟΥΠΟ-ΛΕWСΝΕΑС-ΡWΜΗС. The inscription reads, [+῾Υ]πε[ρα]γία Θεοτόκε, βοήθει Φωτίῳ ἀρχιεπισκόπῳ Κωνσταντινουπόλεως Νέας ῾Ρώμης ("Most Holy Theotokos, help Photios, Archbishop of Constantinople-New Rome").[125] On the obverse of a second, there is a bust image of the Virgin holding the Christ Child before her and accompanied by the circular inscription +ΘΚΕΒΟΗΘΕΙΤW СWΔΟΥΛW, and on the reverse the inscription in six lines is: +ΦWΤΙ-[W]ΑΡΧΙΕΠΙС-ΚΟΠWΚWΝС-ΤΑΝΤΙΝΟΥΠΟ-ΛΕWСΝΕΑС-ΡWΜΗС; the inscription reads, +Θ[εοτό]κε, βοήθει τῷ σῷ δούλῳ Φωτί[ῳ] ἀρχιεπισκόπῳ Κωνσταντινουπόλεως Νέας ῾Ρώμης ("Theotokos, help your servant Photios, Archbishop of Constantinople-New Rome").[126] As with the two different iconographic types of seals of Ignatios described above, here, too, with the two different Marian sphragistic types, it is impossible to assign a type to one of Photios' two patriarchal terms of office.[127] It is possible, however, that the seal with the image of the standing Virgin and Child belongs to Photios' first term on the patriarchal throne because it most closely resembles that of Methodios' seal with respect to both image and inscription; both have a similar standing image of the Virgin and Child accompanied by the same incipit of the invocative inscription:

+Ὑπεραγία Θεοτόκε, βοήθει ("Most Holy Theotokos, help").[128] As outlined above, Photios and Ignatios became rivals for the patriarchal throne and represented differing ecclesio-political policies. Photios would naturally reject Ignatios' practice of placing an image of Christ on his official seals as a visual expression of breaking with Ignatios. He returns, therefore, to the sphragistic practice established by Methodios, whom he meant to recall for reasons set forth below.

The previous Iconophile patriarch Tarasios, under the empress Irene, had been a relative, possibly a great-uncle, of Photios and now stood in a venerable line of Iconophile patriarchs.[129] During the time of the Stoudite schism, Methodios had been a staunch defender of Tarasios, as well as of Nikephoros.[130] Furthermore, it is known that Photios' mother was related by marriage to the empress Theodora who had selected Methodios as patriarch.[131] Photios was also close to the small group of individuals who orchestrated the Triumph of Orthodoxy in 843; when St. Euthymios of Sardis died in 831, Methodios composed his *Vita*, in which one learns that when Euthymios was imprisoned by the emperor Theophilos and interrogated about his associations, Euthymios replied about a female relative by marriage to the emperor.[132] Cyril Mango suggests that it may have been a sister of Theodora or even the mother of Photios.[133] But the lines between Methodios and Photios are more direct. As a young man Photios composed a hymn in memory of Methodios that was sung at the latter's funeral in 847.[134] As outlined above, Gregory Asbestos had been a strong supporter of Methodios but had fallen out with Ignatios. Photios, however, had claimed that Gregory was his mentor, and Gregory in turn consecrated him patriarch.[135] Gregory Asbestos also wrote a now-lost *Vita* of Methodios.[136] Thus Photios assumed the spiritual heritage of Methodios that had been rejected by Ignatios. He spent much of his career reinforcing the condemnation of Iconoclasm, as did Methodios, and he was concerned with the rehabilitation of Methodios' memory.[137]

As the foregoing investigation has demonstrated, the diminutive realm of sphragistic iconography reflects the larger thought-world from which it was produced. This is especially true when the owner of a seal is a leading figure within a particular society. In the case of Patriarch Ignatios, the highest-ranking ecclesiastic in the middle years of the ninth century, the choice of image for his official lead seal would be weighted with much significance. His use of the image of Christ had numerous, complex associations: it proclaimed his privileged imperial lineage, it linked him with other high-ranking individuals who cultivated the use of historiated *enkolpia* as an expression of their Iconophile beliefs, it associated him with the Christ *Chalkites* icon and all its celebrated history, and it announced his allegiance to the Stoudite monks. This last aspect of Ignatios' sphragistic image of Christ was the most critical: it gave official, visual expression to his break with the ecclesio-religious policies of his predecessor, Methodios. Ignatios was deposed and then succeeded by Photios, who in turn was deposed and saw Ignatios restored to the patriarchal throne, only to be followed by Photios once more upon his death. Photios restored the image of the Virgin and Child to patriarchal seals, heralding a return to Methodian policies. The alternating images of the Theotokos and Christ appearing on these small seals of the leading churchmen of the empire testifies to the *rota fortunae* of patriarchal and imperial fortunes in the new world of post-Iconoclasm Byzantium.

Notes

I wish to thank Elena Stepanova for providing the photograph of the Ignatian seal belonging to the Hermitage and Jonathan Shea of Dumbarton Oaks for the photograph of Ignatios' seal from the Fogg collection.

1. For reproductions of Patriarch Ignatios' seals, see G. Zacos, *Byzantine Lead Seals*, vol. 2, ed. J. Nesbitt (Berne, 1984), no. 6a–c, pl. 1; N. Oikonomides, *A Collection of Dated Byzantine Lead Seals* (Washington, DC, 1986), nos. 51 and 52; and J. Nesbitt and C. Morrisson, *Catalogue of Byzantine Seals at Dumbarton Oaks and in the Fogg Museum of Art*, vol. 6 (Washington, DC, 2009) (hereafter *DOSeals* 6), no. 112.1. There is another unpublished specimen in the Bibliothèque nationale de France (Zacos no. 5540), in very poor condition, that is parallel to the seal listed as 6c in the Zacos volume noted above. I wish to thank Jean-Claude Cheynet for bringing this piece to my attention. For earlier publications of these seals, along with the previous misreadings of their inscriptions, see V. Laurent, *Le corpus des sceaux de l'empire byzantin*, 6:1 (Paris, 1963), nos. 5 and 6. For some more recent literature devoted to Patriarch Ignatios, in addition to the information provided in the seal catalogues listed in this note, see P. Karlin-Hayter, "Gregory of Syracuse, Ignatios and Photios," in *Iconoclasm*, ed. A. Bryer and J. Herrin (Birmingham, 1977), 141–146; *Oxford Dictionary of Byzantium*, 2:983–984; M. Vinson, "Gender and Politics in the Post-Iconoclastic Period: The Lives of Antony the Younger, the Empress Theodora, and the Patriarch Ignatios," *Byzantion* 68 (1998): 469–515; *Prosopographie der mittelbyzantinischen Zeit*, Abt. 1; Bd. 2, ed. R.-J. Lilie et al. (Berlin, 2000), no. 2666; L. Brubaker and J. Haldon, *Byzantium in the Iconoclastic Era (ca. 680–850): The Sources, An Annotated Survey* (Al-

dershot, 2001), 52–53, 72–73, 135, 211, 277, 239–240, 260, 263, and 306; *Prosopography of the Byzantine Empire*, vol. 1, *641–867*, ed. J. R. Martindale (Aldershot, 2001), no. 2666; *Dumbarton Oaks Hagiography Database*, ed. A. Kazhdan and A.-M. Talbot (Washington, DC, 2002), http://doaks.org/saints2/dohp.asp?cmd=SShow&key=38 and http://doaks.org/document/hagiointro.pdf, accessed April 18, 2011; H. Chadwick, *East and West: The Making of a Rift in the Church; From Apostolic Times until the Council of Florence* (Oxford, 2003), 119–152 and 164–172; S. Tougher, "Holy Eunuchs! Masculinity and Eunuch Saints in Byzantium," in *Holiness and Masculinity in the Middle Ages*, ed. P. Cullum and K. Lewis (Cardiff, 2004), 98–102; A. Kazhdan, *A History of Byzantine Literature (850–1000)*, ed. C. Angelidi (Athens, 2006), 97–102; and Βίος ἢ Μαρτύριον τοῦ ἐν ἁγίοις πατρὸς ἡμῶν Ἰγνατίου Ἀρχιεπισκόπου Κωνσταντινουπόλεως, ed. P. Kitromelides and Ch. Messes (Athens, 2008), 29–37. For the mosaic image of Ignatios in Hagia Sophia of Constantinople, see C. Mango and E. Hawkins, "The Mosaics of St. Sophia at Istanbul: The Church Fathers in the North Tympanum," *Dumbarton Oaks Papers* 26 (1972): 9–11 and 28–30.

2. For a recent overview of the role of seals in Byzantine studies, see J. Nesbitt, "Sigillography," *Oxford Handbook of Byzantine Studies*, ed. E. Jeffreys, J. Haldon, and R. Cormack (Oxford, 2008), 150–156.

3. For a general discussion of these various types of seals and their use, see N. Oikonomides, *Byzantine Lead Seals* (Washington, DC, 1985), 6–7.

4. W. Seibt and M.-L. Zarnitz, *Das byzantinische Bleisiegel als Kunstwerk* (Vienna, 1997), 20, estimate that possibly 80,000 lead seals exist worldwide, of which only a portion of this sample has been published.

5. Oikonomides, *Byzantine Lead Seals*, 8–9, describes the various uses of seals. For other discussions concerning seals related to officials responsible for commerce and public goods, see N. Oikonomides, "Silk Trade and Production in Byzantium from the Sixth to the Ninth Century: The Seals of *Kommerkiarioi*," *Dumbarton Oaks Papers* 40 (1986): 33–54; J.-C. Cheynet, "Un aspect du ravitaillement de Constantinople aux Xe/XIe siècles d'après quelques sceaux d'hôrreiarioi," *Studies in Byzantine Sigillography* 6 (1999): 1–26; idem, "Épiskeptitai et autres gestionnaires des biens publics (d'après les sceaux de l'IFEB)," *Studies in Byzantine Sigillography* 7 (2002): 87–118; and W. Brandes, "Georgios ΑΠΟ ΥΠΑΤΩΝ und die Kommerkiariersiegel," *Siegel und Siegler, Akten des 8. Internationalen Symposions für byzantinische Sigillographie*, ed. C. Ludwig (Frankfurt am Main, 2005), 31–48. For discussion of both lead and copper tokens, see J. Nesbitt, "Byzantine Copper Tokens," *Studies in Byzantine Sigillography* 1 (1987): 67–76, and S. Bendall and

J. Nesbitt, "A 'Poor' Token from the Reign of Constantine V," *Byzantion* 60 (1990): 432–435.

6. For the image of the cross on lead seals, see I. Koltsida-Makre, "The Representation of the Cross on Byzantine Lead Seals," *Studies in Byzantine Sigillography* 4 (1995): 43–52; and A.-K. Wassiliou-Seibt, "Σύμβολον Ζωηφόρον: Παραστάσεις Σταυρῶν σε Βυζαντινά Μολυβδόβουλλα," in *Φιλοτιμία: Τιμητικὸς Τόμος γιὰ τὴν Ὁμότιμη Καθηγήτρια Ἀλκμήνη Σταυρίδου-Ζαφράκα*, ed. T. Korres (Thessaloniki, 2011), 669–685.

7. Of these, the depiction of the eagle is the most common. Examples are provided by G. Zacos and A. Veglery, *Byzantine Lead Seals*, 1:1 (Basel, 1972), nos. 585–730, pls. 64–72, who acknowledge the religious associations linked with the eagle. See also Seibt and Zarnitz, *Das byzantinische Bleisiegel als Kunstwerk*, 169–178, who also discuss the Christian aspect of the eagle's image. For discussion of the eagle as both an imperial and religious emblem, see *Oxford Dictionary of Byzantium*, 1:669 and I. Koltsida-Makre, "'Η Παράσταση τοῦ ἀετοῦ στά Μολυβδόβουλλα καί ἡ Προέλευσή της," *Δελτίον τῆς Χριστιανικῆς Ἀρχαιολογικῆς Ἑταιρείας* 4, no. 24 (2003): 411–416. For an example of the depiction of an elephant on seals, see C. Stavrakos, "The Elephant: A Rare Motif on the Byzantine Lead Seal ἐπὶ τῶν βαρβάρων," *Proceedings of the 1ˢᵗ International Congress for Sino-Greek Studies, Ioannina, 2–4 October 2004*, ed. C. Stavrakos (Ioannina, 2008) 282–299.

8. G. Zacos and A. Veglery, *Byzantine Lead Seals*, 1:2 (Basel, 1972), no. 1373 and no. 1382, offer examples of a winged victory and a *tyche*, respectively. See also E. Stepanova, "Victoria-Nike on Early Byzantine Seals," *Studies in Byzantine Sigillography* 10 (2010): 15–24.

9. Other than imperial images, secular portraits are extremely rare on Byzantine seals, unlike the medieval Western tradition. For a study of Western medieval seals bearing portraits of their owners, see T. Heslop, *Image and Authority: English Seals of the Eleventh and Twelfth Centuries* (London, 1997). For two Byzantine examples, see Zacos and Veglery, *Byzantine Lead Seals*, 1:2, no. 1386, and N. Oikonomides, "Theophylact Excubitus and His Crowned 'Portrait': An Italian Rebel of the Late Xth Century?" *Δελτίον τῆς Χριστιανικῆς Ἀρχαιολογικῆς Ἑταιρείας* 4, no. 12 (1986): 195–202. For the reassigning of the later seal to an individual of the twelfth century, see O. Kresten and W. Seibt, "Theophylaktos Exubitos (kein 'italienischer Rebell des späten 10. Jahrhunderts,' sondern ΜΕΓΑΣ ΔΙΕΡΜΗΝΕΥΤΗΣ unter Kaiser Manuel I. Komnenos) und seine Siegel," *Jahrbuch der österreichischen Byzantinistik* 52 (2002): 231–241.

10. One eleventh-century example is provided by J. Nesbitt and N. Oikonomides, *Catalogue of Byzantine Lead Seals at Dumbarton Oaks and in the Fogg Museum of Art*, vol. 2 (Washington, DC, 1994), no. 44.9, where the image of the Virgin is found on the seal of a Niketas, *proedros*,

strategos of Samos and *logothetes* of the *dromos*, and the invocative inscription begins, Θεοτόκε βοήθει ("Theotokos, help"). For some general remarks about the repertoire of religious images on lead seals, see Oikonomides, *Byzantine Lead Seals*, 10–15; Seibt and Zarnitz, *Das byzantinische Bleisiegel als Kunstwerk*, 103–106, 121–122, and 135–136; and V. Penna, "The Iconography of Byzantine Lead Seals: The Emperor, the Church, the Aristocracy," Δελτίον τῆς Χριστιανικῆς Ἀρχαιολογικῆς Ἑταιρείας 4, no. 20 (1998): 261–274.

11. Zacos, *Byzantine Lead Seals*, vol. 2, no. 6a–c and *DOSeals* 6, no. 112.1.

12. T. Whittemore, "An Unpublished Seal of the Patriarch Ignatios," *Byzantina/Metabyzantina* 1 (1946): 266, admits the impossibility of assigning the different seals to the two different patriarchates but then hypothesizes that the seals with the bust image of Christ may have been the earliest because the coins of the emperors Michael III and Basil I also display bust images of Christ; Laurent, *Corpus*, 5:1, nos. 5 and 6, however, prefers to assign both types of Ignatios' seals to his second term in office because the patriarch's title on the seal includes the phrase "New Rome," a term for Constantinople that Laurent considers more likely to have been employed by Ignatios' successor Photios and then also employed by Ignatios during his second term in office; however, at the time of Laurent's publication, the seal of an earlier patriarch, John VII (837–843), that bears the title "bishop of Constantinople-New Rome" was unknown and was only later published by Zacos (no. 4); Zacos, *Byzantine Lead Seals*, vol. 2, no. 6a–c, likewise refrains from placing the two types of Ignatian seals in a chronological sequence but does offer the three well-known contemporary figures of Christ as a possible dating guide: that of the presumed *standing* figure of Christ of the Chalke gate (843–847); that of the enthroned Christ in the restored *chrysotriklinos* of the Great Palace (856–866); and that of the bust image of Christ in the dome of the church of the Theotokos of the Pharos (ca. 864), therefore implying a preference for the standing figure of Christ to be selected for the earlier Ignatian seal. When citing these images, Zacos referred to earlier scholarship that interpreted the Byzantine sources as indicating the Christ *Chalkites* was a standing figure, whereas most recently B. Pentcheva, *The Sensual Icon: Space, Ritual, and the Senses in Byzantium* (University Park, PA, 2010), 88–96, has demonstrated that the Christ *Chalkites* icon was that of a relief bust image of the Lord, thereby weakening Zacos' argument for an earlier Ignatian seal with the standing figure of Christ. Oikonomides, *Byzantine Lead Seals*, nos. 51 and 52 and *DOSeals* 6, no. 112.1, refrains from

attempting to assign the different types of seals to one or the other of Ignatios' patriarchates.

13. Whittemore, "An Unpublished Seal," 262.

14. Zacos, *Byzantine Lead Seals*, vol. 2, no. 553.

15. Whittemore, "An Unpublished Seal," 262, where he cites one example of ἡγοῦμαι appearing on a seal.

16. *Thesaurus Linguae Graecae*, http://stephanus.tlg.uci.edu/inst/ browser, accessed April 15, 2011.

17. For a recent discussion of Methodios and his lead seals, see J. Cotsonis, "The Imagery of Patriarch Methodios I's Lead Seals and the New World Order of Ninth-Century Byzantium," *Legacy of Achievement: Metropolitan Methodios of Boston Festal Volume on the 25th Anniversary of His Consecration to the Episcopate 1982–2007*, ed. G. Dragas (Boston, 2008), 366–387.

18. Zacos, *Byzantine Lead Seals*, vol. 2, no. 1. This specimen had been previously published by Laurent, *Corpus*, 5:1, no. 1, who suggested that the image could possibly be either that of John Chrysostom or Christ. Because the portrait type is rather generic and there is no accompanying identifying inscription, the identity of the figure is uncertain. Zacos also notes that another specimen bearing an image of John Chrysostom, previously described by Laurent, *Corpus*, 5:1, no. 2, is actually an eleemosynary ticket, or charitable token, and should be assigned rather to the late seventh or early eighth century. A similar token is also listed by Zacos and Veglery, *Byzantine Lead Seals*, 1:2, no. 1247, pl. 99. For a discussion of Byzantine charitable tokens, see Nesbitt's article cited in note 5 above. For the sequence of known Constantinopolitan patriarchal seals, from the pre-Iconoclastic period to the end of the empire, see Laurent, *Corpus*, 5:1, nos. 1–48, pls. 1–7; Zacos, *Byzantine Lead Seals*, vol. 2, nos. 1–54, pls. 1–11; and *DOSeals* 6, nos. 110.1–130.1.

19. Zacos, *Byzantine Lead Seals*, vol. 2, nos. 2, 3 and 4, respectively; Oikonomides, *Dated Byzantine Lead Seals*, nos. 43, 45, and 49; and *DOSeals* 6, nos. 110.1 and 111.1. The specimens belonging to Theodotos and Anthony were previously published by Laurent, *Corpus*, 5:1, nos. 3 and 4, respectively, who erroneously read the cruciform invocative monograms as Θεοτόκε Βοήθει ("Theotokos, help").

20. For reference to the patriarchal seals of the Byzantine period, see note 18 above. For examples of post-Byzantine Constantinopolitan patriarchal seals with images of the Virgin, see K. Regling, "Byzantinische Bleisiegel III," *Byzantinische Zeitschrift* 24 (1923/24): 106–107; F. Dölger, *Aus den Schatzkammern des Heiligen Berges: 115 Urkunden und 50 Urkundensiegel aus 10 Jahrhunderten* (Munich, 1948), 122; and *Treasures of Mount Athos*, ed. A. Karakatsanis (Thessaloniki, 1997), nos. 13.40, 13.51, 13.56, and 13.60. For a discussion of the chronologi-

cal variance of the Marian iconography found on patriarchal seals as a reflection of the diachronic changes of the apse mosaic decoration in Hagia Sophia in Constantinople, see G. Galavaris, "The Representation of the Virgin and Child on a 'Thokos' on Seals of the Constantinopolitan Patriarchs," Δελτίον τῆς Χριστιανικῆς Ἀρχαιολογικῆς Ἑταιρείας 4, no. 2 (1962): 154–181; and idem, "Observations on the Date of the Apse Mosaic of the Church of Hagia Sophia in Constantinople," *Actes du XIIe congrès international d'études byzantines, Ochride, 10–16 Septembre, 1961*, vol. 3 (Belgrade, 1964): 107–110. Galavaris' fourteenth-century dating of the apse mosaic in Hagia Sophia is erroneous. For the commonly accepted ninth-century dating of the mosaic, see R. Cormack, "Interpreting the Mosaics of S. Sophia at Istanbul," *Art History* 4 (1981): 135–138 (repr. in his *The Byzantine Eye* [London, 1989]), who also provides the relevant bibliography 147 for the study of the church's mosaics; and idem, "The Mother of God in the Mosaics of Hagia Sophia at Constantinople," *Mother of God: Representations of the Virgin in Byzantine Art*, ed. M. Vassilaki (Athens, 2000), 108–113. For a dating of the apse mosaic of Hagia Sophia to the years of the Iconophile interlude, more specifically between 787–797, also employing the iconography of patriarchal seals, see N. Oikonomides, "Some Remarks on the Apse Mosaic of St. Sophia," *Dumbarton Oaks Papers* 39 (1985): 111–115. For criticism of Oikonomides' dating, see Cormack, "Additional Notes: Study VIII," *The Byzantine Eye*, 14.

21. For the seals of post-Iconoclastic emperors, see Zacos and Veglery, *Byzantine Lead Seals*, 1:1, nos. 56–128bis, pls. 18–31; I. Sokolova, *Byzantine Imperial Seals* (St. Petersburg, 2007), nos. 74–210; and *DOSeals* 6, nos. 49.1–109.1.

22. Zacos and Veglery, *Byzantine Lead Seals*, 1:1, nos. 4–33 and pls. 9–14; Sokolova, *Byzantine Imperial Seals*, nos. 17–61; and *DOSeals* 6, nos. 6.1, 8.1–28.2. Seal no. 4 in the Zacos and Veglery volume, assigned to Justinian I, has been a matter of some dispute. W. Seibt, *Die byzantinischen Bleisiegel in Österreich*, vol. 1 (Vienna, 1978), 59n10; idem, "Review of G. Zacos and A. Veglery, *Byzantine Lead Seals*, 1:1–3," *Byzantinoslavica* 36 (1975): 208–209; idem, "Die Darstellung der Theotokos auf byzantinischen Bleisiegeln, besonders im 11. Jahrhundert," *Studies in Byzantine Sigillography* 1 (1987): 36–37; and J.-C. Cheynet and C. Morrisson, "Texte et image sur les sceaux byzantins: les raisons d'un choix iconographique," *Studies in Byzantine Sigillography* 4 (1995): 10, prefer to assign this seal to Justin II (565–578). Although V. Pentcheva, *Icons and Power: The Mother of God in Byzantium* (University Park, PA, 2006), 19 and fig. 13, assigns the seal to Justin II in her text, in her caption accompanying the photograph of the seal, she acknowledges a possible Justinianic issuance. According to Zacos and Veglery, the

inscription of the emperor's name is incomplete (DNIVSTIN . . .). Due to the arrangement of the letters, however, they conclude that the intended name is Justinian rather than Justin. The same position of letters is found on Justinianic coinage. I wish to thank John Nesbitt for this verification. Seibt based his attribution on the seal's imperial portrait, which he claims has a light beard. He also rules out the possibility of the letter "A" preceding the "N" in the inscription. Upon examination of the specimen, however, no trace of a beard can be detected, and the letter "D" preceding the "N," for *Dominus Noster*, read by Zacos and Veglery, is correct. More recently, in *DOSeals* 6, no. 6.1, the editors have assigned the seal to Justinian I.

23. Examples can be found in Zacos and Veglery, *Byzantine Lead Seals*, 1:1, nos. 1–3 and 5, pl. 9. See also Stepanova, "Victoria-Nike," 15–24.

24. Zacos and Veglery, *Byzantine Lead Seals*, 1:1, nos. 34bis–39 and nos. 49–54, pls. 15–17; Sokolova, *Byzantine Imperial Seals*, nos. 64–66 and no. 71; and *DOSeals* 6, nos. 31.1–34.1, 42.1–42.8, and 44.1–47.2. The Trinitarian phrase is written with Latin characters but phonetically transcribes the Greek phrase Ἐν ὀνόματι τοῦ Πατρὸς καὶ τοῦ Υἱοῦ καὶ τοῦ Ἁγίου Πνεύματος ("In the name of the Father and of the Son and of the Holy Spirit").

25. Zacos and Veglery, *Byzantine Lead Seals*, 1:1, nos. 43, 46, and 48, and pl. 16; Sokolova, *Byzantine Imperial Seals*, no. 70; and *DOSeals* 6, nos. 38.1 and 40.1 It is interesting to observe here that the two ruling empresses who ended the two phases of Iconoclasm (Irene in 787 and Theodora in 843) did not place holy figures on their seals. For Irene's and Theodora's seals, see Zacos and Veglery, *Byzantine Lead Seals*, 1:1, nos. 40, 41, 54, and 55, and pls. 15–18; Sokolova, *Byzantine Imperial Seals*, nos. 68, 69, and 73; and *DOSeals* 6, nos. 36.1–36.5 and 47.1–48.3.

26. P. Grierson, *Catalogue of the Byzantine Coins in the Dumbarton Oaks Collection and in the Whittemore Collection*, 3:1 (Washington, DC, 1973), 454, 463–464, pl. 28. See also L. Brubaker, *Vision and Meaning in Ninth-Century Byzantium: Image as Exegesis in the Homilies of Gregory of Nazianzus* (Cambridge, 1999), 148. For a discussion comparing imperial seals and coins, see C. Morrisson and G. Zacos, "L' image de l'empereur byzantin sur les sceaux et les monnaies," *La monnaie miroir des rois*, ed. Y. Goldenberg (Paris, 1978), 57–72, and see the contemporaneous imperial seals and coins published together throughout *DOSeals* 6.

27. J. Breckenridge, *The Numismatic Iconography of Justinian II (685–695, 705–711 A.D.)* (New York, 1959), passim; and P. Grierson, *Catalogue of the Byzantine Coins in the Dumbarton Oaks Collection and*

in the Whittemore Collection, 2:2 (Washington, DC, 1968), 568–570, 578–580, 581–582, 644–646, and 648–649, pls. 37–38.

28. Breckenridge, *The Numismatic Iconography of Justinian II*, 86, concludes that Justinian's first coin type with the "Pantokrator" form of Christ is contemporary with or reflecting the same thought-world, but not necessarily the direct result of canon 82 of the Quinisext Council of 691/692 that preferred representations of Christ in His human nature over that of symbols. Grierson, *Catalogue of the Byzantine Coins*, 2:2, 570, accepts Breckenridge's view, as does J. Haldon, *Byzantium in the Seventh Century: The Transformation of a Culture* (Cambridge, 1990), 370–371, where he also sees the rejection of the use of the image of Christ on the coins of Justinian's immediate successors as a sign of returning to a previous imperial policy in which the emperor legitimizes his own authority; and idem, "Constantine or Justinian? Crisis and Identity in Imperial Propaganda in the Seventh Century," *New Constantines: The Rhythm of Imperial Renewals in Byzantium, 4th–13th Centuries*, ed. P. Magdalino (Aldershot, 1994), 106n32, where he suggests that the new coin type likely precedes the council. In addition, P. Yannopoulos, "Le changement de l'iconographie monétaire sous le premier règne de Justinien II (685–695)," *Actes du XIe congrès international de Numismatique organisé à l'occasion du 150e anniversaire de la Société Royale de Numismatique de Belgique, Bruxelles, 8–13 septembre 1991*, vol. 3, ed. T. Hackens and G. Moucharte (Louvain-la-Neuve, 1993), 35–40, concluded that Justinian II's coin with the image of Christ had no connections with canon 82, but rather the numismatic innovation was a response to the Arabo-Byzantine coinage issued by Abd al-Malik whose reverse bore the inscription, "In the name of Allah." For coins issued by Abd al-Malik, see C. Foss, *Arab-Byzantine Coins, An Introduction with a Catalogue of the Dumbarton Oaks Collection* (Washington, DC, 2008), 58–83. Breckenridge, *The Numismatic Iconography of Justinian II*, raises the problem of the coinage of Abd al-Malik as one possibility for understanding the new coin type of Justinian II but then rejects this hypothesis and concludes that the sequence of events was reversed. Grierson, *Catalogue of the Byzantine Coins*, 2:2, 570, accepts Breckenridge's order of the coinage.

29. See Brubaker, *Vision and Meaning*, 147–152.

30. For a detailed explanation of these trends, see Cotsonis, "The Imagery of Patriarch Methodios I's Lead Seals," 366–387.

31. For significant literature devoted to this much-studied topic, see A. Cameron, "The Theotokos in Sixth-Century Constantinople: A City Finds its Symbol," *Journal of Theological Studies* n.s. 29 (1978): 79–108 (repr. in her *Continuity and Change in Sixth-Century Byzantium* [London, 1981]); V. Limberis, *Divine Heiress: The Virgin Mary and the Creation*

of Christian Constantinople (New York, 1994); C. Angelidi, *Pulcheria: La castità al potere (c. 399–c. 455)* (Milan, 1998), 120–139; K. Cooper, "Contesting the Nativity: Wives, Virgins, and Pulcheria's *imitatio Mariae*," *Scottish Journal of Religious Studies* 19 (1998): 31–43; A. Weyl Carr, "Threads of Authority: The Virgin Mary's Veil in the Middle Ages," *Robes and Honor: The Medieval World of Investiture*, ed. S. Gordon (New York, 2001), 59–94; A. Cameron, "The Cult of the Virgin in Late Antiquity: Religious Development and Myth-Making," *The Church and Mary* (Woodbridge, 2004), 1–21; K. Cooper, "Empress and Theotokos: Gender and Patronage in the Christological Controversy," *The Church and Mary*, 39–51; C. Mango, "Constantinople as Theotokoupolis," *Mother of God*, 17–25; Pentcheva, *Icons and Power*, 11–108, passim; L. James, "The Empress and the Virgin in Early Byzantium," *Images of the Mother of God*, ed. M. Vassilaki (Aldershot, 2005), 145–152; N. Koutrakou, "Use and Abuse of the 'Image' of the Theotokos in the Political Life of Byzantium (with Special Reference to the Iconoclastic Period)," *Images of the Mother of God*, 77–89; L. Brubaker and M. Cunningham, "Byzantine Veneration of the Theotokos: Icons, Relics, and Eighth-Century Homilies," *From Rome to Constantinople: Studies in Honour of Averil Cameron*, ed. H. Amirav and B. ter Haar Romeny (Leuven, 2007), 235–250; L. M. Peltomaa, "Romanos the Melodist and the Intercessory Role of Mary," *Byzantina Mediterranea: Festschrift für Johannes Koder zum 65. Geburtstag*, ed. K. Belke, E. Kislinger, A. Külzer, and M. Stassinopoulou (Vienna, 2007), 495–502; and M. Rubin, *Mother of God: A History of the Virgin Mary* (New Haven, 2009), 63–82. For a criticism of an earlier version of Pentcheva's work, "The Supernatural Protector of Constantinople: The Virgin and Her Icons in the Tradition of the Avar Siege," *Byzantine and Modern Greek Studies* 26 (2002): 2–41—in which she argued that prior to Iconoclasm the cultic processions dedicated to the Virgin did not include her images and that her images had no significance in the protection of the capital city, but rather these were later tenth-century projections back onto earlier sources—see P. Speck, "The Virgin's Help for Constantinople," *Byzantine and Modern Greek Studies* 27 (2003): 266–271. In her *Icons and Power*, 47–49, Pentcheva maintains her earlier position in response to Speck's criticism. See also C. Angelidi and T. Papamastorakis, "Picturing the Spiritual Protector: From Blachernitissa to Hodegetria," *Images of the Mother of God*, 209–223.

32. The complex parsing of the Iconoclast and Iconophile texts concerning the Theotokos, her images, and her intercessory powers can be found in S. Gero, *Byzantine Iconoclasm During the Reign of Constantine V: With Particular Attention to the Oriental Sources* (Louvain, 1977), 143–151; A. Giakalis, *Images of the Divine: The Theology of Icons at the Seventh Ecumenical Council* (Leiden, 1994), 10, 22, 28, and 101; K.

Parry, *Depicting the Word: Byzantine Iconophile Thought of the Eighth and Ninth Centuries* (Leiden, 1996), 191–201; N. Tsironis, "The Mother of God in the Iconoclastic Controversy," *Mother of God*, 27–39; and Koutrakou, "Use and Abuse of the 'Image' of the Theotokos," 77–89. See also L. Brubaker and J. Haldon, *Byzantium in the Iconoclast Era, c. 680–850: A History* (Cambridge, 2011), 192.

33. *Oxford Dictionary of Byzantium*, vol. 2, 846. See also Tsironis, "The Mother of God in the Iconoclastic Controversy," 36.

34. For discussion of the Synod and the Iconophile writers, with reference to their Marian defenses, see Parry, *Depicting the Word*, 7–80, 125–132, and 191–201; Tsironis, "The Mother of God in the Iconoclastic Controversy"; C. Barber, *Figure and Likeness: On the Limits of Representation in Byzantine Iconoclasm* (Princeton, 2002), 68–70, much of which is repeated in his "Theotokos and Logos: The Interpretation and Reinterpretation of the Sanctuary Programme of the Koimesis Church, Nicaea," *Images of the Mother of God*, 51–59; and Koutrakou, "Use and Abuse of the 'Image' of the Theotokos," 81–89. See also N. Tsironis, "From Poetry to Liturgy: The Cult of the Virgin in the Middle Byzantine Era," *Images of the Mother of God*, 92–95.

35. Zacos and Veglery, *Byzantine Lead Seals*, 1:2, nos. 1325–1349A, pls. 103–104, and 1:3, nos. 2979–2985, pls. 202–203.

36. See also J. Cotsonis, "The Contribution of Byzantine Lead Seals to the Study of the Cult of the Saints (Sixth–Twelfth Century)," *Byzantion* 75 (2005): 404. The sphragistic evidence supports similar views articulated by R. Cormack, *Painting the Soul: Icons, Death Masks and Shrouds* (London, 1997), 89–92, and A. Weyl Carr, "Thoughts on the Economy of the Image of Mary," *Theology Today* 56, no. 3 (1999): 359–378.

37. "Τὴν βασίλειον στολὴν ἐκ σοῦ, Παρθένε, Θεός φορέσας, ὤφθη τοῖς βροτοῖς ἀνθρωπόμορφος, διπλοῦ κατ' οὐσίαν· οὗ τὸ εἶδος τῆς μορφῆς ἐν προσκυνήσει ἔχομεν" (PG 99:1769); "ὡς αὐτὸν κυήσασα τὸν Πλάστην σου, διὸ τὴν ἁγίαν μορφήν σου, Θεογεννῆτορ, ἐν προσκυνήσει ἔχομεν" (ibid., 1772); and "Ἡ πάντων βοήθεια, καὶ σκέπη καὶ ἀντίληψις, δεῖξον, ὅτι δύνασαι πρεσβεύειν ὑπὲρ πάντων" (ibid., 1780). See also Koutrakou, "Use and Abuse of the 'Image' of the Theotokos," 81. For attributing the canon to Methodios, see J. Gouillard, "Deux figures mal connues du second Iconoclasme," *Byzantion* 31 (1961), 380–387, and idem, "Le synodikon de l'Orthodoxie. Édition et commentaire," *Travaux et mémoires* 2 (1967): 134–136.

38. Limberis, *Divine Heiress*, 62–97; Angelidi, *Pulcheria*, 120–139; Mango, "Constantinople as Theotokoupolis," 17–25; James, "The Empress and the Virgin in Early Byzantium," 145–152; and Pentcheva, *Icons and Power*, 11–36.

39. Cooper, "Contesting the Nativity," 42.

40. James, "The Empress and the Virgin in Early Byzantium," 150–152.

41. Koutrakou, "Use and Abuse of the 'Image' of the Theotokos," 88.

42. The phrase appears in the second letter of Pope Gregory II to Leo III, in which the pontiff repeats the emperor's claim only to refute it. See J. Gouillard, "Aux origines de l'iconoclasme. Le témoignage de Grégoire II?," *Travaux et mémoires* 3 (1968): 299. Gouillard, 275–277, demonstrates that although the two letters supposedly of Pope Gregory are forgeries, they were written by a Byzantine Iconophile, possibly a monastic, of the late eighth or first half of the ninth century. See also the discussion of these letters and their historical setting by G. Dagron, *Emperor and Priest: The Imperial Office in Byzantium* (Cambridge, 2003), 158–191, passim, and Koutrakou, "Use and Abuse of the 'Image' of the Theotokos," 88.

43. *Jus graecoromanum*, ed. I. Zepos and P. Zepos, vol. 2 (Athens, 1931; repr., Aalen, 1962), 12, and Koutrakou, "Use and Abuse of the 'Image' of the Theotokos," 88. See also D. Simon, "Legislation as Both a World Order and a Legal Order," *Law and Society in Byzantium: Ninth–Twelfth Centuries*, ed. A. Laiou and D. Simon (Washington, DC, 1994), 12–16.

44. Βίος Νικήτα Μηδικίου, *Acta Sanctorum*, Aprilis I, XXIXE (at end of volume), and Koutrakou, "Use and Abuse of the 'Image' of the Theotokos," 88. See also D. Afinogenov, "Κωνσταντινούπολις ἐπίσκοπον ἔχει, II," *Erytheia* 17 (1996): 47 and 51–52, and M. Kaplan, "Le saint, l'évêque et l'empereur: l'image et le pouvoir à l'epoque du second iconoclasme d'après les sources hagiographiques," *Les images dans les sociétés médiévales: Pour une histoire comparée: Actes du colloque international organisé par l'Institut Historique Belge de Rome en collaboation avec l'École Française de Rome et l'Université Libre de Bruxelles (Rome, Academia Belgica, 19–20 juin 1998)*, ed. J.-M. Sansterre and J.-C. Schmitt (Brussels/Rome, 1999), 187–188.

45. See J. Haldon, "Ideology and Social Change in the Seventh Century: Military Discontent as a Barometer," *Klio* 68 (1986): 145 and156–157, 188, and 190; idem, *Byzantium in the Seventh Century: The Transformation of a Culture*, 19, 26, 283, and 441; M.-F. Auzépy, "Le Christ, l'empereur et l'image (VIIe–IXe siècle)," *ΕΥΨΥΧΙΑ: Mélanges offerts à Hélène Ahrweiler*, ed. M. Balard (Paris, 1998), 1:35–38 (repr. in her *L'histoire des iconoclastes* [Paris, 2007], 77–80); K. Pitsakis, "Sainteté et empire: A propos de la sainteté impériale: formes de sainteté 'd'office' et de sainteté collective dans l'Empire d'Orient?" *Bizantinistica: rivista di studi bizantini e slavi* 3 (2001): 155–161; Dagron, *Emperor and Priest*, 82 and 127–157, passim; and M.-H. Congourdeau, "L'empereur et le patriarche dans l'empire byzantin," *Istina* 40, no. 1 (2005): 9–10.

46. See also Haldon, "Ideology and Social Change in the Seventh Century," 170 and 188; idem, *Byzantium in the Seventh Century*, 14, 365–366, and 370–371; and Congourdeau, "L'empereur et le patriarche dans l'empire byzantin," 10. For a criticism of Haldon's emphasis on the potency of the religious symbol over that of the imperial (here, that of Constantine the Great) in the seventh century, see M. Whitby, "Images for Emperors in Late Antiquity: A Search for New Constantines," *New Constantines*, 93.

47. J. Haldon, "Ideology and the Byzantine State in the Seventh Century: The 'Trial' of Maximus Confessor," *From Late Antiquity to Early Byzantium*, ed. V. Vavřínek (Prague, 1985), 87–91; idem, "Ideology and Social Change in the Seventh Century," 170 and 173–174; and idem, *Byzantium in the Seventh Century*, 56–59, 285–286, and 364–366. For the relevant charges against Maximos, see PG 90:109–112 and 168–169. A more recent edition of the Greek text and English translation of these charges against Maximos are provided by *Maximus the Confessor and His Companions: Documents from Exile*, ed. P. Allen and B. Neil (Oxford, 2002), 48–51 and 114–117. For those brought against Pope Martin, see Mansi, 10:849–850. For an English translation of a portion of the trial against Maximos as it relates to a discussion of Leo III's policies, see Dagron, *Emperor and Priest*, 166–173, and *Maximus the Confessor and His Companions*, 54–59.

48. See note 19 above.

49. For a critical edition of the preamble of the *Eisagoge*, see A. Schminck, *Studien zu mittelbyzantinischen Rechtsbüchern* (Frankfurt am Main, 1986), 1–15, who assigns the text to the years 885–886. T. van Bochove, *To Date and Not to Date: On the Origin and Status of Byzantine Law Books* (Groningen, 1996), 7–27, concludes that the text belongs to the years 880–883. For the complete text of the *Eisagoge*, see *Jus graecoromanum*, 2:229–368. For introductory remarks on the *Eisagoge*, see the *Oxford Dictionary of Byzantium*, 1:703–704. For some discussion of the *Eisagoge* as regards its major conceptual developments over the earlier legislation of Justinian I and the *Ecloga* of the Isaurians, especially regarding the concept of the separate powers of authority (of the law, the emperor, and the patriarch), see Simon, "Legislation," 16–18; J. Lokin, "The Significance of Law and Legislation in the Law Books of the Ninth to Eleventh Centuries," *Law and Society in Byzantium*, 76–80; G. Dagron, "Lawful Society and Legitimate Power: Ἔννομος Πολιτεία, Ἔννομος Ἀρχή," ibid., 30; M.-T. Fögen, "Reanimation of Roman Law in the Ninth Century: Remarks on Reasons and Results," *Byzantium in the Ninth Century: Dead or Alive?*, ed. L. Brubaker (Aldershot, 1998), 19, where she suggests that the concept of the two distinct powers between emperor and patriarch became known in Byzantium through the letter

of Pope Nicholas I to the emperor Michael III; van Bochove, *To Date and Not to Date*, 57–81; and Dagron, *Emperor and Priest*, 223–235, who also assigns the *Eisagoge* to the years 879–886, but like Fögen sees the ideology of the two separate powers of emperor and patriarch as stemming from the Roman pontifical model. According to Dagron, the concept of the dual spheres of power already begins to appear by 806, in Letter 16 of Theodore Stoudites addressed to Emperor Nikephoros I. For the text of this letter, see *Theodori Studitae epistulae*, vol. 1, ed. G. Fatouros (Berlin, 1991), no. 16, 46–48. On the other hand, C. Pitsakis, "La 'ΣΥΝΑΛΛΗΛΙΑ', principe fondamental des rapports entre l'Église et l'État (Idéologie et pratique Byzantines et transformations contemporaines)," *Kanon* 10 (1991): 20–21, and idem, "Empire et Église (le modèle de la Nouvelle Rome): La question des ordres juridiques," *Diritto e religione da Roma a Costantinopoli a Mosca. Da Roma alla Terza Roma. Documenti e Studi. Rendiconti dell'XI Seminario, Campidoglio 21 Aprile 1991*, ed. M. Baccari (Rome, 1994), 107–109, argues that even in the *Eisagoge*, the Byzantine understanding of governance is not that of two separate powers of Church and State, but rather one entity with two aspects that relate through συναλληλία, or "consonance." S. Troianos, "Ό Μέγας Φώτιος καὶ οἱ Διατάξεις τῆς Εἰσαγωῆς. Μερικὲς Παρατηρήσεις ὡς πρὸς τὶς Σχέσεις Ἐκκλησίας καὶ Πολιτείας," *Ἐκκλησία καὶ Θεολογία* 10 (1989–1991): 498, had already employed the word συναλληλία once in his earlier discussion of the *Eisagoge* when concluding that the text was attempting to restore an earlier pre-Iconoclastic balance to the spheres of action that operate as an inseparable union, not two separate powers.

50. *Jus graecoromanum*, 2:240.

51. Ibid., 241, and Schminck, *Studien*, 6.

52. Simon, "Legislation," 16–18; Dagron, "Lawful Society," 30; Lokin, "The Significance of Law and Legislation," 78–80; Auzépy, "Le Christ, l'empereur et l'image," 45–47; Brubaker, *Vision and Meaning*, 158–159; Dagron, *Emperor and Priest*, 230–231; and Congourdeau, "L'empereur et le patriarche dans l'empire byzantin," 12.

53. See Brubaker, *Vision and Meaning*, 147–159. I. Kalavrezou, "Images of the Mother: When the Virgin Mary Became *Meter Theou*," *Dumbarton Oaks Papers* 44 (1990): 171, noted the new, post-Iconoclast pattern of imperial sphragistic imagery and suggested that the image of Christ was appropriate for the emperor because the latter was invested with power by Christ. She does not, however, offer any further discussion on this relation, nor does she discuss the relative positions of the images of Christ and the emperor on the coins and seals.

54. *Jus graecoromanum*, 2:242.

55. Ibid.

56. Ibid.

57. Ibid., 243.

58. Ibid.

59. Auzépy, "Le Christ, l'empereur et l'image," 46.

60. Dagron, *Emperor and Priest*, 23.

61. See also D. Afinogenov, "Κωνσταντινούπολις ἐπίσκοπον ἔχει: The Rise of the Patriarchal Power in Byzantium from Nicaenum II to Epanagoga, I," *Erytheia* 15 (1994), 45–65 and idem, "Κωνσταντινούπολις ἐπίσκοπον ἔχει, II," 43–71.

62. Kalavrezou, "Images of the Mother," 171, suggested that the image of the Virgin was adopted by the patriarchs since that of Christ was taken up by the emperors and that the Virgin's image was more appropriate for the patriarch who stood as the mediator between God and His people. She, however, provided no further discussion for this suggestion.

63. Fögen, "Reanimation of Roman Law in the Ninth Century," 19; Dagron, *Emperor and Priest*, 223–235. See note 54, *supra*.

64. Afinogenov, "Κωνσταντινούπολις ἐπίσκοπον ἔχει, II," 65–66, who provides the translation of the pertinent text. The Greek text is edited by J. Darrouzès, "Le Patriarche Méthode contre les Iconoclastes et les Stoudites," *Revue des études byzantines* 45 (1987): "οἱ ἀπόστολοι καὶ οἱ τῶν ἀποστόλων διάδοχοι, ἤγουν οἱ πατριάρχαι" (45), and "Καὶ μὴν ἐπίσκοπος πολλοστὸν καὶ πρᾶγμα καὶ ὄνομα, ὀλιγοστὸν δὲ καὶ λίαν βραχύτατον τὸ τῶν ἀποστόλων καὶ τὸ τῶν διαδόχων αὐτῶν ἀρχικόν τε καὶ αὐτεξούσιον" (49). As Afinogenov observes (66n108), this Methodian reference as the earliest Constantinopolitan patriarchal claim to apostolic succession does not appear in the classic study of F. Dvornik, *The Idea of Apostolicity in Byzantium and the Legend of the Apostle Andrew* (Cambridge, MA, 1958), but it does reinforce Dvornik's overall thesis that the ninth century witnessed the eastern Church's growing concern for apostolicity, in response to and long after similar claims by the See of Rome.

65. *Oxford Dictionary of the Christian Church*, 3rd rev. ed., 710.

66. For the more recent literature, see H. Belting, *Likeness and Presence: A History of the Image Before the Era of Art* (Chicago, 1994), 126–129; M. Stroll, "Maria *Regina*: Papal Symbol," *Queens and Queenship in Medieval Europe: Proceedings of a Conference Held at King's College London, April 1995*, ed. A. Duggan (Woodbridge, 1997), 173–177; J. Osborne, "Images of the Mother of God in Early Medieval Rome," *Icon and Word: The Power of Images in Byzantium*, ed. A. Eastmond and L. James (Aldershot, 2003), 136–140; G. Wolf, "Icons and Sites: Cult Images of the Virgin in Medieval Rome," *Images of the Mother of God*, 37–39; and Pentcheva, *Icons and Power*, 21–26, who elaborates on the significance of either the presence or absence of the Byzantine imperial *loros* in the various depictions of the Roman examples of the *Maria Regina*.

67. The likelihood that Methodios would appropriate the use of religious imagery as employed in Rome is further strengthened by the studies of K. Corrigan, *Visual Polemics in the Ninth-Century Byzantine Psalters* (Cambridge, 1992), 131–134, and J. Anderson, "The Creation of the Marginal Psalter," *Ritual and Art: Byzantine Essays for Christopher Walter*, ed. P. Armstrong (London, 2006), 44–65, who credit Methodios with the invention of the Byzantine marginal psalter, a manuscript tradition imported from the West.

68. R. Cormack, *Writing in Gold: Byzantine Society and Its Icons* (London, 1985), 159–165, where he mistakenly claims that the emperor Michael III also put the image of the Virgin on his seals, and idem, "The Mother of God in the Mosaics of Hagia Sophia," 107–123.

69. See note 20 above for the references to the articles by Galavaris, Oikonomides, and Cormack, and the problems concerning their dating of the apse mosaic.

70. N. Oikonomides, "Leo VI and the Narthex Mosaic of Saint Sophia," *Dumbarton Oaks Papers* 30 (1976): 151–172, and idem, "The Mosaic Panel of Constantine IX and Zoe in Saint Sophia," *Revue des études byzantines* 36 (1978): 219–232.

71. Dagron, *Emperor and Priest*, 95–124.

72. Cormack, "Interpreting the Mosaics of St. Sophia at Istanbul," and idem, "The Mother of God in the Mosaics of Hagia Sophia," 107–123, and especially 116–117, where he elaborates that though the images may be due to initial imperial sponsorship, they reflect a broader public symbolic character as to the ways that the community at large would view the Virgin, representing embedded social attitudes.

73. A. Schminck, " 'Rota tu volubilis': Kaisermacht und Patriarchenmacht in Mosaiken," *Cupido Legum*, ed. L. Burgmann, M.-T. Fögen, and A. Schminck (Frankfurt am Main, 1985), 211–234.

74. A. Lidov, "Leo the Wise and the Miraculous Icons in Hagia Sophia," *The Heroes of the Orthodox Church: The New Saints, 8th–16th c.*, ed. E. Kountoura-Galake (Athens, 2004), 393–432, where the author stresses the emperor's desire to create a miraculous framework for the Great Church.

75. Dagron, *Emperor and Priest*, 99. For a general discussion of this mosaic, see Cormack, "The Mother of God in the Mosaics of Hagia Sophia," 107 and 113–114.

76. For the dedication of the cathedral, see G. Downey, "The Name of the Church of St. Sophia of Constantinople," *Harvard Theological Review* 52 (1959), 37–41.

77. An early association between the Theotokos and the text of Proverbs 9:1 is provided by Chrysostom, PG 64:680. For literature dealing with Wisdom, its personification, and the Virgin, see L. Bouyer, *Le trône*

de la sagesse: essai sur la signification du culte marial (Paris, 1957; repr., Paris, 1987), 39–50 and 74–78; F. von Lilienfeld, " 'Frau Weisheit' in byzantinischen und karolingischen Quellen des 9. Jahrhunderts: allegorische Personifikation, Hypostase oder Typos?" *Typus, Symbol, Allegorie: bei den östlichen Vätern und ihren Parallellen im Mittelalter,* ed. M. Schmidt and C. Geyer (Regensburg, 1982), 146–186; S. Bulgakov, *Sophia: The Wisdom of God* (Hudson, NY, 1993 [rev. ed. of his *The Wisdom of God: A Brief Summary of Sophiology* (London, 1937)]), 114–132; J. Meyendorff, "L'iconographie de la sagesse divine dans la tradition byzantine," *Cahiers archéologiques* 10 (1959): 259–277; idem, "Wisdom-Sophia: Contrasting Approaches to a Complex Theme," *Dumbarton Oaks Papers* 41 (1987): 391–401; D. Pallis, "Ὁ Χριστὸς ὡς ἡ Θεία Σοφία: Ἡ Εἰκονογραφικὴ Περιπέτεια μίας Θεολογικῆς Ἐννοίας," *Δελτίον τῆς Χριστιανικῆς Ἀρχαιολογικῆς Ἑταιρείας* 15 (1989–1990): 119–144; and *"Die Weisheit baute ihr Haus": Untersuchungen zu hymnischen und didaktischen Ikonen,* ed. K. Felmy and E. Haustein-Bartsch (Munich, 1999).

78. A. Kniazeff, "Mariologie biblique et liturgie Byzantine," *Irénikon* 28 (1955): 277–278.

79. Cormack, *Writing in Gold,* 160, in his caption for fig. 56, also suggests that in the mosaic of the southwest vestibule the Virgin receives the offering of Justinian's church because she is the female personification of the Wisdom of God.

80. For the *ekklesiekdikoi,* see J. Cotsonis, "The Virgin and Justinian on Seals of the *Ekklesiekdikoi* of Hagia Sophia," *Dumbarton Oaks Papers* 56 (2002): 41–55.

81. For examples of seals belonging to officials linked to Hagia Sophia, see E. McGeer, J. Nesbitt, and N. Oikonomides, *Catalogue of Byzantine Lead Seals at Dumbarton Oaks and in the Fogg Museum of Art,* vol. 5 (Washington, DC, 2005), nos. 42.1–42.45.

82. *The Synodicon Vetus,* ed. J. Duffy and J. Parker (Washington, DC, 1979), no. 156. For a discussion of the events concerning 843 and the appointment of Methodios and of the various primary sources from which they are drawn, see Gouillard, "Le synodikon de l'Orthodoxie," 119–129; B. Zielke, "Methodios I.," *Die Patriarchen der ikonoklastischen Zeit: Germanos I.–Methodios I. (715–847),* ed. R.-J. Lilie (Frankfurt am Main, 1999), 216–230; and P. Karlin-Hayter, "Icon Veneration: Significance of the Restoration of Orthodoxy?" *Novum Millennium: Studies on Byzantine History and Culture Dedicated to Paul Speck,* ed. C. Sode and S. Takács (Aldershot, 2001), 171–183. See also C. Mango, "The Liquidation of Iconoclasm and the Patriarch Photios," *Iconoclasm: Papers Given at the Ninth Spring Symposium of Byzantine Studies, University of Birmingham, March 1975,* ed. A. Bryer and J. Herrin (Birmingham, 1977), 133–135; P. Karlin-Hayter, "Gregory of Syracuse, Ignatios and Photios,"

ibid., 141; eadem, "Methodios and His Synod," *Byzantine Orthodoxies: Papers from the Thirty-Sixth Spring Symposium of Byzantine Studies, University of Durham, 23–25 March 2002*, ed. A. Louth and A. Casiday (Aldershot, 2006), 55–74; eadem, "Restoration of Orthodoxy, the Pardon of Theophilos and the *Acta Davidis, Symeonis et Georgii*," *Byzantine Style, Religion and Civilization: In Honour of Sir Steven Runciman*, ed. E. Jeffreys (Cambridge, 2006), 361–373; and Brubaker and Haldon, *Byzantium in the Iconoclast Era, c. 680–850: A History*, 449.

83. *Vita Methodii*, PG 100:1252C; *Iosephi Genesii Regum Libri Quattuor*, ed. A. Lesmueller-Werner and I. Thurn (Berlin, 1978), 53 (for an English translation, see *Genesios: On the Reigns of the Emperors*, trans. and ed. A. Kaldellis [Canberra, 1998], 3.21); *Theophanes Continuatus*, ed. I. Bekker (Bonn, 1838), 116; Pseudo-Symeon, in *Theophanes Continuatus*, 644–645; and George the Monk, in *Theophanes Continuatus*, 811. See also F. Dvornik, *The Photian Schism: History and Legend* (Cambridge, 1948; repr., Cambridge, 1979]), 13; Gouillard, "Le synodikon de l'Orthodoxie," 123; Mango, "The Liquidation of Iconoclasm," 134; Afinogenov, "Κωνσταντινούπολις ἐπίσκοπον ἔχει, II," 59, who contends that Methodios was not actually part of the inner imperial circle and that he had been brought to the palace so that greater control could be exercised over him, because he was the most distinguished and influential leader of the Iconophiles and simultaneously a symbol of continuity with the patriarch Nikephoros; Zielke, "Methodios I.," 214–215, where she rejects the primary sources' claim that Methodios was brought to the palace to make use of his knowledge for the emperor and instead suggests that the emperor instead wanted Methodios' advice while keeping a more secure watch over him; Karlin-Hayter, "Icon Veneration," 178, who states that Methodios' later zeal as patriarch in expelling the Iconoclastic clergy was an attempt to compensate for having lived in the palace under the Iconoclast emperor Theophilos; W. Treadgold, "The Prophecies of the Patriarch Methodius," *Revue des études byzantines* 62 (2004): 232, who objects to Zielke's reinterpretation of Theophilos' motives regarding the transfer of Methodios to the palace and states that his suggested motives and those of the primary sources are not incompatible; Karlin-Hayter, "Methodios and His Synod," 55 and 61; and Brubaker and Haldon, *Byzantium in the Iconoclast Era, c. 680–850: A History*, 397–398.

84. Dvornik, *The Photian Schism*, 13–18, 24, and 68. Yet this view has been repeated more recently by Chadwick, *East and West*, 120–121.

85. V. Grumel, "La politique religieuse du patriarche saint Méthode," *Echos d'Orient* 34 (1935): 385–401 (although earlier than Dvornik's classic study, he had already come to the conclusion that Methodios was not a moderate who sought compromises with the former Iconoclasts);

Gouillard, "Synodikon," 127–129; Karlin-Hayter, "Gregory of Syracuse," 141–142; Darrouzès, "Le patriarche Méthode," 15–57; D. Afinogenov, "The Great Purge of 843: A Re-Examination," *ΛΕΙΜΩΝ: Studies Presented to Lennart Rydén on His Sixty-Fifth Birthday*, ed. J. O. Rosenqvist (Uppsala, 1996), 79–91; idem, "Κωνσταντινούπολις ἐπίσκοπον ἔχει, II," 58–71; Zielke, "Methodios I.," 231–244; Karlin-Hayter, "Icon Veneration," 178; and eadem, "Methodios and His Synod," 55–74.

86. *Vita Ioannikii a Petro, AASS* Nov 2:1, 69, 431A. See also Grumel, "La politique religieuse," 385, and Karlin-Hayter, "Methodios and His Synod," 66.

87. *Theophanis Chronographia*, ed. C. de Boor (Leipzig, 1883), 481.22, and *The Chronicle of Theophanes Confessor*, trans. and ed. C. Mango and R. Scott (Oxford, 1997), 661. See also Karlin-Hayter, "Methodios and His Synod," 66; P. Hatlie, *The Monks and Monasteries of Constantinople, ca. 350–850* (Cambridge, 2007), 369–370; and Brubaker and Haldon, *Byzantium in the Iconoclast Era, c. 680–850: A History*, 360.

88. Grumel, "La politique religieuse," 386 and 399; P. Karlin-Hayter, "A Byzantine Politician Monk: Saint Theodore Studite," *Jahrbuch der österreichischen Byzantinistik* 44 (1994): 217–232; Afinogenov, "Κωνσταντινούπολις ἐπίσκοπον ἔχει, I," 51–52 and 55; T. Pratsch, *Theodoros Studites (759–826): zwischen Dogma und Pragma* (Frankfurt am Main, 1998), 76–81 and 135–146; R. Cholij, *Theodore the Stoudite: The Ordering of Holiness* (Oxford, 2002), 48; Karlin-Hayter, "Methodios and His Synod," 66; and Dagron, *Emperor and Priest*, 225–226.

89. For the "Moechian" schism, see P. Henry, "The Moechian Controversy and the Constantinopolitan Synod of January A. D. 809," *Journal of Theological Studies* 20 (1969): 495–522; the summary by Afinogenov, "Κωνσταντινούπολις ἐπίσκοπον ἔχει, II," 52–65, where he critiques some of Henry's treatment of the earlier scholarship devoted to these events; Karlin-Hayter, "A Byzantine Politician Monk," 217–232; R.-J. Lilie, *Byzanz unter Eirene und Konstantin VI. (780–802)* (Frankfurt am Main, 1996), 71–78; Pratsch, *Theodoros Studites*, 83–178, passim; and Cholij, *Theodore the Stoudite*, 38–53.

90. From the surviving sources, the specific canonical questions concerning Methodios' election put forth by the Stoudites are not explicitly mentioned but can be deduced from the responses found in the correspondence of Ioannikios to Methodios: *Vita S. Ioannikii a Saba, AASS* Nov 2:1, 373; and in Methodios' two letters addressed to the Stoudites: Darrouzès, "Le patriarche Méthode," 34–35 and 42–43. See also Grumel, "La politique religieuse," 394–396; idem, *Les regestes des actes du patriarcat de Constantinople*, 1:2 (Paris, 1936; repr., Paris, 1989), nos. 427, 429, 431–434, and 436; Afinogenov, "The Great Purge of 843," 81

and 89; and Karlin-Hayter, "Methodios and His Synod," 67–71. See also K. Maksimovič, "Patriarch Methodios I (843–847) und das studische Schisma: Quellenkritische Bemerkungen," *Byzantion* 70 (2000): 422–446, where corrections are also provided for Darrouzès' edition of Methodios' letters to the Stoudites; and Hatlie, *The Monks and Monasteries of Constantinople*, 392–393.

91. *Vita Ignatii*, PG 105:489C; Βίος ἢ Μαρτύριον τοῦ ἐν ἁγίοις πατρὸς ἡμῶν Ἰγνατίου, 58–59. For an English translation, see A. Smithies, "Nicetas Paphlago's *Life of Ignatius*: A Critical Edition with Translation," PhD dissertation (State University of New York at Buffalo, 1987), 77; *Iosephi Genesii Regum Libri Quattuor*, 6; *Genesios: On the Reigns of the Emperors*, 8; and *Theophanes Continuatus*, 193. See also *Prosopographie der mittelbyzantinischen Zeit*, no. 2666, and *Prosopography of the Byzantine Empire*, no. 2666. Ignatios' mother, Prokopia, was the daughter of the emperor Nikephoros I. For the most recent dating of the *Vita Ignatii* to the years 886–901/902, see I. Tamarkina, "The Date of the Life of the Patriarch Ignatius Reconsidered," *Byzantinische Zeitschrift* 99, no. 2 (2006): 615–630, where the earlier scholarly literature concerning the date of the *Vita* is discussed.

92. Zacos and Veglery, *Byzantine Lead Seals*, 1:1, nos. 43 and 46 and pl. 16 (for Nikephoros I); Sokolova, *Byzantine Imperial Seals*, no. 70 (for Michael I); and *DOSeals* 6, nos. 38.1 and 40.1 (for Nikephoros I). For earlier misattributions of the seal belonging to Michael I, see Seibt, *Die byzantinischen Bleisegel in Österreich*, 1:85n11, and Zacos, *Byzantine Lead Seals*, no. 7.

93. B. Caseau, "L'iconographie des sceaux après la fin de l'iconoclasme (IXe–XIe S.)," *Proceedings of the International Symposium Dedicated to the Centennial of the Birth of Dr. Vassil Haralanov Held in Shumen September 13th–15th, 2007*, ed. I. Jordanov et al. (Shumen, 2008), 230, offered Ignatios' imperial lineage as a possible explanation for his sphragistic iconograhic choice but then immediately rejected it in favor of another motive: that of referencing the prestigious image of Christ at the Chalke gate or that of Christ in the *chrysotriklinos* of the Great Palace. Although there are associations with Ignatios and the icon of Christ of the Chalke gate, as discussed below in the present paper, this does not exclude the significant allusions to Ignatios' imperial dynastic connections, especially in light of his father's policies as outlined below in this paper.

94. *Iosephi Genesii Regum Libri Quattuor*, 70–71; *Genesios: On the Reigns of the Emperors*, 88; and Vinson, "Gender and Politics in the Post-Iconoclastic Period," 490.

95. *Vita Ignatii*, PG 105:540B and 541D; Βίος ἢ Μαρτύριον τοῦ ἐν ἁγίοις πατρὸς ἡμῶν Ἰγνατίου, 100 and 103; and Smithies, "Nice-

tas Paphlago's *Life of Ignatius*," 122 and 125. For the history of the Mangana, especially its early period, see R. Janin, *La géographie ecclésiastique de l'empire byzantin*, pt. 1, *Le siège de Constantinople et la patriarcat oecuménique*, vol. 3, *Les églises et les monastères*, 2nd ed. (Paris, 1969), 70–76; P. Lemerle, *Cinq études sur le XIe siècle byzantin* (Paris, 1977), 273–283; E. Malamut, "Nouvelle hypothèse sur l'origine de la maison impériale des Manganes," Αφιέρωμα στὸν Νίκο Σβορῶνο (Rethymno, 1986), 127–134; M. Kaplan, "Maisons imperiales et fondations pieuses: Réorganisation de la fortune impériale et assistance publique de la fin du VIIIe siècle à la fin du Xe siècle," *Byzantion* 61 (1991): 353–357, where Ignatios is discussed; and *Oxford Dictionary of Byzantium*, 2:1283–1284.

96. *Vita Ignatii*, PG 105:492B–C; Smithies, "Nicetas Paphlago's *Life of Ignatius*," 77–79; *Theophanes Continuatus*, 20; *Iosephi Genesii Regum Libri Quattuor*, 6; and *Genesios: On the Reigns of the Emperors*, 8.

97. *Theophanis Chronographia*, 498, and *The Chronicle of Theophanes the Confessor*, 682. See also Henry, "The Moechian Controversy," 519; Afinogenov, "Κωνσταντινούπολις ἐπίσκοπον ἔχει, I," 63; idem, "Κωνσταντινούπολις ἐπίσκοπον ἔχει, II," 43–44; E. Kountoura-Galaki, "Ὁ Μάγιστρος Θεόκτιστος καὶ ὁ Θεόδωρος Στουδίτες. Μοναστηριακὸς βίος καὶ Πολιτική," Σύμμεικτα 12 (1998): 43–55; Pratsch, *Theodoros Studites*, 179–199; idem, "Nikephoros I. (806–815)," *Die Patriarchen der ikonoklastischen Zeit*, 124–126; Cholij, *Theodore the Stoudite*, 52–54 and 142–143; Hatlie, *The Monks and Monasteries of Constantinople*, 373–374 and 398; and Brubaker and Haldon, *Byzantium in the Iconoclast Era, c. 680–850: A History*, 362. For a discussion of Michael I's reign, see W. Treadgold, *The Byzantine Revival, 780–842* (Stanford, 1988), 177–189.

98. *Vita Theodori Studitae*, PG 99:272D: "'Ὅστις Μιχαὴλ Χριστιανικώτατος ὑπάρχων . . . καὶ γίνεται πρέσβυς χριστομίμητος καὶ μεσίτης τῶν διεστώτων." See also Cholij, *Theodore the Stoudite*, 142n89, and Koutrakou, "Use and Abuse of the 'Image' of the Theotokos," 88–89.

99. *Vita Ignatii*, PG 105:493D–496D; Βίος ἢ Μαρτύριον, 62–64; and Smithies, "Nicetas Paphlago's *Life of Ignatius*," 82–83. See also Mango, "The Liquidation of Iconoclasm," 139–140; Karlin-Hayter, "Gregory of Syracuse, Ignatios and Photios," 142; and Brubaker and Haldon, *Byzantium in the Iconoclast Era, c. 680–850: A History*, 396. On Ignatios' monastic career and the communities that he founded, see J. Pargoire, "Les monastères de saint Ignace et les cinq plus petits îlots de l'archipel des Princes," *Izvestija Russkogo Arheologičeskogo Instituta v Konstantinopole* 7 (1901): 56–91. See also R. Janin, *Les églises et les monastères des grands centres byzantins* (Paris, 1975), 42–43, 61–63, 65, and 67; and Hatlie, *The Monks and Monasteries of Constantinople*, 328–330.

100. See note 16 above and *Theodori Studitae Epistulae*, vol. 2, ed. G. Fatouros (Berlin, 1991), 538.12, 703.11, and 706.49.

101. As implied by the *Vita Ignatii*, PG 105:501D–504A; ; Βίος ἢ Μαρτύριον, 69; and Smithies, "Nicetas Paphlago's *Life of Ignatius*," 89. See also Karlin-Hayter, "Gregory of Syracuse, Ignatios and Photios," 142.

102. *Vita Ignatii*, PG 105: 512B–C; Βίος ἢ Μαρτύριον, 76–77; and Smithies, "Nicetas Paphlago's *Life of Ignatius*," 96–97. See also Karlin-Hayter, "Gregory of Syracuse, Ignatios and Photios," 142–144, where the nature of Gregory Asbestos' problematic ecclesiastical status is discussed in light of the conflicting primary sources. G. Dagron, "Le traité de Grégoire de Nicée sur le baptême des Juifs," *Travaux et mémoires* 11 (1991): 341–343, describes how Gregory, prior to Ignatios' consecration ceremony, had already been accused of celebrating uncanonical ordinations but had not yet been brought before an ecclesiastical trial and so was not deposed when the patriarch excluded him from the consecration ceremony. It was not until the end of 847 or early 848 that Ignatios, by synodal decision, deposed Gregory Asbestos. See Grumel, *Les regestes*, no. 445; and idem, "Le schisme de Grégoire de Syracuse," *Échos d'Orient* 39 (1940): 257–267. In the opening summary of the Constantinopolitan synod of 869, which restored Ignatios to the patriarchal throne, it is recorded that Photios had used the word "parricide" to describe Ignatios' rejection of Methodios' policies. For this accusation, see Mansi, 16:2–3.

103. D. Afinogenov, "Did the Patriarchal Archive End Up in the Monastery of Stoudios? Ninth-Century Vicissitudes of Some Important Document Collections," *Monastères, images, pouvoirs et société à Byzance*, ed. M. Kaplan (Paris, 2006), 125–133.

104. For the legendary nature of the account of the destruction of the icon of Christ of the Chalke gate during the reign of Leo III, and its reception as fact during the post-Iconoclastic period, see M.-F. Auzépy, "La destruction de l'icône du Christ de la Chalcé par Leon III: Propagande ou réalité?," *Byzantion* 60 (1990): 445–492 (repr. in her *L'histoire des iconoclastes* [Paris, 2007], 145–178, 160–164, and 170); eadem, *L'hagiographie et l'iconoclasme byzantin: Le cas de la Vie d'Étienne le Jeune* (Aldershot, 1999), 193–194, 202, and 298–300; L. Brubaker, "The Chalke Gate, the Construction of the Past, and the Trier Ivory," *Byzantine and Modern Greek Studies* 23 (1999): 258–285; J. Haldon and B. Ward-Perkins, "Evidence from Rome for the Image of Christ on the Chalke Gate in Constantinople," ibid., 286–296; Brubaker and Haldon, *Byzantium in the Iconoclast Era (ca. 680–850): The Sources*, 71, 219–220, and 226–227; and Brubaker and Haldon, *Byzantium in the Iconoclast Era, c. 680–850: A History*, 128–135. One the other hand, several scholars writing after the pub-

lication of Auzépy's seminal article have maintained that Leo III did actually remove an image of Christ from the Chalke gate in either 726 or 730: G. Dagron, "L'iconoclasme et l'établissement de l'Orthodoxie (726–847)," *Histoire du christianisme des origines à nos jours*, vol. 4, ed. J.-M. Mayeur et al. (Paris, 1993), 100–101; P. Speck, "Τὰ τῇδε βατταρίσματα πλάνα: Überlegungen zur Aussendekoration der Chalke im achten Jahrhundert," *Studien zur byzantinischen Kunstgeschichte: Festschrift für Horst Hallensleben zum 65. Geburtstag*, ed. B. Borkopp et al. (Amsterdam, 1995), 211–220; and M. Lauxtermann, *Byzantine Poetry from Pisides to Geometres: Texts and Contexts*, vol. 1 (Vienna, 2003), 274–284.

105. For the text of the *Passion*, which includes an internal reference to the date and occasion of its commission, see *AASS*, August, 2:434–447. See also C. Mango, *The Brazen House: A Study of the Imperial Palace of Constantinople* (Copenhagen, 1959), 116–117, who at the time of his writing accepted the existence of the Christ Chalkites icon at the time of Leo III; Auzépy, "La destruction de l'icône du Christ de la Chalcé," 466–472 and 491; eadem, "De Philarète, de sa famille et de certains monastères de Constantinople," *Les saints et leur sanctuaire à Byzance: textes, images et monuments*, ed. C. Jolivet-Lévi, M. Kaplan, and J.-P. Sodini (Paris, 1994), 131–135 (repr. in her *L'histoire des iconoclastes*, 193–198); and eadem, *L'hagiographie et l'iconoclasme byzantin*, 193–194. For the monastery of Saint Aninas, see Janin, *La géographie ecclésiastique*, 34–35.

106. Auzépy, "La destruction de l'icône du Christ de la Chalcé," 471 and 491; and eadem, "De Philarète," 131–132; eadem, *L'hagiographie*, 193–194; and Vinson, "Gender and Politics," 471n8.

107. See Auzépy's article, "La destruction de l'icône du Christ de la Chalcé," for the sequence of events and the approximate date for the first icon of Christ *Chalkites*.

108. For these epigrams, see PG 99:440D–441C. For their dating, see P. Speck, *Kaiser Konstantin VI. Die Legitimation einer fremden und der Versuch einer eigenen Herrschaft*, vol. 2 (Munich, 1978), 614–617; idem, "Τὰ τῇδε βατταρίσματα πλάνα," 211–220; Barber, *Figure and Likeness*, 92; Lauxtermann, *Byzantine Poetry*, 276; and Pentcheva, *The Sensual Icon*, 83 and 249n175. Pratsch, *Theodoros Studites*, 123n44, however, prefers to leave the exact dating of these epigrams open, stating that they could also be assigned to the years of Michael I (811–813).

109. In the second of Theodore's poems in this group, however, the verses form the acrostic Θεοτόκῳ αἴνεσις ("Praise to the Theotokos"). For the poem and acrostic, see PG 99:441A; and Speck, *Kaiser Konstantin VI.*, 614 and 616, who states that this is only an allusion to the Theotokos and not to any image of her associated with the Chalke gate.

110. For the dating of the removal of the icon, see F. Iadevaia, *Scriptor incertus* (Messina, 1987), 62–64. See also P. Alexander, *The Patriarch Nikephorus of Constantinople* (Oxford, 1958), 129, and Mango, *The Brazen House*, 122.

111. For Theodore's five refutational epigrams and text, see PG 99:437C–440D and 441D–477A. The five Iconoclastic epigrams, which he critiqued, appear just before those of Theodore, 436B–437C. See also Barber, *Figure and Likeness*, 92–95, where each of the five Iconoclastic epigrams is provided in English translation and commentary provided for each, in which the Iconoclasts' preference for the *typos* of the cross and Christ as the Logos or Word is highlighted, and 165–167, ns. 48, 52, 55, 56, and 59; and Pentcheva, *The Sensual Icon*, 77–83, who also provides English translations of the Iconoclastic epigrams, slightly different from those of Barber; a commentary on each poem, emphasizing the difference between the *typos* of the Cross and the painted *graphe* image of Christ; as well as a hypothetical reconstruction (fig. 24) of the image of the cross surrounded by the Iconoclastic epigrams as it might have appeared on the Chalke gate. For the dating of the Iconoclastic epigrams to ca. 815, see Mango, *The Brazen House*, 123–124; P. Speck, "Die ikonoklastischen Jamben an der Chalke," Ἑλληνικά 27 (1974): 376–380 (for the English version of this article see "The Iconoclastic Iambic Verses on the Chalke," *Understanding Byzantium: Studies in Byzantine Historical Sources*, ed. S. Takács [Aldershot, 2003], 17–21); and idem, "Τὰ τῇδε βατταρίσματα πλάνα," 211–220; and Lauxtermann, *Byzantine Poetry*, 274–276, who assigns the writing of Theodore's epigrams to 816–818, when he was in exile in Boneta. For an earlier, alternate dating of the Iconoclastic epigrams, see S. Gero, *Byzantine Iconoclasm During the Reign of Leo III: With Particular Attention to the Oriental Sources* (Louvain, 1973), 113–126, who assigns the poems to the reign of Leo III (717–741) and provides yet another translation of the poems slightly different than those given by Barber and Pentcheva. Gero's dating of the poems is no longer accepted.

112. PG 99:437D–440B, 444A, 445A, and 472B–473A. See also Speck, *Kaiser Konstantin VI.*, 616.

113. *Theophanes Continuatus*, 103. See also Mango, *The Brazen House*, 125, who, relying on the tenth-century compilation of the *Patria* (see *Scriptores originum Constantinopolitanarum*, ed. T. Preger [Leipzig, 1901–1907; repr., New York, 1975], 2:219), concluded that Theodora's image was a mosaic depicting the full-length Christ, whereas the previous image had been a bronze statue; A. Berger, *Untersuchungen zu den Patria Konstantinupoleos* (Bonn, 1988), 252–255, concluded that Irene's image was a bronze relief of the bust of Christ whereas that of 843 was a mosaic. Writing before Auzépy's landmark article of 1990,

Berger, too, believed the sources were correct in claiming that Leo III removed an image of Christ from the Chalke gate in 726 and that this image also was a bronze relief; and B. Pentcheva, "The Performative Icon," *Art Bulletin* 88, no. 4 (2006): 636–638; and eadem, *The Sensual Icon*, 88, who interprets the sources as describing both Irene's and Theodora's icons as bronze relief medallions depicting a bust of Christ.

114. For the full Greek text, an English translation, and commentary, see Mango, *The Brazen House*, 125–132; and Pentcheva, *The Sensual Icon*, 89–93, where she provides only a portion of Methodios' epigram, in a different English translation, with the Greek original of this section appearing on 251n206, and commentary.

115. Mango, *The Brazen House*, 125–126; and Pentcheva, *The Sensual Icon*, 89 and 251n206, whose translation appears here.

116. For the chronological appearance of historiated reliquaries and their use by Iconophiles, especially high-ranking individuals, during the eighth and ninth centuries, see A Kartsonis, *Anastasis: The Making of an Image* (Princeton, 1986), 118–123; eadem, "Protection Against All Evil: Function, Use and Operation of Byzantine Historiated Phylacteries," *Byzantinische Forschungen* 20 (1994): 73–102; Vinson, "Gender and Politics," 474–475; and Brubaker and Haldon, *Byzantium in the Iconoclast Era, c. 680–850: A History*, 350–351.

117. *Vita Antonii Iunoris*, ed. A. Papadopoulos-Kerameus, *Pravoslavij Palestnskij Sbornik* 19, no. 3 (1907): 195.11 and 200.32; *Vita Theodorae*, ed. W. Regel, *Analecta Byzantino-Russica* (Saint Petersburg, 1891–1898; repr., New York, n.d.]), 10.11 and 10.13; Theognostos, *Libellus*, PG 105:860D; *Vita Ignatii*, PG 105:525B (for the English translation, see Smithies, "Nicetas Paphlago's Life of Ignatius," 109); and the Acts of the Synod of 869/870, Mansi, 16:79. See also M. Vinson, "The Terms ἐγκόλπιον and τενάντιον and the Conversion of Theophilus in the *Life of Theodora* (BHG 1731)," *Greek, Roman and Byzantine Studies* 36 (1995): 94–96; and eadem, "Gender and Politics," 475.

118. See Kartsonis, *Anastasis*, figs. 24–27, 31, and 33; eadem, "Protection Against All Evil," figs. 1–17; Vinson, "The Terms ἐγκόλπιον and τενάντιον," 91–99; and B. Pitarakis, *Les croix-reliquaires pectorals byzantines en bronze* (Paris, 2006), nos. 1–651, passim.

119. "βλέπει τό τοῦ ἐγκολπίου τενάντιον ἐν τῷ τραχήλῳ αὐτοῦ τὴν ἁγίαν καὶ ἀπαράλλετο εἰκόνα τοῦ ὑψίστου ἐμφαίνοντα ...τὴν τοῦ σωτῆρος ἡμῶν καὶ θεοῦ εἰκόνα τὴν ἁγίαν καὶ σεβασμίαν φέροντος" (*Vita Theodorae*, 10). For an English translation, see M. Vinson, "Life of St. Theodora the Empress," *Byzantine Defenders of Images: Eight Saints' Lives in English Translation*, ed. A.-M. Talbot (Washington, DC, 1998), 372–373. See also Vinson, "The Terms ἐγκόλπιον and τενάντιον," 91–99; and eadem, "Gender and Politics," 475. For more recent discussion of

the pardon of Theophilos, see Karlin-Hayter, "Restoration of Ortho-doxy," 361–373.

120. *Vita Ignatii*, PG 105:525B; and Smithies, "Nicetas Paphlago's *Life of Ignatius*," 109, where the *enkolpion* is misleadingly translated as "reliquary box." See also Kartsonis, "Protection Against All Evil," 82; and Vinson, "The Terms ἐγκόλπιον and τενάντιον," 95.

121. Kartsonis, "Protection Against All Evil," 82, also claims that the *enkolpion* was most probably historiated.

122. *Vita Ignatii*, PG 105:501; and Smithies, "Nicetas Paphlago's *Life of Ignatius*," 87–88. See also Dvornik, *The Photian Schism*, 17–18; and Vinson, "Gender and Politics," 490. Yet the *Synodikon Vetus*, no. 157, whose writer was an Ignatian sympathizer, just as Niketas David Paphlagon for the *Vita Ignatii*, emphatically claims that Ignatios was ca-nonically elected.

123. The events are narrated in *Vita Ignatii*, PG 105:504–521; Smith-ies, "Nicetas Paphlago's *Life of Ignatius*," 89–106; *Iosephi Genesii Regum Libri Quattuor*, 70–71 (for an English translation, see *Genesios: On the Reigns of the Emperors*, 87–88); and *Theophanes Continuatus*, 193–196. For an analysis and comparison of the historical sources dealing with the fall of Ignatios, see P. Karlin-Hayter, "Études sur les deux histoires du règne de Michel III," *Byzantion* 41 (1971): 475–484 (repr. in her *Studies in Byzantine History: Sources and Controversies* [London, 1981]). See also Grumel, *Les regestes*, no. 455; Dvornik, *The Photian Schism*, 35–51, where analysis from numerous sources is given in order to reconstruct an unbiased sequence of events; idem, "The Patriarch Photius in Light of Recent Research," *Berichte zum XI. internationalen Byzantinisten-Kon-gress*, 3:2 (Munich, 1958), 10–12 (repr. in his *Photian and Byzantine Ecclesiastical Studies* [London, 1974]); idem, "Patriarch Ignatius and Caesar Bardas," *Byzantinoslavica* 27 (1966): 7–22 (repr. in his *Photian and Byzantine Ecclesiastical Studies*); Vinson, "Gender and Politics," 486–493, where Theodora's female sex and Ignatios' neutered condition and monastic state are contrasted with the masculine and worldly ste-reotypes of Michael, Bardas, and Photios; and Chadwick, *East and West*, 124–133.

124. For the events see *Vita Ignatii*, PG 105:540–545; Smithies, "Nicetas Paphlago's *Life of Ignatius*," 121–122, 125–128, and 149; *Syno-dikon Vetus*, no. 166; and *Theophanes Continuatus*, 276 and 353–354. See also Grumel, *Les regestes*, no. 589; Dvornik, *The Photian Schism*, 132–173, passim, and 241–251, where the primary sources are dis-cussed; idem, "The Patriarch Photius in Light of Recent Research," 31–32, 35–36, and 44–45, where he claims that Photios died most probably in 891; however, R. Jenkins, "A Note on Nicetas David Paphlago and the *Vita Ignatii*," *Dumbarton Oaks Papers* 19 (1965): 244 (repr. in his *Stud-

ies on Byzantine History of the 9th and 10th Centuries [London, 1970]), states that Photios' death cannot be before 893; Vinson, "Gender and Politics," 471–472; Chadwick, *East and West*, 162–183; and Tamarkina, "The Date of the Life of the Patriarch Ignatius," 618, concludes that Photios must have died after 893.

125. Zacos, *Byzantine Lead Seals*, vol. 2, no. 7a.

126. Ibid., 7b.

127. Ibid., where similar caution is given along with an example of the dangers of attempting to assign a sequence to the two types of Photian seals found in the earlier literature when one of the seals was compared to a similar but misidentified specimen.

128. For Methodios' seal, see ibid., no. 5.

129. PG 102:609B and 817B, where Photios refers to Tarasios as τὸν ἡμέτερον πατρόθειον; Mango, "The Liquidation of Iconoclasm," 137; and W. Treadgold, "Photius Before His Patriarchate," *Journal of Ecclesiastical History* 53 (2002): 1. See also *Prosopographie der mittelbyzantinischen Zeit*, Abt.1; Bd. 4, ed. R.-J. Lilie et al. (Berlin, 2001), no. 7235; and *Prosopography of the Byzantine Empire*, no. 7235.

130. For example, see Darrouzès, "Le patriarche Méthode," 22 and 36–37; and Afinogenov, "The Great Purge of 843," 79 and 86–90.

131. *Theophanes Continuatus*, 174–175. See also Mango, "The Liquidation of Iconoclasm," 137–138, who offers two possible Photian genealogical trees; Treadgold, *The Byzantine Revival*, 436–437n386, where he accepts only the second of Mango's genealogical trees for Photios' family as possible; idem, "Photius Before His Patriarchate," 1–2; and *Prosopography of the Byzantine Empire*, no. 1450, where the first alternative offered by Mango is accepted. See also *Prosopography of the Byzantine Empire*, no. 6253.

132. J. Gouillard, "La vie d'Euthyme de Sardis (+831): un oeuvre du patriarche Méthode," *Travaux et mémoires* 10 (1987): 47; and Mango, "The Liquidation of Iconoclasm," 139.

133. Mango, "The Liquidation of Iconoclasm," 139.

134. "Εὐφροσύνως σήμερον ἡ Ἐκκλησία τοῦ Θεοῦ στολίζεται, ἀγαλλομένη κραυγάζουσα· Ἐλαμπρύνθη μου τὸ κάλλος ὑπὲρ πᾶσαν πόλιν· ἰδοὺ γὰρ τῶν ἀρχιερέων τὸ μέγα κειμήλιον, ὁ ἔνδοξος Μεθόδιος, τὴν πορείαν πρὸς οὐρανὸν ἐποιήσατο. Δεῦτε οὖν, φιλέορτοι, τῶν ὀρθοδόξων τὸ σύστημα, χοροστατήσαντες ἅμα τὴν θείαν λάρνακα, ἰαμάτων πλημμύραν λαβόντες παρ' αὐτῆς, ἱκετεύωμεν αἰτήσασθαι Χριστὸν τὸν Θεὸν τοῦ ῥυσθῆναι τὴν οἰκουμένην ἀπὸ πάσης αἱρέσεως" (PG 102:576–577). See also Mango, "The Liquidation of Iconoclasm,"139; and Treadgold, "Photius Before His Patriarchate," 14.

135. *Vita Ignatii*, PG 105:512; Smithies, "Nicetas Paphlago's *Life of Ignatius*," 96–97; Mango, "The Liquidation of Iconoclasm," 139; Karlin-

Hayter, "Gregory of Syracuse, Ignatios and Photios," 144–145; Dagron, "Le traité de Grégoire de Nicée," 342–345; and Treadgold, "Photius Before His Patriarchate," 14.

136. J. Gouillard, "Deux figures mal connues du second iconoclasme," *Byzantion* 31 (1961): 373–376; Mango, "The Liquidation of Iconoclasm," 139; and Dagron, "Le traité de Grégoire de Nicée," 341–342. The *Vita Methodii*, PG 100:1244–1261, is considered the surviving, anonymous abridged version of the longer *Vita* composed by Gregory.

137. Karlin-Hayter, "Gregory of Syracuse, Ignatios and Photios," 145.

Chapter 4

THE SEAL OF THE GIFT OF THE HOLY SPIRIT: THE SACRAMENT OF CHRISMATION

Rev. Dr. George Dion. Dragas
Professor of Patrology/Patristics

1. *Chrismation and Christian Initiation*

In the Orthodox Church, the sacrament of Chrismation is inseparable from the sacraments of Baptism and Divine Communion. There is an essential unity in the origins of all three, so that any attempt to see them outside this unity would create serious theological and historical problems.[1] Baptism and Chrismation constitute one rite, or one sequel of initiation of believers into the supreme sacrament of the Lord and Savior Jesus Christ and His Church,[2] which is fully realized in the Divine Eucharist. Indeed, a person that receives Baptism and Chrismation also receives Holy Communion.

In the Orthodox perception, Baptism is a kind of personal Pascha, a participation in the death and Resurrection of Christ, whereby the person baptized dies to sin (is forgiven) and rises (is born or reborn) into newness of life in Christ. By the same token, Chrismation is a kind of personal Pentecost, whereby the person chrismated receives the gift of the Spirit, so that he may live the new life in Christ. Communion is the beginning of the new life in the whole sacrament of Christ, the Church. The *praxis* of Christian initiation in the Orthodox Church proclaims that the newly baptized has been united with Christ and anointed with the Holy Spirit, and is called to grow as a child of God the Father in a process of sanctification that is accomplished within the life of the believing community for the sake of the entire world.[3]

This threefold Christian initiation is rooted in the holy gospel, that is, in the saving Person, life, and ministry of Christ, particularly in His birth (the Incarnation), in His Baptism in the River Jordan, in His death and Resurrection, and in His final glorification through his Ascension into heaven and His outpouring of the Spirit at Pentecost (the birth of the Church); but it is also rooted in the saving apostolic mission and ministry, as these are well attested in the sacred literature of the Church, from the earliest apostolic writings to other early (especially those of the fourth century) and later patristic works.

This ancient rite of Christian initiation is maintained today in its original integrity only in the Orthodox Church, although certain criticisms have been raised about some aspects of contemporary Orthodox practice, not without good justification.[4] The Roman Catholic Church and the Protestant churches have broken its unity and have altered its meaning, especially with regard to Chrismation/Confirmation, which is no longer clearly seen as being primarily a free (unconditional) gift of divine grace, but rather as an act centered on man, nor as an indissoluble bond between Baptism and the Eucharist. The result is that the place and role of the Spirit in the sacrament of the Lord Jesus Christ and His Church is not properly understood, and therefore initiation into this sacrament is at least deficient, if not distorted. From an Orthodox point of view, a fundamental recovery of the original integrity of Christian initiation, especially through the restoration of the sacrament of Chrismation, is an urgent need.

Orthodox symbolics specify three Roman Catholic innovations in the celebration of Chrismation: (1) first, we have the innovation that (since the thirteenth century) Chrismation is not given immediately after Baptism in the case of infants, but when they become twelve (or seven in cases of emergency) years old, because infants are not yet self-conscious enough to undertake responsibility for the spiritual battle involved in the Christian life. This is very precarious, because it introduces into this sacrament a subjective criterion and thus strips it of its real character, namely that of being a free divine gift, a seal and confirmation of Holy Baptism. (2) The second innovation is that only bishops and not presbyters normally give Chrismation, although very rarely and as a matter of exception presbyters may also give it by papal permission. This practice contradicts the historic tradition of the Church, which (according to St. John Chrysostom) sees only the sacrament of ordination as the exclusive right of the bishops over the presbyters. Besides, the pope's intervention seems to add a further contradiction to the new Roman Catholic practice. (3) The third innovation is that Chrismation is administered twice, by the use of Chrism and by the laying on of hands.[5]

As regards Protestant Christians, Orthodox symbolics notes that they reject the sacramental character of Chrismation/Confirmation despite the biblical witness to it[6] and the practice of the early Church. Furthermore, it is pointed out that some Protestants (especially Anglicans) have introduced since the seventeenth century a sort of Confirmation ceremony, which is connected with the official entry into the Church of those who had been baptized as infants on the basis of their confession of accepting Christ or the Church's faith.[7] Such a practice clearly indicates that Baptism is not sufficient for entry into the Church, that this entry is conditioned by a subjective human response, although the objective ground to which this response is directed is not so clearly or concretely established. In some cases this point of entry is a confession of the faith, which is signified by Baptism, and a resolve to follow it in life. In other cases it entails a second baptism "*in the Spirit*," which "*confirms*," as it were, the first baptism "*in water*," which was only a sign.

2. The Administration of Chrismation and Its Meaning

In the Orthodox Church, Chrismation takes place within the celebration of Baptism as the newly baptized rises from the font after the third immersion. It takes the form of a cross-wise anointing with Myrrh on the forehead, the eyes, the nostrils, the mouth, the ears, the breast, the hands, and the feet of the baptized, an anointing that is accompanied by the words, "The Seal of the gift of the Holy Spirit, Amen."[8] These words clearly indicate the fundamental connection of this sacrament with the gift of the Holy Spirit. Furthermore, these words are so explicit that no doubt is left as to their meaning, which is the actual conferral of the gift of the Spirit on the newly baptized, whereby he is adopted by God and becomes a beloved son by grace (a Christian).

The "Prayer of the Myrrh," which is said by the celebrant on this occasion, also indicates the particular nuances of meaning of this sacrament in relation to the sacrament of Baptism, which is recognized as a prerequisite to it, and the Eucharistic sacrament of Communion of the Holy Body and precious Blood of Christ, which is its sequel:[9]

> Blessed are you, Lord God Almighty, Fountain of Blessings,
> Sun of Righteousness, Who made to shine forth for those

in darkness a light of salvation through the manifestation of Your Only-begotten Son and our God, granting unto us, though we are unworthy, blessed cleansing in Holy Baptism, and divine sanctification in the life-effecting Chrismation; Who now also has been well-pleased to regenerate this Your servant newly illuminated through Water and Spirit, giving him (her) forgiveness of his (her) voluntary and involuntary sins: do You yourself, Sovereign Master, Compassionate King of all, bestow upon him (her) also the seal of the gift of your omnipotent and adorable Holy Spirit, and the Communion of the Holy Body and Most Precious Blood of Your Christ; keep him (her) in your sanctification; confirm him (her) in the Orthodox Faith; deliver him (her) from the Evil One and all his devices; preserve his (her) soul, through Your saving fear, in purity and righteousness, that in every work and word, being acceptable before You, he (she) may become a child and heir of Your Heavenly Kingdom.

In light of this prayer, the nuances of meaning of this sacrament include the following: the "divine sanctification in the life-effecting Chrismation" that follows "the blessed cleansing (forgiveness of sins) granted through Holy Baptism"; and "the seal of the gift of [God's] omnipotent and adorable Spirit" following the regeneration of the person baptized and the forgiveness of his or her sins, which secures the newly born Christian's safe keeping in a divinely granted sanctification, confirmation in the Orthodox faith, deliverance from the Evil One, and adoption, whereby one becomes "a child and heir of [Christ's] heavenly Kingdom." Basically, however, Chrismation is the anointing of the newly baptized with the Holy Spirit, whereby he is fully conformed to Christ and becomes a Christian, a participant in the gift of the life-giving Spirit that was manifested after Christ's Baptism in water in the form of a dove and after His Baptism into death through the Resurrection, and finally at His final glorification at Pentecost, when He sent the promised Spirit to be with and remain in His Church. Although it has been practiced from the beginning in slightly variable forms, Chrismation has always carried this basic meaning and significance. It is generally accepted that it was first conferred through the laying on of hands on the newborn Christians by the apostles, but was also connected with anointing with Myrrh very early in the apostolic age, as several Church authors have pointed out.

3. The Biblical Roots of the Sacrament of Chrismation

The first roots of Chrismation are traced back to the Old Testament. Chrismation is connected with the Hebrew priests, kings, and prophets. All of them are "christs" by virtue of their Chrismation, but all of them also anticipate or foreshadow the One who is to come, *the Christ*, the Messiah. This is particularly brought out in the book of Isaiah, where the Christ of God is also a Servant, indeed, a suffering Servant who is chrismated with the Spirit of God and who will bring forth justice to the nations but after suffering.[10]

It is in the Law that we first find chrismation being connected with the consecration of Aaron to the priesthood. Exodus 29 informs us that this consecration consisted first in "washing in water"[11] and then in "pouring chrismation oil on the head."[12] Leviticus 8 offers a further elaboration of this act of chrismation in the context of consecration to the priesthood. In Leviticus 21 we come across the interesting phrases "oil of christ" (ἔλαιον τοῦ χριστοῦ) and "holy oil of the christ of God" (τὸ ἅγιον ἔλαιον τοῦ χριστοῦ τοῦ Θεοῦ) being used in connection with the consecration of the High Priest. Finally, the verse that sums up this OT priestly Chrismation is found in Psalm 132/133:2: "It is like the precious oil on the head, running down from the beard, on the beard of Aaron, running down on the collar of his robes." It is important to note here that this verse is repeated by all Orthodox priests when they put on their stoles (which signify the grace of the Spirit) in order to engage in priestly functions, with the addition before it: "Blessed is our God, who pours His grace on His priests, like oil (Myron) running down on the beard of Aaron."

Another use of chrismation in the OT is that of consecration of kings. It is in 1 Kings (1 Samuel) 10 that we read about this in the story of the consecration of Saul as the first Hebrew king. What is particularly interesting here is to observe the explicit connection between this chrismation and the gift of the Spirit of the Lord, which is granted on this occasion and also results in the gift of prophesying. 1 Kings 16 describes how King David was also consecrated with chrismation and how, on this occasion, "the Spirit of the Lord came mightily upon him from that day forward."[13] The same applies to Solomon, as we see in 3 Kings 1:34. It is in the so-called Royal Psalms, however, that we find a particular stress being placed on the chrismation of the Hebrew kings, which is connected with the Spirit of the Lord and with divine sonship as a characteristic of their office. Psalm 2, for example, speaks of "the

kings of the earth who set themselves against the Lord and his chrismated one," and also of "the decree of the Lord" that says to the Hebrew
king (who is the chrismated one of God), "You are my Son, today I have
begotten you; ask of me and I will make the nations your heritage."[14]
Psalm 45 speaks of the king as "the one who is chrismated by God with
the oil of gladness above his fellows"[15] (cf. verses 6–7). Similar statements are found in Psalms 18:50; 20:6; 89:20ff.; and 132:10. It is particularly important to note here that all these verses are seen and used
in the early Church as references to Christ.

Finally, the OT connects chrismation with the Hebrew prophets,
who together with the priests and the kings become the forerunners of
types of the Christ who is to come. The important point in all this is that
chrismation is connected with the grace of God and especially with the
Holy Spirit.

The New Testament begins with the ministry of John the Baptist,
who announces the coming of the (expected) Christ whose distinctive
mark is His Chrismation with the grace of the Holy Spirit. John 1:33f.
is characteristic: "And John testified, 'I saw the Spirit descending from
heaven like a dove, and it remained on Him. I myself did not know Him,
but the One who sent me to baptize with water said to me, "He on whom
you see the Spirit descend and remain is the One who baptizes with the
Holy Spirit." And I myself have seen and have testified that this is the
Son of God.'" A little further on, Andrew the *Protocletos* appears, telling
his brother Simon (Peter), "We have found the Chrismated One" (the
Christos, John 1:41). Jesus is the Christ, the One who is anointed with the
Holy Spirit. The Baptism of Jesus reported in Mark 1:9ff. plainly declares
the same message. Thus it is plain that in the New Testament the grace
of the Spirit is fundamentally linked with the identity of Jesus Christ.
But why is Jesus anointed, why is He the Christ? The Baptist said it: "He
on whom you see the Spirit descend and remain is the One who baptizes
with the Holy Spirit." In other words, Christ was baptized that He may
baptize others in the Holy Spirit. He Himself was chrismated that He
may chrismate others.

It is in the so-called Paraclete passages of St. John that this is most
clearly brought out. Christ, who received the Spirit, is to give the Spirit,
but this cannot be done before He is exalted, and for this to happen He
first has to suffer. "If I do not go away, the Paraclete will not come to you,
but if I go I will send him to you."[16] Indeed, the Paraclete was to be given
not only to the disciples, but also to all those who would believe in Him
through their preaching. This is indeed what happened. It happened

at Pentecost, and Peter declared it plainly in his first sermon, which is recorded in the book of the Acts of the Apostles: "This Jesus God raised up, and of that all of us are witnesses. Being therefore exalted at the right hand of God, and having received from the Father the promise of the Holy Spirit, He has poured out this that you see and hear. For David did not ascend into the heavens, but he himself says, 'The Lord said to My Lord, "Sit at My right hand until I make Your enemies Your footstool."' Therefore, let the entire house of Israel know with certainty that God has made Him both Lord and Christ this Jesus whom you crucified."[17]

It is clear in the New Testament that Christ's work, which began publicly with His Baptism in the Jordan and the descent of the Spirit upon him, was not concluded at the Baptism of His death and Resurrection, but at Pentecost, when the Spirit descended upon the Church. Through His death and Resurrection, death was abolished and mankind was justified. Through His Exaltation at the right hand of the Father, the gift of the Spirit was granted, that He might remain safely in the Church, sanctify her, and operate through her the salvation of the world. This clear link between Christology and Pneumatology is reflected in the early Church's practice of initiation into Christ. This initiation included Baptism and Chrismation/Confirmation.

Baptism is more connected with Pascha, and Chrismation with Pentecost. St. Paul says to the Roman Christians about Baptism: "All of us who have been baptized into Christ Jesus were baptized into his death. We were buried therefore with Him by Baptism into death, so that as Christ was raised from the dead by the glory of the Father, we too might walk in newness of life. For if we have been united with Him in a death like His, we shall certainly be united with Him in a resurrection like His."[18] The same St. Paul also speaks about our Chrismation with the Spirit to the Corinthians: "But it is God who establishes us with you in Christ and has commissioned us. He has put His Seal upon us and given us His Spirit in our hearts as a first installment"[19]; and to the Ephesians: "In Him you also, when you had heard the word of Truth, the gospel of your salvation, and had believed in Him, were marked with the Seal of the promised Holy Spirit: this is the pledge of our inheritance towards redemption as God's own people, to the praise of His Glory."[20] And also: "Do not grieve the Holy Spirit of God, with which you were marked with the Seal for the Day of Redemption. Put away bitterness and wrath and anger and wrangling and slander together with all malice, and be kind to one another, tenderhearted, forgiving one another, as God in Christ has forgiven you."[21]

The Acts of the Apostles clarifies the necessary connection between Baptism and Chrismation (anointing) with the Holy Spirit. Acts 8:12–17 reports the case of the Samaritans who had believed and been baptized but had not received the Spirit. Peter and John went there in order to lay hands on them, that they may receive the Spirit. Acts 19:1–6 reports the case of those Ephesians who had been baptized only into John the Baptist's baptism of repentance and who knew nothing about the Spirit: "They were baptized in the name of the Lord Jesus, and when Paul had laid hands upon them, the Holy Spirit came upon them." It is crystal clear here that Baptism into Christ has as a necessary sequel the reception of the gift of the Holy Spirit. This gift was not given by Baptism, but by the laying on of hands of the apostles. The gift of the Spirit through the laying on of hands of the apostles and the Seal of the Spirit given as a sequel to Baptism, both of which appear to be connected with the Apostle Paul, suggest an early transition from laying on of hands to Chrismation, possibly due to the growth of the Christian mission. This is actually the clear witness of the post-apostolic ecclesiastical and patristic literature.

4. *The Evidence from Early Church Practice*

In the second century AD we have the evidence of St. Irenaeus of Lyons and of Tertullian in Carthage. The former refers to Chrismation in his *Demonstration of the Apostolic Preaching*, an early second-century work, which has survived in an Ethiopic translation. He states in chap. 47 that the Father anointed the Son with the Holy Spirit above His fellows (the saints of the Old and the New Testaments) so that they may be chrismated by Him with the same blessing. Tertullian refers to Chrismation in his treatise *On Baptism*.[22] He explicitly states, "We do not receive the Spirit from the waters of Baptism which prepare us for it," but "through the Holy Chrism, as did Aaron at his consecration to the priesthood by Moses." Tertullian also mentions the laying on of hands as a means of transmission of the Holy Spirit. Notwithstanding the double act of Chrismation and laying on of hands, what is very interesting here is the distinction of the water from the Spirit, and also their interrelation, which Tertullian traces to the dove of the flood at the time of Noah.

Other early (third century, but really going back to the second century) witnesses to Chrismation and the reception of the gift of the Spirit as a necessary sequel or complement to Baptism are to be seen in St. Cyprian of Carthage, Hippolytus of Portus (near Rome), and Serapion of Thmuis. In his *Letter* 77, the former refers to the transmission of the

Spirit immediately after Baptism through the laying on of hands of the Church leaders, but he also refers to the Seal (*signaculum*) of the Lord, which strongly implies Chrismation with consecrated oil. Hippolytus mentions in his *Apostolic Tradition* both "laying on hands" and "two chrismations" with the "oil of gladness" after triple immersion at Baptism as the means for the transmission of the gift of the Spirit.[23] Bishop Serapion, St. Athanasius' friend, includes in his *Euchologion* a "Prayer over the Chrismation with Oil after Baptism."[24] This prayer makes clear reference to the Chrismation after Baptism, whereby the newly baptized receive "the Seal of the gift of the Holy Spirit."

In the fourth century we have the clear testimony of the Church of Jerusalem in the person of St. Cyril of Jerusalem. In his *Catechetical and Mystagogical Instructions*, St. Cyril gives us an account of the practice of initiation in his Church at that time—a practice that had been received from earlier generations. The key text here is his *Catechetical Instruction* 21, which brings out the rich biblical Christological and Pneumatological background to Chrismation as a sequel to initiation into Christ through Baptism. Perhaps the most important comment that St. Cyril makes in this connection is that Christians owe their name to their Chrismation with the Holy Spirit. Indeed, Christians, Chrismation, and Christ are all three connected with anointing with the Holy Spirit.

Another important fourth-century witness to the apostolic necessity of conjoining Chrismation with Baptism is found in St. Ambrose of Milan, particularly in his two treatises *De Sacramentis* and *De Mysteriis*, which supply parallel accounts.[25] Here Chrismation, which entails the gift of the Holy Spirit, is administered twice, as in Hippolytus, by the bishop; and it is directly linked with priestly and royal status, as in the OT, and with the "royal priesthood" (βασίλειον ἱεράτευμα) of 1 Peter 2:9, which is understood in "*spiritual*" terms. St Ambrose, being a great biblical scholar, brings in other interesting verses in order to elaborate the deeper spiritual meaning of Chrismation. Some of them are from the Song of Songs.[26] The final point that we should note from St. Ambrose is his correlation of the Trinity with the calling, the baptizing, and the chrismating of a new Christian candidate.

In spite of the noted differences between East and West in the practice of Chrismation, the basic rite of initiation was the same. A more radical differentiation was introduced in the fifth century. It is at this time that Western bishops allowed their priests to carry out Baptism and first Chrismation but reserved for themselves the second Chrismation and the laying on of hands. What the bishops actually did acquired a new name at this time, that is, confirmation (*confirmatio*).[27] This was done for the good reason that by then it became impossible for the bishop to attend every Baptism. Nevertheless, this provision introduced a separation of Baptism and Confirmation and led to the position of seeing them as two separate sacraments. The confusion that resulted from the introduction of such a strong separation of Confirmation from Baptism came to a head in the thirteenth century (the heyday of Thomas Aquinas and Scholasticism), as we have already noted. Confirmation appeared to be unnecessary, as it had become in the fifth century for St. Jerome. It is in light of this background that we can understand why the Reformed Churches came to regard Confirmation as a non-existent sacrament.

5. *Conclusions*

The Orthodox sense of the necessity of Chrismation in Christian initiation was brought out in the Orthodox reactions to the Lima document. Fr. Thomas Hopko of St. Vladimir's Theological Seminary articulated certain concerns that are typical of these reactions. He found that the greatest concern of the Orthodox in the Section on Baptism had to do with the distinction and relationship between Baptism and Chrismation; the relationship of Baptism and Chrismation to the Eucharist; and the place of children, particularly infants, relative to these statements. His following statement seems to bring out very succinctly the Orthodox position:

> Orthodox hold that Baptism by immersion is a person's Easter (Pascha) and that Chrismation, which is a person's Pentecost, must necessarily accompany Baptism in every instance as a distinct act. As Christ and the Spirit are not the same— yet never separated—and as the Passover of Christ's death and resurrection is distinct from the coming of the Holy Spirit—yet never divided from it—so Baptism and Chrismation (which is not easily identified with the "confirmation" of any of the Western Churches, varying as the understanding and practices are) must also always be united with appropriate theological, liturgical, and spiritual distinctions that allow each act to be what it is in harmony with the other. The Orthodox generally find the Baptism statement greatly lacking at this point. There is also a lack of clarity about the relationship of Baptism (and Chrismation) with the Eucha-

rist. Orthodox hold that baptized (and chrismated) people, including infants, are led directly and necessarily to the Eucharistic table of Holy Communion. They find it incomprehensible that a baptized person would be denied access to the Eucharist.[28]

I believe that the key to the understanding of the Orthodox view of sacraments, and in this case, of Chrismation, lies in their Christological and ecclesiological foundation. This point is most eloquently brought out by Fr. George Metallinos in one of his recent magnificent volumes. He quotes the following statement of one of the greatest liturgiologists of the Orthodox tradition, St. Symeon of Thessalonica:

> Christ is everywhere by means of the ceremony and the communion . . . This was the will of the Artificer of all that the same liturgy should be celebrated both above and below. He Himself appeared doing this, and having been seen as man He accomplished through Himself His union with us . . . He assumed our created nature, and was hypostatically united with us, and He transmitted to the mortal nature the glories of the Godhead, having been clothed without separation and without confusion with it. For in Him, he says, dwells the whole fullness (*pleroma*) of the Godhead bodily (Col 2:9). He was seen and again He is seen, as He is well pleased. And He has given Himself to us, and for us, and even now He gives Himself to us again. Of these works we are liturgists (ministers) and servants and initiators . . . What a miracle! He becomes, and appears, and is self-given, and is carried, and redeems and is communicated through the sacraments.[29]

The logic and purpose of the Incarnation of Christ is, according to St. Symeon, the regeneration and sanctification of the world.[30] This is naturally most evident in the Divine Liturgy: "Christ, becoming like us, in order to sanctify us in our dual nature, was in need of sacraments, and dispensed the grace in a double manner."[31] He is the One who actually operates all things in the celebration of the sacraments: "Hence He grafted His grace inside us [that is, inside the priests] so that He might operate through us . . . Thus, it is not we ourselves who operate the sacraments, but we simply liturgize, that is, we serve. It is He Himself who operates through us."[32] This is how the holy liturgiologist presents the Christological character of the sacraments, which is also the presupposition of their ecclesial character. Church and sacraments are organically connected, because the Church herself, established on the event of the Incarnation, is by her nature sacrament and source of grace, "beginning and end of all the sacraments."[33]

Notes

On our beloved Ecumenical Patriarch Bartholomew's completion of twenty years at the helm of the Orthodox Church, my soul is filled with feelings of thanksgiving and jubilation. His Holiness' unwavering leadership has brought to the Great Church of Christ and to the Orthodox Churches in the Ecumene, as well as to the world at large, many blessings and hope for the present and the future. I had the single privilege of being one of the first visitors to congratulate him at the Phanar very shortly after his enthronement, and I remember his words: "We have now resolved to give everything to the Church." This has clearly been the signal of his patriarchal ministry, following the sacred apostolic tradition of his many and saintly predecessors, who lived entirely for Christ and the Church. I am deeply grateful to him for having summoned me on many memorable occasions to share in serving him and the Great Church. I pray that the Lord of the Church may grand him health and many years, and the joy of seeing fulfilled all his ecumenical aspirations for the Great Church and Orthodoxy at large. The present essay was read at the Pittsburgh Theological Seminary (USA) Meeting, April 3–7, 2000, of the Joint Commission of the Dialogue between the Orthodox Church and the World Alliance of Reformed Churches, and was also presented in a modified form at the Faculty of Theology of the University of Veliko Ternovo in Bulgaria in the year 2000 at the celebrations of the new millennium. It is here updated and published for the first time.

1. See the profound essay of Dr. John Zizioulas (now Metropolitan of Pergamum), "Some Reflections on Baptism, Confirmation and Eucharist," *Sobornost* 5, no. 9 (1969): 644–652. See also Paul Verghese, "Baptism, Confirmation and the Eucharist in the in the Syrian Orthodox Church," *Studia Liturgica* 4 (1965): 81–93; Thomas FitzGerald, "The Orthodox Rite of Christian Initiation," *St. Vladimir's Theological Quarterly* 32 (1988): 309–327, at p. 313; and Hieromonk Hilarion Alfeyev (now Metropolitan of Volokolamsk of the Moscow Patriarchate), "Membership of the Body of Christ: Sacraments of initiation," *Greek Orthodox Theological Review* 43 (1998): 565–572.

2. The word "sacrament" in the Greek New Testament is the word «μυστήριον» ("mystery"), and it appears twice, in connection on the one hand with the Incarnation, or the appearance of God in the flesh, and

on the other hand with the Church. In other words, it has a double signification, both Christological and ecclesiological; hence the adoption of the term "supreme sacrament" in the above text.

3. FitzGerald, "The Orthodox Rite."

4. Cf. Zizioulas, "Some Reflections," 650, which states: "It is an unfortunate development which has been established in the Orthodox Church itself to offer the Holy Eucharist to the newly baptized individual outside the Eucharistic assembly." See also FitzGerald, "The Orthodox Rite," 324, which discusses the problem of the separation of the baptismal service from the Eucharistic Liturgy.

5. See Andreas Theodorou, *Notes on Comparative Symbolics* (Athens, 1985), 290–293.

6. The following verses are directly related to this: (1) Acts 2:38: "Peter said to them, 'Repent, and be baptized every one of you in the name of Jesus Christ, so that your sins may be forgiven; and you will receive the gift of the Holy Spirit.'" (2) Acts 8:14–15: "Now when the apostles at Jerusalem heard that Samaria had accepted the word of God, they sent Peter and John to them. The two went down and prayed for them that they might receive the Holy Spirit (for as yet the Holy Spirit had not come upon any of them; they had only been baptized in the name of the Lord Jesus). Then Peter and John laid their hands on them and they received the Holy Spirit." (3) Acts 19:2–9: "While Apollos was in Corinth, Paul passed through the interior regions and came to Ephesus, where he found some disciples. He said to them, 'Did you receive the Holy Spirit when you became believers?' They replied, 'No, we have not even heard that there is a Holy Spirit.' Then he said, 'Into what, then, were you baptized?' They answered, 'Into John's Baptism.' Paul said, 'John baptized with the baptism of repentance, telling the people to believe in the one who was to come after him, that is, in Jesus.' On hearing this, they were baptized in the name of the Lord Jesus. When Paul had laid his hands on them, the Holy Spirit came upon them, and they spoke in tongues and prophesied—altogether there were twelve of them. He entered the synagogue and for three months spoke out boldly, and argued persuasively about the Kingdom of God." (4) Heb 6:1–6: "Therefore let us go on toward perfection, leaving behind the basic teaching about Christ, and not laying again the foundation: repentance from dead works and faith toward God, instruction about Baptisms, laying on of hands, resurrection of the dead, and eternal judgment. For it is impossible to restore again to repentance those who have once been enlightened, and have tasted the heavenly gift, and have shared in the Holy Spirit, and have tasted the goodness of the word of God and of the powers of the age to come, and then have fallen away, since on their own they are crucifying again the Son of God and are holding Him in contempt."

7. Cf. Theodorou, *Notes on Comparative Symbolics*, 293f.

8. Cf. *Mikron Euchologion* [An Orthodox Prayer Book], trans. John von Holzhausen and Michael Gelsinger (N & T Publications, 1985), 65.

9. Ibid.

10. Isa 42:1; see also 11:1ff.

11. Exod 29:4.

12. Exod 29:7.

13. 1 Kgs 16:13.

14. Ps 2:2, 7f.

15. Ps 45:6f.

16. John 16:6f.

17. Acts 1:32ff.

18. Rom 6:3–5.

19. 2 Cor 1:21f.

20. Eph 1:13f.

21. Eph 1:30ff.

22. Chap. 6ff.

23. Chap. 21.

24. Chap. 15.

25. See esp. *De Sacramentis* 2.24, 4.1, 3, 4; and *De Mysteriis* 6.29, 30.

26. For example, Song of Songs 1:3–4.

27. Cf. Cyril Argenti, "The Sacrament of Chrismation," *Sourozh* 14 (November 1984): 49.

28. See his "The Lima Statement and the Orthodox," in *St. Vladimir's Theological Quarterly* 27, no. 4 (1983): 284.

29. PG 155:956–957.

30. PG 155:181A.

31. PG 155:156

32. *Dialogue* 41 (PG 155:181).

33. See his book *The Theological Witness of Ecclesiastical Worship* (Athens: Armos, 1995), 246f.

Chapter 5

Hospitality: Keeping a Place for the "Other"

Dr. Kyriaki Karidoyanes FitzGerald
Adjunct Professor of Theology

Setting a Place at the Family Table

Growing up as the eldest sibling in a very large extended Greek-American family, it was often my responsibility to help my mother or grandmother set the table for the family supper. This was often a wonderful time of the day, when we would also find moments to laugh, share, and listen to important stories that mattered to who we were as a family. On special occasions such as Christian holy days, name days, birthdays, anniversaries, Thanksgiving, as well as weekly Sunday dinners, extra care and deliberation were given to the choice of foods to be prepared, how they were prepared, the placement of the table seating, and who would be coming. No matter how large the expected dinner company would be, my mother or grandmother would count the settings to be sure everyone was included, and then one of them would ask me to set one more place. Sometimes I would be chastised because I did not do this so well. My way of setting the extra place often caused it to blend in with all of the others, as a result of my young and careless hands. Mama or Yiayia would correct the settings so that the extra addition would be discreetly, yet visibly, more prominent than the other place settings. "You have to clearly make sure this table setting is left open, as we may have to receive the *ksenos* [the stranger] who may be coming, and who knows? The stranger may be Christ Himself," she would advise. This always confused me, because extra people would usually come, but none of them were Christ, I thought. Nevertheless, the seriousness with which she would express this message made me feel very special, as if I just happened to be at an important place at an important time. Making room for the stranger who could be God changes everything . . .

These sweet kitchen memories are a reflection of a whole demeanor of life, as well as an approach to hospitality. With profound, yet subtle, intentionality, perhaps even humbly reverberating the echo of the hospitality of Abraham and Sarah, we hosts would sacrifice time, energy, resources, even adjust our usual daily priorities, in order to open ourselves to receiving the stranger, the other—the other who could be God.

Setting a Place at the Monastic Table

Since ancient Christian times, there has been a strong analogous belief and practice common among monastic communities regarding hospitality. The early monastic tradition placed particular emphasis upon the virtue of hospitality toward visitors. Monasteries were primarily communities of monastics whose lives centered upon regular prayer offered for the whole Church and for the world. At the same time, monasteries were often the destination of pilgrims who sought spiritual nourishment or guidance. Likewise, monasteries were often a safe place of rest for weary travelers.

St. Benedict of Nursia (ca. 480–ca. 547), for example, paid particular attention to the importance of hospitality. He directed that pilgrims and travelers be welcomed and honored by the monastery. In this expression of hospitality, the monastics bore witness to the gospel in a very practical way. To the monks, Benedict said, "All guests who present themselves are to be welcomed as Christ . . . Great care and concern are to be shown in receiving poor people and pilgrims, because in them more particularly is Christ received."[1] Perhaps not too differently from my mother and grandmother, St. Benedict also drew a direct connection between Christ and the alien visitor. Affirming the relationship between Christ and the guest, St. Benedict said, "All humility should be shown in addressing a guest . . . Christ is to be adored [in guests] because He is indeed welcomed in them."[2]

About a century and a half earlier, St. Basil the Great (329–379), the bishop of Caesarea in Cappadocia, Asia Minor, was renowned as a loving pastor and thoughtful theologian. At the same time, he also was known for his compassion and care for those in need. With remarkable devotion and foresight, Basil established a community of care, known as the *Basileias*. Centered around a beautiful church, this village included a hospital, a home for the poor, a home for the elderly, an orphanage, and a home for lepers. Residences were also provided for the staff of clergy, doctors, nurses, and other caregivers. Hospitality was also provided for visiting relatives, clergy, and government officials. Basil himself frequently visited with the sick, poor, and outcast who lived in this special community of care. He directed that hospitality and care be offered to all those in need regardless of their religious conviction or cultural backgrounds. Speaking of the care for those in need, he wrote, "The goal which everyone ought to have in their work is to help the needy, more than to provide for oneself. In this way, we shall avoid the accusation that we are attached to our own personal advantage and we shall receive the blessing that the Lord gives to those who love their brothers and sisters."[3] Remarkable as it may seem, St. Basil's actions and words demonstrate powerfully that every person in need was his brother and sister.

The Hospitality of God: A Revolutionary Understanding

Our humble, human attempts at hospitality point to a revolutionary understanding of the hospitality of God. It is the human response to the God who loved us first and who still keeps reaching out to us first that undergirds our vision of hospitality. There is nothing in creation that even compares to the hospitality of God! The Triune God's invitation to us is not formal or obligatory, neither is it tentative or timid, nor is it unenthusiastic or conditional. Scandalous as it may sound, the living God of love invites each of us to enjoy complete fellowship with Him as adopted sons and daughters. In many ways, God's seeking to share His "home" with us is not unlike a beggar who is personally deeply vulnerable, while desperately seeking our love. He begs us to join Him by loving Him and thus one another.

Here the example of our Lord is especially important. Jesus is the one who honored persons of different cultures, nationalities, and religions. He honored and respected not only his fellow Jews, but also the women of Samaria, the Roman centurion, and Simon the Cyrenian. He accepted men and women, the righteous and sinners, the outcasts and the insiders. Christ was able to see each as a child of God the Father and blessed with the "image and likeness" of God.

During the late sixth to early seventh centuries, St. Maximos the Confessor bore witness to this astounding teaching: "God made Himself a beggar by reason of His concern for us . . . suffering mystically through His tenderness to the end of time according to the measure of each one's suffering."[4]

The ineffable God, while fully present within creation in a mysterious way and abiding eternally outside of time and space, is in countless ways a "fool" in love with us! This teaching helps us put into perspective the ancient Christian affirmation that "the Word became a human person so that the human person may become divine." God was so "foolish" as to utterly empty Himself (*ekenosen eauton*, Phil 2:7) and become one of us, one with us, God Emmanuel. There are no conditions to this love. Creation will never be the same again, as every molecule and electron of created existence has been touched profoundly by the Incarnation. The living God of love freely initiated this inexpressibly unique and astounding action in order to restore our broken relationship with Him and with all creation due to human sin and fallenness.

With this in mind, it is absolutely not because of religious or ethical obligation that our Lord offers us His greatest commandment: "You shall love the Lord your God with all your heart, with all your soul, with all your mind, and with all your strength . . . You shall love your neighbor as yourself" (Mark 12:30–31). His reason for giving us this prime directive is far more personal, or more accurately, inter-personal! In order for us, as individual persons and as members of the Church, to take up our abode in eternal communion with this divine "fool," *we too are called to imitate Him*. In a very real sense, we too must become fools. Humility and feeling foolish are very often deeply interrelated.

Unwelcomed Hospitality

Any outreach toward the "other"—whether it be a personal expression of recognition and connection or one conducted through a group of persons, or even one initiated through ecclesial expressions of outreach—has in common a real risk of making "fools" of ourselves. Any conscious gestures of outreach or hospitality toward persons who were previously considered "strangers" challenge our fallen human frozen concepts of the *status quo*, usually resulting in some kind of separation. Gestures of recognition, and hence of at least rudimentary hospitality toward estranged brothers and/or sisters, are typically treated as "foolish" by at least some persons, at first.

Surely, most of us have experienced gestures of "hospitality" that have left us cold. Perhaps the contact felt superficial or insincere. In some instances, maybe there was no sense of warmth, connection, or freedom in the encounter. Sometimes we can tell that there is clearly no genuine interest in acknowledging the other who does not fit into our preferred niche of persons. This is especially difficult whenever we happen to be the one on the receiving end of this kind of cool, perfunctory "reception." People can often sense when they are devalued and not really wanted, or when they actually may be more of an inconvenience than a welcomed guest or newly discovered loved one.

Still, many of us may have unconsciously conducted such unkind transgressions at one time or another. There are numerous reasons why this may happen. Many times, these reasons may be fairly benign. We may be distracted or diminished for reasons of health or a human crisis that somehow temporarily disables our usual abilities to connect and "see" the other person. Other times, and for various reasons, the "other" makes us feel uncomfortable. These uncomfortable situations often prove to be opportunities for growth. By thoughtfully exploring the various possible reasons that underlie our personal discomfort, we may come face-to-face with some aspect of our own unresolved doubts from the past, our brokenness, sinfulness, and/or hardness of heart. This may have much or little to do with the stranger before us. This added discipline of asking ourselves in the presence of the loving God, "Why do I feel this way?" may offer us new insights into how we may improve our efforts of reaching out to others.

Because of this self-evaluative process, we can learn more about what may impede or assist our side of the dynamic when seeking renewed and more authentic relationships. In assisting us with this self-examination, we would do well to remember the ancient adage made famous by Saint Maximos the Confessor: "Nothing has caused divisions in the Church more than the fact that we do not love one another."[5] It is the very same astounding human failing of lack of love that has kept us from one another *and* from experiencing the embrace of the divine Fool, the ineffable "Other," the Three-in-One who longingly waits to welcome us into the very depths of His life.

Seeking Sustenance

Truly, many Christians think that they desire to love God and others. Perhaps they do. Cultivating this desire, however, is much, much harder than it seems, as "it is a fearful thing to fall into the hands of the living God" (Heb 10:31). By our striving to befriend God, we risk the end of life as we know it. There are no certainties on this path. This is because, as we seek out the beloved divine Fool who fashioned us, we realize once again that we are not the ones who define who we are. Still, we are finite. We are sinners. Despite our best efforts, we are grossly undeserving. Even so, we strive to wait with extreme perseverance, with extreme sacrificial patience (*en ypomone*). Not unlike the five wise virgins (see Matt 25:1–13) who waited through the long, long dark night for their Bridegroom, we too wait a seemingly impossibly long wait: alert, hands raised, open, and outstretched, offering up all that we are through our finite limitations as cherished sons and daughters of the loving Most High God, humbly seeking to receive what God desires so much to give us, the unending gift of the divine Other, His very Self.

In some ways, in seeking God we are not unlike little hatchlings waiting eagerly in the nest, mouths open, tiny wings fluttering, stretching out to receive the nourishment of their lives. They wait with desperation for their mother, who offers them their very sustenance. The mother bird's unconditional "hospitality" is a matter of life and death for her little hatchlings. Such is the offering of God's "sustenance" toward us. This is a God whose hospitality offers us His very Self. For all humankind, this is, likewise, a matter of life and death, of life in abundance or spiritual death (cf. Matt 10:39).

This lifelong humble effort of consciously turning ever toward the living God of love is a universe away from assumptions that are very popular today among many, such as "this is what I am, take it or leave it" or "nothing personal, it's only business" or even "we have to wait for the 'fallen' culture to change." These hardened declarations depict a virtual independence from the love of the living God and encapsulate in their own manner the essence of the fatal sin of pride, that is, the desire to be god without God.

By pursuing instead the "narrow path" (Matt 7:13), we willingly risk our very selves, as we surrender consciously the very core of our finite, personal conceptions of our identity into the hands of the One who created us. Clearly, we are not in charge of this journey! For many of us, this effort may sometimes feel like an indescribably sweet, yet terminally loving, sacrifice, but at other times like a pulverization or crucifixion.

Nevertheless, the reward is infinitely greater than the relatively small personal price paid. This is where we engage the journey harnessed by the "sweet yoke" (cf. Matt 11:30). This is the path that leads to joyful "life in abundance" (John 10:10) as we discover the personal vocation to which each of us has been called. This call is reflected in the ancient guidance offered by St. Gregory of Sinai, who seven centuries ago instructed Christians to seek the Other who is already waiting for us in our depths:

Become what you already are,
Find him who is already yours,
Listen to him who never ceases speaking to you,
Possess him who already possesses you.[6]

The Cross of Hospitality

More political changes, as well as social, economic, and environmental upheavals, have occurred during this young century than could have before been imagined by this generation. We must bear faithfully in mind that despite human sin and limitation, the living Triune God rises to every occasion, in His way and time. God is not bound by human timetables, demands, and objectives. Nothing, not a single thing, escapes the attention of the God of love. It is we human beings who fail both God and one another miserably.

Even as we begin sincerely to reach out to the estranged "other," new difficulties seem to arise simultaneously. To our surprise, at some point in the journey of reaching out we may receive the "blessing" of coming face-to-face with the depths of our own deepest fears, limitations, attachments, sin, and hard-heartedness. We find that we may be afraid to acknowledge certain aspects of ourselves, even to our own selves. Acknowledged or not, these still impede our growth toward God and one another. We may become deathly afraid of forever losing cherished assumptions that are deeply and comfortably familiar to *us*. This course leads to more exquisitely experiencing our personal finiteness. Inexplicably, through the effort of reaching out to the "foreign" O/other, we also encounter ourselves anew. Our journey leads us somewhere we have never been before. Easily forgetting how we each have our own unrepeatable path, we enter these dark and unknown places in which we see no one else; worse yet, we "feel" that no one else is there, and this awareness of isolation is unbearable. And so, in our creaturely uncertainty, we so easily forget that we are not alone. What could be waiting for us just beyond our reach in this darkness? Are our wavering human hearts truly ready and able to bear this "cross" of hospitality?

Relying on "the Foolishness of God"

A healthy response to this question can only come from God. Nevertheless, this question is also an invitation to each one of us to summon—to the best of our ability—the courage to surrender impediments that compromise our progress. We can be sure that, as we strive to respond in this manner, life will sometimes present us with unexpected opportunities that invite us to discern. These opportunities no doubt will include taking uncomfortable risks. Many of these risks may be imperceptivity small, and some great. They may include personal change, increased vulnerability, exposure, loss, and appearing irresponsible or even reckless to friends, family, and the powers that be. Sometimes these risks have enduring consequences. The witness of St. Paul encourages us regarding the ways of God for our lives. He reminds us, "the foolishness of God is wiser than human wisdom, and the weakness of God is stronger than human strength" (1 Cor 1:25).

Pursuing this direction will at some point bring us to decisions and courses of action that will defy conventional wisdom, causing us to appear foolish. Such is the case with the ways of God. "Where is the wise? Where is the scribe? Where is the debater of this age? Has not God made foolish the wisdom of this world?" (1 Cor 1:20). Authentic Christian hospitality is a discipline and virtue possible only for such "fools." The Great Fool, our divine Beloved, even now begs us to imitate and follow Him.

All of us are invited to prepare our own hearts and lives, knowing that we may be taking on foolishness itself. New commitments may be discerned that cause us to reach out and receive the Other through newly found gestures of welcome and hospitality. By so doing, we prepare to receive the divine Great Fool, who is also the Author of Life. For this miracle to occur, our previous personal conventions will no longer be adequate.

The ongoing, daily choices confronting each one of us vis-à-vis hospitality are countless and uniquely personal. Nevertheless, every one of these choices somehow may also impact the entire creation. It matters what each one of us does with our choices of reaching out, from the depths of our hearts outward, to "our" ksenos, our alien brothers and sisters, and this affects others, perhaps even "everyone" in some mysterious manner. At this point it may help us to recall the teaching of St. Benedict that was related earlier: "All humility should be shown in addressing a guest . . . Christ is to be adored [in guests] because He is indeed welcomed in them."[7]

Who are the alien strangers seeking refuge under our tents or seeking to share a meal with us at our table, or merely asking to know the time of day? Largely through the discipline and virtue of hospitality, we Christians are obliged to remain open to see who the Lord would have us engage in loving encounter. This is no easy task. There are going to be consequences for each of our active choices. There will also be consequences when we choose a passive lack of response through the various domains of our existence, including our personal lives, our lives within the Church, our lives in our families, and our lives in society. It is here where we must listen, understand, and thoughtfully respond to the "signs of the times" (Matt 16:3) as identified by the Lord. These various domains of human interaction in the presence of God truly offer us unforeseen opportunities, responsibilities, and challenges for encountering the O/other.

An Inhospitable Response

A number of years ago, in a report that is recorded in *Orthodox Women Speak: Discerning the "Signs of the Times,"*[8] the participants at the October 1996 international Orthodox women's conference in Damascus, Syria, made a remarkable announcement. This related to how easy it is for women who are striving to serve faithfully within the life of the Church could be made so readily "dispensable."[9] There was a sudden electrifying moment of silence in the room, as if a collective scab was ripped off a tender wound, and every one of the sixty-plus women in the conference hall gasped simultaneously in surprise and pain. I will never forget that moment . . . and praise God for the sister who was a native from one of the Orthodox "homelands" (and was also the wife of an Orthodox priest) who courageously declared this.

The women invited to serve as delegates at this event were sent by their respective hierarchs. They were not self-selected. As they were chosen by their bishops, we can safely assume that their fidelity to the faith and to their bishops was unquestioned. It strikes me in an incredulous manner—yes, even today—how the first concern for hospitality declared by St. Benedict, "All humility should be shown in addressing a guest," has not been adequately demonstrated in response to their collective stated concerns. Discussions requesting that the leadership in various Local Churches welcome women more fully in such active ministries as education, pastoral care, theological education, interfaith discourse, ministry to clergy families, as well as the possibility of rejuvenating the ministry of women ordained to the diaconate in those places where this may be needed, were some of the compelling, important issues identified by the group that have not been given the attention they deserve. If "Christ is to be adored because He is indeed welcomed in them," why is it that we have largely ignored Christ as seen through the participants' straightforward and sincerely expressed statements? This is perplexing and disconcerting.

Hope and Hospitable Dialogue

Perhaps in a way that expands on St. Benedict's teaching that "all humility should be shown in addressing a guest," His All-Holiness Ecumenical Patriarch Bartholomew offers an important teaching that delves more deeply into this matter. He states,

> We hear it stated often that our world is in crisis. Yet, never before in history have human beings had the opportunity to bring so many positive changes to so many people simply through encounter and dialogue . . . Accordingly, then, we do not approach dialogue in order to set our arguments against those of our opponents in the framework of conflict. We approach in a spirit of love, sincerity and honesty. In this respect, dialogue implies equality, which in turn implies humility. Honesty and humility dispel hostility and arrogance. Just how prepared are we in dialogue to respect others in dialogue? How willing are we to learn and to love? If we are neither prepared to receive nor willing to learn, then are we truly engaging in dialogue? Or are we actually conducting a monologue?[10]

In a manner that expounds on St. Benedict's "Christ is to be adored because He is indeed welcomed in them," our prayer is that this principle includes dialoguing with sincere Orthodox Christian women who are constructively engaged in the affairs of the Church and who may also echo the concerns voiced in Damascus and elsewhere. With the help of God, it is important to develop our discerning abilities in order to perceive these and other persons who may easily be marginalized and rendered dispensable, and instead reach out and come to know them through authentic dialogue. Ecumenical Patriarch Bartholomew continues this teaching by stressing,

> True dialogue is in fact a gift from God. According to St. John Chrysostom, fourth-century Archbishop of Constantinople, God is always in personal dialogue with human beings. God always speaks: through Prophets and Apostles, through saints and mystics, even through the natural creation itself;

> for, "the heavens declare the glory of God" (Psalm 19.1). Dialogue is the most fundamental experience of life and most powerful means of communication. Dialogue promotes knowledge, abolishes fears and prejudice, and broadens horizons. Dialogue enriches; whoever refuses dialogue remains impoverished. Finally, dialogue seeks persuasion, not coercion.[11]

He may be offering a foundational methodology that may assist us through our various difficult encounters:

> We would not be so naïve as to claim that dialogue comes without cost or danger. Approaching another person—or another belief, another culture—always comes with a risk. One is never certain what to expect: Will the other suspect me? Will the other perceive me as imposing my own belief or way of life? Will I compromise—or perhaps lose—what belongs uniquely to my tradition? What is the common ground on which we can converse? What, if any, will be the fruitful results of any dialogue? These questions plague the mind when we approach for dialogue. Yet, we are convinced that, in the moment when one surrenders one's mind and heart to the possibility of dialogue, something sacred happens. In the very willingness to embrace the other, beyond any fear or prejudice, a mystical spark is kindled and the reality of something—or Someone—far greater than us takes over. Then, we recognize how the benefits of dialogue far outweigh the risks.[12]

A Vocation of Foolishness, A Merciful and Open Heart

With divine assistance, we each can summon the courage to foster this eternally new walk with *the* Someone: the Lord, Jesus Christ. Perhaps a unique characteristic, quite absurd to the conventional world, that this journey will cultivate within us will be a merciful heart. A truly merciful and open heart makes no sense and perhaps even defies the fallen human *status quo*, because it expresses love from within the very heart of God. To our indescribable surprise, through the pleasure of the living God, the human heart now contains the uncontainable, where the love of God, others, and even all of creation itself has found the space and place to dwell and dine through living encounter.

Writing in the fourth century, St. Gregory of Nyssa reminds Christians of this amazing assertion. Through the wisdom and folly of God, our very hearts are able to contain Him. Our very beings are created to be hospitable to God. Although this may not always be so easy, His directive is uncomplicated. We need only "look to Him." St. Gregory writes,

> Realize how much your Creator has honored you above all creatures. He did not make the heavens in His image, nor the moon, the sun, the beauty of the stars or anything else which surpasses understanding. You alone are a reflection of eternal beauty, a receptacle of happiness, an image of the true light. And, if you look to Him, you will become what He is, imitating Him who shines within you, whose glory is reflected in your purity. Nothing in the entire creation can equal your grandeur. All the heavens can fit into the palm of the hand of God . . . Although He is so great that He can hold all creation in His palm, you can wholly embrace Him. He dwells within you.[13]

Even with our very best efforts, this amazing gift will not take place as a result of our own doing, but rather through the divine intervention of the Beloved Fool Himself, by the action of the Holy Spirit. Writing also about the merciful and "without measure" open heart, St. Isaac the Syrian of Nineveh in the seventh century teaches:

> And what is a merciful heart? The burning of the heart on account of all creation, on account of people and birds and animals and demons, and for every created being. Because of their remembrance, the eyes fill with tears. Great and intense mercy grasps the heart and wings it out, for the person who is merciful is not able to bear or hear or see any harm, or the slightest sorrow taking place in the created world. This holds true on behalf of those who harm him. For these, the person offers prayers continually with tears for their protection and redemption. He does so even for the snakes that crawl upon the ground. All of this the person does out of his great mercy, which moves in his heart without measure in the likeness of God.[14]

Through the gracious activity of the Holy Spirit, we are called today in our daily personal journey to seek Christ, our Ultimate Stanger, in every relationship and through every aspect of life. By pursuing this path, we too may find that it not only leads us to Christ, but also to one another, male and female human persons created "in the image" of God (Gen 1:26). In regard to this gift of ultimate encounter, we can learn much from the fourteenth-century teaching of St. Nicholas Cabasilas, who reminds us to seek Christ first in everything we do. He writes,

> Christ gives to human persons life and growth, nourishment and light and breath. He opens their eyes and gives them light and the power to see. He gives to human persons the bread of life, and this bread is nothing else than Himself. He is life for those who are living and a sweet scent for those who breathe. He clothes those who desire to be clothed. He strengthens the traveler, and He is the way. He is at once both the inn along the road and the destination of the journey . . . When we struggle, He struggles at our side. When we argue, He is the reconciler. And when we win the victory, He is the prize.[15]

Making room for the stranger who could be God changes everything . . .

Notes

1. St. Benedict, *Rules* 53.1, 15.
2. Ibid., 53.6–7.
3. St. Basil, *The Great Rules* 42.
4. St. Maximos the Confessor, *Mystagogia* 24.
5. St. Maximos the Confessor, cited in John Moschus and Sophronius, *Pratum Spirituale* [Spiritual Meadow], PG 87:2925.
6. St. Gregory of Sinai, cited in Archbishop Paul of Finland, *The Faith We Hold* (Crestwood, NY: St. Vladimir's Seminary Press, 1980), 96.
7. St. Benedict, *Rules* 53.6–7.
8. *Orthodox Women Speak: Discerning the "Signs of the Times,"* ed. Kyriaki Karidoyanes FitzGerald (Geneva: WCC Publications; Brookline, MA: Holy Cross Orthodox Press, 1999), 21–26.
9. Ibid., 23.
10. Ecumenical Patriarch Bartholomew, "The Imperative of Inter-Religious Dialogue in the Modern World," August 20, 2010, Luben, Poland.
11. Ibid.
12. Ibid.
13. St. Gregory of Nyssa, *On the Song of Songs* 2.
14. St. Isaac the Syrian, *Concerning the Distinction of Virtues* 91.
15. St. Nicholas Cabasilas, *The Life in Christ* 1.4, adapted.

Chapter 6

"TURNING TOWARD" AS A PASTORAL THEOLOGY OF MARRIAGE

Dr. Philip Mamalakis
Assistant Professor of Pastoral Care

M uch has been written about the Orthodox theology of marriage, its historical developments, its ecclesial dimensions, its
ceremony and symbolism, and its eternal implications.[1] Much less
has been written for pastors charged with guiding couples through
the inevitable challenges and irreconcilable differences that occur in
marriage. The intent of this paper is to offer an Orthodox theology
of marriage useful for pastors guiding couples along the path of marriage. A pastoral theology of marriage serves to provide a theological
framework for understanding the sacrament of married life and how
it is that couples form "themselves by God's grace in the likeness
of Christ."[2]

A young couple in their thirties, married for ten years with three
children, whom we will call John and Becky, met with me because they
could no longer endure the constant conflict between them. He was
a successful businessman and she a stay at home mom with a college
degree. They reported that they were stuck and all attempts to communicate ended in conflict. They fought about everything and felt very
disconnected. In the first few sessions it was clear, as they exchanged
sarcastic comments, that they had grown apart as the stresses of running a household and raising children entered their marriage. They
married because they enjoyed each other's company, playing tennis
and skiing, but over the course of their marriage, according to their
reports, they clashed over a number of issues and struggled with the
personal weaknesses that they discovered in each other. They accused
each other: he worked too much, could never relax, and turned the

kids against her. She was disorganized, lazy, and unable to keep the household on schedule and clean. They exchanged criticism and complaints interspersed with insults and judgments yet reported that, with three kids and a mortgage, and hopes of building a summer home, divorce was not an option. They were stuck, and they listed all the issues on which they had reached an impasse, including parenting, planning vacations, scheduling the day, and finances.

In the most extreme pastoral cases, a spouse will approach a pastor to report that the other spouse has emotionally or physically "checked out" of the marriage either through work or recreation or, more critically, pornography, infidelity, or addiction. In the best cases, both partners are involved in the Church or the pastor has a relationship with the prodigal spouse. More typically, the pastor is restricted to working with only one spouse, most often the wife. In these dramatic cases, often the only perceivable options are staying in a "dead" marriage or divorcing. Understanding the theology of the Church of marriage as sacrament or as a theophany provides little guidance to the pastor charged with guiding the spouse. Espousing the sanctity of marriage rings hollow to the lonely, abandoned wife, who faces not only the death of her marriage, but also the death of the hopes and expectations about marriage that she had on her wedding day.[3]

The Spiritual Life and How to Be Married in It

Our theology of marriage provides the starting point for a discussion. "As a sacrament, marriage is a direct revelation of the kingdom of God in two specific persons."[4] "When husband and wife are united in marriage, they form an image of no earthly reality, but of God himself."[5] Marriage is sustained by the Holy Spirit, and is a vehicle of the Holy Spirit. It is transfiguring. "According to faith, marriage in Christ raises man and wife to share in the divine nature."[6] And the divine nature, we know, is love (1 John 4:16). "He who possesses love possesses god Himself, for God is Love."[7]

"The way of life and love of two people is sustained and perfected in their oneness with God's love."[8] It is not so much that divine love is imposed on human love, as it is that human love is transformed in union with divine love. Marriage transfigures "human love into a new reality of heavenly origin."[9] Divine love sustains marriage by transforming the person of husband and wife in divine love and with divine love. Marriage, then, is a journey of love.[10]

The end result is that through the mystery of marriage we come to love in a divine way such that, to paraphrase Galatians 2:20, it is no longer I who loves my wife, but Christ who loves in me. More specifically, marriage is a journey of acquiring perfect love, of becoming perfect love toward our spouse. "The couple's gift of self to each other is to come to love in a divine way."[11]

That perfection is not simply an outward perfection of a couple who never fights, but an essential transformation of the persons of the husband and wife who participate through grace in the divine nature of God (cf. 2 Pet 1:3–4). St. John Chrysostom says, "If you ask Him, He will work an even greater miracle than He worked in Cana: That is, He will transform the water of your unstable passions into the wine of spiritual unity."[12] Yet, in my marriage, I still love my wife imperfectly. And, more noticeably at times, she loves me imperfectly. We know that this is because "only the perfect person, with a perfect conscience, a perfect mind, and perfect power can have perfect love. Such a person is our God."[13] Within the sacrament of marriage, my spiritual journey of acquiring perfect love intersects with her journey. The daily struggles of marriage are situated within this call to acquire perfect love (cf. Matt 5:48).

This journey of acquiring perfect love for our spouse is a journey toward the Kingdom of God, a journey that we can say with certainty is far from free of struggles, because the Kingdom of God suffers violence and the violent take it by force (Matt 11:12). However, the distinct nature of the struggle is not against our spouse, but against the flesh (cf. Gal 5:13–25). It is not that there are struggles along the path of marriage, but that the struggles are the path of marriage.

For the Orthodox, Christ is the celebrant of wedding ceremony, and it is Christ who is at the heart of marriage. "In fact, this wedding is the wedding of the spouses to Christ."[14] In and through marriage, each person is wedded to Christ, in and through their union with each other. "I am married, then, means that I enslave my heart to Christ . . . I am the slave of Christ."[15] We find our fulfillment as husbands and wives as we are united with Christ and perfected in Christ.

We live out the sacramental life of the Church in our daily lives of marriage as we live out our vocation to love our spouse as unto the Lord. "Love her, not so much for her sake, but for Christ's sake. That is why he [St. Paul] says, 'be subject . . . as to the Lord.'"[16] "Do everything for the Lord's sake, in a spirit of obedience to Him."[17] Within the sacrament of marriage, our love for God is expressed through our love for our spouse, and our love for our spouse witnesses to our love for God. Marital struggles are, specifically, the struggle to love our spouse as unto the Lord (Eph 5:20–22).

It is also in this sense that we can say that marriage is not an end in and of itself. The goal of the Christian life is not to remain married, for that might be outside our control, but to be united with God, perfected in love, and to inherit of the Kingdom of God. To sustain a marriage requires that two persons choose to engage each other. Each one is free to turn away from the other and from Christ, most dramatically through infidelity or abuse. The victim of this is not, in any way, obstructed on the path of salvation, even if the marriage ends.

This divine vocation to love our spouse as unto the Lord serves as the orientation of marriage. It is by loving Christ first and foremost that we understand how to love our spouse. This love for Christ is lived out, and expressed, daily through the prosaic, ostensibly insignificant events of married life.

"Turning Toward" in Marriage

To look more specifically at the sacramental nature of married life, I turn to the work of Dr. John Gottman, one of the foremost marital researchers in the United States. He discovered that, contrary to conventional wisdom, happily married couples had as many pervasive problems as distressed couples and did not maintain their connection through deep, heart-to-heart talks. Rather, healthy couples nurtured intimacy in their relationship through the small, simple exchanges that occur throughout the day, such as: "When are you coming home?" "Don't forget to take out the trash." "Demetri is sick?" "Can you pick up milk on the way home?"

He discovered that these small exchanges were, in fact, bids for connection that spouses make to each other. "A bid can be a question, a gesture, a look, a touch, any single expression that says, 'I want to feel connected to you.' "[18] He considers bids for connection "the fundamental unit of emotional communication."[19] He submits that we make bids to each other out of our natural desire to connect, to be in relationships with people. At the heart of the marital union are these hundreds of small bids for connection between couples.[20]

"Turning toward" includes making eye contact, simple nods, attending, listening, and engaging responses, which communicate care, respect, and love. Turning toward communicates, "I hear you," "I am interested in you," "I am on your side," "I accept you," "I'd like to be with you." The daily communicating in marriage, as bids for connection, are not just about sharing information, but about nurturing connection and intimacy.[21]

Often in couples counseling, when I suggest to a husband that he ask his wife what she is feeling, he will tell me that he already knows how his wife is feeling, so why should he ask? I remind him that we ask her how she is doing to express care and concern, to connect, rather than to get information. When a wife is struggling with something, she turns to her husband to connect, rather than to be told what to do. The loving response is not to solve the problem, but to be present and attentive, and to listen. The nature of sharing and listening is that it is a turning toward, and as such, expresses care and love.

"Turning away" refers to the distracted, preoccupied, disregarding, or interrupting responses, which, although not as destructive as turning against, communicate a lack of interest. Turning away communicates, "I don't care about your bid," "I want to avoid you," "I am not really interested in you," "I've got more important things on my mind," "I'm too busy to pay attention to you." We have all experienced this turning away when talking to someone who is watching television or checking his or her cell phone. Although it is not a turning against, it is certainly not a turning toward.

"Turning against" bids for connection are contemptuous putdowns, and belligerent, combative, contradictory, domineering, critical, defensive, angry, or blaming responses. These hostile and aggressive reactions are the most damaging to relationships and communicate disdain, disrespect, and hatred. They communicate, "Your need for attention makes me angry," "I don't respect you," "I don't value you or this relationship," "I want to hurt you," "I want to drive you away," and even, "I hate you."

Spouses are tempted to turn against each other when they are angry, overwhelmed, stressed, hurt, hungry, or tired. Spouses are deceived into believing that they are too tired, too hurt, or too angry to turn toward each other, so they turn against with comments such as: "I don't have time now!" "You're lazy." "Why can't you help?" "You don't care!" "Can't you see I'm busy!" Although feeling overwhelmed or angry are common experiences in marriage, in those moments love demands that in our anger, we turn toward, not against, our spouse (Eph 4:26).

Other times, a spouse might feel that he or she does not have the time to turn toward. Yet, it takes as much time to turn toward, with a statement like "I'm too angry to talk now" as it does to turn against, with a statement like "Get out of here!"

At the heart of marriage, Dr. Gottman discovered, are the seemingly mundane interactions of daily life through which couples grow in intimacy and closeness as they turn toward each other. Far from being insignificant, these interactions are the context for building oneness, expressing love, and growing in love. In his research Dr. Gottman found that couples who turn toward each other most demonstrated the greatest capacity for affection when difficult issues arose in their marriages. Couples who turned away, or against, each other most often seemed to disconnect and experienced greater difficulty in working through major challenges.[22]

Turning Toward as a Theology of Marriage

"The beginning of the spiritual life is conversion (ἐπιστροφή), an attitude of the will turning toward God and renouncing the world."[23]

At the heart of marriage is turning toward one another, without ceasing, as unto the Lord. Paul Evdokimov notes that the biblical term for Eve, *Ezer Ke-negdo*, means "a helper turned toward him" (Gen 2:18).[24] The Latin root of the word "divorce" means "to turn apart" (*divertere*).[25]

Every moment, every exchange, within married life becomes a decisive moment for God to act (καιρός). "In marriage, the Holy Spirit unites the present with the future, as well as every moment of our lives with eternity."[26] It is when couples turn toward each other each moment that their life rises up like a royal doxology, like an unending liturgical chant. In this sense, "marriage is a mysterious icon of the Church."[27]

Turning toward Christ in marriage goes beyond listening to one another and is at the heart of our life in Christ. "Unless you turn (στραφῆτε) and become as children you cannot enter the kingdom of God" (Matt 18:3). For a Christian marriage, turning toward Christ is a self-offering to spouse and Christ. It is an act of openness, an act of opening the heart to Christ, an act of prayer. Turning toward is a self-giving and an act of love. "Love is more than warm feelings. It is an attitude and a disposition of illuminated self-giving."[28] Yet, that self that I have to offer is often angry, frustrated, hurt, or overwhelmed—broken—and spouses, at times, cannot, or do not want to, turn toward the other.

Turning Toward and the Way of the Cross in Married Life

The invitation to acquire perfect love for my spouse, to turn toward my spouse as unto the Lord, without ceasing, is an invitation to do the impossible. The impossible nature of the marriage vocation creates a tension within each of us between our call to love and the inevitable feelings of disappointment, betrayal, rejection, and pain that we experience in marriage. This tension within us is the cross of Christ. The cross of Christ in marriage is not our spouse or our unmet needs, but this tension between our vocation to love and our painful experience. This tension is not a problem to be solved but a mystery to be encountered and lived.

The goal of marriage is not to change our spouse to meet our needs, but to allow the Holy Spirit to change us as we live and love in that tension, as we turn toward Christ and our spouse in the face of disappointments and unmet needs. The way of the cross is the way of life. Marriage is a journey of turning toward Christ within this tension, rather than away or against. We cannot escape the cross of Christ. Rather, by walking the way of the cross, we encounter Christ. When we are crucified with Christ, daily, we rise with Christ. We know that through the cross joy comes to all the world, including our marriages.

To turn toward in this tension is to offer my self—including my sins, my struggles, my pain, my disappointments, my illnesses of my soul, and my brokenness—to Christ and my spouse. Rather than turning against my spouse by reacting out of my brokenness, marriage is a journey of learning how to turn toward our spouse as unto the Lord in our brokenness. To turn toward, in this tension, is to acknowledge or confess (ὁμολογῶ) what is on my heart to Christ and to my spouse with statements such as: "I'm too angry to talk now." "I don't like what you're doing." "It hurts me when you talk like that." "I'm afraid to tell you what I'm really feeling."

No matter how worn down we find ourselves in marriage, we have a choice, even in our exhaustion, to fall away or to fall toward Christ. "Is not repentance [turning toward] only a fall into the hands of God and at his feet in a fainting of the will, with a wounded heart bleeding in regret, members being shattered by sin having no power to rise except by God's mercy?"[29]

Confessing, as a turning toward, is not simply about sharing information, but bidding for connection with God and spouse, which nurtures intimacy and oneness. Paradoxically, confessing my brokenness (turning toward), rather than acting out of my brokenness (turning against) communicates, "I care about you," "You are important to me," "I love you." In and through acknowledging or confessing our brokenness to each other daily (cf. Jas 5:16), rather than acting out of our brokenness, we open our hearts to God's healing Spirit. In that confession we encounter Christ and His Holy Spirit. Turning toward one's spouse is our assent to Christ, the assent of the soul to receive the Holy Spirit in order to be healed, to be transformed.

Marriage as a journey of love becomes a journey of discovery, discovering the person of the spouse and discovering myself, becoming increasingly aware of my brokenness in the context of turning toward my wife in her brokenness. This can be a frightening endeavor, or, in the context of Christ's unfailing love, a journey of transformation. St. Dionysios the Areopagite writes that God is always "imparting Himself with unbending power for deification of those turned toward Him."[30]

The differences of opinion and personalities, the stresses of life, and the disagreements within married life create tension between husband and wife. Couples are tempted to avoid that tension or to blame each other, and pastors are tempted to view that tension as negative or as a problem to be solved. However, this tension is, at another level, the same cross of marriage. It is not a problem to be solved, but a mystery to be lived. In that tension we are called to turn toward, to confess to, our spouse and to Christ. It is precisely in that tension where we, as spouses, encounter Christ. In that tension we are crucified with Christ and we rise with Christ. The journey of marriage is the way of the cross, and in that tension we turn toward Christ through prayer, confession, and repentance. "It is indispensable for every Christian to acquire the habit of turning quickly to God in prayer about everything."[31]

By the third meeting with John and Becky, I shifted the conversation from blame and criticism of the other to confession their own disappointment and pain, inviting them to face the tension that existed within themselves and between them. By blocking the turning against of insults and sarcasm, each one was invited to confess, to share, their feelings of hurt and betrayal. As the conversation shifted to a mutual confession, John gathered the courage to confess that he no longer loved Becky. Her quiet tears validated the fear that John had of hurting her, a fear that had kept him from acknowledging his own tension. She immediately confessed (turned toward him) that she already knew that, and it was better to hear it. In that mutual confession something occurred. They connected for the first time in years. This connection nurtured a sense of intimacy and closeness reminiscent of their early years together.

Keeping the conversations focused on continuing to turn toward each other, they gently shared more of themselves around several of the issues that they had been unable to resolve. We stayed in that tension between them, keeping the conversations focused on turning toward each other. In that tension they chose to confess rather than attack, to love rather than hate, and to turn toward, rather than away from or against, each other. Together, in that tension, they met Christ. They encountered each other, and they left feeling closer. I did not solve any problems, but guided them in the mystery of the cross of marriage, turning toward each other in that creative tension that is the path of intimacy, oneness, and healing. John reported that he never liked coming to my office, but it always made him feel better, and now he feels closer to his wife, able to work together on the challenges in front of them. Today they remain happily married.

To turn toward Christ demands meekness, but at times it means to stand up to or against our spouse's sinful or destructive behavior. Turning toward Christ serves to guide persons in dealing with abuse, infidelity, and addiction that occurs in marriage. Rather than passively acquiescing to sinful conduct, or criticizing or attacking our spouse, to turn toward is to speak up, or to take action, and to set limits to sinful conduct within marriage. "I do not support your pornography use." "I will not participate in that." "If you raise your voice I will leave." "I am not OK with secret cell phones or e-mail accounts." Saying no to sin is a turning toward Christ. Turning toward Christ might mean leaving the home in the face of violence and abuse of any kind. It might mean leaving the marriage when our spouse insists on turning against Christ without ceasing. The goal of married life is not to stay married, but to turn toward Christ without ceasing. St. John Chrysostom contends that it is better to break up a marriage for righteousness' sake than to suffer abuse. "The unbelieving spouse, in these cases, is as much to blame for the separation as the partner guilty of infidelity."[32] Turning toward Christ means seeking pastoral and professional help when we witness our spouse become ensnared in sin or when we, ourselves, become ensnared in sin.

Marital spirituality as it is lived out becomes a constant journey of re-turning toward Christ by re-turning toward the spouse. "Of the many things that impede our salvation the greatest of all is that when we commit any transgression we do not at once turn back to God and ask forgiveness."[33] Re-turning toward is the realization, the acknowledgment, that we have turned away and against Christ and our spouse. Marriage is a journey of re-turning, like the prodigal, to our home and our Father's love. The sacrament of confession finds its place in the heart of the marital journey. As Orthodox we approach confession therapeutically. We don't confess to God to give Him information, but we confess as a turning toward God, opening ourselves up to the healing that comes from His ceaseless bids for connection. Confessing is our response to the tension that exists within us and between spouses, and our participation in the sacramental life of union with God. "The word penitence does not properly express the idea of this fundamental attitude of every Christian soul which turns to God."[34]

In this sense, couples who seek to re-turn toward, daily, in the sacrament of married life "become the image [not] of anything on earth, but of God himself."[35] "When you see a couple who are conscious of this, it is as if you are seeing Christ. Together they are a theophany."[36]

The Role of the Priest

A full understanding of the role of the priest in helping couples walk in the tension of marriage cannot be summarized in a few paragraphs, nor can it be reduced to a series of steps to follow. Essentially, the role of the priest is to hold couples in their tension by blocking the turning away and against that frequently accompanies marital conflict and by facilitating a mutual turning toward Christ and each other. The pastor must, initially, prohibit attacks and criticism and invite the turning toward of sharing personal hurt and pain. This requires that the pastor resist, in himself, the temptation to try to solve problems, and instead focus on listening to struggles. Attempts to solve the complex and intractable problems of marriage usually fail and lead to feelings of frustration, confusion, and failure in the pastor and the couple.

A pastor must understand that the tension within, and between, the husband and wife are not problems to solve, but the cross of Christ. This is the crowning of husband and wife as king/queen and martyr that they receive on their wedding day. Couples need to be taught and encouraged that the cross cannot be avoided and is not a problem to be solved, but the path to intimacy and happiness. Pastors need to guide couples to turn toward Christ and each other in that tension as the way of the cross.

Holding individuals and couples in the tension requires that a pastor have the strength and wisdom to love the couple in his own tension between the desire to solve a couple's problems and the call to listen to people's pain and suffering. This tension in the pastor represents the cross of pastoral care. The greater a pastor's ability to listen in the face of the temptation to solve problems, the more he will be able to help couples live in their tension and experience God's healing grace.

Pastors must resist the temptation to solve the problem, because the problem of marriage is the cross of Christ, which has no solution. Rather, it is the solution. In that tension he must invite each person to confess, to acknowledge their burdens, their struggles, their pain, and their mistakes to the pastor and to the listening spouse. The pastor gives each person the opportunity to confess, and in hearing those confessions, he points to the path of love. He cuts off, or redirects, any blame, attacks, judgments, or turning against that he witnesses, and facilitates a mutual process of turning toward each other. The pastor eases their burdens through listening, and guides them toward repentance, teaching each of the spouses how to listen, silently, as an act of venerating the icon of Christ in the other.

The challenge for pastoral care is to meet couples on this path, keeping the vision of marriage clear, and to guide couples not to endure the struggles, but to be transformed and healed in the midst of the struggles. God did not create marriage that we might endure it, but that we might have eternal life. After a pastor has heard the struggles of each individual, he must guide the persons to understanding how to turn toward Christ and spouse. This requires the wisdom to understand that at times turning toward Christ means setting limits to sinful behavior and standing up to a spouse, and at other times it means patiently enduring a spouse who goes through a struggle. It is the role of the pastor or pastoral counselor to hold a person in the tension and discern what constitutes a turning toward Christ. In that tension we turn toward Christ in prayer and turn toward the spouse in love.

On one level, this does not necessarily solve the problem, because marriage is not a problem to solve, but a mystery to be lived. On another level, this is the solution, because this is the path of the mystery of marriage; it is the way of the cross and the Resurrection.

Notes

1. See Alkiviadis C. Calivas, "Marriage: The Sacrament of Love and Communion," *Greek Orthodox Theological Review* 40 (1995) for a thorough articulation of an Eastern Christian theology of marriage and a comprehensive list of resources on the topic.

2. Calivas, "Marriage: The Sacrament of Love and Communion," 249.

3. The implications for proper marital preparation are evident here. Preparing couples for marriage requires that we address the unrealistic expectations of marriage that many engaged couples have, such that the challenges of marriage are not accompanied by severe disappointment, but mature preparation. Proper marriage preparation plays a key role in teaching couples about the nature and purpose of marriage such that they establish appropriate patterns for identifying and addressing the inevitable challenges that arise. See Philip Mamalakis and Charles Joanides, *The Journey of Marriage in the Orthodox Church* (New York: Greek Orthodox Archdiocese, 2010).

4. John Chryssavgis, "The Sacrament of Marriage: An Orthodox Perspective," *Studia Liturgica* 19, no. 1 (1989): 17.

5. St. John Chrysostom, PG 61:215 and 62:387, quoted in Stephanos Charalambidis, "Marriage in the Orthodox Church," *One in Christ* 15, no. 1 (1979): 204.

6. Charalambidis, "Marriage in the Orthodox Church," 207.

7. St. Maximos the Confessor, *Selected Writings* (New York: Paulist Press, 1985), 122.

8. Calivas, "Marriage: The Sacrament of Love and Communion," 250.

9. Charalambidis, "Marriage in the Orthodox Church," 206.

10. Archimandrite Aimilianos of Simonopetra, *The Church at Prayer* (Athens: Indiktos, 2005), 120.

11. Calivas, "Marriage: The Sacrament of Love and Communion," 254.

12. St. John Chrysostom, *Marriage and Family Life* (Crestwood, NY: St. Vladimir's Seminary Press, 1986), 78.

13. Bishop Nikolai Velimorovich, *The Collected Writings of Nikoli Velimirovich* (Seattle: St. Nectarios Press, 1995), 45.

14. Paul Evdokimov, *The Sacrament of Love: The Nuptial Mystery in the Light of the Orthodox Tradition* (Crestwood, NY: St. Vladimir's Seminary Press, 1986), 123.

15. Aimilianos, *The Church at Prayer*, 125.

16. Chrysostom, *On Marriage and Family Life*, 58.

17. Ibid.

18. John H. Gottman, *The Relationship Cure: A Five Step Guide to Strengthening Your Marriage, Family and Friendships* (New York: Three Rivers Press, 2003), 4.

19. Ibid.

20. A comprehensive overview of Dr. Gottman's research findings on marital intimacy is outside the scope of this paper. For more informa-

tion, see J. Gottman, *The Marriage Clinic: A Scientifically Based Marital Therapy* (New York: WW Norton and Co., Inc., 1999) and *The Relationship Cure*.

21. Dr. Gottman observed that husbands heading for divorce disregard their wives' bids for connection 82% of the time, whereas husbands in stable relationships disregard their wives' bids just 19% of the time (*The Relationship Cure*, 4).

22. Dr. Gottman makes the point that spouses are not the only ones who bid for connection. Children bid for connection through their interactions with parents. Students bid for connection with teachers, and, most relevant for pastors, parishioners are continuously bidding for connection in their exchanges, requests, and demands on pastors. How a pastor responds to these bids communicates powerful messages, often unintentionally.

23. Vladimir Lossky, *The Mystical Theology of the Eastern Church* (Crestwood, NY: St. Vladimir's Seminary Press, 1997), 199.

24. Evdokimov, *The Sacrament of Love*, 32.

25. *The Oxford Latin Dictionary* (Oxford: Oxford University Press, 2002), 533.

26. Aimilianos, *The Church at Prayer*, 127.

27. Evdokimov, *The Sacrament of Love*, 35.

28. Calivas, "Marriage: The Sacrament of Love and Communion," 255.

29. Matthew the Poor and Matta El-Maskeen, *The Communion of Love* (Crestwood, NY: St. Vladimir's Seminary Press, 1984), 98.

30. *The Works of Dionysius the Areopagite*, pt. 1, *The Divine Names, The Mystic Theology, The Epistles and The Liturgy*, trans. John Parker (London: James Parker and Co., 1897), 9.5, quoted in Georgia Williams, "An Exploration of Hierarchy as Fractal in the Theology of Dionysios the Areopagite," paper presented at The Sophia Institute, Fourth Annual Conference, New York, December 11, 2010, p. 6.

31. St. John of Kronstadt, *My Life in Christ* (Jordanville, NY: Holy Trinity Monastery Press, 1984), 132.

32. Chrysostom, *On Marriage and Family Life*, 33.

33. Nicholas Cabasilas, *The Life in Christ* (Crestwood, NY: St. Vladimir's Seminary Press, 1974), 168.

34. Lossky, *The Mystical Theology of the Eastern Church*, 204.

35. Chrysostom, *On Marriage and Family Life*, 75.

36. Aimilianos, *The Church at Prayer*, 123.

Chapter 7

IMPEDIMENTS OF RELATIONSHIP IN THE SACRAMENT OF MARRIAGE

Dr. Lewis J. Patsavos
Professor of Canon Law

A mong the impediments to marriage in the practice of the Orthodox Church, those of relationship present the most perplexing problem. Belonging to this category of impediments are relationship by blood (consanguinity), relationship by marriage (affinity), and relationship by sponsorship at baptism (spiritual relationship). Many relationships traditionally constituting impediments to marriage are self-evident, such as a father and son marrying a mother and daughter. Others are less obvious, such as marriage between relatives of the seventh degree (separated from a common ancestor by seven births, e.g., a son or daughter of one's second cousin), or between persons with the same baptismal sponsor.

In reflecting upon the latter prohibitive regulations of a bygone era, one understandably questions their significance in our present age. Are they simply the residue of long-forgotten social mores, or do they reflect timeless moral truths that must be upheld in every age and every land? Does the broad array of marriage impediments resulting from blood, marital, or spiritual relationships serve the Church's aim of maintaining an undefiled, sacramental state of marriage? If not, does it obstruct this noble goal by frustrating those whose status does not conform to this ancient discipline? Are these prohibitions enforced in a consistent and reasonable manner, which underscores their continuing significance? If not, does the Church's contemporary practice in these matters reveal a tacit conviction that they are of little significance today?

These are some of the questions that beg a response in order to render the Church's practice intelligible. So often, it is the weight of tradition alone that compels us to act as we do. For this reason, it is necessary to pursue a close examination of the canonical regulations regarding impediments to marriage and reflect upon the culture that shaped them. The purpose of this study, therefore, is to provide a better understanding of an area of canonical discipline that may appear incongruous to our contemporary cultural context. Our investigation begins with a thorough review of the canons that prohibit marital union on the basis of previously existing relationships.

I

When one considers the number of relationships that constitute an impediment to marriage, the actual number of canons addressing this subject is surprisingly limited. Among the canons issued by Ecumenical Councils, only two establish impediments due to relationship. They are canons 53 and 54 of the Council in Trullo (692). In view of the fact that these canons are not necessarily listed contextually, they will be examined in inverted order for purposes of convenience. Canon 54 enumerates marital prohibitions as a consequence of relationship by blood or a previous marital union:

> The divine scriptures plainly teach us as follows, "Thou shalt not approach to any that is near of kin to thee to uncover their nakedness." Basil, the bearer-of-God, has enumerated in his canons some marriages which are prohibited and has passed over the greater part in silence, and in both these ways has done us good service. For by avoiding a number of disgraceful names (lest by such words he should pollute his discourse) he included impurities under general terms, by which course he shewed to us in a general way the marriages which are forbidden. But since by such silence, and because of the difficulty of understanding what marriages are prohibited, the matter has become confused; it seemed good to us to set it forth a little more clearly, decreeing that from this time forth he who shall marry with the daughter of his father; or a father or son with a mother and daughter; or a father and son with two girls who are sisters; or a mother and daughter with two brothers; or two brothers with two sisters, fall under the canon of seven years, provided they openly separate from this unlawful union.[1]

Canon 53, on the other hand, addresses the issue of spiritual relationship:

> Whereas the spiritual relationship is greater than fleshly affinity; and since it has come to our knowledge that in some places certain persons who become sponsors to children in holy salvation-bearing baptism, afterwards contract matrimony with their mothers (being widows), we decree that for the future nothing of this sort is to be done. But if any, after the present canon, shall be observed to do this, they must, in the first place, desist from this unlawful marriage, and then be subjected to the penalties of fornicators.[2]

These two canons of the Council in Trullo were not the first of their kind. One senses in their wording the influence of earlier canonical decrees and decisions of the fathers, principally those of St. Basil (ca. 330–379). In his Epistle to Diodorus (canon 87), St. Basil discusses at some length the status of a man who has married the sister of his deceased wife. He in fact condemns this marriage as a reprehensible breach of Christian morality. His opening words, which ascribe the teaching on this matter to authorities more ancient than himself, contain the essence of his reply:

> First, then, let it be said (which is also the most important thing to note) that the custom amongst us which we have to propose in regard to such cases, having as it does the force of a law, on account of the fact that the institutions were handed down to us by saintly men. This may be described as follows. If anyone suffering from filth and overcome by it should ever fall into the unlawful state of having married two sisters, this is not to be deemed either a marriage nor may he be admitted to the congregation and membership of the Church until they have first separated from each other.[3]

He continues to acknowledge that the moral standard which he enjoins is at variance with the principles of Levitical law. Based on what is written in Leviticus 18:18, marriage with two sisters appears to be prohibited only when both are living. He argues, however, that in this case, as in many others, Christian standards of purity are higher than those of Mosaic law. Moreover, he affirms that his prohibition is supported by natural law, not to mention common logic:

Those . . . who disregard nature entirely, and devour the soul
with a passion for dishonoring women, again are compelled
to distinguish the two sexes. To which of the two sexes shall
they ascribe the offspring? Shall they say that they are brothers and sisters of each other, or that they are cousins? Make
not, O man, the aunt a mother-in-law [i.e., stepmother] of
the infants, whose duty it is not even to nurse it in the capacity of a mother; you will only be imbuing the latter implaca-
bly jealous.[4]

Other canons of St. Basil forbid marriage between a man and his
half-sister (canon 75), a man and his sister-in-law or daughter-in-law
(canon 76),[5] and a man and his mother-in-law (canon 79). Strict pen-
ances are foreseen for those who would violate these canonical rules.
St. Basil's prohibition against a man marrying two sisters in succession
is strengthened further by canon 19 of the Holy Apostles: "He who has
married two sisters, or a niece, cannot become a clergyman."[6] In addition, canon 2 of Neocaesarea (ca. 315) contains a similar prohibition,
although with reference to a woman marrying two brothers: "If a woman
shall have married two brothers, let her be cast out [i.e., of communion]
until her death. Nevertheless, at the hour of death she may, as an act of
mercy, be received to penance, provided she declare that she will break
the marriage, should she recover. But if the woman in such a marriage,
or the man, die, penance for the survivor shall be very difficult."[7]

With regard to the canon's concluding comment, St. Nicodemus the
Hagiorite (18th c.) provides the following interpretation. The principle
expressed here is that for such an irregular marriage, penance must begin with authentic repentance. This in turn requires a voluntary separation of the spouses. If restoration to communion is sought only after the
death of one's spouse, the sincerity of repentance is put in question. In
such a circumstance, one cannot be certain that the separation would
have taken place without the death of the spouse.[8]

Based on the canons examined thus far, impediments to marriage
due to relationship are relatively few. Actual prohibited relationships
identified are the following:

1. A man may not marry his sister or half-sister (canon 54 of Trullo).
2. A father and son may not marry a mother and daughter (canon
   54 of Trullo).
3. A father and son may not marry two sisters (canon 54 of Trullo).

4. A mother and daughter may not marry two brothers (canon 54 of Trullo).
5. Two brothers may not marry two sisters (canon 54 of Trullo).
6. A man may not marry the sister of his deceased wife (canon 87 of St. Basil).
7. A woman may not marry the brother of her deceased husband (canon 2 of Neocaesarea).
8. A man may not marry his niece (canon 19 of the Holy Apostles).
9. A man may not marry the mother of his godchild (canon 53 of Trullo).

Understood, although not stated in the above list, are the corresponding relationships involving the opposite sex, such as a woman who may not marry her nephew (see no. 8 above).

Despite their absence in the canonical texts that are the basis of the Church's practice, the number of prohibitions is clearly limited. Underlying all of them are several basic principles:

1. One may not marry a brother/sister, or a brother-in-law/sister-in-law;
2. One may not marry a parent or child, or a mother-in-law/father-in-law;
3. One may not marry a close relative by marriage (e.g., the parent of one's son-in-law/daughter-in-law);
4. One may not marry someone in a quasi-parental relationship (e.g., one's aunt or uncle);
5. One may not marry the baptismal sponsor of one's child.

What appears in these principles to be simple and direct has in practice become difficult and complex. This reality is what led to the current exposition of facts, in the hope that it might cause reflection upon their meaning today. What began as an attempt to prevent specific relationships considered inappropriate in the distant past developed into a complicated system of prohibited marriages of dubious meaning in the present.

As already seen in canons 53 and 54 of Trullo, specific instances of prohibited marriages reflected in the canons were remarkably limited. With the progression of time, however, it became the practice in the East to expand these instances by extending their underlying principles to include more and more relationships. The Byzantine state contributed to this process by promulgating legislation that then became the basis of the Church's practice thereafter. Thus, from the time of the Penthekti

Ecumenical Council (in Trullo, 692) onward, the number of relationships considered by the Church as an impediment to marriage gradually but steadily increased. A leading factor in this state of affairs was the mutual impulse of both Church and state in the Byzantine Empire to prohibit any marriage deemed scandalous, as contributing to familial or social instability. As a result, contemporary canonical discipline, based on traditional practice as opposed to actual canons, is remarkably restrictive in both number and type of relationships considered impediments to marriage.[9]

II

At this point, it will be helpful to review the categories of relationships that are used in the canonical tradition of the Orthodox Church to determine the permissibility of marriage. The most basic among them is blood relationship, or consanguinity. Marriage between close blood relatives was generally prohibited by all societies, exceptions in the primitive era of humanity notwithstanding. Thus, there can be no doubt that such marriages have been impermissible from the very beginning of the Christian era as well.

Consanguineous relationships make a distinction between those of a direct line and those of a collateral line. The distance of relationships is measured by degrees, which correspond to the number of intervening births. Each birth is one degree removed from the common ancestor.[10] In the direct line, marriage is strictly forbidden between a person and his or her progenitors (parent, grandparent, etc.), and between a person and his or her descendants (child, grandchild, etc.). This basic prohibition has always been strictly upheld in the Church's moral teaching. In the collateral line, where relationship arises between a person and those with whom he or she shares a common ancestor (sibling, cousin, nephew/niece, etc.), there is a less restrictive policy governing marital unions.

Roman law on marriage, from which later Byzantine law derives in large part, prohibited marriage between siblings and their immediate descendants. This, however, did not deter the Emperor Claudius (41–54) from marrying his niece following legislation permitting such a marriage introduced for his benefit. Emperor Theodosius I, in 384, extended the principle prohibiting marriage between siblings to include first cousins also. Emperor Justinian (527–565) extended this ban further to include marriages in which one of the spouses was only one degree removed from the common ancestor. This effectively prohibited marriage not only between an uncle and a niece, but also between a great-uncle and his grand-niece.

Two centuries later, a collection of laws known as the *Ecloga*, issued by Leo III and Constantine V in 741, added to the hitherto list of impediments due to relationship that of children of first cousins (i.e., second cousins). This relationship in the collateral line extends to the sixth degree. Practically speaking, this means that each of the related persons is separated from the common ancestor by three births. The total number of births between them is six; hence, they are relatives of the sixth degree to each other.[11]

In her enumeration of impediments to marriage due to consanguinity in the collateral line, the Eastern Church has followed a more strict policy than the Western Church. As a consequence, prohibited marriages include relatives up to and including the seventh degree in the collateral line (e.g., the offspring of a niece or nephew twice removed) according to the principle of exactness (*akriveia*).[12] Marriage between relatives in the direct line of consanguinity continues to be strictly forbidden regardless of degree of relationship.

III

In addition to consanguinity, certain relationships of affinity have also come to be recognized as constituting impediments to marriage. Relationships of affinity arise between persons through marriage. Hence, a spouse enters into a relationship of affinity with the blood relatives of his or her partner. Here again, ecclesiastical practice followed Roman and Levitical law, both of which considered relationships of affinity analogous to relationships of consanguinity. As such, they, too, constituted an impediment to marriage. In view of this, the book of Leviticus prohibits marriage between a man and his stepmother, his daughter-in-law, and his sister-in-law.[13]

Roman law was not so restrictive as Levitical law, prohibiting only marriages between persons related in the first degree of affinity in the collateral line. This relatively lenient restriction, however, was extended by the *Ecloga* to also include other relatives by affinity. Thus, marriage was prohibited between a stepfather and stepdaughter, a father-in-law and daughter-in-law, a son-in-law and mother-in-law, a brother-in-law and sister-in-law, a father and son with a mother and daughter, and two brothers with two sisters.[14]

As seen in canon 54 of Trullo, the Church adopted the more restrictive practices of both Roman and Levitical law in matters of prohibited
marital relationships. The normative practice, as developed over time,
has been to prohibit all marriages between persons related by affinity in
the direct line up to and including the seventh degree in the collateral
line. Strict and consistent application of this practice was not always upheld. History provides us with ample instances of this fact, as does the
variation in practice up to the present among some of the Autocephalous Churches.[15]

IV

A third category of relationship that constitutes an impediment to marriage is that caused by baptismal sponsorship.[16] Understandably, there
is no precedent in Roman or Levitical law for the spiritual relationship
caused by baptismal sponsorship, a purely Christian commitment. Although its roots are found in the Church's rite of Baptism, spiritual relationship as impediment to marriage was first introduced by the state.
Emperor Justinian's *Code* first recognized its legal status, identifying
it with blood relationship. As a consequence, it led to a series of prohibited marriages. This included the sponsor with the woman he had
sponsored in Baptism, as well as godparents and their children with the
person sponsored in Baptism and his or her relatives.[17] Similarly, it forbade a sponsor from marrying the widowed mother of a child whom he
had sponsored.[18] Canon 53 of Trullo quoted earlier adopted the latter
restriction, while passing over in silence the case of a sponsor marrying
his godchild.[19]

Not long after, the *Ecloga* decreed that "the man who has baptized
a woman cannot marry her, or her mother or her daughter, nor can his
son do so, for the marital relations cannot be combined with the spiritually paternal."[20] Still another decree attributed to Patriarch Nicephorus
of Constantinople (806–815) extended this category of impediment. It
"forbade a man to marry the sister of the man who had baptized his son
and imposed a penalty of five years' penance on the one who entered
such a marriage."[21]

In current practice, marriage between spiritual relatives up to the
third degree in either the direct or the collateral line is prohibited. Such a
case would be the marriage between the son of a sponsor and the daughter of a godchild, or between a godchild and the sister of his sponsor.[22]
Within these boundaries of proscription, of course, are second-degree

spiritual relatives in the collateral line. These include godchildren of the same sponsor with each other, or a son/daughter of a sponsor with one's godchild. It is these cases that present the greatest pastoral difficulties today.[23] Persons so related spiritually are often of similar age and likely to live in the same community. As such, there is the possibility that they might meet and develop a relationship that could lead to marriage.

V

Canons that are the basis for impediments to marriage due to bonds of relationship have been cited, categories of these bonds of relationship have been named, and contemporary ecclesiastical practice with regard to the categories has been identified. It now remains to examine carefully the principles underlying the canons in question in order to determine whether contemporary ecclesiastical practice is in harmony with them.

As observed, the canons that prohibit close consanguineous marriages or marriages between persons closely related by affinity are by no means an exception. On the contrary, they reflect a near-universal predisposition within most societies that rejects such marriages as conflicting with natural law. Nearly every culture throughout history has recognized that marriages between a parent and child or between siblings are reprehensible and not to be tolerated under any circumstance. Not only would such marital unions undermine the basic structure of the family, and by extension society as a whole, but they would also bring with them very real health risks. The offspring of such unions would be susceptible to defective genetic traits that might otherwise have remained recessive within the gene pool. Although the modern scientific understanding of this genetic phenomenon was unknown when the applicable canons (and their precursors in Jewish and Roman law) were adopted, instinct alone would appear to preclude such behavior.[24] Thus, there is a fundamental moral standard universally upheld in this regard not only by the institution of the Church, but by all human institutions as well.

The concern of the Church, as expressed in her canons, extends far beyond the most basic level of instinctive morality, however. Following the pattern of Levitical law, the Church has sought to prohibit any scandalous unions or those that might possibly lead to dissension or strife within the family. Censuring the Christians in Corinth for tolerating in their midst someone who had married his stepmother, St. Paul wishes to preserve the Church from public scandal and notorious immorality. "It is widely reported," he laments, "that there is sexual immorality among you, immorality of a kind that is not found even among gentiles" (1 Cor 5:1).[25] The issue of family strife is addressed by St. Basil in his Canonical Epistle 87. Stating that one who marries his wife's sister is creating a "confusion of names," his concern is not with nomenclature, but with disordered family relations. Is this woman mother or aunt to her husband's children? How do they relate to her? Will not all their relationships be marked by confusion and dissension?

> Make not, O man, the aunt a stepmother of the infants, whose duty it is not even to nurse it in the capacity of a mother; you will only be imbuing the latter implacably jealous. It is only hatred of stepmothers that arouses animosity even after death. Rather might one say, in fact, that those who are foes in other respects join hands in pouring peaceful libations to the dead, whereas stepmothers excite hatred after death.[26]

Levitical and Roman laws that limited consanguineous marital unions and marriages between relatives by affinity addressed a particular need. Created in cultures where extended families lived in close contact and where the need to preserve family relationships was strongly felt, their purpose was to ensure family solidarity. Among the higher classes in Roman society particularly, there was yet another motive for proscribing marriages between close relatives. This was a way to create political unions between families. Although this may not have been an important consideration for the Church, the stability of the family was. For this reason, canonical interpretations, ecclesiastical decrees, and imperial laws prohibited certain consanguineous marriages and marriages between relatives by affinity. In doing so, they extended these proscriptions far beyond the general societal prohibitions of the late antique world. As already mentioned, the desire of avoiding even the hint of scandal was a prime concern. However, a constant care was the maintenance of peace and concord within extended families, which in the Byzantine period would have been living in close proximity to each other. Understood in this context, the broad marital restrictions of the Orthodox Church based upon blood relationship and affinity by marriage are quite comprehensible.

In addition to fostering general family concord, there may be yet another reason for both ecclesiastical and civil restrictions on marriage between family members. This is not a reason attested to in the legal sources, but it is one about which one might profitably speculate. In a society in which early and sudden death was not uncommon, the need would have arisen for close relatives to assume responsibility for the financial affairs and legal defense of orphaned minors.[27] In such cases, potential conflicts of interest might arise if a relative serving as guardian were to wed a widowed mother or an orphaned child. It would be most undesirable for one in a quasi-parental relationship with legal responsibility for a child's care and upbringing to enter into marriage with either child or widowed mother. Legislation prohibiting marriage to the furthest degree of relationship may have been intended to protect against family discord in the event of such guardianship and the related matter of inheritance.

Within the societal context in which it was formulated, the marriage impediment of collateral relationship by birth or marriage up to the seventh degree is practical and meaningful.[28] The question, however, remains: to what avail does its continued application, even in theory, serve the needs of the faithful today? It cannot be denied that social norms in the industrialized world of the twenty-first century differ greatly from those of late antiquity or medieval Byzantium. In our highly mobile world, it is quite possible that persons may go through life without ever encountering relatives of distant collateral degrees of relationship by birth, let alone by marriage. If they do, it is likely that they would know them more as mere acquaintances than as relatives. This being the case, one might ask what ought the Church's position to be regarding the marriage of such relatives, were they to seek her blessing.

In our cultural context today, marriages between distant relatives would hardly constitute a scandal or lead to family strife. In view of this, the practice of the Orthodox Church, especially in the Western world, where she constitutes a minority, is surprisingly tolerant. In fact, it is not uncommon for the traditional canonical discipline prohibiting marriages between collateral relatives up to the seventh degree according to *akriveia* to be overlooked. As a result, marriages between distant relatives, which in the past would have been prohibited as a matter of course, today are usually permitted through the liberal exercise of *oikonomia*.[29] This, however, gives the impression that the granting of *oikonomia* has become institutionalized, rendering the prohibition of certain marriages up to the seventh degree meaningless. We are thereby given cause to consider the matter carefully. When contemporary ecclesiastical practice implies the automatic granting of *oikonomia*, either the Church's traditional canonical discipline is being wantonly violated, or it no longer serves the purpose for which it was originally instituted.

It is this writer's contention that the latter is the case. A response must therefore be found which neither scandalizes the sensitivities of traditionalists nor minimizes the concerns of relativists. The strength of our canonical tradition is its ability to adapt to the needs of the Church in any given moment in history. Ample precedent exists to bear out this principle, providing no fundamental truth is thereby compromised. When determined by the hierarchy in synod that a traditional canonical discipline no longer corresponds to the need for which it was originally intended, its recourse is limited. This is due to the fact that canons of universal authority that have been ratified by an Ecumenical Council may be modified or rescinded only by a council of equal authority.

With regard to relational impediments to marriage, the matter varies. As observed, the actual canons restricting marriage between relatives are few and limited in scope. Canons with ecumenical authority that restrict marriage between certain relatives are canon 54 of the Council in Trullo and canons 23, 75, 76, and 78 of St. Basil. Canon 54 of Trullo speaks of relatives by consanguinity in the collateral line up to the fourth degree (first cousins with each other) and of certain relatives by affinity (a father and son with a mother and daughter or with two sisters, among others). The several canons of St. Basil listed refer to similar relatives by affinity who are prohibited from intermarrying.

Prohibitions extending well beyond the above have their origins in the synodal decrees of Local Churches, Byzantine civil law, or practice hallowed by time. It ought not therefore to be a matter of overwhelming consequence for the Church locally to consider adjusting some of these prohibited practices.[30] Any such relaxation of this discipline, however, must take account of local variations where close family ties necessitate the traditional norms. Under no condition ought the Church's willingness to entertain change, where justifiable, be occasion for scandal. In addition, care must be taken not to relax canonical guidelines to such a degree as to give the impression of compromising the Church's moral principles under pressure by society at large. Based upon the Pauline principle of avoiding scandal or the appearance of evil at all costs,[31] it would be wrong to sanction a union generally frowned upon by the faithful. On the other hand, prohibited marriages not stemming from a decree of an Ecumenical Council could be sanctioned. Such marriages might be those between certain persons related by affinity.

Were such a step to be taken, care must be given to identify the specific marriages that are permissible and those that are not, as in the canonical decrees themselves. This is in contrast to invoking prohibited degrees of relationship in general terms, without defining which specific marriages are prohibited. Understandably, a bold proposal such as the adjustment of marriage impediments based upon collateral relationships should only be made for the Church on the local level initially. The day must come, however, when it is addressed for the Church Universal on a pan-Orthodox level.[32] Not only are the canonical decrees regulating marriage long overdue for revision, where necessary, but even the relevant canons themselves.

A case in point is canon 54 of Trullo, which forbids the marriage of two brothers with two sisters.[33] Given the mores and sensitivities of the times in which this canon was adopted, one can understand the reason for its acceptance then. One must ask, however, whether the same holds true today. The sister-in-law or brother-in-law of a spouse was a collateral relative in the second degree to both spouse and sibling. It did not matter whether the relationship was by affinity or by consanguinity. Regardless of the case, marriage with such a close relative was prohibited.

Despite this prohibition, the instances of two brothers marrying two sisters simultaneously, especially in our day, are not unknown. The absence of an impediment, it is held, is due to the simultaneous occurrence of the marriages. However, this begs the question of whether rationalizing legitimacy in this way is not adequate cause for their prohibition to be reconsidered. In view of the fact that no doctrinal principles are involved, an adjustment should not be insurmountable.[34]

Revision of the Church's canonical discipline in this matter could occur on the local level as a first step. There is ample precedent for such a cautious approach.[35] On the other hand, perpetuating a policy that appears meaningless in our time risks the chance of compromising its integrity. Although in theory the claim is made solemnly that certain marriages are prohibited, a satisfactory explanation as to why this holds true in our contemporary context is lacking. Adding to this paradox is the apparent ease with which permission is granted to abrogate this supposedly established canonical discipline. Such inconsistency in canonical practice related to certain impediments of relationship by marriage raises serious questions about their legitimacy and significance at all.

Similar reforms need to be considered with regard to impediments arising from spiritual relationship between potential spouses as well. Significantly, the category of spiritual relationship is addressed by a canon of universal authority, canon 53 of Trullo. An initial reading of the canon, therefore, would appear to preclude any kind of reform. A closer investigation, however, reveals a specific purpose for its adoption.

The Church's principal motive in prohibiting a sponsor at Baptism from marrying the mother of one's godchild was didactic. The prohibition was intended to demonstrate that the "spiritual relationship is greater than fleshly affinity." Insofar as the canon still maintains this premise, it is relevant and spiritually beneficial.

In order to fully appreciate the meaning of the canon, it is necessary to revisit the context from which it comes. In Byzantine society, a sponsor at Baptism might have been called upon to serve as guardian to his godchild in the event of the death of the natural parents. Hence, the prohibition of marriage of a sponsor with the widowed mother of his godchild protected against a potential conflict of interest. Similarly, a sponsor is prohibited from marrying his godchild. Because of the priority given to the spiritual relationship between sponsor and godchild, one may affirm with certainty the appropriateness of canon 53 of Trullo and its derivative decrees. Not only is the prohibited marriage of a sponsor with his godchild appropriate for medieval Byzantine society, but for any society in any age.[36]

In a commentary of canon 53 of Trullo, the case for the imperial law of Justinian prohibiting marriage between a sponsor and godchild is summed up concisely as follows: "The imperial law forbade the adopter parent to marry his or her adopted son or daughter; for the godchild was thought a sort of an adopted child."[37] Yet extensions of this canonical principle to prohibit marriage between two persons sponsored by the same godfather, or between a son/daughter of the latter with his godchild, seem today to be excessive. This leads one to ask: what bearing would such marriages have upon the spiritual bonds of a godparent/godchild relationship? Or, let us consider the hypothetical situation in which very few Orthodox in a given region are available as eligible spouses. Restrictions such as the above limit their availability even more, thereby contributing to the ever-increasing number of heterogeneous marriages (marriages with non-Orthodox spouses).

In view of the fact that most restricted marriages stem from time-hallowed, extra-canonical sources, not from canons of Ecumenical Councils, they should not be beyond the possibility of adjustment. Furthermore, one must question their significance today. The complexities of finding a suitable spouse in our contemporary, pluralistic society are such that it is not helpful to add to them by imposing outdated restrictions that no longer serve a useful purpose.

Marital impediments that resulted from blood, marriage, and spiritual relationships and were upheld for centuries by tradition had their purpose. Most of the impediments mentioned in canons of Ecumenical Councils continue to serve an important purpose up to the present. The proliferation of these impediments in other sources, however, is more due to changeable social and historical circumstances than to immutable moral principles. Such impediments, which in other times and places were understandable, are both difficult to understand and to uphold today. The same can be said of some canons of Ecumenical Councils, which may need to be revised if and when a council of equal authority is ever convened.[38] This is an area where one must come to terms with the need to modify practices not enjoined by Scripture and not intrinsically joined to eternal dogmatic principles. It is only in this way that the Church's canonical corpus can remain meaningful in a world of changing historical and social circumstances. In the words of the eminent theologian Nicholas Afanasiev:

> Orthodox teaching recognizes in principle the alterability of canonical decrees. It would be more exact to say that the Church demands a creative attitude towards contemporary life. The Church examines contemporary life as a theme and as material for its creativity. For this reason the doctrine of the immutability of the canons, which we often come across at the present time, represents a rejection of creative activity and creative attitude towards contemporary life. Nonetheless, it is impossible to avoid the historical situation in which one lives, since the modern life itself enters the Church, and if a creative attitude toward it is lacking, a passive acceptance of it is inevitable; there will simply be an adjustment to it, and *passive* adjustment is always detrimental to Church life.[39]

Requirements of the past regulating impediments to marriage due to relationship by blood, marriage, or baptismal sponsorship may have outlived their usefulness. Revision, where possible, of some of these requirements is but one step that might be taken by the Orthodox Church today to promote the sensitivity of her teachings and relevance of her practical discipline in every age.[40] A revised marriage discipline that responds to contemporary social realities would still uphold the high moral standards of Christian marriage and familial relationships. At the same time, it would serve to underscore the fact that the Church's canonical tradition continues to be a trustworthy guide for Orthodox Christians in their struggle to lead virtuous lives.

Notes

The occasion for submitting the present article, the twentieth anni-versary of the accession of His All-Holiness Ecumenical Patriarch Bar-tholomew to the patriarchal throne of Constantinople, gives cause for joy and thanksgiving. One rejoices in the many great accomplishments of the past two decades and gives thanks to our loving God for them. At the same time, one is reminded of the special training of His All-Holi-ness in the science of the canonical tradition of the Orthodox Church. In view of this, he has been particularly sensitive, among other concerns, to the pastoral problems confronting the Church in our age.

With this in mind, selection was made of a topic, the context for which was a research paper entitled "Analysis of the Canons and Re-lated Ecclesiastical Legislation regarding Marriage Impediments of Re-lationship." Submitted for the course "Canonical Aspects of Marriage" by my former student Alban West, it has been expanded and revised. The timeliness of this topic is further heightened by a recent encyclical of the Holy and Sacred Synod of our Ecumenical Patriarchate regard-ing the impediment of spiritual relationship. Its appearance at this time underscores both the urgency of the matter and the sensitivity of those addressing it.

1. H. Percival, ed., *The Seven Ecumenical Councils*, vol. 14 of Nicene and Post-Nicene Fathers, Second Series (reprint, Grand Rapids, MI: Ee-rdmans, 1956), 390–391.

2. Percival, *The Seven Ecumenical Councils*, 390.

3. D. Cummings, trans., *The Rudder* (Chicago: Orthodox Christian Educational Society, 1957), 842.

4. Cummings, *The Rudder*, 844.

5. Canon 78 of St. Basil repeats the prohibition of a man marrying his sister-in-law.

6. Percival, *The Seven Ecumenical Councils*, 595.

7. Ibid., 79.

8. Cummings, *The Rudder*, 508.

9. One need only consult the maze of *prohibited* and *unprohibited* marriages listed in *The Rudder* (Cummings, 977–996) to acquire a sense of the degree to which impediments due to relationships have prolifer-ated over the centuries.

10. P. Rodopoulos, *An Overview of Orthodox Canon Law* (Rollins-ford, NH: Orthodox Research Institute, 2007), 196.

11. In the Eastern Church, degrees of relationship have always been calculated according to the ancient Roman method, which counts all persons on both sides of the collateral line except the common ances-tor. Thus, a brother and sister are second-degree collateral relatives, first cousins are fourth-degree collateral relatives, and second cousins are

sixth-degree collateral relatives. See J. Marbach, *Marriage Legislation for the Catholics of the Oriental Rites in the United States and Canada* (Washington, DC: Catholic University Press, 1946), 13–14.

12. Following established practice in Roman law, marriage was permitted between relatives of the fourth degree, i.e., first cousins, in the early centuries of the Byzantine Empire. See Ph. Georgiades, *To ek syggeneias haimatos hebdomou bathmou kolyma gamou kai he prostaxis, etous 1186, tou Autokratoros Isaakiou II tou Aggelou* (Athens: Academy of Athens [6, 2], 1937), 5. But between the seventh and twelfth centuries, restrictions were introduced excluding marriage between relatives up to the seventh degree of consanguinity, as well as between certain relatives of affinity. See C. Pitsakis, "Législation et stratégies matrimoniales: Parenté et empêchements de mariage dans le droit byzantin," *L'Homme* 154–155 (2000): 677–696. See also by the same author, *To kolyma gamou logo syggeneias hebdomou bathmou ex haimatos sto byzantino dikaio* (Athens-Komotini: A. Sakkoulas, 1985). Despite these restrictions, it appears that the prohibition of such marriages was not always strictly upheld. See J. Meyendorff, "Christian Marriage in Byzantium: The Canonical and Liturgical Tradition," *Dumbarton Oaks Papers* 44 (1990): 103.

13. The well-known exception to this principle is the "Levirate marriage" defined in the book of Deuteronomy (25:5–10). According to its teaching, a man whose brother dies without offspring is required to marry his brother's widow in order to perpetuate the brother's name through children to be born of the marriage.

14. "Those who are recognized as relations by marriage, stepfather and stepdaughter, father-in-law and daughter-in-law, son-in-law and mother-in-law, brother and bride, that is to say, a brother's wife, likewise father and son of one family and mother and daughter of another family, two brothers of one family with two sisters of another family" (Marbach, *Marriage Legislation*, 12).

15. In her article "Further Notes on Byzantine Marriage: Raptus-αρπαγη or μνηστειαι?" (*Dumbarton Oaks Papers* 46 [1992]: 134), P. Karlin-Hayter notes that various patriarchal *endemousa* synods held in the eleventh and twelfth centuries considered whether or not to treat relationships of affinity with the same rigor as those of consanguinity. Thus, it appears that even then there were those in the Church who thought some of these standards were too extreme.

16. On the important role played by baptismal sponsorship in the Byzantine Church, see R. Macrides, "The Byzantine Godfather," *Byzantine and Modern Greek Studies* 11 (1987): 139–162. See further by the same author, *Kinship and Justice in Byzantium, 11th–15th Centuries*, Variorum Collected Studies Series (Ashgate Publishing, 2000).

17. See Meyendorff, "Christian Marriage in Byzantium," 103.

18. Marbach, *Marriage Legislation*, 18.

19. A possible explanation of this glaring omission might be that such a prohibition is self-evident.

20. Marbach, *Marriage Legislation*, 18.

21. Ibid., 19.

22. In the calculation of degrees of spiritual relationship, the spiritual bond between a sponsor and godchild is equivalent to physical parenthood. Consequently, a sponsor and godchild are in a first-degree relationship to one another.

23. It is this reality that prompted the Holy and Sacred Synod of the Ecumenical Patriarchate to issue a recent encyclical (on January 12, 2011) permitting marriage between godchildren of the same sponsor.

24. An instinctive sense of the risk of genetic disease due to close inbreeding may be the inheritance of the human species as a whole, and indeed of mammals as well. Nearly all highly developed animal species shun inbreeding by instinct.

25. *New Jerusalem Bible*.

26. Cummings, *The Rudder*, 844. The word "stepmother" in place of "mother-in-law" is used in this translation as the more appropriate term for the relationship described by St. Basil.

27. Life expectancy in late antiquity and the middle ages was about half what it is in today's industrialized world.

28. A relative of the fifth collateral degree of relationship is the son or daughter of one's first cousin. A relative of the sixth degree is a second cousin with whom one is separated from a common ancestor by six intervening births.

29. This becomes apparent when consulting the current Yearbook of the Greek Orthodox Archdiocese of America (2011), where on p. 264 it is stated which marriages are prohibited. With regard to marriages between collateral relatives, noticeably missing is any mention of relatives beyond the fourth degree of relationship (first cousins).

30. Here come to mind the degrees of relationship within the collateral line that stand as a bar to matrimony.

31. 1 Cor 8:13.

32. The first step in this process has already been taken by unanimous decision of the representatives of the Autocephalous Churches in attendance at the Second Pan-Orthodox Preconciliar Conference in Chambésy (1982). The document on *Marriage Impediments* thereby approved for discussion will constitute the basis for an eventual resolution of this pivotal topic.

33. As indicated by Fr. John Meyendorff in reference to Byzantine polemics against the West ("Christian Marriage in Byzantium," 103), "The

ban established by the Council in Trullo against the marriage of two brothers with two sisters seems to have been applied strictly, since the non-application of the rule in Western Christendom is often mentioned by Byzantine polemicists as one of the 'Latin heresies.' "

34. Commenting on the strict observance of such prohibited marriages today, Fr. Meyendorff (*Marriage: An Orthodox Perspective*, 2nd ed. [Crestwood, NY: St. Vladimir's Seminary Press, 1975], 54–55) has noted, "Obviously, today it does not seem either necessary or desirable to apply strictly those canons which are based on social and legal principles of the past, and which do not correspond to any permanent theological or spiritual value."

35. From the recent past there comes to mind a decision on the matter of fasting by the Third Pre-Synodal Pan-Orthodox Conference held in 1986 in Chambésy, Switzerland. In anticipation of a definitive position on this vital issue by a council of pan-Orthodox dimensions, a preliminary approach is recommended. Accordingly, each Local Orthodox Church would have the right to determine an interim practice serving its particular needs until such time as a common practice becomes binding.

36. See R. Macrides, "The Byzantine Godfather," 147–148, for the variety of ways in which the role of a sponsor was expressed in the Byzantine Church.

37. Percival, *The Seven Ecumenical Councils*, 390.

38. A case in point is canon 72 of Trullo. This is canon calls for marriage of Orthodox Christians with only those of the same faith. Were it to be upheld today strictly (*kat' akriveian*), especially in lands where Orthodox Christians constitute a minority, the Church would be confronted with grave pastoral problems.

39. N. Afanasiev, "The Canons of the Church: Changeable or Unchangeable?" *St. Vladimir's Seminary Quarterly* 11 (1967): 65.

40. As mentioned elsewhere (see note 33), a preliminary investigation of this vital matter has already taken place. One hopes that an eventual definitive decision that is binding upon all the Autocephalous Churches will be reached in the near future.

Chapter 8

"HOLDING SWAY IN COMPANIONSHIP": GENESIS 1:26 REVISITED

Rev. Dr. Eugen J. Pentiuc
Professor of Old Testament

Orthodox theology regards humanity as possessing a royal, but not a tyrannical dimension. Belief in the stewardship and ministry of humanity within creation is marked by a profound sense of justice and also moderation. We can be neither prideful in our authority nor falsely humble in our self-limitations. We are called to preserve creation by serving its Creator.

(His All-Holiness Patriarch Bartholomew)[1]

On June 6, 1989, the Holy and Sacred Synod of the Ecumenical Patriarchate in Constantinople declared September 1 to be the *Feast of Creation*. His All-Holiness Ecumenical Patriarch Bartholomew asked all the Orthodox churches to observe this feast. Through his rich and untiring activity on various fronts, His All-Holiness has repeatedly warned the world of the perils menacing our planet (our *oikos*, or "home," as the Patriarch likes to call it) and discussed the concrete measures that should be taken for its preservation. By this token, His All-Holiness gained unequivocally and justly the title "the Green Patriarch."

***

In her article "Orthodox Ecological Theology: Bartholomew I and Orthodox Contributions to the Ecological Debate,"[2] Crina Geschwandtner shows that Orthodox tradition has a great potential to contribute to the current debate on how might Christianity respond to environmental crisis. After examining the ecological vision of Ecumenical Patriarch

Bartholomew I, the author argues that Orthodox theological contributions to the ecological debate occur in the areas of ethics, asceticism, and Eucharistic and liturgical ethos.

Although I agree with Geschwandtner on her keen observation, I might emphasize that Eastern Orthodox tradition is well impregnated with Scripture in all the areas mentioned above. My intent is to bring forward some of biblical material in support of the traditional Orthodox view on God's creation and human responsibility toward it.

In the ensuing paragraphs, I would like to dwell on a pivotal and much debated scriptural text, Genesis 1:26, that has been often and abusively interpreted as an open invitation to a triumphalist and careless exploitation of nature by means of technology with exaggerated focus on humanity as God's sole representative on earth.[3] My special emphasis will be on the idea of "ruling" in companionship and how this idea plays lexically and interpretively within the wider context of Scripture and its Semitic matrix.

Textual Witnesses

"And God said, 'Let us make humanity in our image, according to our likeness: and let them rule (*we-yirdû*) over the fish of the sea, and over the fowl of the air, and over the cattle, and over all the earth, and over every creeping thing that creeps upon the earth.' " (Gen 1:26)

This rendition is based, following a well-established scholarly convention, on the Masoretic Text (i.e., the Hebrew text as vocalized and accented by the Masoretes). The main textual witnesses listed below differentiate primarily—and if I may add, lightly—with respect to their lexical choice for the idea of "ruling."[4]

As one can notice from the main textual witnesses, MT, LXX, S, and T use verbs denoting the idea of "ruling" or "exercising authority," whereas V prefers *praesum*, "to take the lead." According to the first group of witnesses, the divine mandate given to the newly fashioned humanity seems to be one of authority and dominion over the rest of creation. However, this remark could lead to a rushed conclusion that is unfortunately so widespread among the general readership, that humans received from God the unlimited right to "conquer" or "trample down" the creation by misusing and wasting its resources in ways that go beyond any rationality or ethical concerns.

Although at first sight the text quoted above seems to refer to man's despotic rule over the non-human creatures, the vocabulary choices made by various textual witnesses alone would require refining this statement for a better understanding of "ruling" in its Semitic and biblical environments.

There are three arguments supporting the idea that Genesis 1:26 is not about absolute ruling with no concern at all for the other creatures. The text under analysis seeks to convey a more nuanced idea of "ruling," or "holding sway in companionship," with the rest of creation and in light of God's laws and precepts.

Below is a succinct discussion of these arguments.

1. *Etymology*

The Hebrew verb *radah*, "to have dominion, rule, dominate,"[5] found in the MT should be related to the Akkadian verb *redu*, "to accompany"[6] (cf. Syriac *rdā'*, "to go, run, flow; to drive"; Mandaean "to travel on, move on, wander"; but note Arabic *radā* [*rdy*], "to tread, trample").

Robert Alter, in his beautiful translation of the book of Genesis,[7] renders the verb *radah* in Genesis 1:26, 28 with "to hold sway," noticing, "The verb *radah* is not the normal Hebrew verb for 'rule' (the latter is reflected in 'dominion' of verse 16), and in most of the contexts in which it occurs it seems to suggest an absolute or even fierce exercise of mastery." In Genesis 1:16 the Hebrew noun *memsheleth* (*memshalah*), rendered "dominion," derives from verb *mashal* III, "to rule, have dominion, reign" (cf. Gen 3:16; 4:7; 45:8; Deut 15:6; Josh 12:5; Judg 8:22; 1 Kgs 5:1).[8] Following on the footsteps of Alter's fine rendition, *radah* may refer to the controlling influence of human beings over other living creatures.

Etymologically and semantically, the verb *radah* used in Genesis 1:26 is not the *terminus technicus* of the Hebrew lexicon for the idea of "ruling, having dominion." The mere fact that the author of Genesis 1:26 (and v. 28) chose such a peculiar verb, and not the more common *mashal* attested in the same chapter, v. 16, has to make one think of the main reason for such a lexical choice.

In light of the Akkadian etymology, the Hebrew verb *radah* should perhaps be understood in the sense of controlling, surveying, or caring for living creatures. The one who "rules" (*radah*) is the one who actually escorts, accompanies, or brings along persons or living creatures entrusted to him to a certain destination. Hence the sense of trust, task, or duty laid upon the one commissioned to escort and exercise controlling influence (an authority of sorts) over his charges.

2. Context

Pascal was right when he declared rather emphatically, "*Man* is neither angel nor beast."

The two juxtaposed accounts of creation in Genesis 1–2 point to humanity's peculiar place and function within God's creation almost echoing another scriptural musing, "For here have we no enduring city, but we are longing for the one to come" (Heb 13:14)

The first account of creation Genesis 1:1–2:4a (P)[9] depicts God the Creator as an Oriental king who while giving orders through his powerful word, does really work to reach his goals. Creation in the P account is a combination of orders and concrete actions. God is both a ruler and a worker. Being created in the image of God, man is called to do the same: to use God given authority yet with discretion. This discretion is required by the fact that ruling is not inherent to humanity. It derives from God, and it should be used in a creative way to the benefit of others. For this reason, man's kingship is subject to accountability. For this humanity needs a divine blessing (Gen 1:28) that equips its members with the ability to function as God's agents on earth. Moreover, man should follow God's *imperium* in Genesis 1:26–28 unpretentiously and with discretion, given the Creator's self-restraining way of bringing His creation out of nothingness through means of concrete work.

The second account of creation, Genesis 2:4b–25 (J),[10] describes humanity within its natural environment. The destiny of the human creature, according to the J account of creation, is to live in God's world along with other creatures while ruling over and caring for them, according to God's well-thought design.

Commenting on Genesis 1:26, John Chrysostom (347–407 AD) explains man's authority over creation as a gift, namely, as God's loving kindness toward His rational beings:

> Even before creating them, he makes them share in this control and bestows on them the blessing. "Have control," the text says, "of the fish of the sea, the birds of heaven and all the cattle, the whole earth and all the reptiles creeping on the earth." Did you notice the definitive character of this authority? Did you notice all created things placed under the

control of this particular being? So no longer entertain ca-
sual impressions of this rational being but rather realize the
extent of the esteem and the Lord's magnanimity toward it
and be amazed at his love beyond all telling. (*Homilies on
Genesis* 10.9)[11]

If man has any authority over creation, underscores this Church Father, is due to "God's magnanimity" and "love beyond all telling" toward
humanity.

The P account introduces us to a theology of blessing that is meant
to downplay the ontological gulf between Creator and creation and thus
make this chasm more bearable. Of the entire creation, God blesses only
three samples: the living creatures (v. 22), the humans (v. 28), and the
Sabbath (2:3). This theology of blessing is characteristically unique to
Israel in the context of other ancient Near-Eastern religious traditions.
Its provenance is situated in the harsh experience of the Israelite exiles
in Babylon (sixth century BC). And it functioned at that time of confusion and distress as a way of survival for ancient Israel. Its quite balanced
and realistic optimism may be still employed today as response to any
disruptive or nihilist ideology.

In the P account, God scrutinizes each of His creatures and pro-
nounces them "good" (1:10, 12, 18, 21, 25), and in 1:31 He proclaims the
whole of creation "very good." The adjective "good" employed in Genesis
1 is not a moral, but rather an aesthetic, qualifier (cf. Eccl 3:11) conveying
that something is "beautiful, pleasant."[12]

The divine pronouncement on the "good" creation, along with the
heptad[13] structure and symbolism permeating the P account of creation,
intimates the idea of design and movement from chaos to order, from
inferior to superior, from beginning to completion on the exciting path
of continuous perfecting.

In the divine pronouncement lies man's responsibility to preserve
God's creation within God's "goodness." Humanity's authority over the
rest of creation has a relative character and should not lead to an irrational exploitation of the latter, because it is to be exercised within a "very
good" world that consists of harmonious interrelationships between its
components. Any despotic ruling runs the risk of altering and even vio-
lating God's pronouncement on the pre-sabbatical state of His creation.

The opening words of the P account, "In the beginning God created the heavens and the earth" (the traditional English translation),[14]
enunciate the fundamental postulate of Israel's faith, a postulate that

infused the whole of biblical literature: creation depends on its Creator. Thus rendered, Genesis 1:1 stands as a complete independent sentence depicting God[15] above time and space.[16] Therefore, creation is neither an autonomous reality nor a simple derivation from God. Creation in Israel's memory is between the state of autonomy and divine emanation. And the only biblically correct way to speak of creation is to use the sentence "God created creation," where the two nouns defining quite different realities are inseparable; or, better put, it bridged via a significant verb, "created" (*bara'*), in the biblical theological Hebrew lexicon.[17]

It is noteworthy that Genesis 1:27 twice uses the same verb *bara'*, "to create," which is found already in v. 1 to describe the creation of humanity. Thus, humanity is set apart from the rest of creation as a reflection of God's powerful creative work. By comparing the two places (i.e., v. 1 with v. 27) where the verb *bara'* is used, one cannot help but thinking of humanity as the summary, reflection, or climax of God's whole creation.[18]

As for the Hebrew word *'adam*, this is a generic term for "humanity." In Genesis 1:26–28 and 5:1–2 this word refers to both man and woman. Thus humanity in its entirety and unity, not individually—males and females—received the ineffable "image and likeness"[19] of the Creator.

Hans Wilderberger gathered a rich list of ancient Near-Eastern inscriptions from Mesopotamia and Egypt, where the divine image was shared only with the king. Here are two examples. Pharaoh Thutmosis IV, also known as Menkheperure (1398–1388 BC), of the famous Eighteenth Dynasty, is described as "the image of Re, son of Amun, who tramples down foreigners." As for the Mesopotamian evidence, in an Assyrian letter dated to the seventh century BC, the priest Adad-shum-utsur calls the king "the image" (*tsalam*, an Akkadian cognate of the Hebrew word *tselem* in Genesis 1:26–27) of the god Bel. Wilderberger, like the medieval Jewish philosopher Saadya (882–942 AD), connects the image of God in humanity (Gen 1:26–27) with the latter's rule over creation. Note that in Genesis 1:28 humanity is blessed and commissioned by the Creator to hold sway over the earth.

If the divine "image" in Mesopotamia and Egypt was exclusively conferred to the king (and this remains to be further investigated), in the Hebrew Bible this royal title becomes democratized, that is, extended to all humans. An early biblical example is the notion of God's "son," which initially referred to the Davidic monarch and then was extended to all Israel (e.g., 2 Sam 7:14; Deut 14:1; Ps 89:28; Exod 4:22). However, according to Wilderberger, this notional democratization can be also detected outside the Hebrew Bible. In *The Instruction for King Meri-Ka-Re*, a late twenty-second-century-BC Egyptian text, one reads, "Well directed are men, the cattle of the god. He made heaven and earth according to their desire, and he repelled the water-monster. He made the breath of life [for] their nostrils. They who have issued from his body are his images. He arises in heaven according to their desire. He made for them plants, animals, fowl, and fish to feed them."[20]

Because in Genesis 1:26–27 all humans were created to bear the image of their Creator, they are all mandated by the latter to exercise authority over His creation. Nevertheless, their authority is always limited by their special position between the heavens and earth.[21]

The juxtaposition of the qualifying phrase "in His image, according to His likeness" with the remark "and let them rule over" shows that between the dignity of humanity created in the image of God and its leading role and destiny, there is a logical correlation.

This correlation between "image" and "authority" or "merit" and "dominion" surfaces in one of the earliest *haggadic midrashim*, that is, *Genesis Rabbah* (ca. 425–500 AD).[22] To express this idea, the ancient Jewish interpreters resort to a pun between two verbs similar in sound and consonantal fabric: *radah* ("to rule, have dominion") and *yarad* ("to descend"):

> R. Hanina said, "If he merits it, [God says,] '*uredu*' (have dominion); while if he does not merit, [God says,] '*yerdu*' (let them descend)." R. Jacob of Kefar Hanan said, "Of him who is in our image and likeness [I say,] '*uredu*' (and have dominion); but of him who is not in our image and likeness [I say,] '*yerdu*' (let them descend)." (*Genesis Rabbah* 8:12)[23]

This *midrashic* interpretation underscores the practical truth that man is to hold sway over creation as long as he produces fruit out of the gifts given by God. If he neglects these gifts up to the point of rendering them fruitless, man is prone to descend beneath the level of other living creatures.

A similar hermeneutical maneuver linking authority over beasts with the image of God that reflects the royal nature of humanity may be found in Gregory of Nyssa (ca. 335–385 AD):

> Let us add that [man's] creation in the image of the nature that governs all demonstrates precisely that he has from the beginning a royal nature. Following common usage, painters of portraits of princes, as well as representing their features,

express their royal dignity by garments of purple, and before this image one is accustomed to say "the king." Thus human nature, created to rule the world because of his resemblance to the universal King, has been made like a living image that participates in the archetype by dignity and by name. He is not clothed in purple, scepter and diadem, for these do not signify his dignity (the archetype himself does not possess them). But in place of purple, he is clothed with virtue, the most royal of garments. Instead of a scepter, he is endowed with blessed immortality. Instead of a royal diadem, he bears the crown of justice, in such a way that everything about him manifests royal dignity, by his exact likeness to the beauty of the archetype. (*On the Making of Man* 4)[24]

Psalm 8 is another text, though not directly related to Genesis 1:26–28, that envisions human destiny in terms of ruling over God's handiwork. Here, the idea of ruling is rendered with the technical verb *mashal*, "to rule, have dominion," and not with the peculiar verb *radah* as in Genesis 1:26.

When I behold Your heavens, the work of Your fingers, the moon and stars that You set in place, what is mortal man (*'enosh*) that You have been mindful of him, human be-ing (*ben 'adam*) that You have taken note of him? You have made him lack little (*meat*) of God, while adorning him with glory and majesty. You have made him have dominion (*mashal*) over Your handiwork, placing everything under his feet. (Ps 8:4–7)

The psalmist speaks of the mysterious duality of humanity, power-ful and weak at the same time. When compared with the rest of creation, humanity looks powerful and noble. When likened to God, it is lacking a "little" (*meat*) in order to become like God, and this missing element brings to humanity continuous struggle and tension, translated into its restrained power and authority over the rest of creation. The relative stamp of human authority is due also to the fact that this authority is not inherent in humanity but rather offered by God as a gift. Or, to use Lev-enson's inspired phrase, humanity in its mastery over creation remains, nothing more, nothing less than "the highest ranking commoner."[25]

In Genesis 1:30 God prescribes for man and beasts the same vegetar-ian diet. This is a reminder for man that, even though created in the image of God and mandated by the latter with authority over the animal world, he is still a creature and hence is dependent on God's mercy.

In light of the above remarks, humans are called by the Creator to be shepherds, stewards, and companions of the non-human creatures while struggling to attain the likeness with the Creator, who takes care of His creation up to its least samples.

3. King-Shepherd Imagery

Any careful reader knows that God is depicted from the first pages of the Scripture as a leader or king, but "this king will never coerce but only invite, evoke, and hope."[26] Consequently, the humanity created in God's image is called to rule over creation as representative of the Creator-King. Genesis 1:26–31 is in fact humanity's enthronement as king of the entire creation.

The kingly authority pattern in Genesis 1:26 is Israelite. In Israel's view on monarchy, the king, far from having unrestricted authority, is called to rule his subjects according to the precepts of the divine law. Thus, the king's authority is exercised with discretion and responsibility and always aimed at the well-being of all. Isaiah's vision (Isa 11:1–9) mirrors an idyllic situation and ideal king projected for a future time.

As Jon D. Levenson[27] well noticed, the use of the verb *radah*, "to rule, hold sway," (Gen 1:26) occurs also in those texts where God, the sovereign King, delegates the Davidic monarch, His viceroy on earth, to rule over His creation (Ps 72:8–11; 110:2; cf. Yahweh's decree in Ps 2:7–9).

It is noteworthy that in Israel, as in the Semitic world at large, the king was seen as a shepherd accompanying his flock; he was to care for, and to sleep and eat along with, his sheep. The kingly dominion or leadership was understood as co-habitation rather than pre-eminence.

In his famous code of laws, Hammurabi, King of Babylon (ca. 1795–1750 BC), introduces himself as follows: "I am Hammurabi, the shepherd of the people." In the epilogue, the same king emphatically proclaims,

> The great gods have called me, I am the salvation-bearing shepherd, whose staff is straight . . . on my breast I cherish the inhabitants of the land of Sumer and Akkad; in my shelter I have let them repose in peace; in my deep wisdom have I enclosed them. That the strong might not injure the weak, in order to protect the widows and orphans, I have in

Babylon the city where Anu and Bel raise high their head, in E-Sagil, the Temple, whose foundations stand firm as heaven and earth, in order to bespeak justice in the land, to settle all disputes, and heal all injuries, set up these my precious words, written upon my memorial stone, before the image of me, as king of righteousness.[28]

Second Isaiah juxtaposes two metaphors, king and shepherd, as describing Yahweh, the Lord of Israel: "Behold, the Lord God comes with might, and His arm rules (*mashal*) for Him; behold, His reward *is* with Him, and His recompense before Him. He will tend His flock like a shepherd (*ro'eh*); He will gather the lambs with His arm, and carry them in His bosom, and gently lead the nursing *ewes*" (Isa 40:10–11).

If in Isaiah 40:10 Yahweh is depicted as a victorious king returning from battle, in v. 11 He is portrayed as a shepherd caring for His flock. He carries gently the lambs and leads the nursing ewes to their resting place. For the sixth-century-BC exiles in Babylon, long-awaited victory and safety represented the most important gifts, hence the portrayal of Yahweh as powerful and gentle at the same time (cf. Deut 1:30–31).[29]

God calls humanity in the vocation of shepherd as a viable and constructive alternative to "an ideology of grasping exploitation and against retreat into irresponsible self-indulgence."[30] Therefore, God's mandate to humanity to rule over creation is really a mandate to serve the other creatures. In support of this view, one may adduce the use of verb *radah* in Genesis 1:26. According to Claus Westermann,[31] this verb designates the traveling of a shepherd along with his flock. There is no pre-eminent position for a genuine shepherd. There is no front, no back, no left, no right, but only *around* and *along with* his sheep.

Psalm 23 depicts God as the model shepherd who cares unceasingly for His sheep so that they may not lack anything. Instead of rough ruling, God the King-Shepherd "leads" (*nahal*), "guides" (*nachah*), and "comforts" (*nacham*) His sheep while offering protection and overflowing prosperity. On the contrary, the bad shepherds do not care for their sheep, but "rule them with cruelty" (Ezek 34:1–4).

In the same Semitic vein, Jesus uses the image of the good shepherd when He speaks of Himself. He is the good shepherd who came to serve instead of being served (John 10).

* * *

As carriers of the image of *Deus absconditus* (Isa 45:15), and through Baptism, of the image of Jesus Christ, Christians (and not only

Christians) have the duty to tend God's creation as a good shepherd tends his flock.

Man's authority over other living creatures is obviously restricted by the command and prohibition of Genesis 2:15–17, and the prohibition of murder (this refers only to human beings; killing animals is not considered murder) and the protection of human life of Genesis 9:1–6. The verbs in Gen 2:15, 'abad ("to work") and shamar ("to keep"), do not evoke an exploitative human activity, but rather care for the earth given to humanity's custody. The first human beings become the stewards of God's creation.

W. Brueggeman invites one to reflect on God as Creator and model in our stewardship for the well-being of the entire creation:

> Yahweh as Creator of humankind and of each human person is sovereign in that relationship. Human persons are creatures who are dependent on and created for obedience. Even before any concrete content is applied to the commands of Yahweh and the obedience of human persons, the category of sovereignty and obedience is a crucial and definitional mark of humans. The One who makes human life possible is holy, glorious, and jealous. Consequently, the force, possibility, and significance of human life are not lodged in an autonomous agent who has been either given full freedom or abandoned, but are lodged in and with the One who makes human life possible by the constant, reliable giving of breath. The human person is not, and cannot be, sufficient to self, but lives by coming to terms with the will and purpose of the One who gives and commands life.[32]

What better way to finish up these brief ruminations on holding sway in companionship with God's other creatures than to offer Isaac the Syrian's inspired words to a world menaced by chaos, hatred, and destruction?

> And what is a merciful heart? It is the heart's burning for the sake of the entire creation, for men, for birds, for animals, for demons, and for every created thing; and by the recollection and sight of them the eyes of a merciful man pour forth abundant tears. From the strong and vehement mercy that grips his heart and from his great compassion, his heart is humbled and he cannot bear to hear of or to see any in-

jury or the slight suffering of anything in creation. For this reason he offers up tearful prayer continually even for irrational beasts, for the enemies of truth, for those who harm him, that they be protected and receive mercy. And, in like manner, he even prays for the lowest as a result of the great compassion, which—after the likeness of God—is poured out beyond measure within his heart. (*Homily* 71)[33]

Notes

This paper is but a modest homage to His All-Holiness Ecumenical Patriarch Bartholomew honoring his genuine love and indefatigable care for God's graceful creation. I would like also to take opportunity to thank His All-Holiness for the hospitality shown to me during my short visit at the Phanar (December 2009) as a Fulbright Fellow conducting research for my fourth book, *The Old Testament in Eastern Orthodox Tradition*, under contract with Oxford University Press.

1. His All-Holiness Ecumenical Patriarch Bartholomew, *Encountering the Mystery: Understanding Orthodox Christianity Today* (New York, NY: Doubleday, 2008), 97.

2. *International Journal for the Study of the Christian Church* 10, nos. 2–3 (2010): 130–143.

3. John Chryssavgis (*Cosmic Grace, Humble Prayer: The Ecological Vision of the Green Patriarch Bartholomew I* [Grand Rapids, MI: Eerdmans, 2009], 20) pertinently remarks, "Perhaps it is natural, or perhaps it is a sign of our arrogance, that we tend to overemphasize our creation 'in the image and likeness of God' (Gen 1:26) and overlook our creation from the dirt and 'the dust of the ground' " (Gen 2:7).

4. Masoretic Text (MT): "let them rule" (*we-yirdû*); Septuagint (LXX): "let them rule" (*archetôsan*); Peshitta (S): "let them exercise authority" (*wa-nshaltun*); Targum Pseudo-Jonathan (T) expands interpretively, "And the Lord said to the angels who ministered before Him, who had been created in the second day of the creation of the world, 'Let us make man in our image, in our likeness; and let them exercise authority (*wa-yishlatun*) over the fish of the sea' "; Vulgate (V): "so that he may take the lead" (*praesit*).

5. F. Brown, ed., *The Brown-Driver-Briggs Hebrew and English Lexicon: With an Appendix Containing the Biblical Aramaic* (Peabody, MA: Hendrickson, 1997), 921–922; henceforth abbreviated BDB.

6. CAD 14:226 (*The Assyrian Dictionary*, ed. R. D. Biggs et al. [Chicago: The Oriental Institute of the University of Chicago, 1999]) lists the following meanings for a quite well-attested verb, *redu* A (*rada'u*,

radu): "to drive animals, wagons, boats, to take along, escort persons, to send, convey merchandise, to guide, control, oversee, to follow a road, to pursue a person." As one may glean from perusing this semantic list, the basic meaning of the verb *redu* (transitive use) is the idea of "escorting" or "accompanying."

7. *Genesis: Translation and Commentary* (New York: W. W. Norton & Co., 1996), 5 and n. 26.

8. Cf. BDB 605.

9. Labeled by biblical scholars the "priestly account of creation" (P), Gen 1:1–2:4a, probably composed during the Babylonian exile (sixth century BC) by a "priestly" author, describes the creation of "heavens and earth" (the Hebrew idiom for the entire creation) in six days, with the seventh day as the crown of God's creative activity.

10. Termed by biblical scholars as the "Yahwist account of creation," Gen 2:4b–25 is commonly dated to the tenth century BC (Solomon's reign). Quite vivid as narrative style, the J ("Jahweh" is the German spelling of "Yahweh") account places humanity at the center of God's creative work.

11. A. Louth, *Genesis 1–11*, vol. 1 of Ancient Christian Commentary on Scripture: Old Testament (Downers Grove, IL: InterVarsity Press, 2001), 40.

12. "In the aesthetic perspective, the distinction of God from God's creature is not nullified. But the friendly disposition of God toward the world is affirmed. God is satisfied that the world he has evoked in love is attuned to his purposes. The blessed world is indeed the world that God intended. Delighting in the creation, God will neither abandon it nor withdraw its permit of freedom" (W. Brueggemann, *Genesis*, Interpretation: A Bible Commentary for Teaching and Preaching [Atlanta, GA: John Knox Press, 1982], 37).

13. The seven-day (heptad) structure attested in Gen 1:1–2:4a is widespread in the ancient Near-Eastern world. In the twenty-second century BC, Gudea, King of Lagash, dedicated a temple during a seven-day festival. Characteristic of the biblical account is that every day something else happens, with a break on the seventh day. See N. M. Sarna, *Genesis: Be-reshit*, JPS Torah Commentary (Philadelphia: Jewish Publication Society, 1989), 4.

14. The first words in the Hebrew Bible—*be-re'shit bara' 'elohim* ("In the beginning God created")—may be also rendered, "When God began to create." If one follows this translation, then there is a grammatical and logical link between v. 1 and what follows in v. 2, with an emphasis that "when" God began to create, there "was" (the verb "to be" with reference to "deep" is missing conspicuously in both MT and LXX of Gen 1:2) some mysterious, watery deep covered by "darkness" to be surveyed or

controlled by *ruach 'elohim* ("wind/spirit of God") moving as a security guard "back and forth" over the menacing vastness of the primordial deep. The root *r-ch-p* (Piel conjugation), "to hover," connotes the idea of vibration. The inert matter is put in motion by God's *ruach*-agent. The Hebrew word for "deep," *tehom*, is treated as a proper noun with no definite article. Though not feminine in form, it is construed with feminine adjectives, a possible hint at the Mesopotamian goddess Tiamat, the female dragon representing the primordial salt water. The same word *tehom* appears in Isa 51:10 in a mythical setting. Gen 1:2 is silent on how this deep came about, but Prov 8:22–24 tries to fill this lacuna by depicting the deep as God's creation. N. M. Sarna (*Genesis: Be-reshit*, 4) argues that Gen 1:3 is the completion of the sentence opened in v. 1, with v. 2 as parenthetical, depicting the state of things in the moment God uttered His first creative words. The rendition beginning with "When . . ." is supported, notices Sarna, by other ancient Near-Eastern literary works, such as *Enuma Elish*, "When above . . ." (the Mesopotamian creation epic known by its opening words). The peculiar syntax, i.e., a noun in *status constructus* (*be-re'shit*) with a finite verb (*bara'*), is attested in other texts (Lev 14:46; Isa 29:1; Hos 1:3). Note that *bara'* refers only to the final product and not to its previous, constitutive elements—another proof that this verb designates a powerful activity.

15. "God" is rendered here by a common noun, *'elohim*. This is a double plural marked noun (something like the ungrammatical English **childrens*, with two markers of plurality on it) that derives from a verbal root, *'-w-l*, "to be strong, mighty, powerful," hence the rendition "All Mighty" ("God" is merely a conventional English rendition of the Hebrew *'elohim*). The double plural marker on this noun accents God's might, so obvious in the creation account.

16. Hebrew *be-re'shit* ("in the beginning") is taken as indicating the beginning of time.

17. The Hebrew verb *bara'* (e.g., Exod 34:10; Num 16:28–30; Isa 65:17; Jer 31:22; Ps 51:12) is exclusively employed with God as subject. Ibn Ezra notices that the verb itself does not indicate the idea of creation out of nothing (*creatio ex nihilo*), unequivocally expressed in 2 Macc 7:28 ("Look up to heaven and earth and see all that is therein, and know that God made them out of things that did not exist [*ouk ex ontôn*]"), but at least it conveys that creation is the product of an almighty God, thus it cannot be reduplicated by human efforts, no matter how strong and persistent they might be.

18. Note that verb *bara'* with regard to particular creatures appears only one time besides Gen 1:27, i.e., in v. 21, on the fifth day of the heptad, when God "created" (*yibra'*) the "great sea monsters" (*hattanninim haggedolim*). The term *tannin* ("sea monster") is elsewhere equated with

Leviathan (Isa 27:1), the terrifying monster symbolizing the evil powers at work (Job 40). Yet Leviathan in Ps 104:26 is emasculated into an object of amusement at the hands of his powerful creator. Unlike the other creatures, which are either called into existence by a command (word) or "made" (*'asah*) by God, humanity and these monsters are the only ones to be "created" (*bara'*). In other words, *'adam* and the *tanninim* are the result of a powerful creational work. Jon D. Levenson (*Creation and the Persistence of Evil: The Jewish Drama of Divine Omnipotence* [Princeton, NJ: Princeton University Press, 1994], 34) sees in the use of *bara'* with respect to the "great sea monsters" (v. 21) the intent of the priestly author who "wishes us to know explicitly that these monsters are not primordial and neither free of God's rule nor an embarrassment to it." The notice (v. 21) that God "created" the "monsters" (*tanninim*—a generic name!) should be read as polemic against the Mesopotamian creation epic *Enuma Elish*, in which Tiamat (the Akkadian common noun *tiamtu* means "sea"), the sea monster, predates the creation.

19. The terms "image" (*tselem*) and "likeness" (*demut*) are used interchangeably (cf. Gen 5:1). Here, as in the ninth-century Assyrian-Aramaic bilingual inscription on a statue at Tell Fekheriyeh in Syria, the pairing of the terms is for emphasis. The whole phrase in Gen 1:26 could be rendered "in His [God's] very image."

20. For rendition in English and discussion of these ancient Near-Eastern texts collected by Wilderberger, see Jon D. Levenson, *Creation*, 114–115.

21. In a canonical reading of Scripture, as intrinsic unity rather than mosaic of various "sources," Gen 2:7 (J) may be adduced as a significant caveat to the optimistic P view on humanity's rule over God's creation (Gen 1:26–27). Gen 2:7 points to humanity, a composite, yet consolidated, creature fashioned out of "dust" (*'apar*) and Yahweh's life-giving "breath" (*neshamah*). A *haggadic midrash* explicates this unique mix on the creation map of Gen 2 in terms of mortality versus immortality: "R. Tifdai said in R. Aha's name: 'The Holy One, blessed be He, said: "If I create him of the celestial elements he will live [forever] and not die, and if I create him of the terrestrial elements, he will die and not live [in a future life]. Therefore I will create him of the upper and of the lower elements: if he sins he will die; while if he does not sin, he will live" ' " (*Genesis Rabbah* 8.11); cf. H. Freedman and M. Simon, eds., *Midrash Rabbah: Genesis*, trans. H. Freedman (London: Soncino Press, 1939; reprint, 1961), 1:62. On humanity as God's "living breath" and some of the theological ramifications of this powerful metaphor, see E. J. Pentiuc, *Jesus the Messiah in the Hebrew Bible* (New York: Paulist Press, 2005), 10–14.

22. Shmuel Safrai et al., eds., *The Literature of the Sages*, vol. 2, *Midrash and Targum, Liturgy, Poetry, Mysticism, Contracts, Inscriptions, Ancient Science, and the Languages of Rabbinic Literature*, Compendia Rerum Iudaicarum ad Novum Testamentum (Amsterdam: Royal Van Gorcum; Minneapolis, MN: Fortress Press, 2006), 149.

23. Freedman and Simon, *Midrash Rabbah: Genesis*, 1:62.

24. Louth, *Genesis 1–11*, 34.

25. Levenson, *Creation*, 112.

26. Brueggemann, *Genesis*, 39.

27. Levenson, *Creation*, 112–113.

28. *The Code of Hammurabi*, trans. L. W. King (reprint, Kessinger Publishing, 2004), 1, 28.

29. W. Brueggemann notices, "In our theological discourse, we are characteristically tempted to pick one of these in preference to the other, to let our preferred one crowd out the other, and to absolutize the preferred one. The witness of Israel, by the rich diversity of nouns, makes such a reductionism in any direction impossible. Thus, one may say that Yahweh is something of a warrior and something of a shepherd, but not finally shepherd and not fully warrior, something of each but not fully either" (*Theology of the Old Testament: Testimony, Dispute, Advocacy* [Minneapolis: Fortress Press, 1997], 232).

30. Cf. Brueggemann, *Genesis*, 38.

31. Westermann, *Genesis 1–11*, Biblischer Kommentar Altes Testament (Neukirchener Verlag, 1999), I/1:218.

32. Brueggemann, *Theology of the Old Testament*, 454.

33. *The Ascetical Homilies of Saint Isaac the Syrian*, trans. D. Miller (Boston, MA: Holy Transfiguration Monastery, 1984), 344–345.

Chapter 9

THEORIA AND PRAXIS IN ST. MAXIMOS THE CONFESSOR'S QUAESTIONES ET DUBIA

Dr. Despina D. Prassas
Adjunct Assistant Instructor of Church History

Douglas Burton-Christie, in his study entitled *The Word in the Desert* on the use of Scripture in the writings of the early Christian monks, describes the importance of the relationship between the words spoken by an elder (γέρων) to a disciple and the actions of that same elder. For the desert monks, holiness of life involved the integration of one's actions and one's words. Burton-Christie cites the example of Abba Moses, for whom the disconnect between one's words and actions was "disastrous."[1] According to Abba Moses, "If a person's deeds are not in harmony with his prayer, he labors in vain."[2] When we come to the seventh century and look at the writings of St. Maximos the Confessor, who will meld together the desert monastic tradition with the writings of Greek patristic tradition,[3] the focus will shift from that of deeds and prayer to action and contemplation. In response to the Origenism of his day, he will emphasize the importance of both *praxis* and *theoria* for living the monastic life.

Theoria, a term that can be defined in many ways,[4] in the ancient world was considered the "highest form of knowledge attainable by the human mind."[5] However, it is Aristotle in particular who describes *theoria* as the supreme end of the human being, and considers the engagement in *theoria* to be associated with a love of knowledge;[6] *theoria* is what brings about pleasure and happiness.[7] Among the Greek patristic writers, the term was primarily understood as spiritual contemplation; the organ which engages in this activity is the *nous*, and it is through the *nous* that one accesses the transcendent realities that exist in the divine Logos.[8]

St. Maximos will develop his own understanding of the role of *theoria* when describing the various stages of the Christian life. Drawing upon the writings of earlier Christian writers,[9] he develops the three stages:[10] the first stage is called πρακτική (but more often, πρᾶξις); the second stage is called γνῶσις, φυσικὴ θεωρία, φυσικὴ φολοσοφία, θεωρία γνωστική, or θεωρητική; and the third stage is called μυστικὴ θεολογία or θεολογία.[11] The term θεολογία is also found in the writings of Evagrios of Pontus,[12] someone from whom Maximos will adopt many ideas regarding the spiritual life, although Maximos "is more precise . . . by choosing his terms more carefully."[13]

In the *Quaestiones et dubia* (henceforth QD), 239 interrogations and responses that address biblical and patristic exegesis and that were most likely directed to a monastic community,[14] St. Maximos outlines the use of the two terms *theoria* and *praxis*. This discussion becomes a paradigm for his biblical interpretation. One point should be made clear: although *theoria* is mentioned fifty-one times in the text and *praxis* is mentioned sixty-one times, both words appear in the same question only thirteen times.[15] This paper will focus on two aspects of Maximos' teaching on *theoria* and *praxis* found in the QD: (1) the relationship between *theoria* and *praxis*, and (2) *theoria* and *praxis* as reflected in the structure of the response to each interrogation.

The Relationship between Theoria and Praxis

In QD 190, Maximos provides a good example of the relationship between the two terms. The interrogation raises concerns about the inconsistency between two biblical passages, Mark 9:1 and Matthew 16:28, which refer to the end times. Will the *eschaton* be marked by the coming of the Kingdom (Mark 9:1) or the coming of the Son of Man (Matt 16:28)? The response specifically refers to a person who engages in action, ὁ πρακτικός, who leaves behind the battle with the passions in order to engage in natural contemplation, τὴν φυσικὴν θεωρίαν. Ὁ πρακτικός dies to the former self and becomes preoccupied with contemplation.[16] Then, such a person passes through natural contemplation, leaving behind all things that have been caused, moving toward the Cause—namely, God—by means of *apophasis*.[17] No longer does this person move among created things.[18] All movement has been transferred to the Creator of all, and any positive, or *kataphatic*, statement regarding the Creator is unnecessary; any understanding of the Creator takes place according to the "theology of negation" (*apophasis*). The conclusion here is that movement from *praxis* to *theoria* progresses in a linear fashion, where *praxis* precedes *contemplation*.

Another example is found in QD 87. After comparing the various elements that constitute the body with those that constitute the soul, Maximos states that the elemental matter of the soul is derived from the four universal virtues (prudence, courage, discretion, and justice) and the right ordering of one's ethical behavior.[19] After the author discusses ethical behavior, the text refers to the habit of engaging in the virtues, and the importance of knowledge, which he defines as contemplation (θεωρία); he concludes the response with "for action is the entryway to contemplation."[20] One proceeds from action to contemplation; *praxis* precedes *theoria*.

However, there are several questions where the order of the progression from *praxis* to *theoria* is not clear. In QD 145, for example, there is a request for a clarification of a passage in Amos (4:8).[21] The request is for an explanation of the two cities. Maximos identifies the two cities as "souls" that have been built by action and contemplation. Any city that does not pursue action, fails.[22] The response draws a close connection between knowledge and action, both of which are necessary for success; neither one is given preference over the other. QD 162 (I, 65) addresses a biblical passage from the Gospel of Mark (2:4).[23] The story tells of the paralyzed man who was lowered by his four friends into a house where Jesus was staying in order to be healed. Maximos equates the paralytic with a *nous* "sick with sin and unable . . . to see the Logos."[24] Natural contemplation (τῆς φυσικῆς θεωρίας) is the door that enables one to see the Logos. The *nous* only receives healing by "faith and [by engaging in] action."[25] There is a coming together of natural contemplation, faith, and action to bring about the healing of the *nous*. The response gives no sense of preference for contemplation, faith, or action; the work of all three is cooperative and seemingly takes place simultaneously. The *nous* is lowered toward the Logos, and in doing so engages in contemplation; the *nous* is able to be healed by faith and action.

In one final example, QD 185, which questions why the raven feeds Elias with bread in the morning and meat in the afternoon (3 Kgdms 17:6), there is still confusion as to the relationship between *theoria* and *praxis*. In the first interpretation of the passage, the bread represents a particular type of nourishment. Elias is nourished by gathering knowledge from "the natural contemplation of the things that exist."[26] In the second interpretation of the passage, Elias is nourished by knowledge and action, where "knowledge is signified by the bread and action by the meat."[27] The knowledge comes about as a result of contemplation; but action is as necessary as knowledge, and perhaps more so, given the association of action with meat. There is no preference for either contemplation or action, and one does not lead to the other, according to the interpretation.

Finally, in QD 130, Maximos addresses the matter directly. He asks, "Whether contemplation (*theoria*) precedes action (*praxis*)?"[28] The response refers to two specific modes of contemplation: that which precedes action, and that which arises out of action.[29] *Theoria* and *praxis* are not understood in terms of a linear progression from one to the next; one (namely, contemplation) does not have precedence over the other (action). In this response, there seems to be an intermingling between the two and a parallelism with regard to significance.[30]

This confusion within the same text with regard to the interrelationship of *theoria* and *praxis* may speak to manuscript transmission issues. In terms of the history of the manuscript tradition, *Vat. gr. 1703*, although the most complete and largest attestation to the QD, is the only manuscript (out of a total of seventeen manuscripts) that includes this question.[31] Although the goal of this paper is not to examine the manuscript tradition, it is important to consider sources that present material that is inconsistent with information found elsewhere in the text. At the same time, there are other possible reasons for the variety of responses regarding the same topic.

There are several references to encounters that Maximos has had with Origenist monks, in particular in *Ambiguum* 7,[32] and also *Ambiguum* 42,[33] where he attempts to clarify the teaching of Gregory of Nazianzus, and to explain the henad of rational beings and the relationship between the body and the soul. Polycarp Sherwood, in his study on Maximos' Origenism, provides a full explanation of the sixth-century controversy and the unresolved issues that Maximos would have inherited.[34] In the sixth century, John of Scythopolis will write a commentary in support of Dionysios the Areopagite's theology in order to mitigate Origenist interpretations of the Areopagite's work.[35] Defending the writings of Origen, Evagrios, and Didymos the Blind would be more difficult. Even though the three were anathematized in the letter to the assembled bishops at the Fifth Ecumenical Council, held in 553 (Constantinople), and their writings condemned, many monastic communities refused to relinquish their works.[36] Questions were raised regarding the interpretation of biblical passages by these writers because their works were embraced by the Origenist monks.

The concern over the influence of Origenist monks in the monasteries was genuine.

Derwas Chitty relates the story of the development and tonsuring of Cyril of Scythopolis as a monk. Cyril's entire family had supported his choice, and his home was often visited by travelers from the wilderness. Among the stories found in the *Vita Euthymii* and the *Vita Johannis Hesychastae*, there is a reference to the concern of Cyril's mother that her son might come under the influence of the Origenists, who "were gaining power in Jerusalem"[37] in the sixth century. Such was the very real concern that the Origenists in the Palestinian monasteries, and particularly in Jerusalem, posed.

When John Moschus and Sophronius (who would become patriarch of Jerusalem several decades later) settled at the New Lavra several decades after the expulsion of the Origenist monks, they would have been familiar with the history of the monastery.[38] After moving west to North Africa (ca. 629), Sophronius encountered Maximos, who was among a community of monks there. Sophronius became his teacher and spiritual father,[39] and would have certainly discussed the ongoing difficulties that the Origenist monks were posing in the monasteries.

With the condemnations of the works of Origen, Evagrios, and Didymos, a crisis emerged within the monasteries: what would the monks read?[40] Were all of Evagrios' works to be discarded? Many monks continued to read the *Chapters on Prayer*,[41] yet a cautious approach was necessary. Therefore, the Origenist controversy that emerged in the seventh century was a problematical monastic trend. This was not simply "an intellectual debate, but a concern—at once philosophical and theological—impinging upon significant aspects of monastic, and thus Christian practice."[42] The Origenist monks who adopted a more speculative understanding of prayer emphasized the importance of *theoria* over *praxis*. This divide between *theoria* and *praxis* would not have been unfamiliar to the seventh-century monks, and Maximos is writing to combat this form of Origenism among the monks.

Theoria *and* Praxis *Reflected in the Structure of the Responses*

Theoria and *praxis* serve as a format for the structure of the responses to the interrogations in the QD. Maximos constructs his sentences and responses in a specific way, and this structure is a reinforcement of the importance of the interdependence of *theoria* and *praxis*.

When looking at a specific question, what emerges is a threefold format. The reader finds the following in almost every question: (1) a biblical or patristic quotation upon which Maximos has been asked to comment; (2) a straightforward, technical explanation of the quotation using a well-known interpretive method; and (3) another explanation of the same interrogation that can only be described as practical or "experiential."[43] A few examples will clarify this threefold format.

In QD 21, Maximos provides an interpretation of the passage from 1 Corinthians 15:23–24 ("Christ is the first fruits; then they who are of Christ at His coming; then [comes] the end"). This is the first aspect of the question, namely, the biblical passage to be interpreted. The author then provides the more straightforward explanation of the passage:

> "Christ" became the "first fruits" through His resurrection; "then they who are of Christ" are they who believe in Him; "then the end" which is the salvation of all the nations through faith.[44]

This is a direct, simple explanation of the passage based primarily on the combined use of the literal, allegorical, and anagogical methods of interpreting specific words in the passage.[45] Christ as "first fruits" is interpreted allegorically as the Resurrection. The passage "they who are in Christ" is interpreted literally as the faithful. The interpretation of "the end" speaks to the end times, the *eschaton*, and Maximos interprets the passage in an anagogical way as "salvation for all." This interpretation is clear, more technical, and in keeping with the basic methods of biblical interpretation.

The next few lines provide the third aspect, that of another interpretation of the passage:

> And if you desire to understand the statements relating to each one, "Christ is the first fruits" is the faith in Him, "then they who are of Christ" are the works of faith, "then the end" means being separated from all things, both perceptible and intelligible, and being joined to God by knowledge.[46]

He prefaces this second interpretation with "if you desire to understand," suggesting a deeper, more thoughtful interpretation for the audience. This interpretation is different in character than the previous interpretation. The description of "Christ is the first fruits" as faith provides a simple interpretation and appeals to the uneducated; this can be understood by anyone, and certainly by a monk. The interpretation of the next section of the passage ("then they who are of Christ") as works of faith also provides a simple explanation of the passage.[47] The interpretation of the last section of the passage ("then the end"), however, offers a more complex interpretation involving both the separation from all "worldly" things and the union with God, specifically by "knowledge" (γνώσεως).[48] This interpretation requires some explanation.

Being separated from all "perceptible and intelligible" things would have been an obvious goal of the monk.[49] However, being joined to God by knowledge begs the question: to what type of knowledge is he referring?

In the *Quaestiones ad Thalassium* (henceforth QT) 60, Maximos discusses two types of knowledge of divine things. He mentions relative knowledge, which is "rooted only in reason and ideas, and lacking in the kind of experiential perception of what one knows through active engagement."[50] The second type of knowledge is called authentic knowledge (τὴν δὲ κυρίως ἀληθινὴν), knowledge rooted in actual experience, and takes place by participating in divine things (such as prayer); this occurs by grace. It is through this second type of knowledge that one attains deification (θέωσις).[51]

The knowledge to which Maximos refers in QD 21 is this second type of knowledge mentioned in QT 60, experiential knowledge, even though he does not use the term experience (πεῖρα).[52] One is separated from "perceptible and intelligible" things in QD 21, which would be similar to the "reason and ideas" of QT 60. The connection to God by knowledge takes place through "active engagement."

As if to emphasize the point, Maximos continues the interpretation by adding the following passage from the biblical text, although it was not mentioned in the interrogation: "Death is the last enemy to be destroyed."[53] The enemy is destroyed, he explains, when "we . . . submit the entire self-determining will to God."[54] This explanation clearly speaks to the action in which the monk needs to engage in order to be "joined to God."

What is of importance here, in this second interpretation of the biblical passage of QD 21, is the reliance of this interpretation on, and the appeal to, experience; there is no emphasis on allegorical or literal interpretation. This second type of interpretation is based on experience or activity.

QD 142 (I, 62 II, 21), interprets a passage from the Acts of the Apostles (1:1–4), that of the descent of the Holy Spirit after the ascension of

Christ.[55] The first interpretation associates the nine orders of the angelic powers described by Dionysios[56] with the nine days from the ascension to the day before Pentecost, because the nine orders of angels were "also in need of a visit from the Lord."[57] The Lord then appeared to God the Father, and at that point the Spirit descended. This is a straightforward allegorical interpretation of the biblical passage that provides the answer to the question "What was Christ doing during the nine days between His ascension and Pentecost?"

The second interpretation claims to provide a response according to "another method of contemplation" (κατ'ἄλλον θεωρίας τρόπον).[58] Interestingly, the explanation appeals to the practice of the Ten Commandments (Exod 20:1–17). The word of God that is concealed in the commandments "is embodied in us,"[59] descends in "us" through the practice of the commandments, and raises "us" until we come to "the most lofty of all the commandments, which says, 'The Lord is your God, the Lord is one.' "[60] The interpretation comes to an end by describing the activity of the *nous*, which only by releasing all things and coming to an end in God becomes God through the activity of grace.[61]

Access to the Word comes through participation in the commandments, which are the word of God. The commandments are the agents through which God comes to be embodied in and descends into the human being. This takes place only when one takes part in the practice of the commandments. The emphasis here is on the progression through the commandments if one is to come to the realization of the most "lofty commandment," namely, that God is one. Only in this way is oneness with God possible. The inclusion of the importance of the practice of the commandments turns the focus of the interpretation to that of "action." The monks must engage in action in order to achieve oneness with God.

Lastly, QD 185 also provides two interpretations of the story of Elias and the raven who feeds him (3 Kgdms 17). The raven represents human nature blackened through disobedience, and Elias represents the knowledgeable *nous* "sitting in the gully of temptations and labors of *askesis*."[62] The interpretation outlines the importance of being nourished by gathering knowledge of the natural contemplation of things that exist, and being initiated into the mystery of the Incarnation of the Lord that will occur at the end times.[63]

The second interpretation begins with a typological interpretation of Elias as the Lord.[64] However, the tone of the interpretation changes, and the emphasis is placed on the experiences that Jesus Christ endured. The gully represents the present life, where one is exposed to temptations and sufferings that are to be endured voluntarily. The Lord was not accepted by His own people, and they did not "nourish Him."[65] It was the nations (τὰ ἔθνη) who welcomed and nourished Him through knowledge and action (διὰ γνώσεως καὶ πράξεως), where the bread fed to Elias is knowledge, and the meat is action.[66]

Again, there is an emphasis on the importance of action or behavior for living the Christian life. The life of the monk was not simply one of prayer or contemplation; temptation and suffering are part of the monastic life, and must be addressed through the practice of spiritual disciplines.

There are two formats for the interpretations found in the QD. One format incorporates the interpretive methods that would have been familiar to Maximos' audience: those of typology, arithmology, as well as literal, allegorical, and anagogical interpretation of Scripture.[67] The second format focuses on the more practical interpretation of scripture: how does the interpretation contribute to the daily life of the monk and provide examples for how to live? I label the first format a type of *theoria*, contemplation of Scripture that involves a more intellectual approach. The second format is a type of *praxis* where the understanding of Scripture is based on a more practical approach. This pattern of presenting one after the other, a *theoria*-based approach and a *praxis*-based approach, is repeated throughout the entire *Quaestiones et dubia*. There are multiple interpretations of each biblical passage, but these two formats of interpretation appear in almost every question. What was the motivation for this twofold structure of interpretation? Why was there a need to provide a more practical interpretation?

Perhaps the intention was not to provide an alternate, practical interpretation of Scripture, but rather to offer a more balanced approach to the interpretation of Scripture, and to the monastic life, in general. Maximos encouraged the "middle way," the Aristotelian understanding of the mean[68] that was embraced by many patristic writers, and clearly states the importance of this approach in QD 27.

In QD 27, the interpretation of the story from Exodus (16)[69] refers to "manna" as the word of God that is united to a person when he or she engages in action and knowledge (πράξεως καὶ γνώσεως); this activity nourishes the soul.[70] The appropriate use of the "word of God" takes place when one follows the "middle way of the virtues" (τὴν μεσότητα τῶν ἀρετῶν) and one avoids all excesses or minimal use of the virtues.[71] The person who follows this approach is able to understand and use Scripture properly. Maximos provides an example, however, that does not relate to scriptural interpretation; he is, no doubt, relating a contemporary example from the life of the monk.

Whenever someone who maintains a celibate lifestyle (i.e., a monk) avoids promiscuous behavior but "judges marriage to be abominable" (βδελυκτόν δὲ τὸν γάμον κρινεῖ), he is not using reason properly, but excessively.[72] The "*logos* of continence"[73] becomes "rancid" as a result of his inability to moderate the excessive judgment. Maximos continues that it "not only becomes rancid, but also brings forth worms, that is, gives birth to other passions."[74] The inability of the monk to temper his ability to judge will lead to a struggle with other passions. The move toward the extreme position weakens the monk's ability to control other areas of his spiritual and monastic life, making him susceptible to the fluctuations of the passions. This emphasis on the balance between the extremes returns the discussion to the topic of this paper.

Patristic and biblical interpretation took on a crucial importance in the seventh century; concerns regarding interpretation had been building since the Arian controversies of the early fourth century, especially within the monasteries.[75] Monastic exegesis was of a particular type: "for the monk devoted to the pursuit of perfection it was reasonable to link ascetical progress with scriptural study."[76] The way in which the Bible and the Fathers were understood influenced how the monks lived their lives. With unbridled interpretation came controversy, attacks on the faith, and disagreement about what constituted correct monastic practice. The ongoing discussion of the issue of interpretation would be addressed in the latter part of the seventh century at the Council in Trullo, where canon 19 required that only clergy be allowed to interpret Scripture and that any interpretation should be in accordance with the teachings of the Church Fathers. Improvisation was frowned up. For the monks, the discussion was not a purely intellectual one.

St. Maximos the Confessor, in the *Quaestiones et dubia*, attempts to provide an interpretation of Scripture that upholds the teachings of the Church Fathers, and supports the monastic life by emphasizing the balance between *theoria* and *praxis*. He demonstrates a parallelism between the two concepts that validates the importance of each; this position would not have been acceptable to the Origenist monks of his day. Both *theoria* and *praxis* were necessary for the Christian life, and Maximos outlines this necessity by the three stages of spiritual development: *praktike*, *theoretike*, and *mystike theologia*. For St. Maximos, these stages were essential in order to achieve the most important goal of the monastic, and the Christian, life: "oneness with God."

Notes

1. Douglas Burton-Christie, *The Word in the Desert: Scripture and the Quest for Holiness in Early Christian Monasticism* (Oxford: Oxford University Press, 1993), 145.

2. Abba Moses, *Apophthegmata Patrum* 17, PG 65:288BC, cited in Burton-Christie, *The Word in the Desert*, 145. There is also the story of Antony of Egypt (Antony 1) that describes action as the remedy for the struggle with the thoughts (*logismoi*). Antony, who was struggling with his thoughts, after asking God for help comes upon a man who was calmly alternating work with prayer. The man (an angel in disguise) advised Antony, "Do this and you will be saved" (PG 65:76B).

3. This is one of the themes of Paul Blowers' book *Exegesis and Spiritual Pedagogy in Maximus the Confessor: An Investigation of the Quaestiones ad Thalassium*, vol. 7 of Christianity and Judaism in Antiquity, ed. C. Kannengiesser (Notre Dame, IN: University of Notre Dame Press, 1991), chap. 1, where he discusses the relationship between the patristic exegetical ἀπορίαι tradition and the spiritual pedagogical tradition of monastic questions and responses, "where the *quaestio-responsio* was never destined to be a purely literary genre *per se* but primarily a teaching device adapted to a wide variety of literary formats" (28). For a short but comprehensive history of the *quaestio-responsio* tradition in Christian literature beginning in the third century CE, see John Haldon, "The Works of Anastasius of Sinai: A Key Source for the History of Seventh-Century East Mediterranean Society and Belief," in *The Byzantine and Early Islamic Near East*, vol. 1, *Problems in the Literary Source Material*, ed. Averil Cameron and Lawrence I. Conrad, Studies in Late Antiquity and Early Islam 1 (Princeton, NJ: Darwin Press, 1992), 116–118. For a discussion of Maximos' use of the *quaestiones* genre in the *Quaestiones et dubia*, see André-Louis Rey, "Les Eratopokriseis dans le Monde Byzantin: Tradition Manuscrite des Textes Anciens et Production de Nouveaux Textes," in *Eratopokriseis: Early Christian Question-and-Answer Literature in Context*, Proceedings of the Utrecht Colloquium, 12–14 October 2003, ed. Annelie Volgers and Claudio Zamagni (Leuven, Netherlands: Peeters, 2004), 178–180.

4. The entry occupying almost four columns in G. W. H. Lampe, ed., *A Patristic Greek Lexicon* (Oxford, 1994), but understood by most of the Greek patristic writers as "spiritual contemplation" (ibid., 648); other definitions include "consideration," "investigation," "study." When used in exegetical texts, the word is considered a technical term for the spiritual sense of Scripture, and represents the intermediate position with regard to exegetical style between the so-called schools of Antioch and Alexandria (ibid., 649).

5. A. Di Berardino, ed., *Encyclopedia of the Early Church*, vol. 2, trans. Adrian Walford (New York: Oxford University Press, 1992), 832. This was the consensus of the Presocratics, Platonists, Aristotelians, all the way through to the writings of the Neoplatonists.

6. *Protr.* fr. 6 Walzer, *Aristotelis dialog. fragm.* (Florence, 1934), 35, 13–41, cited in Di Berardino, *Encyclopedia of the Early Church*, 2:832. For a more general explanation of the use of *theoria* in the Greek patristic writers, see Di Berardino (ibid., 2:832).

7. "For there are actual pleasures that involve no pain or appetite (e.g., those of contemplation), the nature in such a case not being defective at all" (*Nichomachean Ethics* VII 1152b36–1153a1, translated by David Ross as *The Nichomachean Ethics of Aristotle* [reprint, London: Oxford University Press, 1972], 185).

8. Di Berardino, *Encyclopedia of the Early Church*, 2:832.

9. See Lars Thunberg's classic study of Maximos' theological anthropology, *Microcosm and Mediator: The Theological Anthropology of Maximus the Confessor*, 2nd ed. (Chicago: Open Court, 1995), where he traces the concepts of the *vita practica*, the *vita contemplativa*, and the *vita mystica* in Maximos' predecessors, 333–335.

10. Thunberg, *Microcosm and Mediator*, 335–338.

11. Ibid., 335–336.

12. Ibid., 335.

13. Ibid., 336.

14. All references to the Greek are from Declerck's critical edition, which henceforth will be referred to as "Declerck": José Declerck, ed., *Maximi Confessoris Quaestiones et dubia*, Corpus Christianorum Series Graeca 10 (Turnhout, Belgium: Brepols, 1982). References to this text will include the question and line number, followed by the page number in the critical edition. In terms of terminology, I use the term "question" to describe the interrogation and response, and will use these last two terms to describe the specific parts of the question.

15. QD 17, QD 29, QD 30, QD 80, QD 87, QD 130, QD 142, QD 145, QD 162, QD 185, QD 187, QD 190, QD I, 68.

16. Ἐνασχολούμενος τῇ τῶν ὄντων θεωρίᾳ (Declerck, 190.119–120, 132).

17. Declerck, 190.21–23, 132.

18. Ἀλλὰ καὶ ὁ περάσας τὴν φυσικὴν θεωρίαν καὶ πάντα τὰ αἰτιατὰ καταλιπὼν καὶ εἰς τὸν αἴτιον ἐλθὼν διὰ τῆς θεολογικῆς ἀποφάσεως, καὶ οὗτος ἔθανεν τῇ προτέρᾳ καταστάσει, μηκέτι ἐν τοῖς πεποιημένοις κινούμενος (Declerck, 190.21–25, 132).

19. Καὶ τῆς ψυχῆς ἡ ἐκ τῶν τεσσάρων ἀρετῶν στοιχείωσις καὶ ἀρχὴ ποιεῖ τὴν τῶν ἠθῶν κατόρθωσιν (Declerck, 87.8–10, 68).

20. Πρᾶξις γὰρ ἐπίβασις θεωρίας (Declerck, 87.12, 68).

21. "And two or three cities will be gathered up into one city to drink water and they will not be satisfied" (Declerck, 145.1–3, 103).

22. Ἐπειδὴ δὲ τὴν πρᾶξιν οὐ μετέρχονται, ἀποτυγχάνουσιν (Declerck, 145.12–13, 103).

23. The same story is found in Luke 5:19.

24. Παραλυτικός ἐστιν πᾶς νοῦς ἐν ἁμαρτίαις νοσῶν καὶ μὴ δυνά μενος . . . ἰδεῖν τὸν λόγον (Declerck, 162.9–11, 113).

25. Καὶ τῇ πίστει καὶ τῇ πράξει λαμβάνει τὴν ἴασιν (Declerck, 162.14–15, 113).

26. Γνῶσιν ἐκ τῆς τῶν ὄντων φυσικῆς θεωρίας συλλέγων (Declerck, 185.8–9, 126).

27. Ἔθρεψαν διὰ γνώσεως καὶ πράξεως, διὰ τοῦ ἄρτου τῆς γνώ σεως δηλουμένης, διὰ δὲ τοῦ κρέατος τῆς πράξεως (Declerck, 185.18–20, 126).

28. Εἰ προηγεῖται ἡ θεωρία τῆς πράξεως (Declerck, 130.1, 95).

29. Διττὸς ὁ τῆς θεωρίας τρόπος. α μὲν ὁ ὁρίζων τοῖς πρακτοῖς τὰ δέοντα, ὅστις καὶ προηγεῖται τῶν πρακτῶν. ὁ δὲ ἕτερος ὁ τὰ πραττόμενος διανοούμενος, ὅστις καὶ μετεπινοεῖται τῆς πράξεως (Declerck, 130.2–5, 95).

30. Thunberg confirms the importance of the parallelism between *theoria* and *praxis* in his examination of Gregory of Nyssa's writings on the *vita practica* and the *vita contemplativa*; see *Microcosm and Mediator*, 334. Evagrios, in a text that has not been confirmed to have come from his hand, agrees with this parallelism, but adds virtue and *gnosis* (PG 40:1278A). Interestingly, Gregory of Nazianzus sees *praxis* as a ladder to *theoria* (*Oration* 4.113 [PG 35:649B–652A] and *Oration* 20.12 [PG 90:1092B]) but considers the *vita practica* as functioning at a lower level than contemplation, even though the two are interrelated.

31. For a thorough analysis of *Vat. gr.* 1703, see Declerck, xxv–xxxiv, xcvii–ci, and for a comparison of the manuscript with the second most reliable branch of the manuscript tradition, Selection I, see ccxxvii–ccxliv.

32. PG 91:1069C.

33. PG 91:1325C.

34. By the seventh century, the Origenist monks were utilizing the teachings of Gregory of Nazianzus and Gregory of Nyssa to support their positions. The starting point for the discussion on the question of Maximos' Origenism and to whom he is responding is Polycarp Sherwood's study, *The Earlier Ambigua of Saint Maximus the Confessor and His Refutation of Origenism*, Studia Anselmiana, Philosophica, Theologica 36 (Rome: Herder, 1955), specifically pt. 2, chap. 1, entitled "Maximus and Origenism," especially 72–92. Sherwood concludes that "Maximus works with a knowledge of the Origenist literature, not improbably

of Origen himself'" (90). Other descriptions of difficult conversations are recorded in *Ambigua* 10, 15, and 39. Although the discussion of Maximos' Origenism has not really progressed significantly (see *St. Maximus the Confessor's "Questions and Doubts,"* trans. Despina D. Prassas [DeKalb, IL: Northern Illinois University Press, 2010], 10, 12; and Joshua Lollar's critique of her position in "Book Reviews," *Journal of Early Christian Studies* 19, no. 1 [Spring 2011], 151), Brian E. Daley, in his article "Apokatastasis and 'Honorable Silence' in the Eschatology of Maximus the Confessor" (*Maximus Confessor: Actes du Symposium sur Maxime le Confesseur, Fribourg 2–5 septembre 1980,* ed. Felix Heinzer and Christoph von Schönborn, Paradosis 27 [Fribourg, Switzerland: Éditions Universitaires, 1982], 309–339), not only provides an excellent history of the discussion on Maximos' Origenism, which often is based on his comments on the topic of the *apokatastasis,* but couches what may be perceived as Maximos' Origenism in his eschatology. He also addresses Maximos' understanding of *apokatastasis* in QD 19. What is probably of equal importance to defining Maximos' Origenism is the development of an understanding of *why* he incorporated the writings of Origen, Evagrios, and Didymos in his works, even though he does not mention these three by name. For the "six successive moments" of Origenism, beginning with the teachings of Origen in the third century, see "Origenism" in Di Berardino, *Encyclopedia of the Early Church,* 2:623.

    35. Sherwood, *The Earlier Ambigua,* 76, citing John of Scythopolis' commentary on Dionysios.

    36. The condemnations of 543 and 553 are found in Hefele-Leclercq, *Histoire des Conciles,* 2.2 (Paris, 1908), 1182–1198. The anathemas of the Fifth Ecumenical Council (as well as Justinian's 543 edict against Origen and his doctrines, specifically that of the *apokatastasis*) reflected the positions and difficulties that arose as a result of the teachings of the "Isochrist" and the "Protoctist" monks with regard to Origenist and Christological issues. Evagrios' Christology would be seen as identical with the position of the Isochrists, and the issue of *apokatastasis* became the primary one that would be condemned in the anathemas of the Council of 553. See the afterword in Elizabeth A. Clark, *The Origenist Controversy: The Cultural Construction of an Early Christian Debate* (Princeton, NJ: Princeton University Press, 1992). But Origen is the person to whom the Isochrists appeal, and this results in his association with them; see "Origenism" in Di Berardino, *Encyclopedia of the Early Church,* 2:623. See also Adam G. Cooper, *The Body in St. Maximus the Confessor: Holy Flesh, Wholly Deified,* Oxford Early Christian Series, ed. Gillian Clark and Andrew Louth (Oxford: Oxford University Press, 2005), 67–73.

37. Derwas Chitty, *The Desert a City* (reprint, Crestwood, NY: St. Vladimir's Seminary Press, 1995), 123. The references to the story of Cyril's mother are found in the *Vita Euthymii*, 71.20–27, and the *Vita Johnnis Hesychastae*, 216.10–15. Chitty outlines the difficulties of the presence of the Origenist monks in the monasteries of Palestine in the sixth century, specifically the battles between the monks of the Old and New Lavras, 124ff. See also Jennifer L. Hevelone-Harper, *Disciples of the Desert: Monks, Laity, and Spiritual Authority in Sixth Century Gaza* (Baltimore: Johns Hopkins University Press, 2005), 24–25 and corresponding footnotes for the response of the monks of Gaza, in particular, of Barsanuphios, who "brought the attention of his disciples back to the practical task at hand—their own spiritual formation" (24).

38. They probably settled at the New Lavra some time between 590 and 603, and stayed at the monastery of Theodosius also (John Patrich, *Sabas, Leader of Palestinian Monasticism: A Comparative Study in Eastern Monasticism, Fourth to Seventh Centuries*, Dumbarton Oaks Research Library and Collection [Washington, DC: Dumbarton Oaks/ Trustees for Harvard University, 1995], 348).

39. Ibid.

40. Hevelone-Harper describes the dilemma at Tawatha and the struggles of the monks to read the works of Origen and Didymos, and the *Kephalia Gnostica* of Evagrios, along with the writings of Evagrios' disciples; see Hevelone-Harper, *Disciples of the Desert*, 24. Chitty cites this same story; see *The Desert a City*, 136. The monks of Tawatha took their questions to Barsanuphios, who refused to discuss the topic of the pre-existence of souls or the final punishment; he advised that they practice humility, obedience, tears, asceticism, poverty, and detachment (Barsanuphios and John, *Letter* 600). However, there is evidence that he was "willing to discuss the nature of the resurrected body" in *Letter* 607 (Hevelone-Harper, *Disciples of the Desert*, 157n64).

41. John of Scythopolis will concede that the monk could read Evagrios for what was useful, although he encourages the monk to discard the rest (*Letter* 602, in Hevelone-Harper, *Disciples of the Desert*, 157n64). Antoine Guillaumont, in his *Les "Kephalaia Gnostica,"* also describes how Evagrios' ascetical works would continue to be read by Greek Christians, but his more speculative treatises would be dismissed; see Guillaumont, *Les "Kephalaia Gnostica" d'Evagre le Pontique et l'histoire de l'origénisme chez les Grecs et chez les Syriens*, Patristica Sorbonensia 5 (Paris: Éditions du Seuil, 1962), 166–167, 170. Some works of Evagrios were preserved under the names of other authors.

42. Cooper, *The Body in St. Maximus the Confessor*, 67.

43. After reading through the responses, one might wonder whether this second type of interpretation is an expression of Maximos' own personal experience.

44. Ἀπαρχὴ Χριστὸς διὰ τῆς ἀναστάσεως γέγονεν, ἔπειτα οἱ τοῦ Χριστοῦ, οἱ εἰς αὐτὸν πιστεύσαντες, εἶτα τὸ τέλος, πάντων τῶν ἐθνῶν ἡ διὰ πίστεως σωτηρία (Declerck, 21.4–6, 19).

45. For a discussion of Maximos' biblical interpretive style, see the chapter on Maximos written by George C. Berthold in Charles Kannengiesser, *Handbook of Patristic Exegesis: The Bible in Ancient Christianity* (Leiden, Netherlands: Brill, 2006), 942–967, especially the subsections on anagogy (sec. II), tropology (sec. IV), and allegory (sec. VI). Often in the QD, Maximos tells his reader exactly what type of exegetical method he is using, for example, in QD 8.9, "κατὰ τὸ γράμμα" and "κατὰ δὲ τὸν τῆς ἀναγωγῆς τρόπον."

46. Εἰ δὲ καὶ εἰς τὸν καθένα θέλεις ἐκλαβεῖν τὰ εἰρημένα, ἀπαρχὴ Χριστός ἐστιν ἡ εἰς αὐτὸν πίστις, ἔπειτα οἱ τοῦ Χριστοῦ, τὰ ἔργα τῆς πίστεως, εἶτα τὸ τέλος, τὸ χωρισθῆναι πάντων, αἰσθητῶν τε καὶ νοητῶν, καὶ διὰ γνώσεως κολληθῆναι τῷ θεῷ (Declerck, 21.6–11, 19).

47. Gaining knowledge of God requires faith itself, as well as works of faith; see *Ambiguum* 10 (PG 91:1148D).

48. " 'Then the end' means being separated from all things, both perceptible and intelligible, and being joined to God by knowledge" (τὸ χωρισθῆναι πάντων, αἰσθητῶν τε καὶ νοητῶν, καὶ διὰ γνώσεως κολληθῆναι τῷ θεῷ; Declerck, 21.9–11, 19).

49. Within the QD, there are several references to the importance of detachment (*apatheia*), usually described as "perfect detachment": QD 10, QD 29, QD 48, QD 61, QD 90, QD 127, QD 167, QD 177, QD III, 1.

50. QT 60.63–66, in *Maximi Confessoris Quaestiones ad Thalassium*, vol. 2, *Quaestiones LVI–LXV, una cum Latina interpretatione Ioannis Scotti Eriugenae iuxta posita*, ed. Carl Laga and Carlos Steel, Corpus Christianorum Series Graeca 22 (Turnhout, Belgium: Brepols, 1990), 77. Henceforth the series will be abbreviated CCSG.

51. CCSG 22.60.67–71, 77. According to A. Cooper, Maximos is indebted to Dionysios the Areopagite for this understanding of knowledge (*The Body in Maximus the Confessor*, 29).

52. For a discussion on the term πεῖρα in the writings of Maximos, see Pierre Miquel, "Πεῖρα: Contribution à l'étude du vocabulaire de l'expérience religieuse dans l'oeuvre de Maxime le Confesseur," *Studia Patristica* 7 (Berlin: Akademie-Verlag, 1966), 355–361.

53. 1 Cor 15:26.

54. Ὅτ'ἂν καὶ αὐτοὶ τὸ αὐτεξούσιον θέλημα ἅπαν τῷ θεῷ παραχωρήσωμεν (Declerck, 21.11–13, 19).

55. Acts 1:1–11.

56. Dionysios the Areopagite, *De cael. hier.* 6.2 (PG 3:200D).

57. Ἑκάστῳ τάγματι μίαν ἡμέραν ἀπένειμεν ἀπὸ τῆς ἐσχάτης ἕως τῆς τελευταίας; ἐδέοντο γὰρ καὶ αὗται τῆς τοῦ κυρίου πρὸς αὐτὰς ἐπιδημίας (Declerck, 142.6–8, 101).

58. Declerck, 142.12–13, 101.

59. Σωματοῦται δὲ ἐν ἡμῖν (Declerck, 142.14, 101).

60. Μέχρις οὗ ἔλθωμεν εἰς τὴν πάντων ὑψηλοτέραν τῶν ἐντολῶν, τὴν λέγουσαν κύριος ὁ θεός σου, κύριος εἷς ἐστιν (Declerck, 142.16–18, 101).

61. Μᾶλλον δὲ πάντα ἀφεὶς ὁ ἡμέτερος νοῦς εἰς αὐτὸν τὸν θεὸν καταλήξει . . . θεὸς κατὰ χάριν γινόμενος (Declerck, 142.19–21, 101).

62. Ἐν τῷ χειμάρρῳ τῶν πειρασμῶν καί τῶν πόνων τῆς ἀσκήσεως ἱδρυμένου (Declerck, 185.6–7, 126).

63. Declerck, 185.7–11, 126.

64. Declerck, 185.13, 126.

65. Οἱ ἴδιοι εἰς τὰ ἴδια ἐλθόντα οὐ παρέλαβον οὐδὲ ἔθρεψαν (Declerck, 185.16–17, 126).

66. Declerck, 185.19–20, 126.

67. For a list of the "tools" Maximos uses to interpret Scripture, see D. Prassas, *St. Maximus the Confessor*, 22–31.

68. Aristotle, *Nichomachean Ethics*, II.8.1108b and II.9.1109a.

69. The story in Exodus 16 refers to the complaints of the Israelites regarding lack of food, and the raining down of manna from heaven. For Maximos, this story will illustrate the importance of moderation, the importance of following the "middle way."

70. Τὸ μάννα σημαίνει τὸν τοῦ θεοῦ λόγον τὸν πᾶσιν διὰ πράξεως καὶ γνώσεως προσφυῶς ἁρμοζόμενον καὶ τὴν ψυχὴν τρέφοντα (Declerck, 27.3–5, 22).

71. Declerck, 27.6–8, 23. Maximos also uses the term "royal middle way" in QD 184: μεσότητι καὶ ὁδῷ βασιλικῇ (Declerck, 184.18, 125).

72. Declerck, 27.8–9, 23.

73. This phrase is also found in Philo (*Leg. alleg.* 2.78) and Chrysostom (*In Ep. I Cor.*, PG 61:152).

74. Καὶ οὐ μόνον ἐπώζεσεν, ἀλλὰ καὶ σκώληκας ἐξῆρψεν, τουτέστιν πάθη ἕτερα γεννήσας (Declerck, 27.13–15, 23).

75. The use of allegory to interpret the biblical narratives was highly problematical and was believed to produce the majority of the errors. The letter of Theophilus of Antioch, found among Jerome's letters (*Letter* 98), saw allegorical interpretation as detrimental for any understanding of the truth of Scripture (Berthold, *Handbook*, 946).

76. Berthold, *Handbook*, 944. Perhaps the word "necessary" should be used instead of "reasonable."

Chapter 10

Sanctity, Asceticism, and the Environment

Dr. James C. Skedros
Cantonis Professor for Byzantine Studies and
Professor of Early Christianity and Byzantine History

O ver the past several decades, the desert ascetical tradition of the
fourth through the seventh centuries has become popular reading for Christians and non-Christians alike. The *Sayings of the Desert
Fathers*, the *Life of Antony*, the lives of the great ascetics of the Palestinian desert Euthymius and Sabas, the spiritual correspondence of Sts.
Barsanuphius and John, the *Life of Mary of Egypt*, and many other texts
have found their way onto the bookshelves of Christians, especially Orthodox, Catholic, and Anglican, looking for spiritual nourishment and
guidance in an increasingly mechanized, digitized, and impersonal
world.[1] The desert wisdom of these early Christian men and women en-
compasses, among other elements, an intense love for God, a self-sacri-
ficial love, an unending struggle with the temptations and attractions of
the world, and an unwavering respect for God's creation. For those of us
living in a world dependent on an economic model of overconsumption,
the simplistic life of the desert ascetics is not only alluring, but may be
our only answer to human-driven environmental catastrophe. Committed to a life of *askesis* and the pursuit of sanctity, these desert ascetics
had a deep love and respect for God and all of his creation (animate and
inanimate, seen and unseen), resulting in a harmonious existence with
God, neighbor, and the world.

The evidence from the teachings and stories of the Desert Fathers
and Mothers is unambiguous: a life of repentance, *askesis*, sacrificial
love, prayer, and so forth has a direct impact on the environment. Their
spiritual struggle for salvation impacted the created world; though they
fled "the world," their theological and spiritual orientation had direct

consequences on their world. Examples abound. In his collection of stories about saintly ascetics of the Palestinian and Syrian deserts, John Moschos, the seventh-century Christian pilgrim and close friend of the future Patriarch Sophronios of Jerusalem, relates the following story:

> Abba Polychronius the priest also told us about another elder living in the same Lavra of Abba Peter who would often go off and stay on the banks of the holy Jordan. There he found a lion's den in which he installed himself. One day he found two lion-cubs in the cave. Wrapping them up in his cloak, he took them to church. "If we kept the commandments of our Lord Jesus Christ," he said, "these animals would fear us. But because of our sins we have become slaves and it is rather we who fear them."[2]

The harmonious encounter with nature, especially wild animals, is common in the writings by and about the desert ascetics. These and other stories serve to illustrate that the saint is capable of participating in a restored natural relationship between fallen humanity and the created cosmos. Yet this does not occur magically. It is the result of a focused commitment of love for God and his creation, self-sacrifice, and an ascetic way of living. In what follows, these three elements will be examined within the context of the writings of and about the Desert Fathers in order to provide a response to the environmental crises that we face today.

Saintly Love

Walk into any Orthodox Church and you are greeted by an array of images depicting Christ, His mother, and the saints. Icons on the screen separating the altar area from the main body of the church, images of the saints in the narthex waiting to be venerated and greeted, and pictures of Christ and His saints on the walls and ceilings of the church are standard fare in an Orthodox church. Saints and sainthood are part of the very foundation of the Church. In his Letters, St. Paul addresses his fellow Christians as "saints." Even in the Liturgy, before the singing of the communion hymn, the priest acknowledges the presence of the consecrated Gifts of bread and wine before him, Gifts that have become the Body and Blood of our Lord: "The holy Gifts for the holy people of God (*ta hagia tois hagiois*)." That is, these consecrated Gifts are for "the saints."

Yet who is the saint, and what constitutes being a saint? Our images of the saints are those who are otherworldly, those whom we try to emulate but whom we will never truly be like. From the great theologians of the Church (like St. Basil, St. Gregory the Theologian, St. Gregory Palamas) to the ascetics or monastics (such as St. Antony, St. Mary of Egypt, St. Silouan the Athonite)—how might we ever live as they did? The common conception of the saint is someone whom we lift up as an example of Christian living but whose life we can only dream of imitating. Such an exalted view of the saints, however, does a disservice to the Christian message. St. John Chrysostom, the well-known fourth-century preacher and archbishop of Constantinople, in his first homily on St. Paul's Letter to the Romans offers a simple definition of a saint. Commenting on the opening verses of the Letter, where Paul addresses "all those in Rome beloved of God, called to be saints" (Rom 1:7), Chrysostom notes that Paul

> did not simply write "to all in Rome," but added "to all God's beloved (*agapetois theou*)." Why? Because this is the best distinction which demonstrates from where sanctification comes. From where, then, does sanctification come? From love. This is why, after having said "beloved," [Paul] added "called to be saints."[3]

For Chrysostom, the definition of a saint is one who loves. The vocation of sanctity is to love.

The goal of the Christian life is love. Our ability to love is the true measure of our spiritual life, the true measure of our worth as Christians, the true measure of our humanity. The "law of love," to borrow a phrase from the spiritual classic *Unseen Warfare*, is the law of the Christian faith. But what is this love, how does one attain it, and to whom is it directed?

An overused and abused term, the word "love" is employed to describe a variety of human emotions. In the Orthodox Christian context, love is unselfish and selfless, sacrificial and giving. Christian love places the emphasis on the other, whether the other is God, one's neighbor, enemy, friend, or the environment. This love is service-oriented and is founded upon respect for the other. In the words of the Orthodox theologian Oliver Clément, love is "a disinterested affection that does not ask to be paid in return . . . It is the ability to discover in the other person an inward nature as mysterious as our own, but different and willed to be so by God."[4]

In the ascetical writings of the Orthodox Church, especially those coming out of the tradition of the Desert Fathers, Christian love is also equated with love for God. The deep ascetic impulse for communion and union with God, which lies at the heart of the monastic enterprise in the Christian East, resounds in these ascetical writings. Yet even in these writings, the love of God—that intense desire for union with the divine that is a universal aspect of mystical writings, be they from the Orthodox East, the Christian West, or even the Islamic Sufi mystical tradition—is never divorced from love of God's creation. St. Silouan the Athonite, the humble Russian monastic who lived on Mt. Athos from 1892 until his death in 1938, reaffirms the traditional ascetic impulse "My soul thirsts for the living God," but only in the context of perhaps his most famous saying: "Blessed is the soul that loves her brother, for our brother is our life."[5] The Christian desire for God—to love God—that yearning of the soul for its Creator, is never complete, never fully realized, except in the context of love for one's neighbor. The metaphor of a circle with God at its center reflects this: as we journey from the outer circle to the center along any one radius, we naturally draw closer to those journeying to the center of the circle along a different radius.[6] The closer we draw to God, the closer we are to our neighbor. Love for God cannot be divorced from love for our neighbor.

Are we to understand the environment as our neighbor? In the sense that the environment is brought into being by the Creator, the answer is yes. Yet, humanity is ontologically different from God's non-human creation in that it is only the human being who is created in the image and likeness of God. Yet within the tradition of the Desert Fathers, God is to be loved and contemplated in His creation. Evagrius of Pontus, the fourth-century ascetic from Sketis in the Egyptian desert, noted,

> There came to St. Antony in the desert one of the wise men of that time and said: "Father, how can you endure to live here, deprived as you are of all consolation from books?" Antony answered: "My book, philosopher, is the nature of created things, and whenever I wish I can read in it the works of God."[7]

For Evagrius, like many of the Desert Fathers, the contemplation of God's creation, what we would call collectively the environment, is a key component of the desert ascetic life. "The goal of practicing the virtues (*praktike*)," writes Evagrius, "is love (*agape*)," whereas the goal of ascetic contemplation is theology, which begins with the "contemplation of nature (*physike theoria*)."[8] Evagrius postulated two stages of the Christian life of the desert ascetic: the first being the practice of virtues (*praktike*), whose origin is based on faith and whose end goal is a sort of elemental grace or peace (*apatheia*). The second stage is that of contemplation (*theoria*), initially of the created natural order (*physis*) and ultimately of God (*theologia*). The contemplation of nature is simultaneously an act of seeing God through His creation and experiencing the created order through God.[9] The duality is significant. The desert ascetic's contemplation of nature is never an end in itself; if it were, it would lead to idolatry. Contemplation of nature leads to knowledge of a certain, yet incomplete, knowledge of God. It is only through faith or belief in God as Creator, the foundation of the ascetic life, that a proper relationship with nature can be maintained.

Sacrificial Love

The object of unselfish love is God, our neighbor, and creation. The attainment of this goal is hard work, and it requires self-sacrifice: "If any man would come after me, let him deny himself, take up his cross, and follow me" (Mark 8:34); "whoever wishes to be great among you must be your servant, and whoever wishes to be first among you must be your slave" (Matt 20:26–27). The call to a life of self-sacrifice, of empathy toward others, is necessary because humanity lives in a fallen state. Fundamental to the Christian understanding of the world is the notion of the Fall of man as depicted in the first two chapters of the book of Genesis. In the garden, Adam and Eve, tempted by the lure of becoming like God and knowing both good and evil, substitute themselves as the end goal of their existence. The reality of the Fall is reflected in humanity's unending struggle to deny the self-idolatry of its own existence and acknowledge that it is the Creator to whom all our desire should lead. Instead of making God the ultimate point of reference, humanity placed itself as the end goal. *Man*, not God, becomes the measure of all things. As such, everything from my neighbor to my family members, from my personal possessions to the environment, exists for my benefit alone, in order to affirm my own self-goodness and worth. This view of human existence has been aptly referred to as the "shattered image."[10] It is a broken image of who we truly are and what our true aim in life ought to be.

In the Gospels, a teacher of the law asks Jesus which is the greatest commandment. The Lord responds by quoting the Hebrew Scripture: love God and love your neighbor. In the Gospel of John, Christ re-emphasizes this commandment by stating, "A new commandment I give to you, that you love one another" (John 13:34). In Luke's account of the encounter, the teacher of the law asks further of Jesus, "Who is my neighbor?" to which Jesus responds with the Parable of the Good Samaritan. The desert tradition takes this teaching one step further. In the words of St. Isaac the Syrian, the merciful heart of a Christian is a heart "which is burning with love for the whole of creation: for humans, for birds, for demons—for all God's creatures."[11] The evangelical imperative to love one another is broadened to include all of God's creation.

The ascetic tradition of the early Church emphasizes that love for God and His creation must be a sacrificial love. Just as Christ's love for humanity and the world is realized through the cross, the same is true for human love. Christ offers us a way, the way of the cross. It is through Christ's death on the cross, the ultimate expression of self-denial, that the brokenness of the Fall of man is healed and the world (the cosmos) is restored to its state of paradise. The sacrificial love of the cross is succinctly expressed in the words of the great Egyptian saint Antony: "Live as though dying daily."[12] Perhaps the most extreme example of this is that of St. Symeon the Stylite, the famous fifth-century ascetic from Syria who lived on top of a pillar for multiple decades. Without the sacrificial love expressed through the cross, the extreme forms of asceticism coming out of the desert tradition make no sense. They simply become aberrant human behavior and ends in themselves. Mary of Egypt's more than forty-seven-year sojourn in the desert is possible only through Christ's sacrificial love for Mary and the sacrificial love that Mary has for God.

The lives of Antony, Symeon, and Mary represent extreme examples of sacrificial love that in their own way put these saints' individual lives in proper balance with the world within and around them. Superficially, Antony's twenty-year seclusion in a deserted fortress, Symeon's voyeuristic life on top of a pillar, and Mary's self-imposed exile to the desert for her past sins appear to be self-centered and to express each saint's own self-absorption. Outside of the context of sacrificial love, such a reading of these saints' lives fails to see the deeper reality of the cross and its transformational power. Upon exiting the fortress after twenty years of solitude, Antony's physical and spiritual state is harmoniously in balance:

> His body had maintained its former condition, neither fat from lack of exercise, nor emaciated from fasting and com-

bat with demons, but was just as they had known him prior
to his withdrawal. The state of his soul was one of purity, for
it was not constricted by grief, nor relaxed by pleasure, nor
affected by either laughter or dejection . . . He maintained
utter equilibrium, like one guided by reason and steadfast in
that which accords with nature.[13]

Unlike Antony, when Mary of Egypt is "discovered" by the priest Zosimas, she is naked, and her entire body is black from the sun.[14] Similarly,
Symeon the Stylite punishes his body through exposure to the elements,
minimal nourishment, and prolonged periods of standing. Yet, for both
Mary and Symeon their sacrificial love for God and neighbor results in
a restoration of their relationship with the natural world. In the case
of Symeon the Stylite, this is expressed in the several natural miracles
that he performs. The life of Mary of Egypt, as we will see below, demonstrates the remarkable ability to sustain life on limited resources
through her harmonious relationship with nature. In all three cases, it
is only by loving sacrificially that concord between humanity and the
world can be realized.

Askesis

It is through Christian *askesis* that we can return to the Garden of Eden.
The Greek term "*askesis*" has a much broader meaning than that implied by the two English derivatives "ascetic" and "asceticism." In Classical Greek the term is frequently used in the context of athletic training
and exercise. It can also simply mean "work." With the arrival of the monastic tradition in the fourth century, the term is used to describe the
spiritual and physical struggle of the solitary hermit or cenobitic monk.
Over time, and most profoundly influenced by the tradition of the Desert Fathers, *askesis* comes to mean within the Orthodox Church the way
in which one puts in practice the vocation of the cross. "Through the
path of asceticism," writes John Zizioulas, "the Church educates man to
sacrifice his own will, his self-centeredness, and subject himself freely to
the will of God, thus showing that man has reversed the attitude of the
first Adam."[15]

Just what does this asceticism look like? For most, the first thing
that comes to mind is fasting. Authentic fasting has very little to do
with rules and regulations about what one can or cannot eat. Fasting is
setting right our relationship with food and everything else. Through

fasting, eating begins to lose some of its self-centeredness and, combined with prayer and love, eating (along with many other daily actions) can be transformed into a sacramental act. *Askesis*, however,
is not limited to what enters the mouth. It is a reigning in of our passions; it is setting aright our relationships with people, our family, our
profession, our hobbies, our responsibilities, the environment—in a
word, with our world. *Askesis* is a response to the physical as well as
to the non-physical passions. It is an attitude by which one is able to
order life, and it provides the foundation for re-establishing the proper
relationship with the world around us, by putting God at the center of
our circle rather than ourselves.

Askesis is a form of self-denial. Although it conjures up images of
extreme self-mortification, it is not this. It can be as simple as turning off
the lights in the house when they are not in use, sharing a cup of coffee
with a longtime enemy, recycling, eating healthy foods, not overeating,
taking shorter showers, giving people the benefit of the doubt, turning
down the thermostat, or not speaking slanderously or negatively about
others. *Askesis* is the unending struggle to deny the self-idolatry of our
existence and acknowledge that it is to the Creator and His creation that
all our love should lead.

Askesis points to a result other than self-idolatry. It not only pre-
serves resources by not wasting them, but sets aright the relationship
between humanity and the created order, resulting in the "miraculous"
sustenance of humanity by nature. It is often expressed as a return to
paradise. A common expression of this found in the ascetical literature
of the desert is that of bread from heaven. Holy men and women received heavenly bread to sustain them, or their bread miraculously never
ran out. The *Life of Mary of Egypt* reflects this return to paradise and
humanity's capability of surviving without the comforts of the world.
After her conversion and departure from Jerusalem for the desert, Mary
took with her three loaves of bread, which lasted seventeen years, after
which she fed herself with wild plants and "whatever else can be found
in the desert."[16] The ascetic reorders the needs of the physical body, and
the hope of salvation serves as an "inexhaustible food." As Mary of Egypt
told Zosimas, "I feed and cover myself with the word of God who governs
the universe."[17]

The sixth-century hagiographer Cyril of Scythopolis expresses the
fruits of *askesis* differently. In his *Life of St. Euthymius*, Cyril emphasizes
the saint's ability to control the created world. For Cyril it is less about
the harmonious relationship between the human person and the animal

kingdom than about the control over nature given to Adam in paradise: "In addition to the other charisms possessed by the godly Euthymius, he also received this one from God—the grace of living with carnivorous and poisonous animals without being harmed by them." Cyril tells his readers they should not be surprised at Euthymius' spiritual gift because anyone familiar with Scripture should have "precise knowledge that when God dwells in a man and rests upon him all beings are subject to him, as they were to Adam before he transgressed God's commandment. Not only the wild animals but the very elements are subject to such a man."[18] These words of Cyril may conjure up images of humanity's "right" to control the created world, yet we must not lose sight of who is exercising dominion and in what way. Euthymius is a monk with little if any temporal authority, a humble desert ascetic who through his *askesis* and love has received the grace of living harmoniously with nature, not in an abusive or destructive manner. Only in this way can one properly understand the natural relationship between humanity and the created cosmos as a return to the Garden of Eden. The relationship is not based on power. The desert ascetic has given up on worldly power. Rather, in the words of Patriarch Bartholomew, it "derives from the fundamental belief that the world was created by a loving God."[19] The world contains "seeds and traces" of God, and as such "the material and natural creation was granted by God to humanity as a gift, with the command to 'serve and preserve the earth' (Gen. 2:15)."[20]

Allow me to share a brief personal experience that may help bring the relationship of *askesis* and the restoration of fallen humanity into sharper focus. At the age of twenty-three, I traveled to Europe along with five other college friends. Having grown up in the western part of the United States in the 1960s and 1970s, I had never been outside of the country. I grew up in a Greek-American family and was raised within the Orthodox Church, but my experience of Orthodoxy was rather limited. I had never visited a monastery, and what I knew about monasticism was what I had read in books. Our trip to Europe included several weeks in Greece. One of our travel companions had been to Greece before and had visited Mt. Athos. Upon his urging, our group spent five days in the summer of 1985 on Mt. Athos visiting three monasteries. It was a remarkable experience. Along with the lengthy and intense liturgical services, what I remember most about the trip was the natural and aesthetic beauty of the place and the way in which the monks whom we encountered perceived the Holy Mountain and everything around them as holy or sacred. They seemed to approach everything that they came into contact with—their work, their food, their worship, their monastic buildings and grounds, and, of course, the beautiful landscape and environment of the Athos peninsula—as sacred. Everything was holy. I had never experienced this before. Only later was I able to attribute this to the reality that through the ascetic life one is set aright with the world. Does this mean that we all must become monks and nuns? Of course not. Yet it does imply that we all must try to live more ascetic lives; we must all practice *askesis*.

Conclusion

The contemporary ecological crisis facing the world is of human origin. It is a direct result of the Fall of man. In its continued state of self-absorption, humanity has and continues to view people, animal and plant life, and inanimate objects as instruments to be used in order to affirm and solidify humanity's own self-worth. The environmental crisis is simply the latest expression of a spiritual crisis that has faced humanity from its beginning. Our response to this crisis must, therefore, be spiritual. The Orthodox Christian tradition offers a response: sanctity and *askesis*. The two are inextricably connected. Sanctity is the tangible result of love for God and His creation; and the most assured path toward this love is through *askesis*, the setting aright of all our encounters with other humans and the rest of God's creation. Through *askesis*, creation ceases to be a vehicle for the preservation and affirmation of our ego and rather becomes what it was created to be: a means to enter into communion with God and our neighbor. If we loved God, our neighbor, and the environment in a sacrificial and ascetic way, there would be no ecological crisis.

Notes

1. The work of Benedicta Ward has been foundational for the English-speaking world in making the genre of the *Apophthegmata Patrum* available to a wider audience; see especially *The Sayings of the Desert Fathers: The Alphabetical Collection*, rev. ed., trans. B. Ward (Kalamazoo, MI: Cistercian Publications, 1984. Additionally, the editing and translating of the lives of many ascetics of the Egyptian, Syrian, and Palestinian deserts have provided a wider context for the famous sayings of the Desert Fathers, as well as providing additional examples of the wisdom of the desert in action.

2. John Moschos, *Pratum Spirituale* 18, translated by John Wortley as *The Spiritual Meadow* (Kalamazoo, MI: Cistercian Publications, 1992), 13.

3. Chrysostom, *On Romans*, Homily 1 (PG 60:399), quoted in Demetrios Trakatellis, "Being Transformed: Chrysostom's Exegesis of the Epistle to the Romans," *Greek Orthodox Theological Review* 36, nos. 3–4 (1991): 220–221.

4. Olivier Clément, *The Roots of Christian Mysticism* (London: New City, 1993), 270.

5. Staretz Silouan, *Wisdom from Mt. Athos* (Crestwood, NY: St. Vladimir's Seminary Press, 1974), 30.

6. Dorotheos of Gaza, *On Refusal to Judge Our Neighbor* 139, in E. Wheeler, trans., *Dorotheos of Gaza: Discourses and Sayings* (Kalamazoo, MI: Cistercian Publications, 1977), 138–139.

7. Evagrius of Pontus, *Praktikos* 92, in Kallistos Ware, *The Orthodox Way*, rev. ed. (Crestwood, NY: St. Vladimir's Seminary Press, 1995), 43.

8. Evagrius of Pontus, *Praktikos* 84.

9. Ware, *The Orthodox Way*, 117.

10. John Chryssavgis, *Beyond the Shattered Image* (Minneapolis: Light and Life, 1999).

11. Isaac the Syrian, *Ascetic Treatises* 48, in John Chryssavgis, *Beyond the Shattered Image*, 9.

12. Athanasios of Alexandria, *Life of Antony* 89.

13. Athanasios, *Life of Antony* 14, in *The Life of Antony and the Letter to Marcellinus*, trans. Robert C. Gregg (New York: Paulist Press, 1980), 42.

14. *Life of Mary of Egypt* 10.

15. John Zizioulas, "Man the Priest of Creation: A Response to the Ecological Problem," in A. Walker and C. Carras, eds., *Living Orthodoxy in the Modern World* (Crestwood, NY: St. Vladimir's Seminary Press, 2000), 185.

16. *Life of Mary of Egypt* 30, trans. Maria Kouli, in Alice-Mary Talbot, ed., *Holy Women of Byzantium: Ten Saints' Lives in English Translation* (Washington, DC: Dumbarton Oaks Research Library and Collection, 1996), 86.

17. Ibid., p. 87.

18. *Life of St. Euthymius* 13, in *Lives of the Monks of Palestine*, trans. R. M. Price (Kalamazoo, MI: Cistercian Publications, 1991), 18–19.

19. His All-Holiness Ecumenical Patriarch Bartholomew, *Encountering the Mystery: Understanding Orthodox Christianity Today* (New York: Doubleday, 2008), 92.

20. Ibid.

Chapter 11

Liturgical Adaptation in the United States: A "Thick Description" of One Greek Orthodox Parish

Dr. Anton C. Vrame
Adjunct Associate Professor of Religious Education

Accepting an honorary doctorate in 1997 from Holy Cross Greek Orthodox School of Theology, His All-Holiness Ecumenical Patriarch Bartholomew delivered an address entitled "Pure Orthodoxy: A Quest of the Times."[1] The address immediately drew attention for its brief references to "liturgical" practices in the United States, such as the quality of chanting and the use of seating, although these practices were seldom referred to subsequently. In the address two issues were discussed in greater depth: the quality of translations of liturgical texts into English and the mixture of local traditions with Orthodox Tradition. On these two points, the address sent a message that attempted to offer a position of more close attention to accuracy on the one hand, while allowing space for the creative developments of a local church.

On the topic of translation the address states, "Already one can note that in many instances, not only are these inferior, but they are even unconsciously introducing wrong beliefs and even heretical notions into Orthodox worship."[2] Yet after making a lengthy critique but offering no particular examples of inferior translation or heretical notions, His All-Holiness supported the principle of translation and the use of a vernacular in a particular place, stating, "Through all of this, we do not take sides *against* translations. Rather, the Orthodox Church *has always recommended that the people be taught the faith, and worship God in their own language.*"[3]

On the matter of local customs being mixed with Orthodox Tradition, His All-Holiness stated,

As is well known, the Orthodox Church came to America through immigrants,[4] who brought to America at the same time their Orthodox Faith and their local or ethnic traditions. We respect these traditions and we congratulate those who make an effort to preserve them. However, we must distinguish them from the Orthodox Tradition. This has special significance for those coming to Orthodoxy from other Confessions, who do not relate with the country of provenance of the community in which they are enrolled, for they have no obligation to follow the local traditions of the national provenance of the community, but only those of Orthodoxy. This certainly does not mean that the other members of the community are deterred in any way, rather we would encourage them to preserve the traditions of their people. As regards, however, our people we encourage them to keep the beautiful traditions of our race.[5] This simply means that whatever traditions do not relate to Orthodoxy, but to other parts of our life, ought not to be imposed on the newcomers as a so-called part of Orthodoxy.

This statement affirms ethnic or local practices for those who seek to preserve them, even while they must be recognized as external to the "pure Orthodoxy" that the title of the address seeks to demand. This could be seen in the ongoing discussions among Orthodox Christians about tradition with a big "T" and with a little "t," that is, the differentiation of *the* Orthodox Tradition from the local customs or traditions of Orthodox people. Simultaneously, the statement affirms that these local customs, largely imported from the Old World, should not be imposed on new members of the Church, because they are not part of *the* Orthodox Tradition. Although the address does not deal with the ongoing acculturation of the Orthodox Tradition to a new cultural milieu, it implicitly seems to affirm the emergence of new local practices in the New World.

Early statements in the address would seem to support this implicit affirmation, but the critiques that followed obscured them. His All-Holiness raised the incarnational principle of the Orthodox Church; that is, the Christian Orthodox Faith is not just an abstract or intellectual proof system, but "truth, which was revealed to us by the incarnate Son and Logos of God, and from that time is confirmed experientially through the heart's assurance by divine grace."[6] This incarnational principle expresses itself in the ongoing life of the believer and the community of Faith, which is handed on from generation to generation, thus *traditio* or *paradosis* in its purist understanding. The reality of Orthodox Christianity is its living expression. As His All-Holiness stated,

> Orthodoxy is a lived truth. This means it is a lived dogma. James, the Brother of God, writes about this in his Catholic Epistle [when he says] "show me your faith by your deeds" (James 2:18). That is, deeds reveal one's faith, not as abstract concept, but as genuine content. For of one sort are the deeds of a believing Orthodox, of another sort are the deeds of one who believes, for example, in Hinduism. Consequently, the deeds of Orthodox Christians reveal to a careful observer what the content of our faith is.[7]

Because the statement refers to Orthodox Christians in the plural, we must also assume that this statement can be expanded to include the deeds of an Orthodox community, from the smallest parish to the entire Church itself.

Thick Description to Understand Local Adaptation

Cultural anthropologist Clifford Geertz made "thick description" the essential tool of ethnography. As he writes, "Doing ethnography is like trying to read [in the sense of "construct a reading of"] a manuscript— foreign, faded, full of ellipses, incoherencies, suspicious emendations, and tendentious commentaries, but written not in conventionalized graphs of sound but in transient examples of shaped behavior."[8] The famous example he draws upon is the simple act of watching two people rapidly contracting one of their eyelids. Is it a wink or a twitch? Are the two somehow communicating? If so, what are they saying to one another? By closely and carefully observing behaviors and describing them in as much detail as possible and beginning to analyze them, we can begin to understand the people and the culture of the people who are performing them. Again, as Geertz states, "Social actions are comments on more than themselves . . . Small facts speak to large issues."[9]

Thick description allows the observer to both describe and analyze, in this case, the liturgical adaptations of one Greek Orthodox parish in the United States. Through thick description we can begin to unravel the threads of visual, verbal, and ritual that weave together in one parish community as it gathers to celebrate the Divine Liturgy on a typical Sunday. Observing a particular community, in concert with the statement of Ecumenical Patriarch Bartholomew, the careful observer can also begin to understand the people who perform them, to learn what they believe and how they express their faith. Over a number of weeks, the liturgical life of St. Gregory the Theologian Greek Orthodox Church in Mansfield, Massachusetts, a parish of the Greek Orthodox Metropolis of Boston of the Archdiocese of America, was carefully observed. Although there are limitations to the objectivity of the observations because the observer is both a member of the Greek Orthodox Church and the particular parish, through the act of thick description, a number of adaptations of liturgical life in the Greek Orthodox Church to an American context can be seen.

Observing St. Gregory's

St. Gregory the Theologian Greek Orthodox Church was first organized in the early 1990s. With the blessing of then Bishop Methodios of Boston, the parish was organized with the specific intention of outreach to English-speaking Greek Orthodox. The community located itself southwest of Boston, where there was no existing Greek Orthodox parish and where growth seemed likely. The weekly parish bulletin contains the parish mission statement: "The mission of St. Gregory the Theologian parish is to serve the religious and spiritual needs of all Greek Orthodox Christians, converts, those of inter-faith marriages, and the 'unchurched' living in the 95/495[10] area, and especially, though not exclusively, those whose mother tongue is English."[11]

The parish held its first Divine Liturgy in May 1992 with a handful of parishioners. Initially located in a rented church space, the parish moved to an office/industrial space, where it held services and programs for a few years. In 1997, the parish purchased the facilities of an Assemblies of God parish, remodeled the space for Orthodox worship and the parish's other needs, and held its first Liturgy there in October. In 2011, the parish has approximately 175 stewards.[12] The parish is noted for its almost exclusive use of English in all its services, almost total reliance on stewardship to meet its financial needs, its excellent religious education program for youth and adults, and its outreach in the local community. There is a full-time *proistamenos* serving the parish. There are no other ordained ministers.

Upon entering the narthex, visitors will notice a "welcome table" that contains a guest book and information about the parish. Members of the parish serve as "greeters," welcoming regular parishioners as well as visitors. The parish weekly bulletin always contains the following message, adding to the sense of welcome from the community:

> We welcome you to worship with us today. Whether you are an Orthodox Christian or this is your first visit to an Orthodox Church, we are pleased to have you with us. Although Holy Communion and other Sacraments are offered only to baptized and chrismated (confirmed) Orthodox Christians, all are invited to receive the *antidoron* (blessed bread) from the priest at the conclusion of the Divine Liturgy. The *antidoron* is not sacramental, but is reminiscent of the agape feast that followed worship in the ancient Christian Church. After the Divine Liturgy this morning, please join us in the Church Hall located downstairs for fellowship and refreshments. We hope that you will return often to worship with us, to grow in Christ and in our Orthodox Faith.[13]

The interior of the worship space is fairly typical of Orthodox church structures in the United States, with seating in pews, a dome with a *Pantocrator*, and a *Platytera* in the apse, etc. There are many icons hanging around the nave. One feature in the sanctuary is quite atypical from other Orthodox parishes. Specifically, the icon screen is quite simple, being a wrought iron "fence" that is approximately forty-eight inches tall, with panel icons hanging on it. The Beautiful Gate is marked as the wrought iron forms a tall arch over the center of the screen, and the wrought iron gates themselves are movable. This creates a completely open sanctuary, and worshippers can see everything that occurs within, from the actions of the clergy and acolytes to the *prothesis* and diaconal apses and to the sides of the holy altar table.[14] In addition, the church has a hall and kitchen for gatherings, classroom spaces for religious education and a Greek afternoon school, a library and bookstore, and offices for the clergy and secretary.

On an ordinary Sunday, the Orthros service is chanted from 8:30–9:30 a.m. The parish has a small group of three volunteer chanters who sing the service in English with the celebrant. Very few people attend. The Divine Liturgy begins at 9:30 a.m. As is found in many parishes, the congregation at the moment of "Blessed is the kingdom" is fairly small, and a steady flow of attendees arrives over the next forty-five minutes. The "inaudible" prayers of the priest are read aloud. Because of the mission of the parish, the Divine Liturgy is celebrated virtually entirely in

English. However, some hymns that repeat a refrain, such as "Through the prayers of the Theotokos," will include one refrain in Greek. The congregation sings the hymns and responses, led by a woman who plays an organ and sings to lead them. People sing the more "popular" hymns and responses, following the lead of the organist. The chanters and the organist will sing the variable hymns—for example, a seasonal communion hymn—after the Small Entrance or at other points in the Divine Liturgy. To guide the congregation, the parish utilizes the *Divine Liturgy Hymnal*[15]—the so-called "green book" because of its green cover—but has inserted and glued new pages to reflect its musical practices and melodies, usually musical adaptations of the hymns developed by the church organist. For example, the *Hymnal* shows the responses to the *Plerotika* in a major key, but the parish sings them in a minor key.

The Apostolic and Gospel pericopes are read in English only,[16] and the sermon follows the Gospel reading. The chanters and the congregation will sing the Old Testament verses and the Alleluia following the Apostolic Reading.[17] The sermon is frequently longer than found in other parishes, lasting sometimes as much as twenty-five minutes. By the time of the Great Entrance, the congregation is full, with many children in attendance. The parish will exchange the kiss of peace before the Creed. The Creed is recited only in English.[18] Following the consecration of the gifts, after the "May the mercies of our Great God . . ." the priest will interrupt the usual order as the parish council approaches the *soleas* with the offering trays. The priest offers a prayer before the tray is passed. The Lord's Prayer will be recited in Greek and English.

While the priest receives Holy Communion and prepares the chalice, the congregation will recite the "I believe, O Lord . . ." Virtually the entire congregation will receive Holy Communion, which can take between fifteen and twenty minutes. Children, who have attended the Divine Liturgy with their families, will go off to Sunday church school after receiving Holy Communion. The parishioners allow children and teachers to receive the Sacrament before the rest of the congregation. Also, the adults participating in religious education class will also move to their classroom at this time. During the distribution of Holy Communion, a group of teenage boys and girls has begun chanting Psalm 136 ("O give thanks to the Lord") in the traditional Byzantine melody. Teenage girls will hold a basket of bread at Holy Communion, while the altar boys will assist the priest. At the end of the Divine Liturgy, before the distribution of the *antidoron*, the priest will usually make announcements of upcoming events in the life of the community. The congregation will then proceed to a fellowship time with coffee and other items in the church hall.

Observers will also witness four other specific adaptations to the liturgical experience that require greater elaboration.

First, during the Great Entrance—or any other procession that involves the priest and acolytes processing from the north door of the sanctuary, down the north aisle, and returning, usually by the center aisle, to the *soleas*—people stand in place, but begin to slowly rotate counterclockwise to face or to follow the procession from their places. Generally, the people seem to want to face the priest and the procession throughout the entire procession. Those on the south side of the church will only need to turn to their left to face the procession. Those on the north side of the church will make a full counterclockwise rotation to remain facing the procession.

The origin of this practice is unclear. It can be seen in many parishes and is not unique to St. Gregory's.[19] No one announces how the procession will move through the church or instructs the people to follow the procession in this manner.

Second, as mentioned above, the congregation will exchange the kiss of peace at the recitation of the Creed. After exclaiming, "Let us love one another . . . ," to which the people respond, "Father, Son, and Holy Spirit . . . ," the priest will proclaim, "Christ is in our midst!" and the congregation will respond, "He is and always shall be!" Then members of the congregation will turn to those standing nearby and greet one another in the same manner.[20] Frequently, one sees husbands and wives or parents and children exchanging a small kiss. Others in the congregation will shake hands. Not everyone will recite the traditional greeting, and you will also hear "Peace to you," "Good morning," or other greetings. Some people seem willing to go a little out of their way to greet those standing off alone or to greet children.

Third, following the consecration of the Holy Gifts, after the "May the mercies of our Great God . . . ," the priest will leave the sanctuary and meet members of the parish who have brought in offering baskets. On occasion there is a second offering tray, usually for a specific purpose. Before collecting the offering, the priest will offer a prayer. It is:

> O Lord our God, You created us and brought us into this life. You showed us the way to salvation and have granted us the revelation of the heavenly mysteries. Accept our Stewardship Offering as an acceptable sacrifice and in return send

down upon us the grace of your Holy Spirit. Look down on us, O Lord, and accept our Stewardship Commitment as You accepted the gifts of Abel, the offerings of Noah, the burnt offerings of Abraham, the priestly sacrifices of Moses and Aaron and the peace offerings of Samuel. Accept also now, in your goodness, O Lord, these gifts from the hands of us sinners, making us worthy of the reward of the faithful and wise stewards on the fearful day of Your just judgment. For You are the God of mercy, love and salvation and we glorify You, the Father, the Son and the Holy Spirit, now and forever and to the ages of ages.[21]

Fourth, should an infant be churched on a Sunday, this service will be conducted before Holy Communion. After the Lord's Prayer and before the "Holy things are for the holy," the priest interrupts the Divine Liturgy, announcing to the congregation that the parish is welcoming a new child into its midst, and welcomes the return of the parents to the parish. The priest then processes to the back of the nave and meets the family with the infant. He will conduct the service of churching from there. During the "churching," the priest carries the infant down the center aisle of the nave reciting the "The servant of God is churched . . ." The parents will follow behind and wait at the steps of the *soleas* while the priest carries the child—whether a boy or a girl—through the south door, behind the holy altar table, pausing beneath the icon of the *Platytera* as if to point her out to the child; he then proceeds through the north door, reciting Simeon's Prayer, to return the newborn to the parents. Then the priest returns to continue the Divine Liturgy. As the priest has stated, the reason for conducting the service at that moment is because the service is aimed at restoring the mother "to communion" with the Church after her forty-day absence, as well as welcoming the infant to the community. By conducting the service before Holy Communion, the mother is able to participate in the Sacrament shortly thereafter. Also, because the entire congregation witnesses the service, the entire congregation can welcome the newborn and parents to the parish once again.

Clues to Understanding the Adaptations

The adaptations at St. Gregory the Theologian Church in the Divine Liturgy focus on three dimensions: (a) participation of the entire congregation; (b) emphasis on the "horizontal," community-building dimension of liturgical actions; and (c) incorporating the talents and abilities of as many people as possible.

Participation of the Congregation

Congregational singing in the Divine Liturgy entered the life of many parishes more than a generation ago in the United States. Two publications supported the effort. The first was the *Divine Liturgy Hymnal* published by the Greek Orthodox Archdiocese in 1977.[22] This book provided congregations and other groups with accessible music, a bilingual text, and a transliteration of the Greek text to assist non-Greek speakers. The both widely accepted and critiqued "green book" has influenced parish life ever since.[23] This is the book in use at St. Gregory's, with modifications. At St. Gregory the Theologian parish, congregational singing was established from the beginning of the parish as a way to involve the entire congregation. In the weekly parish bulletin, the parish calls itself a "singing church," and the congregation is encouraged to participate by singing the hymns. To assist the parishioner, the parish provides a list of the hymns to be sung, especially the variable hymns, and where they are to be located in the hymnal. At some moments, the leader of the singers will announce on which page the hymn can be found.

The second book that has encouraged congregational singing and more general participation in the Divine Liturgy is also from the 1970s. In *Living the Liturgy*, which has not gone out of print in its publishing history, Stanley Harakas names ten ways people can participate in the Divine Liturgy. They are: "(1) Receiving Holy Communion; (2) Being the Church; (3) Sharing in the Symbolism; (4) Responding to Dialogues and Biddings; (5) Singing the Hymns; (6) Reciting the Creed and the Lord's Prayer; (7) Using Your Body in Worship; (8) Listening to the Readings and Sermon; (9) Using the 'Units' of the Divine Liturgy; (10) 'Praying the Liturgy.' "[24] In the book, Harakas argues that the Divine Liturgy is meant for participation. He writes, "These ten ways are the natural and appropriate methods for Orthodox Christians to share in the Liturgy."[25]

St. Gregory's appears to have followed the advice of Fr. Harakas very closely. Because Fr. Harakas was the pastor of the community for a number of the parish's early and foundational years, it could also be said that Fr. Harakas applied the principles of *Living the Liturgy* to the parish. At St. Gregory's we see a very high percentage of the congregation receiving Holy Communion (item 1). Harakas encourages frequent participation with these words: "Frequent and regular Holy Communion is vital. We cannot go Sunday after Sunday to the Divine Liturgy and ignore the invitation 'With the fear of God, faith and love draw near' and think that we can be true participants in the Mystery."[26] Although Harakas does not include sharing the kiss of peace in the book, sharing the kiss of peace could be argued to be one of the following: being the Church, responding to dialogues, or using your body (items 2, 4, and 7). Congregational singing clearly involves responding to dialogues and biddings and singing the hymns (items 4 and 5). About congregational singing Harakas writes, "No one advocates the abolishment of our choirs, but the restoration of congregational singing in one form or another is a real requirement if the Orthodox laity is ever to become involved in the Liturgy in more than a spectator fashion."[27] About responding the bidding and dialogues, Harakas writes, "In fact, certain portions of the Divine Liturgy really don't make any sense without the active participation of the lay people."[28] The entire congregation recites the Creed and Lord's Prayer (item 6). Harakas writes, "It is clear that the recitations of the Divine Liturgy are designed to be said by all the people and not just a single person or a representative group. Pastors should encourage all the people to recite both the Creed and the Lord's Prayer during the Divine Liturgy."[29] Readings are read in English and the sermon is delivered in English, clearly so that the congregation will understand them and can attend to them (item 8). Harakas writes, "For many the readings and the Sermon are occasions for our mind to wander. There is a dimension to participation in the Divine Liturgy which is simply attentiveness. When the Epistle and Gospel are read, we should strain our inner ear to understand the message."[30]

Community Building through Liturgical Action

Observing the parish in action liturgically, the adaptations to the Divine Liturgy that have occurred appear to have a "horizontal" emphasis to them. In other words, the adaptations have helped to build the community and strengthen the relationships among the congregation. This would also appear to be a result of Harakas' work in *Living the Liturgy*. Whereas all of the above examples are evidence of the horizontal dimensions of the life of the church, the second item in the list of how to participate in the Divine Liturgy is "Being the Church." By this Harakas suggests that attending the Divine Liturgy is the gathering, the *ekklesia*—or assembly of the faithful—beyond the vertical or transcendent dimensions of the Liturgy. He writes about this, "The Liturgy, as we have said, is not only the preparation, consecration, and distribution of the Body and Blood of Christ, it is also our affirmation of what we are: the people of God . . . Thus, participation by the Christian in the Divine Liturgy means in part that he goes to Church to be with and to be the Church of God."[31]

The action that most clearly expresses this idea is the sharing of the kiss of peace. As mentioned above, the people of St. Gregory's share the kiss of peace before the recitation of the Creed. Harakas does not mention the kiss in *Living the Liturgy*. As a renewed practice in some Greek Orthodox communities, the kiss of peace began to occur after the book was published. Conducted at the moment after the priest exclaims, "Let us with one mind . . . ," and the people greet one another, they concretely unite with their neighbor. More than just a polite greeting, the kiss of peace is an expression of the unity of the congregation, which will recite the Creed "with one mind and heart" and in one voice. Harakas includes in the discussion on the Creed that the original text is not "I believe" but "We believe," which is an even stronger affirmation of unity of faith.[32] Inviting parishioners to exchange the kiss of peace also can lead to forming new relationships outside of the liturgical experience. During the fellowship hour, parishioners have the opportunity to become better acquainted, thereby moving beyond a brief handshake during the Liturgy.

Incorporating the Talents of the People

During the course of the Divine Liturgy, we see many people involved, from performing routine tasks to more specific roles. As mentioned at the beginning of the description, there are greeters in the narthex, welcoming parishioners and visitors. Typically, young people will be standing at the doors to the nave, distributing the weekly bulletin, but also welcoming parishioners. Parish council members, but also others, will assist with ushering people during Holy Communion or passing the offering tray. Of course there is a group of boys, serving as acolytes. The parish has added opportunities for girls to assist "liturgically" as well. One girl every Sunday will bring the *antidoron* to the priest, who will bless it and place it in a stand on the *soleas*, while the girl waits with a liturgical cloth to cover it. During the distribution of Holy Communion, the same girl will hold the tray of bread for the communicants after they receive the Sacrament. As mentioned above, during Holy Communion a group of teenagers has begun chanting Psalm 136 ("O give thanks to the Lord") in addition to the communion hymn sung by the people or the chanters.

Conclusion

In "Pure Orthodoxy," His All-Holiness Ecumenical Patriarch Bartholomew argues for discerning the Tradition of Orthodoxy that is not bound by local or national customs from one people or place and that does not impose them on another people or place. As a result, he creates space for new customs or forms of expression to begin and to take root in new places or among new people. In this paper, through the act of "thick description," we have seen how one Greek Orthodox parish in the United States has made adaptations in liturgical practices, deeply rooting them in the theology and liturgical knowledge of the Orthodox Church, in order to find new expressions of the same liturgical life for a contemporary American context.

Notes

1. Ecumenical Patriarch Bartholomew, "Pure Orthodoxy: A Quest of the Times," *Greek Orthodox Theological Review* 42, nos. 3–4 (1997): 195–202.

2. Ibid., 199.

3. Ibid., 200. Emphasis added.

4. Of course, this reflects Greek Orthodox history, but in no way diminishes the history of Russian Orthodox missionary activity in Alaska.

5. The term "race" here must be a translation of *genos*, meaning "people" or "nationality."

6. Ecumenical Patriarch Bartholomew, "Pure Orthodoxy," 197.

7. Ibid.

8. Clifford Geertz, "Thick Description: Toward an Interpretive Theory of Culture," http://hypergeertz.jku.au/GeertzTexts/Thick_Description.htm, last accessed May 23, 2011.

9. Ibid.

10. 95/495 is a reference to the two interstate highways that are near the parish.

11. St. Gregory the Theologian Church Sunday Bulletin, vol. 20, issue 36, May 8, 2011.

12. In Greek Orthodox Archdiocese practice, a steward is one household, whether a single individual or a large family.

13. St. Gregory the Theologian Church Sunday Bulletin, vol. 20, issue 36, May 8, 2011.

14. It is well known that in antiquity, the icon screen was much simpler than is typically found today in Orthodox parishes. The icon screen at St. Gregory's attempts a return to that concept.

15. *The Divine Liturgy of St. John Chrysostom: A Hymnal with Texts in Greek, English, and English Phonetics* (Brookline, MA: Greek Orthodox Archdiocese of America Department of Religious Education, 1977).

16. When the Metropolitan visits, the reading of the Gospel will also be in Greek.

17. Although not usually seen in Greek Orthodox parishes, this practice was adopted from the practices of Holy Cross Chapel at the Hellenic College-Holy Cross Greek Orthodox School of Theology in Brookline, Massachusetts, which has subsequently suppressed the practice.

18. When the Metropolitan visits, the Creed will also be recited in Greek.

19. During one Holy Friday evening service at a small church of the Orthodox Church of America near Chicago, I witnessed an entire congregation singing the Lamentations with their backs to the altar, the *kouvouklion*, and the *Epitaphios* icon, but everyone faced the priest, who, because of a particularly long line of acolytes, was standing near the back of the church in the center aisle.

20. Some claim that the kiss of peace among the laity is a contemporary innovation of the Church. However, as Robert Taft has written, "The kiss of peace is one of the most primitive rites of the Christian liturgy. Originally it seems to have been a common greeting, probably exchanged at every Christian synaxis" (R. Taft, *A History of the Liturgy of St. John Chrysostom*, vol. 2, *The Great Entrance* [Rome: Pontificio Istituto Orientale, 2004], 375). Later he writes, "Since it seems that the kiss . . . was exchanged only between neighboring worshippers, the rite could have been accomplished with a minimum of time and confusion" (ibid., 390).

21. The source of the prayer is the Stewardship Booklet of the Greek Orthodox Archdiocese of America, www.goarch.org/archdiocese/departments/stewardship.

22. *Divine Liturgy Hymnal.*

23. It must be noted that earlier efforts at hymnals were also present in the 1970s, and others have been published subsequently, such as those of Holy Cross Orthodox Press. However, none have had the durability of the *Divine Liturgy Hymnal*. The main critique of the *Hymnal* has been the awkward English phrasing, which often repeats phrases or holds long syllables to words so that the musical melodies of the Greek and English can match exactly, note for note.

24. Stanley S. Harakas, *Living the Liturgy* (Minneapolis, MN: Light and Life Publishing, 1974), 70.

25. Ibid.

26. Ibid., 52.

27. Ibid., 62.

28. Ibid., 59.
29. Ibid., 64.
30. Ibid., 67.
31. Ibid., 54.
32. Ibid., 64.

Chapter 12

How Much Do Our Learned Evaluations Influence the Way We Reconstruct the Past?

Dr. Evie Zacharides-Holmberg
Professor of Classics and Ecclesiastical/Patristic Greek Language
and Literature

We usually have problems when faced with concepts that are at odds with our conventional framework of thought, that is, the one we have inherited from our culture. Our learned evaluations tend to influence to a great extent the way we perceive literature, art, politics, and life in general. And when we try to connect with the past, our general tendency is an interpretation into a mode of values that we have formed within our cultural milieu and toward which we feel comfortable relating. Our tendency of translation into "familiar modes" runs wild both with regard to subjects about which we do not have much information and also with regard to areas where the evidence is looking at us straight in the face.

Let us take an example from a well-known literary work: Homer's *Iliad.* Centuries of what we know as the history of reciting and analyzing the Homeric poetry have created innumerable theories as to the composition, transmission, redaction, recension, pronunciation, and authorship of the *Iliad* and the *Odyssey*. The divergence of the conclusions drawn is a staggering example of how our personal tendencies toward "interpretation" can get us lost in details, causing us to miss the beauty of the ancient message. For centuries we have immersed ourselves in "problems" of "inconsistencies" in language, descriptions of equipment, religion, social customs, and the like. We have been divided into "revisionists," "interpolationists," "fundamentalists," and others. We have analyzed to death the evolution and transmission of the Greek epics, carrying within the "methods" of our examination of the text our own perception of what poetry should be, a perception

limited by the confines of our "scholarly understanding" and our position within space and time. The Aeolic, Ionic, and Arcado-Cypriot
elements in the language have been traced, questioned, and recorded.
Archaeological, linguistic, social, and "older" and "younger" elements
have been analyzed.

Questions that shake the beliefs of the ancient society that produced the poems have been raised: are the Homeric poems the result
of joining together "loose songs"? Were they created by one, two, or
more poets? The text, reconstructed by the accepted processes of
textual criticism from Byzantine manuscripts, has been the object of
study for centuries. But how much do we know about the original way
the poems were pronounced and sung? We have lost the music and
to a great extent the actual pronunciation that went along with the
music . . . And in our exhaustive analysis of the text, we forget that the
Iliad and the *Odyssey* were compositions of a glorious combination of
beauty in language, music, and content, with the power to hold cap-
tive their audiences for hours of singing or reciting and inspire them
toward a way of life worth living.

Our tendency toward "interpretation" and "translation" into terms
we can culturally and ideologically "understand" becomes especially
obvious in our translations of what we consider "sacred" texts. To offer
just one example, there is no end to the additions, omissions, and mis-
constructions of the translation of the original Greek of the New Testament texts, all of which depend on the religious message intended to be
portrayed as viewed through the particular intellectual interpretation or
faith of the translator/interpreter.

In no other domain, however, does our tendency toward "translation" and interpretation into terms we can culturally relate to become
more obvious than in the visual arts. It may be that this is a domain
where this tendency can be visually demonstrated, and as the saying
goes, "a picture is worth a thousand words." Also, one could say that
the information we possess is more tangible in the visual arts. We can
actually behold, hold, and reconstruct the object in whole or in part.
Granted, there might be a certain amount of information concerning the
object's original appearance as the artist had intended, an appearance
that has been lost. We can never exactly recreate, for example, the color
combinations that once covered the surface of ancient buildings and
sculpture. They have faded, have been partially or totally abraded and
lost. We can only guess from the remaining traces and other information
that we possess the original appearance of the surface of these artifacts.

In the case of metal objects, time has created a layer of red, blue, and green in various degrees of combinations between the surface of the metal and the environment in which these objects have been exposed. The only art objects of the past that are almost indestructible are the ones made of baked clay, because clay, when baked at a certain temperature, will retain the shape, texture, and color of the time when the piece was originally fired. And yet, even in the case of pottery, our intellectual "translation" of how a reconstructed vase should look like when presented in a museum environment can cloud our judgment during the process of restoration and come between the final product of restoration and the original intention of the ancient artist who produced the vase.

In my conservation work I have examined, run tests, and reconstructed a great number of art objects from various time periods and cultures. My work includes the reconstruction of the facial characteristics of several marble pieces from the permanent collection of the Museum of Fine Arts, Boston. Among those pieces are two Roman copies of classical Greek originals, a fourth-century figure of a woman from a classical Greek funerary monument and a portrait of an official dating from 475 AD. Although I have been working in classics as a classical scholar and as an art conservator and restorer for the past thirty-five years, and have always trusted that I bring into my work the combination of my training and experience in the fields of the classics, art history, applied arts, and art conservation, it is only recently, after I worked on the facial reconstruction of the aforementioned art objects and presented various papers on their history, examination, and treatment, that I began to realize how much our aesthetic and cultural evaluations—as they have been formulated primarily since the time of the Italian Renaissance—have influenced the way we perceive and reconstruct antiquity. Simply put, in spite of our training and practical experience in our relevant field of specialization, we cannot help but "translate" antiquity into the "language" of our culture.

In the domain of the visual arts, this process of "translation" and "interpretation" by the archaeologist, collector, and museum curator becomes even more complicated, because the majority of the information we possess concerning ancient Greek art comes down to us through Roman copies. And although the Roman artist may be as faithful as possible to the Greek original, the fact remains that in the final analysis, what we are looking at is a Roman "translation" of a Greek original.

Since the time the Romans became acquainted with Greek art in the end of the fourth century BC, impressed by the beauty of the Greek culture, they began transporting art works in all media as spoils of war. Wealthy Romans soon started to order copies of famous Greek pieces in bronze, marble, and terra-cotta. Some of these copies are beautiful as pure Roman inspiration pieces, some are faithful copies of the Greek originals, but many are lacking the spirit and the technical skill of their source of inspiration. This becomes obvious, for example, when we compare the Erechtheion Korae in Athens to Roman copies. One of the most obvious differences, even to the untrained eye, is the rendering of the folds in the cloth that covers the body of the maidens. The folds in the Roman copies are simpler and straighter, and they simply cover the body instead of bringing out its shape as in the Greek original:

Pl. 8. Original and Copy of the Erechtheion Korae

Fig. 38. Kore from the Erechtheion. British Museum

Fig. 39. Kore in situ at the Erechtheion, Athens

Fig. 40. Three-quarter back view of Fig. 39

Fig. 41. Copy of Fig. 38. Vatican Museum

Fig. 42. Three-quarter front view of Fig. 41

Fig. 43. Copy of an Erectheion Kore. Villa of Hadrian, Tivoli

Fig. 44. Copy of an Erectheion Kore. Villa of Hadrian. Tivoli

Fig. 45. Copy of an Erechtheion Kore. Villa of Hadrian, Tivoli

Fig. 46. Copy of an Erectheion Kore. Villa of Hadrian. Tivoli

Due to my training and practical experience as a classicist, archaeologist, art conservator, and artist, I have always been confident that I
am able to look at a work of art with the loving respect of the artist and
classicist who is sensitive to the object's inherent beauty but at the same
time perceives the object with the objectivity of the classicist and that
of the examiner and art conservator/restorer. In the final analysis, it is
the art conservator/restorer who will combine the evaluation and experience of the classicist/art historian with the hands-on practical experience of the artist/restorer. It is the artist/restorer who, setting his or her
own aesthetic preferences aside, will reconstruct the object according to
the intent of the artist who originally produced it. This is a painstaking
process, involving a great amount of research, examination, and comparison of the object in question to other existing copies or originals
by the same artist, study of the time period of the production of the
object—if it is an original—and/or of those periods when copies were
produced. This process also includes technical, aesthetic, and moral
considerations with regard to the reconstructions of missing pieces—
especially if these reconstructions include facial characteristics—and
the ability and willingness to determine the feasibility of such reconstructions, making certain that one remains honest with regard to the
original intent of the artist.

Having worked on a great variety of works of art from various cultures and time periods, I cannot say that I have found myself in a difficult position with regard to the objectives described above—that is, until after my recent work on one of the aforementioned four marble pieces
from the Museum of Fine Arts, Boston. It was after I had completed the
research and restoration work and had presented papers on the conservation and reconstruction of the facial characteristics that I began to really question the validity of the reconstructions. Being an artist, I always
held the opinion that one should try to reconstruct the missing areas of
an art object in order to present it as the work of art that it was intended
to be. Presenting an art object broken and disfigured does not do justice to it, to the artist who produced it, or to the period it represents.
The reconstruction of the missing pieces, however, has to be within the
spirit of the culture and the original intent of the artist who produced
the work of art that is under consideration. If there is any doubt as to the
truthfulness of the reconstruction, it should, by all means, be avoided.
However, given the restrictions—cultural, intellectual, political, etc.—
involved in such reconstructions, I reached the conclusion that a reconstruction that only partially satisfies all the considerations mentioned

above should be avoided altogether, because it can dramatically change the character of the work of art itself.

This article traces the various steps leading to this conclusion. It also demonstrates, through comparisons to various works of art and their reconstructions/restorations, the deviations from the original intent of the ancient artist as they appear on the restored works of art. These deviations, based on the aesthetic values of the curator and restorer in combination with various agendas and political directives within the museum environment and the countries where the works of art are exhibited—often different than those governing classical Greek artistic expression—appear to guide our evaluations of what "should be" the accepted and ideal in beauty, art, and art restoration.

Let us consider the following example. We assume that the classical Greek period of the fifth and fourth centuries BC set the standards that underlie the mainstream Western tradition in art, both in painting and sculpture. During my recent research and restoration work, however, I have begun to question the validity of this assumption. As I demonstrated in my presentation at the 2010 Annual Hawaii International Conference on Arts and Humanities, the aesthetic preferences that direct the reconstruction process of at least one feature of the facial anatomy—that of the nose—do not follow those of classical Greek art.

Let us briefly review the major points I made concerning nose reconstructions of ancient Greek and Roman copies in the Museum of Fine Arts, Boston. Most of the nose restorations do not follow the traditional classical Greek shape. The classical Greek nose is straight, it has a relatively wide ridge, and there is no particular accentuation of the nostrils or the tip:

Fig. 2. Aphrodite (Kaufmann Head) presently in the Louvre in Paris, believed to be a very faithful Roman reproduction of the head of the Knidian Aphrodite by Praxiteles

Fig. 3. The Chios Head, presently at the Museum of Fine Arts, Boston, probably an original from the fourth century after the Praxitelean form of expression

Fig. 4. Greek original from the fourth century BC at the Museum of Fine Arts, Boston. The facial characteristics of the proper right side of the face have been reconstructed by the author.

The nose is a very important facial feature. It is the center around which the other portions of the face are arranged and harmonized. And yet, its simple shape—so obviously portrayed in classical works of art— invariably deviates in older and more recent restorations. Let us take some examples from the Museum of Fine Arts, Boston. The tip of the nose on the head shown below (fig. 5) is a restoration. The tip of the nose slightly tilts upward, and the nostrils are more pronounced than on Greek originals.

Fig. 5.

Fig. 6a.

Fig. 6b.

The piece on the left (fig. 6a) is a Greek original; the one on the right (fig. 6b) is a Roman copy with an accentuated tip of the nose following a previous restoration.

With regard to old and new restorations alike, there seems to be a tendency to create something more slender, with the tip and the nostrils more pronounced and "cuter." It seems as if the restorer or copyist has been trying to "ameliorate" the original. There have been obvious unfortunate renderings of this particular facial feature, as it can be seen in the following Hercules head (figs. 15–19), a Roman copy of a Greek original from the fourth century, now found in the Museum of Fine Arts, Boston. The nose restoration is obviously disproportionate to the face and off center. In spite of its awkwardness, however, this restoration displays the tendency of the nineteenth and early twentieth centuries to create a more slender, smaller "sculpted" and "cuter" nose.

In order to demonstrate this point, I will use three art objects from three different museums: our first example is the so-called "Head of Diomedes" from the Museum of Fine Arts, Boston. We are dealing with a copy without a particular date. In the museum's file description it is referred to as "Graeco-Roman." It is a fine-grained marble head that had been broken into four pieces and was then put together at some unknown place and time, and the joins had been filled with plaster. Its dimensions are 27.4 x 18 cm (10 13/16 x 7 1/16 in.). It is listed as a Francis Bartlett donation, and entered the museum in 1900. In the captions that accompany the illustrations, the Museum of Fine Arts, Boston, will be referred to as MFA.

Fig. 7. Head of Diomedes at the MFA (before treatment)

The other two pieces I will be using as points of reference and comparison are named "Roman copies." The first one (fig. 8) is displayed at the Glyptothek in Munich, Germany, and is known as the Munich Diomedes. It is accessed as a "Roman copy after a Greek original from 440–430 BC attributed to Kresilas." It is 1.02 m (3 ft. 4 in.) tall. No date of its production as a copy is given. Its accession number is: inv. 304.

Fig. 8. The Munich Diomedes. The nose is missing, as in the majority of ancient pieces.

The second piece (fig. 9) is on display at the Louvre Museum, Paris, France, and it is referred to as a "copy of Nausykles or Kresilas." Its title reads: "Diomedes stealing the Palladion (now lost). Marble, Roman copy from the 2nd–3rd century CE after a Greek original of the 5th century." It is 1.85 m (6 ft. 1 in.) tall. It comes from the former collections of Cardinal Richelieu and entered the museum in 1801.

The Head of Diomedes from the Museum of Fine Arts, Boston, is made from Pentelic marble, the medium used extensively during the fifth and fourth centuries for the production of sculpture in Athens. Although its description reads "Graeco-Roman," there is a possibility it could have been produced earlier in Athens. The head had been exhibited since its acquisition in the state it had been received: the head had been broken into four pieces, and it must have been glued together, because there was no evidence of pins in the x-rays taken. The adjoining areas of the breaks, as well as missing parts of

Fig. 9. Diomedes at the Louvre. The variation in color starting at the ridge of the nose is a sign of restoration. The whole nose is probably an addition.

the face and hair, had been filled with plaster. This layer of plaster had been thickly applied, and there was no indication of a particular effort of carving it so that it would conform to the details of the original surface. Moreover, this layer of plaster had been painted over, most probably intentionally, in a color that strongly contrasted with the marble surface of the original. This contrast, besides making the restoration obvious, hid the fact that the plaster restoration covered a large portion of the original surface and distorted the shape of the original details; it hid this distortion by directing the eye toward the clashing effect of the difference in coloration between the original and the restoration, and away from a harmonious perception of the surface as a whole.

Restorations with a clear intent of making the reconstruction of missing areas of the original obvious in the name of "honesty" is a well known tendency of the past, occasionally practiced even today. To mention extreme cases, there are examples of restored vases where the surface of the reconstructed areas has been recessed in order to make the restoration as obvious as possible. This practice, besides the disadvantages mentioned above, is completely unnecessary, because any reconstruction/restoration can be detected through the methods of modern examination, and all restoration materials used in the museum labs are readily reversible. Most importantly, such a practice severely alters the original intent of classical Greek art, which in its ultimate expression aims at transcending the practical experience of mortality by aspiring to the creation of ultimate beauty. This aspiration is expressed in Plato's terms in the *Symposium*, through the words of his teacher Socrates:

> And if man's life is ever worth living, it is when he has attained the vision of the very soul of beauty . . . that it is only when he discerns beauty itself through what makes it visible that a man will be quickened with the true, and not the seeming virtue . . . And when he has brought forth and reared this perfect virtue, he shall be called the friend of god, and if ever it is given to man to put on immortality, it shall be given to him.

This is an inspired vision of man's potential to attain a glimpse of immortality through the experience of beauty, a notion with which Aristotle would disagree . . . And yet Aristotle, who considered that artistic craftsmanship belongs to the field of manual labor and that professional skill in any of the arts is a disgrace to a free citizen, had not been initiated in the Mysteries, whereas Pythagoras; Plato; the great painter and sculptor Pheidias; and a great number of artists and free Athenian citizens during the apex of the Periclean golden age had. And Aristotle belonged to the end of the fourth century . . .

One has only to glimpse at the beauty of the Parthenon—in whose structure there does not exist a single straight line, and where the slight inward incline of each column, if projected upward into space, would eventually meet at a symmetrical point in what is perceived as the celestial sublime—in order to relate to the notion that the order and harmony that the Greeks believed pervade the universe coincide with their main aesthetic practice. In such an aesthetic practice, there is no room for disharmony. And a clash in color between restoration and the original surface is obviously a disharmony.

The request for treatment in the case of the Diomedes head at the Museum of Fine Arts, Boston, specified "cleaning." After the initial cleaning of the marble surface, the inevitable step was the cleaning of the surface of the restoration. The cleaning of the plaster restoration was done using acetone and ethyl alcohol alternately on cotton swabs. The cleaning of the dark overpaint revealed the extent of the plaster overfill. The plaster of the restoration, besides covering a large portion of the hair and beard area, created a serious distortion in the area of the eyelids, the proper left temple, and the tip of the nose.

Fig. 10.

Not only did the restoration create a false bulging effect in these areas, but it also concealed the difference between the two eyes with regard to the opening of the eyelids. The proper right eye, for example, seemed to be half closed compared to the proper left one.

Fig. 11.

The area of the hair was first cleaned, and the surface of the plaster was carved in order to conform to the original rendering of the curls.

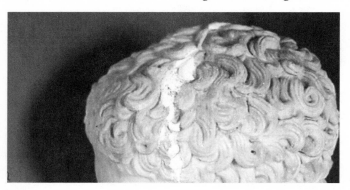

Fig. 12.

Next came the turn of the disfiguring restoration of the face. Even under the disfiguring color of the restoration, the distortion in the tip of the nose can be perceived on both pictures presented below, but especially on the one on the left. Both nostrils are excessively pronounced, and in the picture on the left the tip of the nose is elongated and turns slightly upward (fig. 13).

Fig. 13.

The rendering of the ancient Greek nose has been a bone of contention among copyists, art historians, and restorers. The Christians and time had a lot to do with the condition in which most ancient Greek heads and Roman copies have come down to us. Most ancient Greek and Roman works of art are missing their noses in whole or in part as a result of the fact that a nose can be easily abraded or broken with the passage of time, or because—as it is true in most cases—it was broken and destroyed on purpose in antiquity in an effort to abuse and insult a product of the "pagan" culture. Keeping this in mind, should we wish to reconstruct this feature of facial anatomy in part or in whole, we have plenty of examples to choose from. A Greek nose, in the original or whenever rendered faithfully by the Roman artists who copied Greek works of art, has basically straight lines, and it is rather big compared to later standards of what may constitute an "elegant" or "cute" nose. Take the case of the aforementioned Greek original from the fourth century that represents a female figure (fig. 14).

Fig. 14. Marble figure of a woman from a classical Greek funerary monument at the MFA

The nose is relatively big with straight lines, the nostrils are not overly pronounced, and the mouth is full. All Greek noses are not the same, however. In the case of Hercules, for example, because he is known as a fighter, the nose is bigger, with flared nostrils. Even in this case, however, there are many examples—both original works and copies—representing Hercules, from which information can be obtained for the reconstruction of such a nose, as was the case with a head of Hercules from the Museum of Fine Arts, Boston (fig. 15). The

Fig. 15.

head was made of Pentelic marble, and it is probably a Roman copy of a Greek original dating from around 340 BC. The old restoration, which was done toward the end of the nineteenth century, had produced a nose that was not only disproportionately small, but also off-centered.

After a careful study of the nose of Hercules as it appears in various Greek originals and copies, both in marble and terra-cotta, a final version of the nose was carved, which made this work of art both aesthetically pleasing and close to the original intent of the ancient artist.

Fig. 16. Versions of Hercules compared to the head at the MFA on the lower left

Fig. 17. The nose during the process of reconstruction

Fig. 18. The final version of the nose compared to a Greek original from the fifth century

Fig. 19. Final version of the nose as it is now restored

In the case of the Diomedes head, the rendering of the nose should have been a fairly straightforward process. The ancient Greek nose, as mentioned above, is relatively large and straight with simple lines in most of the examples we possess from both the classical period and their copies. And yet most of the reconstructions of this part of the facial anatomy seem to deviate from this Greek canon, especially the reconstructions from the nineteenth and the beginning of the twentieth centuries.

As mentioned above, the nose of Diomedes at the Louvre appears to be a restoration (figs. 20a and 20b).

Figs. 20a., 20b., and 20c.

When observed in profile (fig. 20b), it exhibits a similar elongation at the tip with a slightly upward incline, as well as a pronounced slender carving of the nostrils. Compared to the simple straight lines of the Zeus of Artemision from the fifth century (fig. 20c), the difference between the ancient and the modern tastes becomes obvious.

In the case of Diomedes from the Museum of Fine Arts, Boston (figs. 21–24), the distortion at the tip of the nose could be discerned after close observation even under the coat of the dark plaster restoration.

Fig. 21. Before treatment

After the dark paint covering the plaster restoration on the
face was removed, besides the
distortions in the area of the eyelids and the nose, it became clear
which portions of the beard and
the cheek were missing.

Fig. 22. The dark paint covering the plaster restoration
hides the distortions created by excess filling material

The excess plaster restoration was removed, and the missing areas of
the face and the beard were reconstructed using a filling material containing alabaster dust, which in a 30% solution of Rohm and Haas Acry-
loid B-72 was transparent enough to match the surface of the marble and
let show through it the underlined plaster fill, which had been painted
with Golden Acrylic emulsion paints imitating the color variations of
the original marble surface. This technique proved to be very satisfactory in creating the illusion of a marble surface in the restored areas.

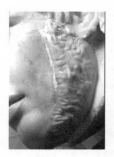

Fig. 23. During and after treatment pictures of the proper left side

After all the missing areas had been reconstructed, there still remained the problem of
reshaping the old restoration of the tip of the
nose. In the new restored version, which kept
the shape of the old restoration only in this
area, the deviation from the classical canon
was not so obvious when the head was viewed
from the proper left side (fig. 24).

Fig. 24.

When viewed, however, from the proper right, the distortion of the
MFA head (fig. 25a) was obvious and even more pronounced than that
of the head at the Louvre (fig. 25b).

Fig. 25a.   Fig. 25b.

In a comparison between the restored head from the Museum of
Fine Arts, Boston (fig. 26a), and the one from the Louvre (fig. 26b), in
the frontal view one can see that the tip of the nose is slightly hanging
over the upper lip. The head of the piece in Munich, which has no nose
addition, is also presented below (fig. 27).

Fig. 26a.

Fig. 26b.   Fig. 27. The head from
                                 the Munich Diomedes

Fig. 28a. Diomedes at the   Fig. 28b. Diomedes at
Louvre, proper left side   the MFA, proper left side

Fig. 29a. Diomedes at the
MFA, proper right side. The
tip of the nose is a restoration.

Fig. 29b. Diomedes at the
Louvre, proper right side.
The nose is a restoration.

Although both noses are partially and totally restored (respectively as presented in the pictures above), they exhibit similarities in the rendering of the nose. In the case of the head from the Museum of Fine Arts, Boston, the tip of the nose is fuller, and its projection out and up more pronounced. If one were to apply the standards of a typical classical Greek nose, the version displayed below on the right with the ruler in front of the protruding edge of the tip of the nose (fig. 30b) would have been closer to the original intent of the ancient artist (both the one who produced the original, as well as the one who produced the Roman copy).

Fig 30a.   Fig. 30b.

During the process of restoration of the Hercules' head discussed above, if we compare the various versions produced before we reached the final desired goal, it becomes obvious how easy it is to be side-tracked into a version conforming to our current visual experience of what a nose should look like:

Fig. 31.

Fig. 32. Various stages during the restoration of the nose of Hercules, with a version similar to the nineteenth-century nose restoration, as shown on the head (left) exhibited at the MFA

Fig. 33. Final version of the nose (right) compared to the previous stage of restoration (left). The one on the left is slightly longer and curvier.

In the case of the Diomedes, the head from the Museum of Fine Arts, Boston, shares certain similarities with the other two heads from the Louvre and Munich. The rendering of the head and beard is very similar in all three, and there are additional similarities in the nose restoration, as well as the slightly opening of the lips between the head from the Museum of Fine Arts, Boston (fig. 34a), and the one at the Louvre (fig. 34b).

Fig. 34a.   Fig. 34b.

The ridge of the nose of the MFA Diomedes is broader than the one at the Louvre. Because only the tip of this nose is a restoration, we can assume that this is our closest version of what the original Greek piece looked like. We can, therefore, appreciate the intentional reshaping of the restored nose on the right (fig. 34b) so that it can appear more elegant.

Fig. 35a.   Fig. 35b.

There is a similarity in the opening of the lips in both pieces. The shape of the eyes and eyelids, however, is different, and it is closer to the head from Munich.

The head from the Museum of Fine Arts, Boston (fig. 35a), shares more similarities with the Munich head (fig. 35b) in the shape of the face and the ears. The nose on the head from Munich has been broken, but one can guess from what still remains that it must have been bigger than the restoration on the head at the Louvre and closer in size to the remaining original portion of the one from the Museum of Fine Arts, Boston.

The final version of the nose restoration of Diomedes at the Museum of Fine Arts, Boston, following the directive from the curator of Greek and Roman Art, kept the shape of the old restoration in the area of the tip of the nose in order to serve as "a case study of old restorations."

As we conclude this study, we cannot help but wonder why one should intentionally choose to keep the version of a nose that deviates from the original intent of the artist. It would have certainly been more honest not to restore the nose at all, as in the case of the head of Diomedes in Munich.

Diomedes at the MFA   Diomedes at the Louvre

Diomedes in Munich

Fig. 36.

It has also become obvious in this study that it is possible to re-create a Greek nose in a way close to the original intent of the ancient artist. This option, when there is enough information for such a reconstruction, is certainly more faithful to the aesthetic notions of the ancient Greeks. When our own aesthetic values, however, the ones of our culture or those of an old restoration, are reflected in the way we reconstruct the past, the final product of what we produce is not a restoration of the past, but a deception.

The final version of the restored Diomedes from the Museum of Fine Arts, Boston, is faithful as to the original intent of the ancient artist with one exception: the tip of the nose, which retains the shape of the old restoration. And whether our final decision to keep this shape can be explained as our intent to retain "an example of a study of a restoration process," or it is due to a reluctance to change a shape that had been accepted for years as the ideal version of a restoration of an ancient Greek nose, or it is simply due to an attempt on our part to make the original better(!)—as is the case in so many translations of the ancient texts—the fact remains that once again we are looking at a second translation of the Greek original: the first being the one of the Roman artist, and the second that of our own cultural preference.

Fig. 37.

Chapter 13

TONSURE AND *CURSUS HONORUM* UP TO THE PHOTIAN ERA AND CONTEMPORARY RAMIFICATIONS

Rev. Dr. Philip Zymaris
Assistant Professor of Liturgics

The Photian era is known as a significant landmark for relations between the Eastern and Western Churches. This has been stressed especially in the work of the distinguished Czech scholar Francis Dvornik. The meeting of East and West that was caused by the conflict between Pope Nicholas I and Patriarch Photios produced correspondence and conciliar literature that put current practices of East and West into relief. This article will attempt to examine only one of those aspects: practices in East and West regarding tonsure, monasticism, and the episcopate, and the significance this may have for today's practice.

The adventure described in the classic book *The Photian Schism*[1] began when Photios, a distinguished layman, professor, and *protospatharios* ("secretary of state") of the imperial court, succumbed to imperial pressure to succeed the ousted Ignatios as patriarch of Constantinople. In order to occupy the patriarchal throne by Christmas 858, Photios was ordained *"athroon,"* that is, directly from the lay state to the episcopal rank in a matter of a few days. This tradition of *athroon* ordinations was not unusual in the ninth century and earlier, as has been described elsewhere;[2] however, what is of interest in the narration of Photios' series of one-day ordinations is the reference to the monastic state as being one of the "grades" that Photios "passed" through in order to become bishop. This mention is paradoxical because the historical context makes it clear that the purpose of this series of ordinations was not to place Photios in a monastery, but on the patriarchal throne. This state of affairs therefore seems to set a strange precedent for an abstract "monasticism" as a kind of title or "grade" totally divorced from the communal life of any monastery. This possibly reflects a shift in mentality regarding monasticism from early Church practice, as will be shown below. Using the events of the ninth century as a springboard, then, an attempt shall be made to explain this phenomenon by examining earlier practices and traditions of the Church in order to offer a possible explanation for this interpretive shift regarding this neuralgic ministry in the Church.

This reference to Photios' one day as a "monk" is recorded in the acts of the Synod of 869–870. This synod was convened in Constantinople eleven years after Photios' ordination and led by papal legates. It was convened for the express purpose of ousting Photios and bringing Ignatios back to the patriarchal throne, and therefore the acts of this council painted everything related to Photios in the darkest of colors.

Because of its significance, the actual narrative of Photios' ordination is worth quoting in full. It reads as follows: "And the saying 'we created a saint in a day' came true, for on the first day he went from the *lay state to the monastic*, on the second day a reader, and then on the next day a subdeacon, on the next day a deacon, after this a presbyter and then, finally, on the sixth day, it being the birthday of Christ, he was promoted to the hierarchical throne, announcing peace to the people but not really meaning this nor being worthy of true peace."[3] Two items of interest regarding this account must be mentioned initially at this juncture. First of all, the mention of the transition from the lay state to the monastic state is not an ordination service; it should be assumed that the rite of monastic tonsure is implied here. Secondly, regarding the historical accuracy of the account, one may reasonably have some hesitation for the following obvious reason: the narrator, Niketas of Paphlagonia, was clearly negatively disposed towards Photios, as is evident in the sarcastic tone of this text as well as in the fact that he was a member of the anti-Photian, pro-Western party responsible for the convening of this synod according to the bidding of Pope Nicholas I.[4] Besides the anti-Photian intent of the narrative, it must be noted that this was written eleven years after the actual event of Photios' ordination, and it is unknown whether Niketas was actually an eyewitness to it or not. Indeed, this narration could perhaps represent an oral tradition as to how a member of Niketas' party *thought* such a series of ordinations would or should be conducted. The caution with which one must read this account is intensified by the fact that the inclusion of the monastic "rank" as the first step in the process of the *athroon* ordination clearly conflicts with opinions of Photios himself regarding monasticism, as recorded in his epistles and in the acts and canons of the "pro-Photian" Council of 879–880, as will be seen below. Therefore, one must not totally exclude the possibility that the account narrated by Niketas reflects a more Western notion of monasticism (and ordination, for that matter) that was trickling gradually into the East, even though Niketas himself was an Easterner. One therefore also cannot totally rule out the possibility that this tonsure never really occurred. However, it must be stressed that, even if this tonsure did not truly occur, the mere existence of this reference in the text does witness at least to the reality of a mentality that was current in some circles. This mentality, which goes against earlier tradition and contemporary notions of Photios himself, gradually made enough headway in the East to the point where, in today's practice in certain Orthodox circles, one does not even bat an eye when confronted by a "monasticism" not dedicated to the desert but to active ministry in the world, that is, a nominal, symbolic monasticism that boils down to a title rather than a form of life. This contemporary attitude today essentially equates monasticism with celibacy, as was the case already in the ninth-century West, as will be demonstrated below. The examination of this phenomenon and its origins is therefore significant not only for a study of the ninth century, but also for an understanding of today's practice in Orthodoxy.

1. A Historical Review of the Notion of "Tonsure"

It has been remarked that a universal characteristic of human life as evidenced in all human societies is the symbolism, importance, and potency attributed to hair.[5] The way in which someone wears his or her hair (the "hairdo") indicates much about that person and his or her position in society. The Church, not of this world but in the world, did not issue forth from a vacuum, and therefore adopts catholic signs of human life consonant with the gospel and transforms them with a Christian meaning and content. In this context the Church also adopted certain current cultural customs regarding hair and gave them a new interpretation.

In the Greco-Roman world, where Christianity expanded and spread, the notion of "*tonsura*" already had a cultural significance. Even before the advent of Christianity, tonsure, which originally signified the *complete shearing of one's hair*, was the characteristic of slaves. The lack of one's hair in effect meant the loss of one's power,[6] and the shearing of one's hair therefore signified servitude and submission.[7] Thus tonsure took on the connotation of the total offering, service, and submission of the servant to his master. One should also note that in the ancient Jewish tradition the shearing of one's hair had the additional connotation of mourning and penitence for one's sins according to the spirit of Isaiah 22. The connotations of these two traditions regarding hair, the Jewish and Greco-Roman, coterminous with the world within which Christianity originated and expanded respectively, eventually combined in religious circles. Indeed, even before the advent of Christianity such a shearing of one's hair came to signify one's offering and submission to a specific deity or was seen as a mark of sacrifice for a special favor asked of a god, much like the votive offerings (τάμα) later common in Christianity.

With the advent of Christianity, this connotation of tonsure was adopted by Christians and transferred to the Christian God. Thus, in Christianity tonsure was understood as an indication of special service or obedience to God as well as an indication of repentance and penitence for sins. Indeed, according to the terminology of canon law, "slavery to God" was denoted by a total shearing of the hair.[8] Thus one finds to this day in the liturgical tradition of the Orthodox Church various tonsures connected to the special service offered by particular orders of the so-called "minor clergy" as well as a tonsure in the context of the rite of initiation. Whereas these forms of tonsure developed gradually by about the seventh century, monastic tonsure developed with the emergence of monasticism in the fourth century. This is because the cultural connotations of total dedication already connected with the total shearing of one's hair were especially appropriate in the case of monasticism. In fact, tonsure in the context of monasticism acquired a major symbolic meaning as the sign of initiation *par excellence* into the monastic state, the rite of passage which introduced one to the so-called "repentant order," to those who are "under obedience," according to the terminology of the Fathers of the Council of 879–880, as we shall see below.[9]

Thus, it is evident that the way one "wore his hair" had significance in Christianity. Indeed, a study of Christian customs regarding hair reveals that this was the case not only regarding monasticism and tonsure, but in all the ministries of the Church. Reference was already made to the various "tonsures" that evolved in later Christianity in connection with the minor clergy. On a broader base, one finds that reference is also made in the literature to characteristic styles, or "*schemata*," current in the early Church and appropriate to the different ministries in the Church besides the monastic one. Thus it seems that clergy and laity had their own appropriate *schemata*, which included a particular "hairstyle" that indicated their particular position in the Church.[10] This is clearly evident, for example, in canon 21 of the Quinisext Council. This canon determined that excommunicated clerics had to change their hairstyles to that of the laity, which implies that there was a difference. In the event that such persons were reinstated as clergy, they would cut their hair once again according to the style, or "*schema*," of the clergy. This distinction is also clear in the case of St. Tarasios, Patriarch of Constantinople, who was Photios' uncle and who was clearly ordained directly from the lay state to the episcopal rank with no intermediary "stages." According to the account of this ordination, it is clear that his *schema* was changed: "In accordance to the will of the State he left behind him the things of the world and having *his hair cut according to the priestly fashion* and having humbly altered his general appearance, through divine and spiritual intercessions, he accepted the honor of the episcopal anointing and was raised to the height of the high pastoral chair."[11]

At this point it is significant to note that in the consciousness of the early Church, the episcopal ministry was clearly distinguished from the monastic, unlike the popular piety today that practically identifies the two. The ancient tradition made a clear distinction between bishops as the presidents of the Eucharistic assembly and monks who were "under obedience." It thus would be illogical for the leader of the community to have his hair shaved in the style of a slave. This clear distinction is therefore reflected in the differing *schemata* of bishops and monks, as is evident in cases where bishops resigned from their episcopal duties in order to retire to a monastery and the reverse case, where monks become bishops.[12]

It should also be made clear at this point that the aforementioned styles examined here belong to the fourth century onward. After the conversion of Constantine and the Edict of Milan, which allowed for the toleration of Christianity, this faith was set free to develop details of day-to-day life unencumbered by the fear of persecution, whereas in eras of persecution it is obvious that Christians did not avidly seek to bring unnecessary attention to themselves. Monasticism also was a post-persecution phenomenon linked to the officialization of Christianity in the Roman Empire. This means that before the legalization of Christianity, Christians, whether lay or clergy, appeared as all other Roman citizens, according to the styles of the day. In accordance with the admonitions of St. Paul,[13] who was a Jew but also a Roman citizen, and also of the fourth-century *Apostolic Constitutions*,[14] this simply meant that men[15] wore short hair.[16]

2. *The Purpose of Monasticism*

As mentioned above, however, after the Edict of Milan different ministries were able to emerge freely, and monasticism was one of these major
ministries that developed. Monasticism clearly began as a lay movement
after the legalization of Christianity, a movement that strove to maintain
the radical newness and power that Christianity possessed in the previous era of persecutions. This was an instinctive attempt from within
the Church to preserve an awareness of "the one thing needful" and the
eschatological perspective that was common to all Christians during the
era of persecutions. In short, this was a reaction against a possible "do-
mestication" of Christianity once it became the state "religion," a state
of affairs which could facilitate its becoming too comfortable with the
ways of power in *this* world. In this sense, the power of monasticism lay
precisely in its "powerlessness"; it was therefore a spontaneous movement that issued forth not from those Church members in positions of
leadership and power in the Church (i.e., the clergy), but rather it was
a lay movement, indeed, not only a lay movement but also a non-Greek
movement. Interestingly enough, this is seen in the fact that early monasticism began with those who were literally on the geographical and
ethnographical fringes of the empire. Hence monasticism was initially
found among the Egyptians (Copts) and then also among the Palestin-
ians (Semites), on the Southern and Eastern fringes of the empire, respectively. Thus, monasticism was initially withdrawal from the world
for the sake of an intense life of prayer and ascesis. In true monasticism,
not blighted by heretical notions, this special withdrawal from the world
was the result of love for God and His world and creation, and not due to
a dualistic rejection of the world. Because of this special role and vocation of monasticism, it is clear that the special vocation of the monk was
not the "active ministry" in the parishes—the parish priests and hierarchy had this specific duty—but rather monastic withdrawal to the desert
for the sake of contemplative prayer.

Monasticism, therefore, was initially a strictly non-clerical movement. Indeed, canon 2 of the Council of 879–880 emphasizes this distinction that has been blurred in later years: that is, that the pastoral
care of the people is the duty first of all of the presidents of the Eucharistic assembly, the bishops and not the monks who live not in circumstances of leadership, but under obedience. As the canon says, "The
situation of the monk is of one who is learning and under obedience to
the word; he is not in a situation of teaching or presidency or minister-

ing of others, rather, such are to be ministered to."[17] For this reason, in early monasticism ordination to the clergy was considered as incompatible with the monastic vocation.[18] If eventually in the subsequent development of early monasticism some monks were ordained, this was exclusively for the serving of the liturgical and sacramental needs of the monastery. A parallel "active" ministry in the surrounding parishes of such a "priest-monk" was therefore unheard of.

3. *Photios and Tonsure*

Taking all of the above into account the inclusion of tonsure as one of the "grades" that Photios had to "pass" through in order to be enthroned as the patriarch of Constantinople is paradoxical. As mentioned above, the rite of tonsure—signifying subjection—for someone destined to be placed on the major episcopal throne of the East is inconsistent and diametrically opposed to Photios' own views, evident in the acts and canons of the Council of 879–880. This is clear because one of the major themes that this council dealt with was the role of monasticism in the Church and the distinction between monasticism and the episcopal ministry. This was in great measure due to the recent precedent set by Patriarch Ignatios. Ignatios, a former monk known for his conservatism,[19] was elected patriarch of Constantinople under the empress Theodora. With the "changing of the guards" in the imperial courts—that is, the usurpation of the imperial throne by Theodora's son Michael III—Ignatios' continued loyalty to Theodora and criticism of the new regime made him unfit for the new situation. He was therefore exiled and replaced by Photios—hence Photios' *athroon* ordination in order to quickly accommodate the new situation. In this context Ignatios resigned as patriarch of Constantinople and withdrew to a monastery. However, when the political situation later changed in his favor, Ignatios abandoned his monastery in order to exercise patriarchal authority once again, and Photios was exiled—the anti-Photian Council of 869–870 was convened to justify this situation. When the climate changed yet one more time, however, Photios was reinstated over against Ignatios, and the Council of 879–880 was convened in order to refute the decisions of the previous "anti-Photian" Council of 869–870 and to normalize the new ecclesiastical situation.

In this context, the council, remembering these recent historical events, dealt with the theme of the place of monasticism. Specifically, it was discussed whether it is lawful or not for a bishop who has resigned to a monastery to return later to episcopal authority. In the acts of the council, Photios characteristically asked the Fathers of the council, "What do you think about those of the episcopal rank who place themselves in the rank of the monastics? *Have they not given themselves over to subjection?* Can they then afterwards regain their former pastorship?" The answer of the Fathers was negative: "This is not the practice amongst us, neither is it known. For whoever goes from the episcopal to the monastic ranks, i.e. to those numbered among the repentants, such a one cannot once again claim the episcopal office."[20] Therefore a clear distinction is made in this council between monks who are under obedience and bishops, who are presidents of the Eucharistic assembly. Because their roles were clearly distinguished, it is logical, as mentioned in passing above, that their external appearances also reflected this. It therefore would not make sense for a bishop to circulate with a monastic tonsure (i.e., totally shorn hair), which had the connotation of servitude and not leadership. This custom is evident in Photios' second epistle to Pope Nicholas I, where the external distinguishing characteristics of the monk and the bishop are distinguished. According to this epistle, on the one hand the monk is known by the tonsure, whereas the bishop, on the other, is known by his own characteristic *schema*. Photios thus describes how, in cases when a monk is compelled to become a bishop, he must change his external appearance to reflect his new role: "Amongst us, we do not transform the monastic schema to that of the clergy; *however, because some have desired to raise monks to the episcopal heights, such a one has his hair cut in a circle, thus changing the former schema."*[21] Again, in this same epistle Photios compares Eastern and Western practices regarding such a change in ministry. It seems that Photios was aware of a general blurring of the external distinguishing marks of the monastic and episcopal ministries[22] that had already occurred in the West but not as of yet in the East. He referred specifically to the fact that, in the West, when a monk became a bishop he would retain the external trappings of a monk, whereas in the East this was not the case. Thus, he compared the seemingly superficial ascetic practice of monks in East and West of abstaining from meat. In the West if such a monk were to become a bishop, he would continue this polity, whereas an Eastern monk-become-bishop would be compelled to even change his diet. To back this up, he cites a rule adhered to in Alexandria where, if a monk were elected to become patriarch of Alexandria, he would first have to declare publicly that he would eat meat![23] The discussions recorded in the acts of the Council of 879–880 time and again corroborate the existence of such clear distinctions between the monastic and episcopal vocations. At one point the Fathers of the council, comparing the customs of East and West regarding this issue, declared that "if one is not tonsured in Christ,[24] he cannot become a bishop or patriarch; in the West monks are also ordained to the clergy, [but] *we do not know of such a custom*."[25]

4. *Suggested Solution to the Problem*

If all of the above is the case, how, then, can one interpret the insertion of the monastic tonsure in the series of "grades" Photios had to "pass" through in order to be enthroned as patriarch of Constantinople? It seems that, judging from the context of this ninth-century clash of Western and Eastern ecclesiastical customs, it is probable that this phenomenon is due in part to the infiltration of Western notions on the priesthood and monasticism into the East. One must remember that the anti-Photian Council of 869–870 was essentially convened according to the bidding of Pope Nicholas I in order impose papal authority, that is, a Western ecclesiology, upon the East. It is therefore not farfetched to opine that in this context even the Eastern Fathers of this council, in supporting a Western ecclesiological policy as a "package" logically adhered—perhaps unconsciously—to analogous Western views on the priesthood, monasticism, and the so-called *cursus honorum*, that is, the order of grades of the priesthood that one must pass through in order to become a bishop. Specifically, the Western practical identification of monk and priest, in contrast to the clear distinction of the two in the Eastern practice, could have led to a description as found in the account of Photios' ordination. This hypothesis seems to make sense because it turns out that the series of degrees, or grades, as presented by Niketas follows exactly a Western *cursus honorum* pattern as exhibited in the Western canonical tradition.

As mentioned above, in early monasticism monks in both East and West were not ordained except for the special exception of a few priest-monks ordained specifically for the liturgical and sacramental needs of the monastery. However, this clear distinction between the roles and vocations of the monk and the clergyman gradually began to erode in the West, especially with the gradual imposition from the sixth century forward of the practice of universal clerical celibacy. Once the early monastic inhibition regarding the incompatibility of being both monk and clergy faded away, there was an analogous increase in ordained monks in monasteries. On the other hand, the so-called "secular" clergy of the parishes also were ultimately understood as belonging to various "monastic" orders, especially with the increase in such orders dedicated to active ministry in the world.[26] In this way the monks and parish clergy began gradually to resemble each other more and more in the West and eventually were practically identified. Ultimately, earlier distinctions between *monks* and *clergy* had no real meaning anymore.[27] Thus, at least on a popular level initially, the distinguishing feature of the monk was not the monastery—because monasteries in the West could take on so many different forms (more or less abstract) depending on the "monastic" order—but celibacy. Because all clergy were celibates, all clergy were therefore considered in some sense monks.

This was in sharp contrast to the Eastern view of monasticism, which never adopted any concept of different "orders" of monasticism, but rather always adhered to one form of monasticism connected with withdrawal to a physical (not theoretical) monastery and a dedication to contemplative prayer life—a form of life clearly distinct from the active ministry of parishes. Indeed, the service of tonsure was done in a monastic context and connected the new monk to that specific monastery. Thus, in the Eastern view, celibacy by itself was not equated with monasticism. The monk is not the celibate, but someone who withdraws from the world to join a specific community and way of life that happens to also include celibacy. Thus, celibacy, as a special calling and eschatological sign of the Kingdom,[28] has always been blessed in the Church to appear in any of the other non-monastic ministries of the Church (i.e., a celibate deacon, a celibate layperson, etc.);[29] indeed, celibacy in the world was eventually connected specifically to the leadership (and therefore by definition non-monastic) ministry of the episcopacy. Indeed, in the East the tradition of both married and celibate clergy serving the Church in the world was a venerable tradition—the celibate clergy serving in the world, however, were not confused with monastics.[30]

On the other hand, the Western identification of monasticism, celibacy, and the priesthood gradually was reflected in the Western interpretation of the *cursus honorum*, or grades of the priesthood.[31] Because of this unofficial identification of monasticism and priesthood, the monastic tonsure was eventually seen as a necessary rite of passage for all entering the clergy—whether they were to serve in a monastery or not. In this sense, tonsure was gradually interpreted as the necessary "first degree" of the priesthood.[32]

5. *The Account of Photios' Ordination in the Tradition of the Western* Cursus Honorum

This Western understanding of the *cursus honorum* eventually found its way into the East, in the acts of the Council of 869–870. Before this Eastern appearance, the development of this *cursus honorum* can be traced in the canonical tradition of the West. Specifically, the 869–870 *cursus* can trace its lineage to a Roman council of 769, which dealt with a similar issue. This council was also convened to justify the ousting of a hierarch who had been ordained *athroon*.[33] The description of the ordination of the upstart Constantine of Nepi is essentially in keeping with the *cursus* tradition described in canon 10 (13) of the Sardican Council of 343, with the difference that *monastic tonsure* is now added as the first step reflecting a departure from the mentality of the fourth century.[34] Thus, according to the Council of 769, the only candidates for the episcopacy who can be installed on the papal throne are those cardinal deacons or cardinal presbyters who serve at the Vatican and who have passed through the following priestly "grades": monasticism (!), subdeacon, deacon, (presbyter not obligatory!), bishop.[35] Thus we find a precedent set for the *cursus honorum* presented in canon 5 and in the acts of the anti-Photian Council of 869–870 one hundred years later. This 869–870 description matches both the earlier tradition as found in the Sardican council (reader, deacon, presbyter, bishop) and the 769 Roman council, which adds "monasticism" as the necessary "first degree" for one to be ordained bishop (!), as well as the degree of subdeacon. It is noteworthy that an epistle written in 866 by Pope Nicholas I addressed to the bishops of the East and read in the context of the 869–870 council imposed this exact *cursus honorum*.[36] Therefore, the actual *cursus honorum* recorded in the Council of 869–870, as a combination of the traditions of Sardica 343 and Rome 769, reads as follows: tonsure, reader, subdeacon, deacon, presbyter, bishop.[37]

As we stated above, this Western abstract understanding of tonsure, although it did not provoke any objection amongst the fathers of the 869–879 council—perhaps because of their ecclesiological tendencies—clearly goes against the earlier tradition of the East. The discussions in the later Council of 879–880 seem to reflect the fact that there was dissonance regarding this tradition, although it apparently was making headway in the East. One must note in all fairness that an earlier precedent coming from the East that could have led to a gradual unconscious acceptance of this innovation in the *cursus* could be the nomocanons of Justinian. In one of these nomocanons, it was determined that all candidates for the episcopacy were obligated either to have served for six months as a clergyman or simply to be a monk. Whereas specifically six months service as a clergyman was required, no time limitation was given for the "monastic road" to the episcopacy. It is therefore possible that some with no serious desire for monastic life saw nominal tonsure as a quick ticket to the episcopacy even before contact with similar Western practices.[38]

6. *Conclusion*

The account of Photios' ordination and the eventual adoption of this *cursus*, then, must be seen at least in part as a result of Western influence. This makes sense in the context of a compromise between two forms of ecclesiology, described elsewhere as "ministerial" and "hierarchical."[39] According to the "ministerial" interpretation, Church life is modeled after the life of the Trinity, where the Persons of the Holy Trinity are one while at the same time remaining unique and unrepeatable. In this context, any "hierarchy" is not a pyramidal hierarchy of "higher" and "lower." Rather, here there is a hierarchy of diversity in unity, where the one ministry completes the other, according to the theology of the body of Christ as seen in St. Paul (1 Cor 12:12f.). No one ministry was seen as the "standard" that all others were to imitate; rather, for the body-Church to be healthy, each ministry had to accomplish its unique role. In this Pauline sense, then, in the early Church different ministries worked together to make the Church "catholic," that is to say, complete. In this context, a hierarchical *cursus* was nonsensical because each ministry was seen as a complete ministry in and of itself, tracing its origins to Christ Himself.[40] Therefore, no ministry was seen as a lower "stepping stone" for another higher "more complete" degree. Members of the Church were "ordained" straightaway to the ministry that they were most fit to serve, as is clear in the ordination prayers of the early Church.[41] All these ministries had meaning and were connected the one to the other in the communal context of the Church. Once this connection with the community—that is, the Eucharistic assembly—was de-emphasized, these various ministries of the Church could easily be construed as an individual "possession" divorced from any communal context. Once this mindset was gradually adopted, then ministries that were once unheard of outside a communal context—such as monasticism connected to the monastery—could be separated from that context and "objectified" as a mere "title." In this way, tonsure could ultimately be construed as a title, and monasticism as a possession that one carries with himself or herself totally independently from the actual monastic setting. According to such an understanding, it was easy for "monasticism" to be construed even as an obligatory "grade" in a series of stepping stones within a Church hierarchy.

It seems clear from the above that this Western conception, although foreign to the pristine Eastern concept of monasticism, has, alas, already from the time of Photios, made headway in the East. Indeed, in contemporary Orthodox practice it is not uncommon for the rite of tonsure to be performed as a supposed necessary prerequisite for a celibate cleric's worldly ministry, or even as a prerequisite for the episcopal rank. In such cases, the service of tonsure, which necessarily mentions a monastery within which the candidate promises to "leave his bones," becomes a hypocritical show,[42] a mere following of the letter of a supposed law that a bishop must be a tonsured monk, for all know that the candidate will either have a very nominal relationship with the "monastery of his repentance" or in fact will never actually set foot in the monastery mentioned.[43] In cases where a bishop is actually taken from a monk residing in a monastery, of course there is no ambiguity—his tonsure "promises" have had true ramifications in his life. In actual fact, though, in today's practice candidates for the episcopate are usually taken from celibates in the world—and there is nothing wrong with this, as this is a venerable tradition of the Church. But in such cases there is no reason to pretend that they are what they are not; that is, there is no reason for them to be tonsured and invested with monastic titles that have no meaning in their context as this adds nothing to their ministry. Indeed, why load them with promises they cannot keep in their holy ministry in the world? In the ancient Church, in cases where candidates for the holy episcopate came from the celibate clergy serving in the world, such candidates—if they had any titles—would possess titles and offices proper to the clergy serving in the world[44] *because that's exactly what they were doing, serving in the world!* So in this clear-cut tradition, the titles of those in the world—whether *celibate or married*—were the same, for it was nonsensical to introduce monastic titles out of context. Indeed, what would be wrong with returning to this unambiguous practice? Is it somehow demeaning for a celibate to have the same titles and offices as the married, as was the venerable tradition of the Church?[45] If this is the case, then psychological issues are involved that are a far cry from Christ's humble ministry and the Gospel injunction that that the "first shall be last and the last first" (Matt 19:30).

Thus, this later practice of introducing monastic titles out of context into the worldly clerical ministries seems to betray an ambiguous theology. One author has coined the phrase "crypto-docetism" to describe this phenomenon. According to the late first-century heresy of docetism, the Incarnation of Christ was not a reality, but a mere appearance, a figment of the imagination. According to Vasilieos Thermos, "St. Ignatios of Antioch suggests the existential consequences of this delusion: 'if our Lord was in the body and crucified only according to appearances then I now am being tied only according to appearances. What then is the use of my being given over to death, fire, sword and the wild beasts?' "[46]

The solid reality of the Incarnation is therefore the unambiguous foundation for an equally solid theology of the Church, a theology based on solid realities and not on appearances. The institutions and practices of the Church—and especially the neuralgic leadership ministries of the Church—should therefore be based on and reflect such solid realities and not appearances and role confusions. Especially in cases where we are dealing with the ministries of the episcopate and monasticism, which are such important gauges for the health of our Church, this should be the case. These ministries should be based on the solid foundation of the venerable tradition of the Eastern Church as expressed in the clear ministerial distinctions of St. Photios and the Fathers of Council of 879–880. Otherwise our *lex orandi* (liturgical prayer and rites) will be shown to be tragically inconsistent with what we claim our *lex credendi* (theology) teaches. In this way, contemporary Orthodox practice will fall into the danger of not serving theology, reality, and truth, but various interests, dubious psychologies, and meaningless, ambiguous customs. Such confused notions will only serve to weaken the witness of contemporary Orthodoxy to the world around us. If we prefer to adhere to customs that make no sense and that, in any case, trace their origins to a foreign context anyway, then the powerful witness of the theological-liturgical tradition of our Church is severely impaired. This holy inheritance bequeathed upon us is thus locked up in a box and rendered inaccessible to the world that so thirsts for the truth of Christ as expressed in His Holy Church, the body of Christ.[47]

Notes

1. Francis Dvornik, *The Photian Schism: History and Legend* (Cambridge, 1948).

2. Philip Zymaris, "*Athroon* Ordinations in the Tradition of the Church," *Greek Orthodox Theological Review* 53, nos. 1–4 (2008): 31–50.

3. Mansi 16:232BC.

4. For details of the complex ecclesio-political dynamics of this Photian controversy, see F. Dvornik, *The Photian Schism*; and idem, "East and West. The Schism of the Patriarch Photius, Restatement of Facts," *The Month* 179 (1943): 257–270.

5. Alexander Schmemann, *Of Water and of the Spirit* (Crestwood, NY), 127.

6. Ibid. See also the account of Sampson and Delilah in the Old Testament book of Judges 16.

7. A. Michel, "Tonsure," *DTC*, vol. 15A, p. 1228; J. Tixeront, *Holy Orders and Ordination* (London, 1928), 133f.

8. 'Αμίλκα 'Αλιβιζάτος, "'Η κουρὰ τῶν κληρικῶν καὶ μοναχῶν κατὰ τὸ κανονικὸν δίκαιον τῆς 'Ορθοδόξου 'Εκκλησίας," *ΕΕΒΣ ΚΓ'* (1953): 235.

9. Mansi 17:501C.

10. 'Αθανασίου Γκίκα, «'Η ἀμφίεσις τοῦ 'Ορθοδόξου κλήρου: 'Ιστορία – παρὸν καὶ μέλλον», *Τὰ ἱερὰ ἄμφια καὶ ἡ ἐξωτερικὴ περιβολὴ τοῦ 'Ορθοδόξου κλήρου* ('Αθῆναι, 2002), 81.

11. Ignati Diaconi, "Vita Tarasii Archiepiscopi Constantinopolitani," ed. I. A. Heikel, *Acta Societatis Scientiarium Fennicae*, vol. 17 (Helsinki, 1891), 401.

12. In cases where a bishop resigns to retreat to a monastery he would receive monastic tonsure, which implies means that the monastic tonsure was different from the episcopal *schema* (Θεοδώρου Γιάγκου, «'Η κουρὰ μετὰ τὴ χειροτονία. 'Η ἐφαρμογὴ τοῦ Β' κανόνα τῆς χυνόδου τῆς 'Αγίας Σοφίας 879/880», *Σύναξις Εὐχαριστίας* ['Ορμύλια, 2003], 365–390). In the opposite case, when a monk becomes a bishop the monastic tonsure is changed to the episcopal *schema*. This is seen, for example, in the case of the Eastern monk Theodore, who was ordained archbishop of Canturbury in 668. The account makes note of the fact that he had to wait four months for his hair to grow into the characteristic episcopal *schema* (H. Leclercq, "Tonsure," *DACL*, 2433). This was not only a Western practice, for it is clear in one of Photios' epistles that this was also the practice in the East: "Because when some would raise the monk to the episcopal heights, such a one would have a big circle cut on the top of his head, thus changing the former schema" (PG 102:605C).

13. 1 Cor 11:14.

14. PG 1:564–568.

15. It is noteworthy that, in accordance with 1 Cor 11, the opposite was the case for women, as even in the case of nuns the usual total shearing of monastic tonsure was prohibited according to canon 17 of the Gangra Council.

16. J. Tixeront, *Holy Orders and Ordination*, trans. S. A. Raemers (London, 1928), 134.

17. Mansi 17:504A.

18. See D. J. Leclercq, "Le sacerdoce des moines," *Irénikon* 36 (1963): 11–12: "Les premiers moines considéraient le sacerdoce comme un état très honorable, mais, à cause de cela meme, comme oppose au leur, qui est caractérisé par la lolitude et la vie pénitente . . . La raison fondamentale de cette attitude semble avoir été celle-ci: le sacerdoce apparaissait contraire au grand principe monastique d'après lesquel les pratiques spirituelles doivent trouver leur expression et leur garantie dans le domaine corporel. L'humilité intérieure pouvait, chez d'autres, s'accomoder des honneurs extérieures; mais chez le moine elle devait se manifester par le fait de vivre dans un état humble, de même que la vigilance se manifestait par les veilles, la pureté du Coeur par le jeûne. Le sacerdoce, en outré, était contraire au propos de solitude et de tranquillité du moine." See also E. Ἰωαννίδου, Ἐπιδράσεις τοῦ μοναχισμοῦ τῆς ἀωατολῆς στὸν κανόνα τοῦ ὁσίου Βενεδίκτου (Κατερίνη, 1995), 105. See also Jean Leclercq, "On Monastic Priesthood According to the Ancient Medieval Tradition," *Studia Monastica* 3 (1961): 139–142.

19. See Ἰωάννου Ζηζιούλα, «Ἰγνάτιος», in Θρησκευτικὴ καὶ Ἠθικὴ Ἐγκυκλοπαίδεια, τόμ. ΣΤ', 716. The same was the case with St. Methodios, who was the patriarch before Ignatios (Ludwig Nemec, "Photius – Saint or Schismatic?" *JES* 3 [1966]: 231–232).

20. Mansi 17:501CD. See also the second canon of this council: "If any bishop or anyone else with a prelatical office is desirous of descending to monastic life and of replenishing the region of penitence and of penance, let him no longer cherish any claim to prelatical dignity. For the monks' conditions of subordination represent the relationship of pupilship, and not of teachership or of presidency; nor do they undertake to pastor others, but are to be content with being pastured" (D. Cummings, ed., *The Rudder* [Chicago, 1957], 478).

21. PG 102:605C.

22. See also the "Second Epistle of Photios to Pope Nicholas I" (PG 102:605A) and the "Encyclical Epistle of Photios to the Eastern Patriarchs" (PG 102:724D–725A and 733BCf.), where Photios makes reference to problems caused in the West by a general leveling of all distinctions between clergy with an active ministry in the world and monastics; specifically, he mentions awareness of scandals that have occurred in the West due to the practice of universal clerical celibacy.

23. "Second Epistle of Photios to Pope Nicholas I" 23 (PG 102:605C).

24. This is an enigmatic phrase: «εἰ μὴ ἐστί τις κεκαρμένος ἐν Χριστῷ, ἐπίσκοπος ἢ πατριάρχης οὐ γίνεται. ἡ δὲ δύσις καὶ τοὺς ὄντας μοναχοὺς κληρικοὺς ποιεῖ. Τοῦτο δὲ ἡμεῖς οὐ γνωρίζομεν». One may only conclude that "tonsured in Christ" is referring to the tonsure received in the context of the rite of initiation eight days after Baptism together with the prayers of ablution. The phrase therefore communicates the obvious fact that only those baptized may become clergy. The second part of the statement is also enigmatic, for it is obvious that patriarchs such as Methodios and Ignatios were taken from the monastic ranks. Many more, however, were taken from the ranks of the laity (see Zymaris, "*Athroon* Ordinations," 43f.). Perhaps the Fathers of this council wanted to stress this latter practice over against the former in support of Photios.

25. Mansi 17:457DE.

26. This notion was strengthened with the advent of the "canons," who, although fulfilling duties belonging to the secular clergy, they lived together as a semi-monastic "brotherhood." The precedent set by the "canons" is especially significant for this development because the principle of their lifestyle was precisely that one may minister to a parish and be a monk simultaneously. See A. Papadakis and J. Meyendorff, *The Christian East and the Rise of the Papacy* (Crestwood, NY, 1994), 64–65.

27. This is clear in the Western canonical tradition. For example, the Fourth Council of Toledo (633) imposed obligatory tonsure on all clergy (A. Michel, "Tonsure," *DTC* 15A:1231), and a later Council of Toledo declared that all parish clergy were to live together in semi-monastic style with the bishop in the bishop's residence, the "conclavium episcopi" (G. B. Ladner, *The Idea of Reform* [Cambridge, MA, 1959], 343). Indeed, eventually the different "monastic" orders with varying contemplative and pastoral duties began to have their own characteristic tonsure as a form of identification.

28. See Matt 19:12 and 1 Cor 7.

29. In this sense, marriage as a sacrament of the Church is also understood as an eschatological sign of the Kingdom. Because the cross will have been transcended in the Kingdom and because there will no longer be need of such symbols or icons of the Kingdom, both monasticism and marriage will be transformed and transcended in the Kingdom. However, the *relationships* contracted in this life—whether monastic or marital—will always be a part of one's identity in the Kingdom. On the equality of both marriage and celibacy as eschatological signs of the Kingdom see Paul Evdokimov, *The Sacrament of Love* (Crestwood, NY, 2001); and S. Charalambidis, "Marriage in the Orthodox Church," *One in Christ* 15, no. 1 (1979); 205–223.

30. On the fact that the Church from time immemorial blessed the celibate vocation for service in the world without equating this with monasticism, see the unique contribution of 'Επιφανίου I. Θεοδωροπούλου, *Μοναχικὸς καὶ ἄγαμος κοσμικὸς κλῆρος* - *Μελέτη κανονικὴ καὶ ἱστορικὴ περὶ διακρίσεως τοῦ ἀγάμου κοσμικοῦ κλήρου ἀπὸ τοῦ μοναχικοῦ* ('Αθῆναι, 1963). See also Βασιλείου Θερμοῦ, *Τὰ ὀφφίκια τῶν πρεσβυτέρων* (Νέα Σμύρνη, 1999), 37–38.

31. For a history of this development see Henri Leclercq, "Ordinations Irrégulières," *DACL* 12B:2345: "On pourrait toutefois soutenir que la profession monastique tenait lieu d'épreuve préparatoire."

32. J. Tixeront, *Holy Orders and Ordination,* 133. According to Leclercq, also from the end of the fourth century tonsure clearly was seen in the West as a rite of passage into the *clergy* and not into a specifically *monastic* lifestyle ("Tonsure," *DACL* 15B:2435).

33. See John St. H. Gibaut, "The Clerical Cursus of Constantine of Nepi: Two Accounts," *Ecclesia Orans* 12 (1995): 196f.

34. L. Duschesne, ed., *Le Liber Pontificalis: Texte, introduction, et commentaire,* vol. 1, 2nd ed. (Paris, 1886), 468–469.

35. According to a later manuscript that perhaps reflected Frankish influence, the series of grades that Constantine passed through was (one day each): tonsure, doorkeeper, reader, exorcist, sacristan, subdeacon, deacon, bishop. See Gibaut, "The Clerical Cursus," 196.

36. Mansi 16:118. See also Gibaut, "The Cursus Honorum," 63–64.

37. Mansi 16:162–163.

38. Archbishop Peter L'Huillier, "Episcopal Celibacy in the Orthodox tradition," *St. Vladimir's Theological Quarterly* 35, nos. 2 and 3 (1991): 288f.

39. Zymaris, "*Athroon* Ordinations," 32f.; Φιλίππου Ζυμάρη, *Ἡ ἱστορικὴ, δογματικὴ καὶ κανονικὴ σπουδαιότης τῆς Συνόδου Κωνσταντινουπόλεως (879-880)* (Θεσσαλονίκη, 2000), 16–31 (doctoral dissertation under publication).

40. Zymaris, "*Athroon* Ordinations," 32.

41. *The Treatise on the Apostolic Tradition of St. Hippolytus of Rome,* ed. Rev. Gregory Dix (New York, 1937), 2, 5 (bishop's ordination); 13 (presbyter); 17 (deacon). See also W. H. Frere, "Early Ordination Prayers," *Journal of Theological Studies* 17 (1915): 324f; Edwin Hatch ("Holy Orders," *Dictionary of Christian Antiquities* [London, 1880], 1475–1476) adds the following: "It was probably not until the clerical office became a regular profession that promotion from one grade to another became an ordinary rule; persons who were well fitted for particular offices sometimes remained in them to the end of their lives. Ambrose (*de Offic. Ministr.* i.44) writes as though division of labour were recognized in the Church, and as though it were a function of the bishop

to find out the office for which each person was best qualified." See also Hamilton Hess, *The Canons of the Council of Sardica, A.D. 343* (Oxford, 1958), 104: "There is little evidence that previous to the fourth century any prescribed order of ascent to the highest office was observed or even expressed as being desirable . . . diverse examples of the omission of one or more offices on the way to the episcopate may be cited, *and these are not exceptional cases.*"

42. Note the moving conversation that occurs between the abbot of the monastery and the candidate for tonsure, which is reduced to the level of mere parody in cases where there is no real intention to stay in the monastery referred to: "Question: Do you agree to remain in this monastery and in its ascesis till your last breath? Answer: Yes, with God's help, honorable father" (Jacobus Goar, *Euchologion Sive Rituale Graecorum* [Graz, 1960], 383, 385). This dialogue is repeated three times, and each time a pair of scissors is placed in the hands of the candidate for him to return to the hands of the abbot as an assurance that all that has been agreed upon in the dialogue is an expression of the free will of the candidate.

43. A typical example of this recent distortion of the tradition, which is understood in popular piety as "Tradition" from time immemorial, even though it is clearly in agreement with the Western tradition outlined above, is the very recent interpretation of the office of archimandrite either as a leadership role in the parishes or as a necessary "intermediary stage" for one preparing for the episcopate. The office of archimandrite was originally an exclusively monastic office, as the etymology of the title implies ("head of the [monastic] walls"). The holder of this office was a head abbot and therefore not necessarily even ordained. For this reason it was not considered a clerical office and is not included in the list of clerical offices seen on p. 223 of the 1992 (1977) edition of the official *Hieratikon* of the Church of Greece ('Αθῆναι: 'Αποστολικὴ Διακονία, ῎Εκδοσις Α' 1962, Β' 1977, Γ' 1987, Δ' 1992). However, in very recent history, influenced by the Western notion that celibate clerical ministries in the world must necessarily be considered *monastic* and be put over other ministries, effort was made to place this *non-clerical* office over all other *clerical* offices. Thus at the bottom of the traditional list on 223 a note is added: "The archimandrite precedes all other offices according to a decision of the Holy Synod." This is in keeping with the very recent decision specific to the Local Church of Greece that has since been assumed to be a universal practice of Orthodoxy from time immemorial. In 1929 the Holy Synod of the Church of Greece officialized the precedence of the "rank" of archimandrite over all other clerical offices. For the full text of this very recent decision see Αἱ συνοδικαὶ ἐγκύκλιοι, τόμος Α' ('Αθῆναι, 1955), 537–538 ('Αριθ. Πρωτ. 695/ Διεκπ. 1337); and Βασι-

λείου Θερμοῦ, *Τὰ ὀφφίκια τῶν πρεσβυτέρων* (Νέα Σμύρνη, 1999, 37–38). It is obvious that, for the sake of consistency, this leadership role could just as well be served by a celibate cleric without the specifically monastic title of archimandrite, which has no real meaning in this context.

44. It is clear that the protopresbyter, whether married or celibate, was an extremely important office in the tradition—with the caveat that the celibate protopresbyters potentially could become bishops. See Βασιλείου Θερμοῦ, *Τὰ ὀφφίκια*, 26ff.

45. In a strange attempt to distinguish married and celibate clergy serving in the world, a paradoxical liturgical practice with no canonical basis is commonly observed, where celibate clergy do not wear the *phelonion*—the vestment required for sacraments—when presiding over the sacraments of marriage and Baptism!

46. Πρὸς Σμυρναίοις 4, *ΒΕΠΕΣ* 2, 313. See Βασιλείου Θερμοῦ, «'Εκκλησιαστικὸς δοκητισμός», *Σύναξη* 58 (1996): 45.

47. The warning of Christ Himself seems fearfully appropriate in this context: "You are the salt of the earth; but if the salt loses its flavor, how shall it be seasoned? It is then good for nothing but to be thrown out and trampled underfoot by men" (Matt 5:13).

Appendix

The Leadership of the Ecumenical Patriarchate and the Significance of Canon 28 of Chalcedon

A Statement by the Faculty
Holy Cross Greek Orthodox School of Theology
Brookline, Massachusetts
April 30, 2009

The Ecumenical Patriarchate of Constantinople is the preeminent Church in the communion of the fourteen Autocephalous Orthodox Churches. Reflecting the witness of St. Andrew, the First-Called Apostle, the enduring mission of the Ecumenical Patriarchate of Constantinople is to proclaim the salutary Gospel of Jesus Christ in accordance with the Apostolic and Orthodox Faith.

The Ecumenical Patriarchate has a particular responsibility to strengthen the unity of the Orthodox Churches and to coordinate their common witness. At the same time, the Ecumenical Patriarchate has a specific responsibility to care for the faithful in lands beyond the borders of the other Autocephalous Churches. This is a ministry of service to the entire Church which the Ecumenical Patriarchate undertakes in accordance with the canons and often under difficult circumstances.

The Faculty of Holy Cross Greek Orthodox School of Theology profoundly regrets that statements recently have been made which misinterpret the canonical prerogatives and distort historical facts related to the distinctive ministry of the Ecumenical Patriarchate. Indeed, some injudicious remarks have insulted the person of Ecumenical Patriarch Bartholomew and have attempted to diminish the significance of his ministry.

These statements, made by bishops, priests, and laity, have been widely distributed. Regretfully, they have done little to advance the cause of Orthodox unity and the witness of the Church today. Indeed, some observations have misrepresented the traditional basis of

Orthodox ecclesiology. They contradict the admonition of St. Paul that "all things should be done decently and in order" (1 Cor 14:40).

Principles of Ecclesiastical Organization

The Church, chiefly through the Ecumenical Councils, has established significant principles of ecclesiastical organization. These principles are expressed in the canons of the Councils and in subsequent historical practices which have been sanctioned by the Church. These principles support the proclamation of the Gospel and strengthen the good order of the Church.

The Ecumenical Patriarch has been accorded specific prerogatives of witness and service from the time of the fourth century. This was a period when the Church was able explicitly to provide for canonical structures following the period of great persecution of the first three centuries. These prerogatives form the basis for his ministry to the entire Orthodox Church. These prerogatives distinguish the responsibilities of the Ecumenical Patriarch from other bishops of the Orthodox Church. They clearly grant to the Ecumenical Patriarch of Constantinople a primacy among the bishops of the Church. This primacy of service brings with it significant authority and responsibilities.

A number of recent commentators have challenged the leadership and responsibilities of the Ecumenical Patriarchate. They have misinterpreted canon 28 of the Council of Chalcedon (451), and related canons and practices. In order to appreciate properly the significance of canon 28 of the Council of Chalcedon, it must be interpreted in the light of other canons and practices of the Church at that time. It is far from being irrelevant as some may claim.

The Second Ecumenical Council in Constantinople (381) in canon 3 acknowledged that the bishop of Constantinople enjoys "prerogatives of honor (*presveia times*)." While recognizing that the bishop of New Rome (Constantinople) ranked after the bishop of Old Rome, a parallel between the primatial positions of the two bishops was affirmed.

At the Fourth Ecumenical Council in Chalcedon, the privileges of the bishop of Constantinople received further elaboration especially in canons 9 and 17. These canons stated that disputes in local churches could be appealed to Constantinople. Canon 28 of Chalcedon continued to draw a parallel between Old Rome and New Rome and reaffirmed the decision of 381. Canon 28 of the Council stated that the bishop of Constantinople had "equal prerogatives" (*isa presveia*) to those of Old

Rome. Over two hundred years later, the distinctive position of Constantinople was also reaffirmed in canon 36 of the Penthekti (Quinsext) Council (in Trullo) in 692.

Furthermore, canon 28 of Chalcedon explicitly granted to the bishop of Constantinople the pastoral care for those territories beyond the geographical boundaries of the other Local (autocephalous) Churches. At the time of the fifth century, these regions commonly were referred to as "barbarian nations" because they were outside the Byzantine commonwealth. (St. Paul in Romans 1:14 also had used the term "barbarians" to refer to those beyond the old Roman Empire.) Canon 28 of Chalcedon appears to clarify the reference in canon 2 of the Council of Constantinople which says that churches in the "barbarian nations" should be governed "according to the tradition established by the fathers."

This interpretation of canon 28 is supported by the fact that the geographical boundaries of the Local Churches are set. Their bishops are not permitted to minister beyond these limits. The Council of Constantinople in canon 2 clearly states: "Bishops should not invade churches beyond their boundaries for the purpose of governing them . . ." This principle is also reflected in canons 6 and 7 of the Council of Nicaea (325) and in the Apostolic Canons 14 and 34, also dating from the fourth century.

The Church invested only the bishop of Constantinople with the responsibility to organize ecclesial life in the places not under the care of other Local (autocephalous) Churches. This is reflected, for example, in the missions to the Goths and Scythians in the fifth century. The pastoral and missionary activities inaugurated by St. John Chrysostom while Patriarch of Constantinople are especially instructive in this regard. One must also take note of the missionary activity of the Ecumenical Patriarchate in Central and Eastern Europe from the ninth under Patriarch Photios and later on through the sixteenth centuries. In these cases, the Ecumenical Patriarchate acted to spread the Gospel in territories beyond the boundaries of other Local Churches.[1]

The Ecumenical Patriarchate granted autocephalous status to the Church of Russia in 1589, confirmed in the Golden Seal Certificate in 1591, which was reaffirmed by a synod in Constantinople in 1593 when patriarchal status was granted. In these Tomes, the territorial jurisdiction of the Church of Russia was clearly defined. This practice was followed in the Tome of Autocephaly for all subsequent Autocephalous Churches which were granted their status by the Ecumenical Patriarchate and confirmed by the assent of the other Autocephalous Churches.

Ecumenical Patriarch Bartholomew has recently said:

> The Orthodox Church is an orderly community of autoceph-
> alous or autonomous Churches, while she is fully aware of
> herself as the authentic continuation of the One, Holy, Cath-
> olic and Apostolic Church. She fulfills her spiritual mission
> through the convocation of local or major Synods, as the ca-
> nonical tradition has established it, in order to safeguard and
> affirm the communion of the local churches with each other
> and with the Ecumenical Patriarchate. The Ecumenical Pa-
> triarchate, as the First Throne in the Orthodox Church, has
> been granted by decisions of Ecumenical Councils (canon 3
> of the II Ecumenical Council; canons 9, 17 and 28 of the IV
> Ecumenical Council; canon 36 of the Quinsext Ecumenical
> Council) and by the centuries-long ecclesial praxis, the ex-
> ceptional responsibility and obligatory mission to care for
> the protection of the faith as it has been handed down to
> us and of the canonical order (*taxis*). And so it has served
> with the proper prudence and for seventeen centuries that
> obligation to the local Orthodox churches, always within the
> framework of the canonical tradition and always through the
> utilization of the Synodal system . . . [2]

History bears this out. It is attested to by innumerable examples of initiative undertaken by the Ecumenical Patriarchate to exercise leadership
for those Local Churches prevented by unusual circumstances from doing so. In this capacity, the Ecumenical Patriarchate elected patriarchs
for other Sees when asked, acted as arbitrator in disputes, deposed con-
troversial patriarchs and metropolitans outside its territory, and served
on many occasions up to the present as mediator in resolving issues of
Pan-Orthodox concern.

Especially important for the well-being of world Orthodoxy in recent times was the role of Ecumenical Patriarch Athenagoras in convening a series of Pan-Orthodox Conferences in 1961, 1963, 1964, and 1968
to address immediate issues requiring a Pan-Orthodox consensus, and
to make preparations for the convocation of a Great and Holy Council.
These Conferences marked the beginning of a new period of conciliarity among the Orthodox Churches. The Ecumenical Patriarchate acted
with wisdom and love to draw the Churches out of their isolation so that
they might address critical issues together.

Numerous consultations have taken place since then to examine the ten themes which were proposed by the Churches in 1976 for study in anticipation of the convening of a Great and Holy Council. Among these themes was the topic of the Diaspora.

When this conciliar process began in 1961, all the Autocephalous Churches recognized that it was the prerogative of the Ecumenical Patriarchate to lead this effort for the good of the entire Church. For over forty years, the Ecumenical Patriarchate has wisely led this conciliar process with the concurrence of the other Autocephalous Churches.

In conjunction with this conciliar process, the distinctive initiatives of the Ecumenical Patriarch, with the collaboration of other Autocephalous Churches, have led to significant events in the life of the Orthodox Church. Among these are: the re-establishment of the Church of Albania (1992); the arbitration of disputed patriarchal elections in the Churches of Bulgaria (1998) and Jerusalem (2005); and the establishment of an orderly succession of the Archbishop of Cyprus (2006). In all of these cases the leadership of the Ecumenical Patriarchate was of singular importance. It was a leadership fully recognized by all the Autocephalous Churches.

Far from acting in an arbitrary manner, Ecumenical Patriarch Bartholomew personally has profoundly contributed to the life of the Orthodox Church through his persistent efforts to deepen the sense of conciliarity and common witness among the Autocephalous Churches. In addition to the above developments, he has visited all the Autocephalous Churches and cultivated a personal relationship with their leaders. Most importantly, he has convened and presided at the historic Synaxis of Orthodox Primates in 1992, 1995, 2000, and 2008.

The wise words of Metropolitan Maximos of Sardis should be recalled:

> The Patriarch of Constantinople rejects any *plenitudo potestatis ecclesiae* and holds his supreme ecclesiastical power not as *episcopus ecclesiae universalis*, but as Ecumenical Patriarch, the senior and most important bishop in the East. He does not wield unrestricted administrative power. He is not an infallible judge of matters of faith. Always the presupposition of his power is that in using it he will hold to two principles: conciliarity and collegiality in the responsibilities of the Church and non-intervention in the internal affairs of the other churches . . . [3]

With these observations in mind, the following must be noted with regard to the distinctive primacy of the Ecumenical Patriarch. Firstly, all the Autocephalous Churches recognize the Ecumenical Patriarch as the "first bishop" of the Church. He has specific responsibilities for coordinating a common witness among the Autocephalous Churches. As such, the Ecumenical Patriarch exercises this ministry first of all in relationship with the Holy Synod of the Ecumenical Patriarchate. The Patriarch is the president of this Synod. He does not act over or above the other bishops. According to the Orthodox perspective, primacy involves conciliarity. He always acts together with the other bishops of the Patriarchal Synod. Likewise, in his relationship with other Orthodox, the Ecumenical Patriarch is honored as the *protos*, the first bishop of the Church. This position gives to the Ecumenical Patriarch the special responsibility for identifying issues requiring the attention of the entire Church and for convening appropriate meetings to address these issues. When the Orthodox meet in a Synaxis, the Ecumenical Patriarch is the presiding bishop of the meeting.

As Ecumenical Patriarch Bartholomew has said, the Ecumenical Patriarchate "constitutes *par excellence* the center of all the local Orthodox churches. It heads these not by administering them, but by virtue of the primacy of its ministry of Pan-Orthodox unity and the coordination of the activities of all of Orthodoxy."[4]

The Development of the Orthodox Church in the United States

At the most recent Synaxis in Constantinople in October 2008, Ecumenical Patriarch Bartholomew proposed to the other Primates that renewed attention be given to the so-called Diaspora. A part of the process leading to the Great and Holy Council, representatives of the Autocephalous Churches had examined the topic of the Diaspora in 1990 and 1993, and made significant recommendations. As one of his proposals, Ecumenical Patriarch Bartholomew called upon the Churches to "activate the 1993 agreement of the Inter-Orthodox Consultation of the Holy and Great Council in order to resolve the pending matter of the Orthodox Diaspora."[5] This was a clear indication that the Ecumenical Patriarchate refused to accept indefinitely the present canonical irregularities in places such as the United States.

Moreover, the Primates in their Statement affirmed the proposal of Patriarch Bartholomew that meetings be held in the year 2009 to resume discussions on this critical issue. They affirmed their "desire for the swift healing of every canonical anomaly that has arisen from historical circumstances and pastoral requirements, such as in the so-called Orthodox Diaspora, with a view to overcoming every possible influence that is foreign to Orthodox ecclesiology. In this respect we welcome the proposal by the Ecumenical Patriarchate to convene Pan-Orthodox Consultations within the coming year 2009 on this subject, as well as for the continuation of preparations for the Holy and Great Council. In accordance with the standing order and practice of the Pan-Orthodox Consultations in Rhodes, it will invite all Autocephalous Churches."[6]

Under the leadership of Ecumenical Patriarch Bartholomew, the Primates indicated that the *status quo* in the so-called Diaspora was not acceptable.

The development of the Orthodox Church in the United States is very complex. The early growth of the Orthodox Church in this country has resulted from immigration, missionary activity, and the return of Eastern Catholics to Orthodoxy. In more recent decades especially, the Church also has received many persons who have found in Orthodoxy the fullness of the historic Apostolic Faith. Truly, the Orthodox Church in this country has become a salutary witness to Our Lord and His Gospel. Through its teachings, ecumenical dialogues, and philanthropic activities, the Orthodox Church has contributed to the process of reconciliation and healing in our society.

At the same time, it must be recognized that the proper development of the Church in this country has not always followed the principles of ecclesiastical organization reflected in the canons of the Councils which have already been mentioned. The presence of multiple jurisdictions from various Autocephalous Churches in the same territory and the presence of multiple bishops in the same territory are clearly contrary to the canonical tradition. The good order of the Church has been shaken by acts which have gone contrary to ecclesiological principles and historical *praxis*.[7]

Among these acts was the grant of "Autocephaly" to the Russian Orthodox Greek Catholic Church (the Metropolia) by the Church of Russia in 1970, thereby renaming this jurisdiction the "Orthodox Church in America." This action had no canonical basis. From that time, the Ecumenical Patriarchate and the majority of other Autocephalous Churches have refused to recognize the "autocephalous" status of this jurisdiction. As a result, this jurisdiction has not been accorded a place in global Pan-Orthodox discussions in accordance with the agreement of the Autocephalous Churches.

Yet, the Ecumenical Patriarchate has exercised restraint and has not broken communion with this jurisdiction. Indeed, in the 1990s the Ecumenical Patriarchate frequently received representatives of this jurisdiction to discuss its irregular status. While recognizing the historical road of this jurisdiction, the Ecumenical Patriarchate has affirmed that the canonical irregularities have not been resolved.

Under the leadership of the Ecumenical Patriarchate, a truly Pan-Orthodox solution must be found for the entire Church in the United States. Recent Ecumenical Patriarchs and their representatives have consistently reiterated this fact. During his pastoral visit to Washington in 1990, Ecumenical Patriarch Dimitrios said:

> It is truly a scandal for the unity of the Church to maintain more than one bishop in any given city; it clearly contravenes the sacred canons and Orthodox ecclesiology. It is a scandal that is exacerbated whenever phyletistic motives play a part, a practice soundly condemned by the Orthodox Church in the last century. The Ecumenical Patriarchate, as a supra-national Church serving the unity of the Church, is not indifferent to the condition that has evolved, and will exert every effort in cooperation with the other Holy Orthodox Churches, and in accordance with canonical order, to resolve this thorny problem.[8]

In order to address the difficult situation in America, the Ecumenical Patriarchate has consistently supported efforts aimed at increasing cooperation among the jurisdictions and at establishing proper order in accordance with the canons. Archbishop Athenagoras proposed a Conference of Orthodox Bishops in 1936. This proposal was the basis for the "Federation" which came into existence in 1943. Archbishop Michael convened a gathering of Orthodox bishops in 1952 with the intention of having regular meetings. Archbishop Iakovos led the establishment of the Standing Conference of Canonical Orthodox Bishops (SCOBA) in 1960. Since that time, the Exarch of the Ecumenical Patriarchate has served as the chairman of SCOBA in accordance with the agreements affirmed in the Pan-Orthodox Conferences.

Moreover, it was under the leadership of the Exarch of the Patriarchate of Constantinople that meetings of all Orthodox bishops were convened in this country. Archbishop Iakovos presided at the meeting in 1994. Archbishop Demetrios presided at meetings in 2001 and 2006.

Members of the Holy Cross Faculty have been actively involved in a number of initiatives of the Ecumenical Patriarchate aimed at addressing the canonical irregularities of church life in America. The Faculty of Holy Cross was invited in 1977 by the Ecumenical Patriarchate to submit a vision of unity for the Orthodox Church in the United States. The draft of this vision constituted one approach to the models of unity under study.[9] Faculty members have been invited to participate in meetings related to the preparation for the Great and Holy Council. The present Dean of Holy Cross was involved in meetings of the Inter-Orthodox Preparatory Commission convened by the Ecumenical Patriarchate in Chambésy, Switzerland, in 1990 and 1993, as well as a related meeting in 1995.

Conclusions

We believe that the Ecumenical Patriarchate possesses distinctive prerogatives to serve the unity and witness of the entire Orthodox Church in accordance with the canons and the *praxis* of the Church. Since the fourth century, the Ecumenical Patriarchate has acted in accordance with the canons to maintain and strengthen the "unity of spirit in the bond of peace" (Eph 4:3) among the Autocephalous Churches.

Directly related to our situation in the United States is the interpretation of canon 28 of Chalcedon and related canons. Although it deals with a specific situation of its time, canon 28 nevertheless safeguards principles which constitute the basis of permanent aspects of our canonical tradition. Other canons do the same. One might consider, for example, canon 6 of Nicaea or canon 3 of Constantinople or canon 39 of the Penthekti (Quinsext) Council (in Trullo), among others. In the first instance, an established order of church government is confirmed; in the second, an adjustment of church order is made to accommodate a special need. In both instances, principles are provided which reveal the manner in which the Church expresses herself in different situations. So it is with canon 28 of Chalcedon. It confirms what in practice was already in progress at that time—a primacy of honor among equals for the bishop of Constantinople, expressed in a way which reflected this reality.

While not diminishing the significance of canon 28 and related canons, the Ecumenical Patriarchate has wisely recognized the distinctive and complex features of Orthodoxy in the United States especially. The

Ecumenical Patriarchate has recommended that a truly Pan-Orthodox solution must be found. It has advocated this perspective in recent Pan-Orthodox discussions. In light of canonical tradition and ecclesial *praxis*, the Ecumenical Patriarchate is alone in the position to guide the Autocephalous Churches toward a proper resolution for the Church in the United States.

We rejoice that much is made of Orthodox unity and the role of the Ecumenical Patriarchate in achieving it. This is good and hopeful, in view of the fact that it keeps alive and at the forefront of our concerns the quest for this noble goal. At the same time, however, it raises, once more, the issue about the way in which this unity should be achieved. At the center of this discussion is our Mother Church, the Ecumenical Patriarchate, and the understanding of its role in initiating the process of the goal towards unity.

We look to the venerable Ecumenical Patriarchate to continue to lead the Autocephalous Churches in addressing the difficult challenge of the Orthodox Diaspora, especially here in the United States. The recommendations of the Inter-Orthodox Pre-Conciliar Consultations in Chambésy in 1990 and 1993, as well as the meeting there in 1995, provide significant proposals for addressing the irregularities of church structures in the United States.

We endorse the proposal of Ecumenical Patriarch Bartholomew to activate the 1993 agreement which proposed the establishment of an Episcopal Assembly in given areas. We look forward to meetings scheduled to take place this year to continue to examine the topic of the so-called Diaspora.

We appeal to all, both clergy and laity, to pray for the unity of the Church and to commit ourselves to words and deeds of healing and reconciliation so that our good and loving God, Father, Son, and Holy Spirit, will be honored and glorified.

Notes

1. See Lewis J. Patsavos, *Primacy and Conciliarity: Studies in the Primacy of the See of Constantinople and the Synodical Structure of the Orthodox Church* (Brookline, MA, 1995).

2. Ecumenical Patriarch Bartholomew, "Address to the Ukrainian Nation," July 26, 2008.

3. Metropolitan Maximos of Sardis, *The Ecumenical Patriarchate in the Orthodox Church* (Thessaloniki, 1976), 236. This outstanding study

documents the historic role of the Ecumenical Patriarchate, especially in relationship with the other Autocephalous Churches.

4. Ecumenical Patriarch Bartholomew, *Encountering the Mystery* (New York, 2008), xl.

5. Ecumenical Patriarch Bartholomew, "Address at the Synaxis of the Heads of Orthodox Churches," Constantinople, October 10, 2008.

6. "Message of the Primates of the Orthodox Church," Constantinople, October 12, 2008.

7. See Thomas FitzGerald, *The Orthodox Church* (Westport, CT, 1995), 101–115.

8. "Remarks of Patriarch Dimitrios," *The Orthodox Church* 26, nos. 9–10 (1990): 9.

9. See Lewis Patsavos, "The Harmonization of Canonical Order," *Journal of Modern Hellenism* 19–20 (2001–2002): 211–228.